W9-BAL-489

Ethical Decisions for Social Work Practice

Sixth Edition

Ethical Decisions for Social Work Practice

Frank M. Loewenberg

Professor Emeritus, Bar-Ilan University

Ralph Dolgoff

University of Maryland, Baltimore

Donna Harrington

University of Maryland, Baltimore

F.E. PEACOCK PUBLISHERS, INC. • Itasca, Illinois

Copyright © 2000 by F.E. Peacock Publishers, Inc.
All rights reserved
Library of Congress Catalog Card No. 00-130327
ISBN 0-87581-431-X
Printed in the United States of America
Printing   10   9   8   7   6   5   4   3   2
Year   04   03   02   01

What is the ethical way for a social worker to respond when:

- Your client tells you that he intends to commit a serious crime.
- A twenty-six-year-old married woman wants a tubal ligation because she does not want to have any more children. She asks you to help her find a physician who will perform this procedure.
- A social worker in a residential detoxification center believes that one of the residents is potentially violent and may become a danger to other residents.
- A client who is HIV-positive tells you that he has unprotected sex with his wife because he does not want her to know of his condition.
- A social worker learns that another social worker knows about a child abuse situation but has failed to report the case to the Child Abuse Center.
- A board member has helped to obtain a substantial grant which has made it possible for your agency to serve adult alcoholics and members of their families. Now this board member wants you to report that more clients have been served by this program than actually did participate so that the agency can receive a larger grant next year.
- Physicians and a nurse in a pediatric hospital believe strongly that a child should have a tracheostomy. The child's parents are resistant because the child's lungs can fail, the procedure looks very painful, and death is possible. The chief physician asks you to convince the parents to agree *no matter what.*

Contents

Figures, Tables, and Exemplars

Preface

Every day, all of the communication media—television, newspapers, radio, and films—are concerned with and present ethical issues from every societal level. Unethical acts are reported that occur in business and industry, academia, scientific research, government, and in the media themselves. Many groups advance and support often conflicting moral claims.

Ethical problems arise whenever and wherever people deal with human lives, human survival, and human welfare. These are activities in which social workers are involved daily. For this reason, we believe that concern for ethical conduct should be included in every curriculum for professional education. But those who teach in the area must keep in mind Thomas Aquinas's caution that when it comes to ethics "we cannot discuss what we ought to do unless we know what we can do" (*Commentary on De Anima*, I. 1.2). In other words, teaching the theory of ethical action is not worth much unless we also teach the skill of making ethical decisions. In this book, therefore, we will follow this dual focus. Some have said that virtue cannot be taught in a college classroom and that ethical dilemmas cannot be resolved by textbooks. However, we believe that the principles and techniques of ethical assessment and ethical decision making do have a place in a professional curriculum.

At the same time, we agree with those who have suggested that the concern of instructors should be less focused on presenting solutions to dilemmas than with efforts to encourage students to be alert in discovering and perceiving ethical issues, in considering competing arguments, in examining both the strengths and limitations of their own positions, and in reaching for thoughtfully reasoned conclusions. Our approach to ethical decision making is designed to assist social workers in reasoning carefully about ethical issues, to help them clarify their moral aspirations at the level demanded by the profession, and to achieve a more ethical stance in practice.

The exercises at the end of each chapter have been prepared to heighten students' sensitivity to the ethical aspects of social work practice, to aid them in developing a personal approach to such issues, and to help them consider the essential elements in ethical decision making in professional practice. Suggestions for additional readings also appear at the end of each chapter.

In our continuing effort to make this book more useful, we have added new material, dropped some dated material that appeared in earlier editions, and rewritten all chapters. We have included new sections on domestic violence and genetics, a glossary of terms, new graphics, a selected list of Internet sources of information about values and ethics, and many new exemplars. In addition, there are expanded sections on managed care and mental health, and technology.

We have retained the two ethical decision screens. We have received numerous comments that the screens have proved helpful in the rank-ordering of ethical principles and ethical obligations, thus helping social work practitioners identify priorities among competing ethical obligations. For this edition, we have created a screen concerning the *continuum of worker values* and the potential implications for social workers of their own values in relation to those of clients and employing agencies. Our intent has been to suggest some principles and guidelines that can substantially help social workers making ethical practice decisions, and we have been gratified by the wide use of the screens. Although ethical and moral perfection remains an unattainable goal, social workers, like all others, must continue to strive toward that goal.

The exemplars in this book are taken from the real world, but none of them occurred in exactly the way described or to the people identified in each situation. Neither names nor other identifying information came from social agency records nor from social workers who worked with these people. Many new exemplars have been added to reflect newer areas of practice. Needless to say, the exemplars do not always typify good or desirable practice. They were chosen simply to illustrate ethical problems occurring in the real world of practice.

We want to thank our colleagues and students for helping us think through many of the issues involved in social work ethics. Thanks are due to the anonymous reviewers of earlier editions; they drew our attention to several topics that should be added. To Dick Welna and Ted Peacock, special thanks for encouraging us to prepare the sixth edition. We also want to express our appreciation to Bernetta Hux for her assistance, to the Health Sciences and Human Services Library at the University of Maryland, Baltimore, and to the Milton S. Eisenhower Library of the Johns Hopkins University.

We want to welcome Dr. Donna Harrington as coauthor of this sixth edition of the book, and we look forward to continued successful collaboration.

The appearance of this edition marks more than a quarter of a century of association with Ted and Sarah Peacock, our publishers. We wish to express our gratitude to them.

Finally, we thank our spouses, Chaya, Sylvia, and Patrick, who have continued their everlasting patience with our not-so-minor foibles.

Frank M. Loewenberg
Ralph L. Dolgoff
Donna Harrington

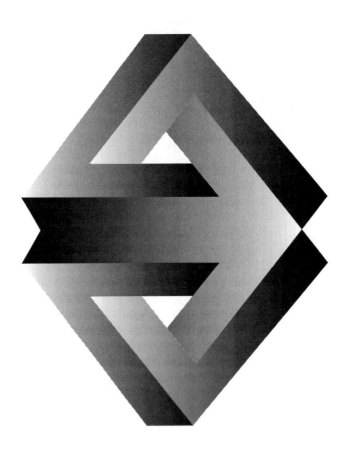

PART ONE

Introduction to
Ethical Decision Making

1. Ethical Choices in the Helping Professions

Every day, most social workers are confronted with the necessity to make ethical decisions. Sometimes they have an opportunity to think about the choices, perhaps to talk things over with a colleague or to consult with an expert. More often, however, social workers—even student social workers—are alone when they must make difficult ethical decisions; they cannot wait because of the immediacy of the problem that faces them. At best, they have a few hours or a few days to consider what should be done.

➤ **1.1 The Guevara Family Struggle: Report or Not?**

The Guevara family is working very hard to get by economically. Mr. and Mrs. Guevara both work full-time. Their four children—three of whom are in elementary school—return home in the early afternoon. The oldest child, Rosa, is 16 years old and expected to feed, supervise, and care for the other children, which she has done successfully. However, a neighbor reported the Guevaras to Child Protective Services, accusing them of neglect. When Morgana Elam, the social worker assigned, met with her, Mrs. Guevara told her that this is the way it is done in their culture. Also, she and her husband want to make a better life for their children. They have explored every possible alternative, and there is none. If one of them has to cut back on employment, a paycheck will be lost without any assurance that other work will be found. After checking,

Ms. Elam found she also could not suggest an alternative. The children all appear healthy and happy.

What ethical issues does this situation pose? Where will the social worker find help with the ethical aspects of this practice problem? How will the social worker decide what course of action to follow?

This situation poses a number of ethical dilemmas for Ms. Elam. One should note that, in addition to the parents, children, and social worker, there are others involved—such as neighbors and society. But, in this case we will limit our focus to the family and social worker. In this book we consider only professional ethical dilemmas, and the social worker is confronted by a number of such dilemmas whose solutions should be congruent with ethical professional practice. We will briefly analyze three of these dilemmas.

The root ethical problem in this situation is that every social worker, including Ms. Elam, fills two professional social work roles: (1) The social worker is both a helper/enabler and (2) a societal/control agent. The conflict between these two roles triggers a number of ethical dilemmas. What is good for one participant is not necessarily what is best for another. A decision that is best for now may not be so for the long run. In addition, since we do not live in a perfect world, we also need to consider the degree of damage that can be permitted to occur before the social worker must intervene.

Competing values.   Client self-determination, protection of human life, and enhancing the quality of life are three values to which all social workers are committed. But as is so often the case, in this instance the social worker cannot honor all of them. If the social worker substantiates the neglect report, she may undermine the family's self-determination and perhaps their long-term quality of life. On the basis of their experience so far, everyone is safe. If she does not substantiate and report the situation as neglectful, there is always the risk that something will occur that Rosa cannot handle. Weighed against that risk is the commitment of the parents to gain through hard work an improved quality of life for their family. There may be good reasons for giving priority to one, rather than the other, of these values. Nevertheless, this is a problem in professional ethics that the social worker must resolve either knowingly or unconsciously.

Multiple-client system.   Ordinarily a social worker gives priority to her client, just as ordinarily she would respect the client's self-determination. These principles are relevant to this situation. However, the social worker also has responsibilities toward others, including the parents, their children, and child protective services, as well as herself. This practitioner must decide to whom she* owes first obligations.

Value dilemma. This situation confronts the social worker with additional value dilemmas. While she is committed to provide service to her clients, she is not at all sure which professional values are relevant in this situation. She does not want to undermine the family's self-determination or the parents' motivation to advance economically and provide a better life for the family. She also does not want to impose her own values on the family, thus undermining their culture. Will the least harm be done by verifying the family neglect report, which means the family may lose an important source of income, or not reporting, in which case there is at least some risk of danger for the children? How can she choose between these conflicting but important values?

In summary, in this situation, the social worker's ethics indicate that in her role as a helper/enabler, she must make certain the family is enabled to make its own thoughtful decisions, she must assist the family to know and analyze alternatives, and she must facilitate access to helping systems that make these decisions possible. In terms of her role as social control agent, the social worker must *not* intervene unless there is clear evidence of imminent and irreversible danger of major proportions.

There are many ways to prepare for this practice reality. First, it is important to recognize that every decision in social work practice includes ethical aspects. Next, social workers need knowledge and skill to clarify these aspects of practice in order to engage in effective ethical decision making. Knowledge and skill in this area (as in all other aspects of social work practice) must be developed and refined throughout a social worker's professional career.

This book has been written to help social workers, students as well as practitioners, prepare for informed and skillful reasoning in ethical decision making. Part of this preparation consists of considering such questions as: Who is my client? What obligations do I owe to my clients? Do I have professional obligations to people other than my clients? What about my family? My agency? My profession? What are my own personal values? Are these compatible with the profession's values?

---

* Some social workers are men, many more are women. In recent years, many writers have used such terminology as *his or her* and *she or he.* Or they have used the plural, such as "social workers believe." However, these usages are clumsy and often tend to interfere with the clarity of the message. Since most social workers are women, we will refer to the social worker as *she* (except in exemplars where the worker has been identified as a man, as in Exemplar 3.2) and to the recipient of the service as *he* (except where the recipient is a woman, as in Exemplar 1.2). We hope that male social workers and female recipients will bear with our usage.

With societal values? What are my ethical priorities when these value sets are not identical? What is the ethical way to respond when I have conflicting professional responsibilities to different people?

In this chapter we will introduce this complex and important topic and define what we mean by *ethical decision making.* There are those who charge that some social workers have not yet developed a strong enough sense of morality, and that therefore they find it hard to cope with the ethical implications of their practice. Others think that social workers are aware of ethical issues that occur in practice, but that they make decisions on the basis of incomplete knowledge, value judgments and biases, and insufficient conscious use of self. Social work students and practitioners have repeatedly asked for guides to help them grapple with ethical practice issues. Until recently, these requests were answered only by the adoption of codes of ethics that were helpful in some ways, but left too many questions unanswered. The requests for help continue because most social workers know instinctively that ethics are supremely important. Even those who have never heard of Gewirth tend to agree with him that ethical requirements "take precedence over all other modes of guiding action" (1978, p. 1).

The very subject of professional ethics was once almost completely ignored in the social work curriculum. But there has been a change. In the past two generations, scientists have cracked the genetic code, put men on the moon, replaced hearts and other vital organs, successfully transferred an embryo from the test tube to the womb, and cloned Dolly, the sheep.

From a technological point of view it is nowadays possible to do almost anything we want to do. The key question now is how to decide what ought to be done. In line with this, more and more social workers have come to recognize that they, too, face questions that go beyond the "techniques" of social work. This recognition has made the subject of professional ethics more visible in the professional social work curriculum. Since 1982, the Council on Social Work Education (CSWE *Curriculum Policy Statement,* 1982, 1992, 1997 Revised) required the inclusion throughout the curriculum of values and ethics that guide professional social workers in their practice.

What does the term *ethics* mean? The word comes from the Greek root *ethos,* which originally meant custom, usage, or habit. In contemporary use it deals with the question of what actions are morally right and with how things ought to be. *General ethics* clarify the obligations that are owed by one person to another person. But some obligations are based on the specific relations between two people (such as a mother and her son), or they are based on a particular role voluntarily accepted by one of the parties. The latter are special obligations that apply only to those who have consented to accept that role position (Fishkin, 1982, pp. 25–27). *Professional ethics* are a codification of the special obligations that arise out of a person's voluntary choice to become a professional, such as a social worker. Professional ethics clarify the ethical aspects of professional practice. *Professional social work ethics* are intended to help social work practitioners recognize the morally correct way of practice and to learn how to decide and act correctly with regard to the ethical aspects of any given professional situation.

CONTEMPORARY INTEREST IN PROFESSIONAL ETHICS

Jane Addams talked many years ago about the importance of ethical practice, but until recently most professional social workers were less than clear about the ethical aspects of practice. Even though it is difficult to avoid ethical problems in everyday practice, a powerful tradition has attempted to deemphasize questions of morals, values, and ethics within the practitioner's purview. Social workers accepted this "scientific" stance and preferred objective explanations over moralistic ones. But this approach has not helped them in making ethical decisions when difficult problems arise, especially in such controversial practice areas as abortion, genetic and other technologies, potential HIV transmission, allocation of scarce resources, and similar situations.

One of the paradoxes of modern times is the fact that the interest in professional ethics is high—even though the level of morality of our society sometimes seems rather low. In this century, more people have been killed by violence than ever before. Genocide was perfected in our own lifetime: the Nuremberg trials after World War II, the Civil Rights movement in the late 1950s and 1960s, killings in Cambodia, Rwanda, and the Balkans as well as those in other nations, the many rapid advances in medical and computer technology, and the impeachment of President William Clinton have all resulted in a greater awareness of human rights, including the rights of clients. The renewed interest in social work ethics is, in part, related to this emphasis on human rights and, in part, it is an expression of the maturation of the social work profession. Another explanation for the growing interest in social work ethics lies in the increasing concern of practitioners with the proclivity of clients to resort to litigation in order to resolve claims of ethical malfeasance and malpractice. As a result, in the last three decades, complaints and lawsuits against social workers insured by the NASW Insurance Trust have increased dramatically (Houston-Vega, Nuehring, & Daguio, 1997).

Unethical conduct, corruption, and scandals in government as well as in industry have become commonplace. Almost daily, newspapers report unethical practices by some scientific researchers, physicians, lawyers, accountants, and other professionals. Media have reported on ethical matters concerning: the impeachment trial of President Clinton, regulation of the oil industry, Olympics corruption, medical research issues, drugs in sports, Kosovo and Serbia, lawyers sharing fees, and political fund-raising. Ethical matters are frequently in the public eye. Courses in ethics are spreading rapidly and are offered today not only by universities but also by businesses, industries, professional groups, and even by the military.

Social work practitioners are searching for guides that will direct their practice behavior along ethical lines. For many, neither science nor religion has provided satisfactory answers to the ethical problems that they face. The renewed emphasis on professional ethics is due to a "desire to retrieve human values and moral concerns from the high-tech influence of science, professionalization and rapid technical innovation" that is so characteristic of all areas of contemporary life, including professional social work (Walrond-Skinner & Watson, 1987, p. 5).

ETHICAL PROBLEMS IN SOCIAL WORK PRACTICE

Some suggest that ethics are a problem that occurs only on very special occasions. In most situations a practitioner requires only a high level of professional skill and insight, since such situations do not involve any ethical questions. This approach to professional practice, established by Sigmund Freud himself, has been accepted by generations of practitioners in all of the helping professions. The assumptions underlying this approach are supported by certain philosophers who argue that most actions do not involve any moral question but are the result of a free choice among the various available alternatives. These alternatives are located in the area that Fishkin (1982) identified as the "zone of moral indifference." But other philosophers insist that there are ethical implications or ethical aspects to almost every professional decision. We follow the latter approach because we believe that professional social workers are not merely technical problem solvers but also moral agents.

An examination of social work practice will reveal that almost all practice principles involve (or are based on) ethical principles. One of the sources for ethical problems in social work practice may be located in the multiplicity and contradiction of values that characterize contemporary society. While we often speak of ethical problems, it would be more correct to speak of the *ethical dimensions or ethical aspects of social work practice problems*. In the past it was assumed that ethical issues arose out of, and were limited to, the dyadic relation between social worker and client. Current ethical concerns also include those that arise out of the newer practice models, which include many participants in addition to client and worker. The breakdown of consensus concerning societal means and goals, the increasing scarcity of resources that are available for social welfare, and the utilization of new technologies not only have intensified traditional ethical dilemmas but also have given rise to what may well be a new generation of ethical issues in social work practice.

In this book we will examine *ethical problems* and *ethical dilemmas*. Ethical problems raise the question: What is the *right* thing to do in a given practice situation? How can a social worker avoid unethical behaviors in that situation? Ethical dilemmas occur in situations in which the social worker must choose between two or more relevant, but contradictory, ethical directives, or when every alternative results in an undesirable outcome for one or more persons. The seedbed for ethical problems in social work practice is graphically portrayed in Figure 1.1.

Any disagreement that different participants of the action system (Group B) have with regard to alternate decision options (Group A) or alternative assumptions (Group C) will intensify the difficulties that social workers will encounter in ethical decision making. Examples of such difficulties occur when

- A client wants a service that may affect another member of the family who does not want to receive that service: An adult daughter may want to place her aged father in a nursing home, but the father wants to remain in his own home.
- Conflicting values impinge on the decision facing the social worker: A young woman asks whether her fiance (who is your client) is HIV positive, while the client wants to keep this information secret.
- The community and the profession have different priorities: Everyone agrees that something must be done about domestic violence, but community leaders believe that better police protection is more important than building another shelter.
- The social agency prescribes a treatment modality based on one social work theory, although the practitioner knows that another approach is indicated for a particular client: The agency is committed to psychodynamic therapy, whereas research evidence indicates that in this situation cognitive-behavioral therapy may be more effective.

Some social workers try to ignore the ethical problems and dilemmas that arise in these and similar situations, either because they are too uncomfortable in making ethical decisions or because they think that they already have the answer. Other social workers are aware of the

Figure 1.1   Ethical Problems in Social Work Practice

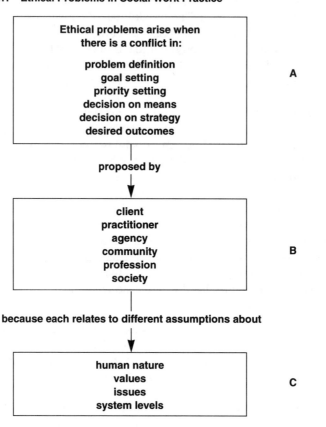

ethical aspects of these problem situations, but are uneasy because they think that they do not yet have the skill to deal with ethical problems of this nature.

Two root causes for ethical problems are (1) competing values and (2) competing loyalties. Social workers may benefit from paying special attention to these root causes.

Competing values.   An ethical dilemma may arise when a practitioner is faced by two or more competing values, such as justice and equality, or confidentiality and protecting life. Similarly, in a period of rapidly shrinking budgets, no practitioner can ignore considerations of efficiency and effectiveness, even though these constraints may do violence to what is thought to be best for a particular client. A worker may feel equally committed to two values, even when both cannot be actualized in a specific situation.

Competing loyalties.   When competing or conflicting groups make claims for the social worker's loyalties, she may face an ethical dilemma. A classic example of this dilemma is the social worker who represents both the agency and the client, with each making conflicting demands. There is little need to point to the more blatant examples of this cause of ethical problems. But even less blatant incidents, such as a request for giving preferential treatment to relatives and friends, can be problematic from an ethical point of view. Multiple loyalties are also a source of ethical quandaries when a social worker serves a multiple-client system, as is so common today. In these circumstances, identifying the person or unit that should receive priority attention becomes a key ethical issue.

Several exemplars from social work practice will now be examined. Consider how ethical issues arise in each exemplar. The ethical problems faced by the social worker who has been assigned to work with Blanca Gabelli are similar to, yet different from, those faced by worker Morgana Elam in Exemplar 1.1.

➤ **1.2 Blanca Gabelli Costs Too Much**

Blanca Gabelli, an 84-year-old retired physician, participates in a day treatment program and resides in an assisted living residence. Recently she has become slightly more forgetful, falls more frequently, and has been somewhat less able to care for herself. She has also become increasingly irascible, and several staff members have complained about her demanding behavior. Your supervisor has asked you, as the social worker who serves the residents, to arrange a transfer to a nursing home because Ms. Gabelli is a "pain" and she is costing the residential program too much. Although you believe that Ms. Gabelli is not yet in need of nursing home care, you contacted the one possible nursing home to arrange for a transfer. You just received a call from Ellen Brito, the nursing home administrator, who is asking about Ms. Gabelli's health, behavior, and attitudes. How should you respond?

Let us consider some of the ethical choices this social worker might make.

Goal Setting

Who should set the goals in this situation? If you comply with your supervisor's demand, you and your supervisor determine Ms. Gabelli's future while also undermining her sense of autonomy. Do you and your supervisor have an ethical right to do so? What part should Ms. Gabelli play in deciding her own living arrangements?

Role Conflict

A social worker is an agency employee. What are the implications if you do not comply with your supervisor's demand? Does the social worker's role require that you always comply with the suggestions of your supervisor or that you always serve as Ms. Gabelli's protector? Whose interests should receive priority consideration? Your supervisor's? The agency's? Yours? Ms. Gabelli's? What role should you play in relation to the nursing home administrator (not a social worker)? Should you share with the nursing home staff some or all of the facts about Ms. Gabelli's behavior?

Value Dilemma

This social worker's supervisor is demanding that the worker comply with the agency's decision rather than with her client's choice. In addition, her supervisor is asking her to lie and manipulate the situation so that the agency can transfer Ms. Gabelli. But this social worker personally places a high value on honesty. In what ways do her professional and personal values clash? Should the social worker tell Ms. Gabelli what her supervisor said? How honest should this social worker be and with whom?

Another set of ethical problems faces Sharon Gillette, the social worker in the following exemplar.

➤ **1.3 A Tornado Hits Warrensville**

It was 7:35 A.M. in Warrensville when the phone in the Gillette home rang. Sharon Gillette rushed to answer because her husband had left for work over an hour ago. About half an hour after he left, the radio and TV aired warnings of tornados in the vicinity. Mrs. Carlyle, who baby-sits for Sharon's children, just called to say she could not get there this morning. Just a few minutes ago fire sirens had sounded indicating that a very dangerous weather condition would hit the town momentarily. All Warrensville families knew they should take cover in their prepared sheltered spaces. Now the phone rang for Sharon. The Civil Emergency Center asked her to report immediately for duty at her assigned Emergency Center because there were already homes destroyed and people in shock.

Competing values. Is it right for Sharon to leave her family? What mother can leave her children frightened and confused by tornados? On the other hand, what are her obligations as a social worker to the homeless families being served at the Emergency Center? This social worker cannot simultaneously be in her shelter with her children and at the Emergency Center.

Ambiguity.   Sharon would have been far less troubled by her decision if she had known that there would be no damage to her house and children or if she had known for certain that her presence at the Emergency Center would make a critical difference in the lives of the homeless victims of the tornados. In addition, this decision had to be made very fast, thus increasing the stressfulness of decision making.

What other ethical issues does this case pose? Where in the *Code of Ethics* will this social worker find help with the ethical aspects of this practice problem encountered in emergency situations such as floods, hurricanes, outbreaks of violence, and war? How will the social worker decide what course of action to follow? The ethical aspects of the situation are relatively straightforward. As a social worker, Sharon is charged with professional responsibilities, perhaps especially in an emergency situation, but she also has responsibilities to her family, which in this case includes very young, frightened, and potentially at-risk children. Which of these two obligations has priority?

CAN PROFESSIONAL ETHICS BE TAUGHT?

Teaching professional ethics is based on the assumption that knowledge about ethics will lead to the acquisition of attitudes and values, and that these, in turn, will produce the desired ethical behavior. But is there any reason to think that studying ethics will motivate ethical behavior any more than studying biochemistry will inspire a person to become a physician? In fact, some have suggested that learning about ethics may not be the best way to promote ethical behavior. Social work students and practitioners who spend too much time reflecting about professional ethics may find themselves in the same situation as the centipede who became incapable of moving about when it tried to understand how its legs worked. Further empirical research is needed to discover whether and to what extent learning about ethics is helpful. Educators still do not know much more about value-and-ethics education than Socrates did more than two thousand years ago when he told Meno that he did not know how values were acquired nor whether they could be taught at all. These questions still require answers.

The widely accepted view is that attitudes determine behavior, but some leading attitude theorists have proposed that behavior determines attitudes. Generally it is held that our behavior is a direct consequence of our attitudes about the world, but the revisionist theorists suggest that a person tends to select beliefs and attitudes that are in consonance with or support his or her behavior (Bem, 1970; Festinger, 1957). Following the traditional theory, it is widely believed that social workers' values influence their professional practice such as the selection of treatment methods. The Council on Social Work Education (CSWE) requirement for curriculum content related to values and ethics is also based on the assumption that a student who learns to value professional ethics will, as a practitioner, choose to behave in ethical ways.

It may be that both approaches are correct. Deutscher, Pestello, and Pestello (1993) indicated that both the attitude → behavior and the behavior → attitude models are far too simplistic and not fully in accord with reality. Under some conditions the relationship is reciprocal or reversed so that, at the same time, attitudes influence behaviors and behaviors influence attitudes. However, attitude is just one determinant of behavior as intentions, expectations of others, and beliefs about outcomes all influence behaviors (Manstead, 1996).

In earlier times, professional ethics were transmitted by watching a master practitioner. This apprentice model was satisfactory for training professionals as long as the new practitioner faced the same type of problems as did the master teacher. Social work's traditional emphasis on concurrent field instruction and educational supervision suggests a partial continuation of the apprentice model. But in today's world of rapid changes, this model may no longer be optimally effective; alternate teaching methods must be developed to supplement this traditional curriculum approach.

The impact of college and university curricula on changes in values and ethics is not entirely clear. Feldman and Newcomb (1994), on the basis of an examination of more than 1,500 empirical studies conducted over four decades in many different parts of the United States, reported some positive findings, though these differed for various types of colleges and curricula. Most interesting was their conclusion that, with few exceptions, faculty members exerted an impact only "where the influence of student peers and of faculty complement and reinforce one another" (1994, p. 330). Feldman and Newcomb surveyed primarily undergraduate colleges and focused on general value systems. There are only a few empirical studies of value changes in professional social work education. These raise some questions about the efficacy of teaching values. A number of studies report either negative outcomes or no significant changes (Varley, 1963; Varley, 1968; Hayes & Varley, 1965; Brown, 1970; Cyrns, 1977; Judah, 1979). Five other studies (Sharwell, 1974; Moran, 1989; Wodarski et al., 1988; Frans and Moran, 1993; Rice, 1994) report some positive findings. However, all of these studies attempted to measure value changes as reflected by answers to a questionnaire and did not assess ethical behaviors in practice settings.

More than 40 years ago, Pumphrey (1959) noted that social work students viewed the teaching of values as something quite apart from (or even irrelevant to) practice. Changes have occurred since Pumphrey undertook her study, but a recent observer noted that too many students still think that the major objective of ethics education is to pass an exam at the end of the semester. It is no wonder that social work students, like medical students, are often unable to recognize ethical problems in practice situations (Reiser et al., 1987).

It is doubtful whether an academic course limited to thinking and talking about professional ethics will suffice to make students more ethical practitioners. Thinking and talking must be supplemented by doing. Skill in utilizing the decision-making tools that we will present in this book, as well as the discussions and exercises, should help to improve the ability of students and practitioners to reason more effectively about ethical issues, improve the quality of ethical decision making, and result in more ethical professional behaviors in day-by-day practice. At the same time we try to avoid giving pat answers. Instead, we hope to convey the need for tolerance of ambiguity when it comes to professional ethics. In professional practice there is rarely, if ever, only one correct ethical way. Our approach is to focus on ethical applications in practice situations rather than merely on the philosophical foundations of professional ethics. We agree with Hokenstad (1987) that instruction that is limited to ethics and values and does not at the same time concern itself with knowledge and practice will not facilitate the development of ethical social work practice. The purpose of teaching professional ethics is to develop not philosophers or ethicists, but more effective and more ethical practitioners.

Social work educational programs are expected to provide specific knowledge about social work values and their implications, to help students to develop an awareness of their personal values, and to clarify conflicting values and ethical dilemmas. One goal of social work education is to educate social workers who are responsible for their own ethical professional conduct (CSWE, 1997 Revised).

The following are reasonable objectives for a course in professional ethics. Students will:

1. become more aware of and more sensitive to ethical issues in professional practice;
2. identify and grapple with competing arguments by examining their limitations and strengths;

3. learn to recognize the ethical principles involved in their practice situations;
4. develop a greater understanding of the complexities of ethical decision making;
5. be able to reach thoughtfully reasoned conclusions and apply ethical principles to their professional activities; and
6. be able to clarify moral aspirations and standards and evaluate ethical decisions made within the context of the profession.

ABOUT THIS BOOK

In this book we try to help students to acquire skill in analyzing ethical quandaries, to become aware of the ethical aspects of practice, and to learn techniques and tools useful for making better ethical decisions. We will not present detailed prescriptions for solving specific ethical problems, nor will we offer a cookbook approach that indicates what to do in every given practice situation. Instead, we will offer various models to help social work students and practitioners gain skill in analyzing and assessing the ethical dimensions of practice problems so that they can develop ethically appropriate professional behavior. We will suggest several analytic schemes that may help social workers resolve the ethical dilemmas that they face in practice.

It is important to recognize that ethical practice is an individual, an organizational, a professional, and a social phenomenon. Though ethical conduct is intentional and willed behavior for which each individual bears responsibility, the professional peer group and the agency setting can and must encourage professional behavior that is ethical. Joseph (1983, p. 47) noted that "ethical concerns are generated by the structural and interactional arrangements of organizations, as well as from their goals and objectives." For too long ethics have been the exclusive concern of the individual. Ethics must become the concern of the social group—in this instance, the concern of each social agency as well as of the total profession.

In Chapter 2 we will review the relation between values, general ethics, and professional ethics. Widespread concern about the relation between law and ethics has led us to include a section on the relationship of ethical and legal behavior. We will also examine the manifest and latent functions of professional ethics as well as present a brief history of the evolution of professional ethics in the field of social work.

In Chapter 3 we will develop our decision-making framework. After briefly presenting several basic ethical theories and various approaches to ethical decision making in the helping professions, we will develop two decision-making screens, specifically designed to help in assessing the ethical alternatives that social workers face in their day-by-day practice.

Part Two of the book will be devoted to the presentation of a number of ethical problems and ethical dilemmas in professional practice. Nine of the chapters in this section cover a variety of practice problems. Each ethical problem and dilemma is important in its own right, but no claim is made that any one is more important than any other. For each dilemma we have presented some relevant background information in order to help the reader examine the ethical dilemmas that arise out of the exemplars presented. The decision screens developed in Chapter 3 should be applied in analyzing each of these ethical dilemmas.

In the thirteenth and final chapter we again discuss the question of who is responsible for professional ethics. From what we have written in this chapter and from the development of our argument throughout the book, it will not come as a surprise that we place the responsibility for professional ethics not only on each individual social worker but also on the employing organization and on the organized professional group.

Exercises and suggestions for additional readings will appear at the end of every chapter. The code of ethics for the National Association of Social Workers (NASW) and for several other social work professional groups, as well as additional exemplars, a glossary, and a list of selected Internet sites will be found in the appendixes.

Ethical issues will continue to cause discomfort even after this book has been completed. This is so because every decision that a social worker makes entails ethical risks. Perhaps the most agonizing of these risks is the danger of making a choice that may hurt or damage a client. Every effort must be made to avoid such dangers; yet these hazards are unavoidable and must not lead to inaction. We hope that the tools for ethical decision making that we will present, as well as the discussions and questions that will be raised, will alert social workers to their ethical responsibilities and help them become more skilled and more ethical practitioners.

EXERCISES

1. Read one exemplar related to your interests in Appendix A. Try to answer the following questions:
   a. What ethical issues are involved in this exemplar?
   b. What provisions of the NASW *Code of Ethics* address themselves to the ethical issues you have identified?
   c. What ethical problems and ethical dilemmas that occur in this exemplar *are not* covered by the NASW *Code of Ethics?*

      d. What do you think is the ethical thing to do? Do you think there is more than one solution?

2. Compare and contrast the ethical principles that relate to confidentiality in the five codes of professional ethics presented in Appendix B.

      a. Which code do you consider most helpful when a practitioner must make ethical decisions involving this principle? Why?

      b. Put yourself in the Morgana Elam situation (Exemplar 1.1). What options are open to you? Analyze these in terms of the four questions raised in Exercise 1 (above).

3. Study your local TV and newspapers for one week. Identify the ethical issues that have implications for social workers.

SUGGESTIONS FOR ADDITIONAL READINGS

A short list of readings that we have found particularly helpful is found at the end of each chapter. Emphasis is given to the more recent literature rather than to the classics. The readings may amplify points that have been made, present other points of view, or raise additional questions. Reference to an article does not necessarily mean that we agree with it. But in each instance we have found that the author has made a thoughtful contribution to one or more of the subjects discussed in the chapter. The articles are mentioned only by author and year; the full citation can be found in the bibliography at the end of the book.

      Goldstein (1998) presents a critical analysis of the moral aspects of social work practice. Dean and Rhodes (1992) suggest that good clinical practice is not necessarily good ethical practice and recommend that ethical deliberation be a more explicit focus of practice and of practitioners' self-examination. Manning (1997) argues for moral citizenship to guide ethical social work practice. Kaslow (1998) considers major ethical concerns that come to the fore across countries. Gambrill and Pruger (1997) present debates regarding 19 issues, including the effectiveness of the NASW *Code of Ethics* as a guide, whether ethical standards are higher than the law, and the relationship of practitioners to the known unethical behavior of their colleagues. Sparse empirical evidence is introduced, but the issues focus on practice, coercion, professional self-regulation, professional education and training, and special client populations.

2. Values and Professional Ethics

Values are a very important element in social work practice. According to Brown (1968), "no other profession, with the exception perhaps of philosophy, concerns itself as deeply with the matter of values as does the profession of social work." Goldstein (1973) described social workers as "value laden individuals." For Vigilante (1974) social work values are "the fulcrum of practice." Frankl (1968) also emphasized the centrality of values, not only for professional practitioners but for everyone. Life without values has no meaning, but only creates an "existential vacuum." For Frankl the "will to meaning" is considerably more important than the "will to pleasure."

VALUES

Social workers, like so many others, often fail to distinguish between such terms as *values, ethics,* and *morality* (or *virtues*). They use them rather loosely. But values are not the same as virtues, though the two terms are often used interchangeably. Neither are values the same as ethics. One popular dictionary offers 17 definitions of *value*. Timms (1983) reviewed reports and publications from a number of social science fields and found no less than 180 different definitions for the term.

A survey of the social work literature suggests that social work writers have used many of these definitions.

Maslow (1962) once observed that values are like a big container that holds all sorts of miscellaneous and vague things. Many philosophers have used the term *value* as if it meant the same as interest, but John Dewey used the term in a more precise way by noting that it must include some element of appraisal or preference. Most social scientists have followed Dewey's definition, indicating that values are meant to serve as guides or criteria for selecting good and desirable behaviors. Kupperman (1999, p. 3) suggests that a value refers "to what is worth having or being" and that it "is preferable that it exist rather than not exist." Values enhance a life or the world and define "those conceptions of desirable states of affairs that are utilized in selective conduct as criteria for preference or choice or as justifications for proposed or actual behavior" (Williams, 1967, p. 23). Kluckhohn adds that "a value is not just a preference but it is a preference which is felt and/or considered to be justified..." (1951, p. 306). Most writers draw attention to the differences between societal values, group values, and individual values. Usually values at these different levels are complementary or reciprocal, though at times they may be in conflict. Within any one society, most people, most of the time, agree about a core of societal values.

PROFESSIONAL VALUES

Social work practitioners take their basic professional values from societal values, that is, from the values held by the larger society in which they practice. These professional values are most often compatible with societal values, but there may be important differences in emphasis, priorities, or interpretation. It stands to reason, just as there is wide agreement about societal values, so is there a wide consensus about basic professional values.

The central role that values play in social work has been recognized by many, as was noted in the beginning of this chapter. According to McGowan (1995), professional values are primary in practitioners' decision making and action. The *Code of Ethics* of the National Association of Social Workers (1996) summarized the core values of the social work profession as follows:

1. Social workers elevate service to others above self-interest. (Service)
2. Social workers pursue social change, particularly with and on behalf of vulnerable and oppressed individuals and groups of people. (Social Justice)

3. Social workers treat each person in a caring and respectful fashion, mindful of individual differences and cultural and ethnic diversity. (Dignity and Worth of the Person)
4. Social workers understand that relationships between and among people are an important vehicle for change. (Importance of Human Relationships)
5. Social workers are continually aware of the profession's mission, values, ethical principles, and ethical standards, and practice in a manner consistent with them. (Integrity)
6. Social workers continually strive to increase their professional knowledge and skills and to apply them in practice. (Competence)

There is a general consensus about social work values. For example, most professional social workers agree that client participation, self-determination, and confidentiality are among basic social work values. However, disagreements are likely to occur when it comes to implementing these generalized professional values. Social workers may differ about priorities, since they are not absolute, specific objectives, and the means necessary to put these generalized values into practice. Furthermore, little is known about how social workers make decisions about values in practice and whether adherence to values differs by practice setting or field (Pike, 1996). Thus the value "enhancing the dignity of life" may be used by one social worker to support a client's request for an abortion, while her social work colleague may call on the same generalized value to support her professional decision to try to persuade the client to go through a full-term pregnancy. This situation led Perlman to conclude that "a value has small worth, except as it is moved, or is moveable, from believing into doing, from verbal affirmation into action" (1976, p. 381).

Vigilante asks whether values can "be transmuted into instruments of professional practice, or do they serve only to guide practice and morally justify the profession" (1983, p. 59)? Bloom suggests that philosophic definitions of values do not really assist practitioners in the helping professions; according to him the focus should be on "what values look like as expressed in action" (1975, p. 138). Professional values that do not provide guidance and direction are only of limited use. Nevertheless, they are important because ethical principles and ethical rules can be derived from these values. When framed as a professional code of ethics, such rules and principles may provide social workers with the ethical criteria necessary for making difficult practice decisions. Note should be taken that ethical principles are always derived from values. A rule or principle that is not derived from values but from another source is not an ethical rule. Such a rule may be a bureaucratic rule, a principle derived from practice wisdom, or something else, but it is not an ethical rule.

ETHICS

How to move from values to behavior is a problem that is not limited to professional practitioners. It is a more general problem that has become the focus of attention of ethicists. *Ethics* are generally defined as that branch of philosophy that concerns itself with human conduct and moral decision making. Ethics seek to discover the principles that guide people in deciding what is right and wrong. Another definition points to a key function of ethics. "Ethics is not primarily concerned with getting people to do what they believe to be right, but rather with helping them to decide what is right" (Jones et al., 1977, p. 8).

Though the terms *values* and *ethics* are often used interchangeably, they are not identical. Ethics are deduced from values and must be in consonance with them. The difference between them is that values are concerned with what is *good* and *desirable*, while ethics deal with what is *right* and *correct*. A person's right to privacy, for example, is an important value of American society. One of the social work ethical rules deduced from this value states, "Social workers should obtain clients' informed consent before audiotaping or videotaping clients or permitting observation of services to clients by a third party" (NASW, 1996, Section 1, 1.03-f).[*] In the same manner *privacy* is a desirable value, while *informed consent* and *confidentiality* are the ethical rules and the correct ways of practice that are derived from this value.

Even though values are meant to serve as guides for selecting desirable behavior, they do not always lead to these results since a person's behavior is not always consistent with his or her professed values. Social workers, like other professionals, at times practice in ways that are inconsistent with professional values or in ways that do not reflect societal values. For example, client participation in decision making is highly valued by social workers, yet some practitioners do not always make sufficient effort to involve their clients fully. One reason for the lack of congruence between values and behaviors may be that values are usually stated at a very high level of generality, while behaviors are very specific. Another reason for this incongruence may be the gap between professed (or public) and real (or personal) values of the person.

There is broad agreement about the most generalized values, such as cooperation and success, but these are not sufficiently specific to help identify appropriate behavior patterns. The more specific a value, the more useful will it be as a behavioral guide. On the other hand, the more specific a value, the smaller the chance that it will gain wide acceptance.

---

*Note: This reference is to the NASW *Code of Ethics* (1996). All such citations encountered subsequently in this work refer to the same source.

For example, everyone agrees that *family life* is a highly desired value—
that is, everyone agrees as long as that value is not defined in more specific operational terms. But this generalized value does not help an adult
son who has to make difficult decisions about how to care for his para-
lyzed, senile father without increasing the tensions that already exist between his present wife and his children from a previous marriage. Nor
will the son's social worker find any specific ethical referents that may
provide her with guidance in this situation.

MORALITY

George Bernard Shaw (1932) once wrote, "I don't believe in morality."
His reference may have been to traditional values and rules of behavior
promulgated by some external authority. Yet it is hard to conceive of life
in a society that is essentially amoral.

Morality consists of principles or rules of conduct that define standards for right behavior. One might hope that morality consists of a set of
general rules that apply to everyone in a society. These rules are neither
enacted nor revoked by a legislature, but are accepted and changed by
general consensus. They define the relationship between the members of
a society. As Goldstein observed, "a moral sense…involves not only individual thoughts and actions but relationships with others" (1987,
p. 181). Athough in the United States there is a broad consensus about
some issues, we are witnessing nowadays a growing diversity and multi-
moralities. There are deep divisions in American society about such issues as euthanasia and the right to commit suicide, abortion, gay and
lesbian marriage, the responsibilities of individuals, families, and governments, and on another level clashing values among immigrant, racial,
generational, religious, sexual-orientation, and ethnic and cultural groups,
among others. Social workers are increasingly confronted by a diversity
of values and moralities; they practice in a society where there is less
and less consensus about what is *the* proper moral stance.

The *Curriculum Policy Statement* of the Council on Social Work
Education (Revised, 1997) expects every social work education program to provide specific knowledge about social work values and their
ethical implications, including assisting students to develop an awareness of their own values and ethical dilemmas. The *Statement* also sets
forth a series of social work professional values such as regard for individual worth and dignity, the individual's right to make independent decisions and to participate actively in the helping process, a commitment
to assisting client systems to obtain needed resources, striving to make
social institutions more humane and responsive to human needs, and

respect for and acceptance of the unique characteristics of diverse populations, as well as responsibility for one's own ethical conduct, the quality of one's practice, and continuous growth in knowledge and skills of the profession.

Curriculum content must be offered so that students can understand and appreciate human diversity. Content must be included about population groups relevant to each program's mission, such as race, color, gender, age, creed, ethnic or national origin, disability, political orientation, and sexual orientation. Such groups represent a diversity of values and perspectives and, for many social workers, raise value dilemmas, both for themselves and for their clients. Such a diversity also complicates their ethical decision making in practice.

PROFESSIONAL ETHICS

Professional ethics provide the guide that enables a social worker to transform professional values into practice activities. Ethical principles do not describe professional practice, but provide screens in terms of which practice options can be assessed as to their rightness or wrongness. Codes of professional ethics identify and describe the ethical behavior expected of professional practitioners.

Professional ethics are closely related to, but not identical with, general societal ethics. Just as social work values are derived from the values held by society but are not necessarily identical with those values, so professional ethics come from the same sources as societal ethics but may differ from them in important details. There may be differences in priorities, emphases, intensities, or applications. Illustrative of these crucial differences are the ethical principles governing the relationships among people. Both societal and professional ethics stress the *principle of equality*, but professional ethics give priority to the client's interests ahead of the interests of all others. Figure 2.1 spells out these differences in concise form.

For social workers, this professional ethics principle is expressed in the standard of the NASW *Code of Ethics: "Social workers' primary responsibility is to promote the well-being of clients"* (NASW, 1996, 1, 1.01). The implications of this professional ethical principle for social workers and their practice are manifold because every social worker is almost continually forced to choose (knowingly or not) between general ethics and professional ethics. It is, of course, often easier to deduce and formulate an ethical principle in theory than it is to apply it in practice. The framers of the CSWE *Curriculum Policy Statement* recognized the importance of professional ethics for social work practice. They therefore mandated that there should be infused throughout the curriculum

Figure 2.1   The Ethics of Interpersonal Relations

GENERAL ETHICS:	All persons shall be respected as equals.
PROFESSIONAL ETHICS:	All persons shall be respected as equals, but priority shall be given to the interests of the client.

the values and ethics that guide professional social workers in their practice (Council on Social Work Education, Revised, 1997).

Some social workers can discuss professional ethics at length at staff meetings but fail to see how these principles affect their own practice. In the following exemplar the situation faced by one social worker will be analyzed; pay particular attention to the questions of professional ethics that this worker faces.

➤ 2.1 Diana Can't Go Out

Ms. Macedonia is a single parent, the mother of three children ranging in age from seven to sixteen. Her oldest daughter, Diana, is a 16-year-old high school student. Until the beginning of this school year she received good grades, but at midterm she was failing all courses. She seems to have lost all interest in school. For the past three weeks she has not been in school at all.

Ms. Macedonia is a clerical worker in the town's only industry. She goes to work early in the morning before her children leave for school, and returns home late in the afternoon, hours after the children finish school. Ms. Macedonia is a good home manager. However, she has no friends and is always at home by herself.

Recently Ms. Macedonia turned to the local family service agency to ask for help. She told the social worker that she felt depressed since she did not know what to do with Diana. By talking with both Ms. Macedonia and Diana the social worker learned that Diana has to stay home every evening and every weekend because her mother does not want to be alone. Even though Diana wants to go out with her friends, her mother never allows her to do so.

Ms. Macedonia's social worker faced a number of practical and ethical questions, including the following: Who is "the client" to whose interest the social worker should give priority? Is it Diana? Or her mother who made the initial request for help? Or both? Is it ethical for the social worker to intervene with Diana even though she has not asked for help and who (on being contacted by the worker) claims to have no need for help? What other ethical considerations are evident in this case?

No profession can establish for itself ethical rules that grossly violate the general ethical standards of the community. If a profession fails to take into consideration general societal ethics, it risks severe sanctions, including the possible revocation of part or all of its professional authority. Yet society recognizes that practice requirements make it impossible for professional practitioners to follow the identical ethical rules that people generally are expected to follow. Social workers, for example, may ask the kind of questions that in general conversation might be considered inappropriate or even an invasion of a person's privacy. However, before asking such questions, a social worker must be certain that this information is necessary and that she can keep it confidential.

Society often sets limits to what a social worker may do. These limits can add to the ethical problems that social workers face. In a number of foreign countries, particularly in some of the developing countries, social workers have been jailed because they chose to follow professional ethics and used a practice modality contrary to their government's expectations. Their fate highlights the fact that ethical problems in professional practice are real and at times can result in dire consequences. In a number of countries, including our own, some social workers have lost their jobs, have not received promotions, or have been shunned because they practiced in accord with professional ethical principles and in this way ran afoul of certain societal values.

LAW AND ETHICS: THE PROBLEM OF UNETHICAL BUT LEGAL BEHAVIOR

Within the last two decades, Congress and all state legislatures have passed a large number of laws that have affected and will continue to affect social work practice. At the same time the various state and federal courts, including the U.S. Supreme Court, have handed down a number of decisions that are of critical importance for social workers. "Good intentions" and "ignorance of the law" are no longer acceptable excuses for social workers who run afoul of the law. Lack of knowledge not only exposes practitioners to possible litigation for malpractice but may also contribute to unprofessional and unethical practices.

The purpose of this section is to help social work students and practitioners understand the interdependence of law and practice. We will also explore a number of key legal principles that are of vital importance for social workers. Less attention will be paid to specific legal questions because (1) in many instances the "law" differs in each of the fifty states, (2) law is constantly evolving, so that if we were to discuss a specific law, there is a real possibility that it would be out of date even before this book is in the hands of the reader, and (3) we do not intend to make lawyers out of social workers.

Characteristics of Law

Law has been variously defined by different authorities. According to Albert (1986), laws are concerned with protecting people against excessive or unfair power—government as well as private power. Black (1972) emphasizes the social control aspect of law; for him, law defines the normative relations between a state and its citizens. Selznick (1961) considers justice to be at the very center of any adequate definition of law. Others note that law tells people what they can and cannot do. The law informs them what is likely to happen if they are caught doing something that is prohibited (Van Hoose & Kottler, 1985). A crucial characteristic of law is that it is enacted by legislatures, interpreted by courts, and enforced by the threat of punishment. Its observance is held to be obligatory.

Law changes continually. At any given time it tries to reflect current knowledge and mores. The adaptation and change of law to reflect contemporary culture is exemplified by the evolution of the laws on abortions. When the California Supreme Court, in the *Belous* case (1969), reversed the lower court conviction of an obstetrician who had been found guilty of procuring an abortion, it discussed at length the history of the statute that classified procuring an abortion as a crime. It noted that when the statute was enacted in 1850, almost every abortion resulted in the woman's death because of the complete lack of modern antiseptic surgical techniques. The legislature in the mid-nineteenth century therefore limited abortions to those rare cases in which the danger to the woman's life from continuing the pregnancy was greater than the danger of her dying from the abortion. The Court noted that nowadays abortions during the first trimester are relatively safe—in fact, statistically safer than going through with the pregnancy. For this and other constitutional reasons the Court reversed the conviction under what it considered the antiquated abortion statute and thus, in effect, revised the law in line with contemporary knowledge and technology.

In societies where the broad moral consensus has eroded, laws may be more effective than "moral persuaders" because they are enforced by the police power of the state. In 1970 the U.S. Supreme Court held in *Goldberg v. Kelly* that the due-process clause of the Fourteenth Amendment of the Constitution also applied to social welfare programs. This new legal protection for the poor resulted in the next decade in an eightfold increase in administrative appeal hearings in the Aid to Families with Dependent Children (AFDC) alone.

No matter how defined, law is of direct and immediate concern to social workers. There are many different ways in which law impacts on social work practice. Laws authorize payment for specified services; laws direct that certain social services be provided for all who need them; laws authorize professional social workers to engage in some activities that other people are not allowed to perform, but they also limit social workers from other activities that can be performed only by practitioners of another profession. Laws require social workers to report certain information to designated government agencies. Since laws differ from state to state, we avoid mentioning specific ones. Our purpose is merely to indicate the importance of laws for all social workers, no matter whether they are agency-employed or in private practice. Yet some social workers remain ignorant of the law. They practice as if the law were of little or no concern to them. Most experts agree that child abuse reports have increased over the past 30 years, but many cases continue to go unreported. Though all states now require that cases of suspected child abuse and neglect be reported to a designated public child protective agency, no matter whether the social worker is employed by a public or voluntary agency or is in private practice, some social workers still are not familiar with this requirement. They are also not aware that most state laws include threats of civil and criminal penalties for those failing to report (Besharov & Laumann, 1996).

Two national studies of the incidence of child abuse and neglect and the reporting patterns of a broad representative sample of professionals who serve children found that many professionals failed to report substantial numbers of the children they saw who had observable signs of child abuse and neglect. Professionals failed to report to authorities 56 percent of apparently abused or neglected children. More than 85 percent of fatal or serious physical abuse cases (life-threatening or requiring professional treatment to prevent long-term impairment) they saw were reported, as well as 72 percent of the sexual abuse cases. However, these data translate for the period studied into 2,000 children with observable physical injuries severe enough to require hospitalization that were not reported and more than 100,000 children with moderate physical injuries that went unreported. Over 30,000 apparently sexually abused children went unreported. Noteworthy is the fact that these nonreporting rates were discovered among relatively well-trained professionals, not among those less well-trained (Besharov & Laumann, 1996).

Researchers are still not certain how to explain this failure to report child abuse and neglect. At one time it was thought that professionals feared that reporting might result in a lawsuit, but nowadays all jurisdictions give immunity from civil and criminal liability to professionals who report child abuse and neglect cases (Daro, 1988).

Differences Between Law and Ethics

What are the similarities and differences between law and ethics? Law has an ethical dimension. Thus Albert insists that "it is altogether misleading to say…that legal duties have nothing to do with moral duties" (1986, p. 9). But there are differences. While law observance is obligatory and enforced by threat of punishment, compliance with ethical principles is voluntary and reinforced only by a moral respect for values. Professional ethics, however, may also be enforced by professional sanctions; such sanctions may range from a simple censure to cancellation of permission to practice. A professional who is guilty of unethical or unprofessional behavior may be punished by a court of law and also may be disciplined for the same offense by her professional association.

Whereas ethics are often characterized by a sense of ambiguity and indeterminacy, law is said to be definitive. Yet the outcome of legal disputes is far from certain or predictable. Legal rules are pliable; whether a particular legal rule will apply often depends on the arguments presented by one or the other side.

Law is enacted by legislatures and can be changed by a subsequent enactment or by legal interpretations. Ethical rules, though they do change over time, are generally immune from deliberate changes. Yet there is a close relationship between law and ethics since laws are often based on ethical principles. Thus, the legal principle of *privileged communication* is based on the *privacy* value and the ethical principle of *confidentiality*. (See Chapter 4 for a discussion of these principles.)

Conflict Between Law and Professional Ethics

Treating people wrongly does not become ethically right even when this is required or sanctioned by law. At times, a practitioner may follow the law and still be guilty of unethical professional behavior. In the past, a number of state legislatures enacted laws that mandated the involuntary sterilization of certain groups of felons and developmentally disabled persons. Can we say that a social worker who participated in these "lawful" programs practiced in an ethical manner? Many social workers claim that compliance with the law requiring the reporting and deportation of those who have entered this country illegally is contrary to professional ethics. Other social workers state that the application of the death penalty, even when authorized by law, is always unethical. Some suggest that there is a moral right, even a moral duty, to violate unjust laws (Pemberton, 1965).

Yet there is a general assumption that human service professionals have an ethical duty to obey the law. From the time of John Locke to our own day there have only been a few who have openly challenged this assumption. Yet "in some circumstances, competing ethical principles may be so fundamental that they justify disobedience of the law" (Melton, 1988, p. 944). This dilemma is highlighted by the *Tarasoff* decision (*Tarasoff v. Regents of the University of California*, 1976, 551 P2nd 334 at 340). The wider implications of this decision will be discussed in greater detail in Chapter 4. Here we will only note that in *Tarasoff* the California Supreme Court held that in some situations the welfare and safety of the community may be more important than the confidentiality principle. Some social workers view this legal requirement to break confidentiality as forcing them to choose in certain cases between the professional helping relationship, professional ethics, and law. Other social workers hold that a law cannot override professional ethical duties. But most have accepted the principles of the *Tarasoff* decision and— as the *Code of Ethics* suggests (NASW *Code*, 1996, 1.07c)—do not think that they have to choose between professional ethics and law, as is the case in reporting child abuse.

Social work with HIV-positive persons may make the dilemma of the *Tarasoff* decision even more critical for many social workers. What are the ethical and the legal requirements when such a client admits to his social worker that he continues to share needles or engage in unprotected sexual relations without notifying his partner of his condition? Should this social worker break confidentiality and warn the endangered partner? This ethical dilemma will be discussed in greater detail in Chapter 11.

Another example of the law/ethics dilemma may arise in connection with the legal requirement to report cases of suspected child abuse. Should a social worker disobey the law requiring that such cases be reported to the child protective agency when she knows (on the basis of past experiences) that the staff of that agency is not competent to deal with this problem? The *Code of Ethics* of the Clinical Social Work Federation (1997) addresses the possible conflict between professional ethics and law in Section VIb:

> Clinical social workers practice their profession in compliance with legal standards, and do not participate in arrangements or activities which undermine the law. When they believe, however, that laws or community standards are in conflict with the principles and ethics of the profession, they make known the conflict and work responsibly toward change that is in the public interest.

Malpractice and Unethical Behavior

A social worker's activities may be unprofessional, unethical, or both. An activity is unprofessional and malpractice when it departs as a result of professional negligence or misconduct from the usual practice that a "prudent professional" would have rendered in the same situation. It is *unethical* when it violates the professional principles and standards promulgated by the profession's *Code of Ethics* in dealing with clients, colleagues, practice settings, the profession, and the broader society.

Failure to provide proper professional service (that is, rendering unprofessional service) can make a social worker liable to civil suits and/or criminal charges. Failure to provide ethical service can make a social worker liable to professional sanctions. In some situations a social worker faces all three risks. For example, a social worker who has sexual relations with a client may face a civil damage suit, criminal charges in at least nine states, and professional sanctions for unethical behavior. (See Chapter 8 for a more extensive discussion of the ethical issues involved in client/social worker relations.) Having sexual relations with a *former* client may also be unethical and illegal, but after a lapse of a period of time there may no longer be a case for civil liability. Thus, in Illinois if sexual contact occurs within *one* year of termination of therapy, there may be grounds for legal action. In Minnesota and California, civil liability is limited to a *two*-year period. But in Wisconsin an action may be brought within *three* years of the sexual contact or up to *15* years after sexual contact occurred if the patient failed to bring the action within the three-year period due to the effects of the sexual contact. Legal remedies available to victims of sexual exploitation by psychotherapists have expanded since the late 1960s, and criminal actions are charged under sexual assault statutes. The question, both legally and ethically, is not the elapsed time, but rather whether such relations still constitute an exploitation of the therapeutic relationship (Perry & Kuruk, 1993).

Civil suits to recover damages resulting from unprofessional actions or inaction are known as *malpractice suits*. The relatively low premium rates for malpractice insurance that social workers pay (in contrast to the premiums paid by physicians and other high-risk occupations) suggest that successful malpractice suits against social workers are still rare, but their number is increasing every year. In the early 1970s there were almost no lawsuits against social workers, but since then the number of suits against social workers insured by the NASW Insurance Trust have increased dramatically (Houston-Vega, Nuehring, & Daguio, 1997, p. 1). It must be remembered that all professions experienced a growth in lawsuits in recent decades, which is characteristic of our increasingly litigious society. In the past there might have been relatively few malpractice suits against social workers because most clients believed in their social workers' selfless dedication to client welfare. Or, the relative scarcity could have been due to a lack of common law to serve as a cause of legal action (Perry & Kuruk, 1993). As more social workers go into private practice (where service is provided for payment of a fee), all social workers may expect to become more vulnerable to malpractice suits.

Social workers who want to protect themselves properly should know what is involved in malpractice. By learning how liability develops, they can take precautions that will reduce the hazards they may face. One need not be a lawyer to understand the principles involved. However, in specific situations, legal consultation is desirable. Nevertheless, it is important to keep one's perspective about malpractice and not panic. Yet social workers should not underrate the potential risks they face.

A client must prove these four conditions in order to win a malpractice suit:

1. The defendant (that is, the social worker) must have a legal duty to provide a professional service to the plaintiff (client). Ordinarily, a social worker has such a legal duty once a person becomes a "client" (whether in an agency or in private practice).
2. The social worker's performance must have been negligent or below generally accepted professional standards of competence. What would other social workers have done under the same circumstances? "Good intentions" or "ignorance" are rarely an effective defense.
3. The plaintiff (client) must have suffered an injury or loss.
4. The social worker's actions or inaction must have "caused" the alleged injury or loss.

There appear to be few limits to the reasons for which malpractice suits can be initiated. The following list, based on Besharov and Besharov (1987, pp. 519–20) and Corey, Corey, and Callanan (1998, pp.141–46) shows the great range of malpractice actions:

1. Failure to obtain or document informed consent
2. Treatment without consent
3. Improper and incorrect diagnosis
4. Inappropriate treatment
5. Failure to consult with a specialist
6. Failure to refer to a specialist
7. Failure to prevent a client's suicide
8. Causing a client's suicide
9. Failure to protect a third party against damage
10. Inappropriate release of client from hospital
11. False imprisonment
12. Failure to provide adequate care for a client in residential care
13. Assault and battery
14. Sexual involvement with a client
15. Breach of confidentiality
16. Defamation

17. Violation of a client's civil rights
18. Failure to be available when needed
19. Abrupt or inappropriate termination
20. Inappropriate bill collection methods
21. Failure to report suspected child abuse
22. Failure to report suspected child neglect
23. Inadequately protecting a child
24. Violating parental rights
25. Inadequate foster care services
26. Failure to cure or failure to achieve satisfactory results
27. Client abandonment
28. Practicing beyond the scope of competency
29. Failure to control a dangerous client

Many social workers are familiar with several of the risks of malpractice listed above and the general principles of malpractice litigation. But fewer are well informed about risk reduction methods (Houston-Vega, Nuehring, & Daguio, 1997, p. 1). In one research study, 105 New Jersey social workers were asked whether a malpractice suit would be successful in the case of a therapist who had asked the police to pick up an emotionally disturbed client. This client had threatened to assault his therapist because he imagined that the therapist had revealed confidential information about him. Only 29 respondents (27.6 percent) gave the correct answer to this vignette—that there was little or no basis for a successful malpractice litigation based on the therapist's actions. However, 61 percent gave the correct answer to another illustrative case example. The second such example involved a case where a depressed client threatened to commit suicide and also kill her two children. Social workers were asked whether there was a basis for a successful malpractice litigation against the worker if she failed to inform the client's husband of the threat. The correct answer was that her actions were a very unlikely basis for a successful litigation. The publicity given to the *Tarasoff* decision in professional journals may explain the higher percentage of correct responses in this instance. Nevertheless, even in this case 40 percent of the social workers did not seem to know what is involved in malpractice litigation (Gerhart & Brooks, 1985).

The question remains: How can a social worker defend herself against the possibility of a malpractice suit? Knowledge, information, and good practice are the best defenses against liability. Additionally, sound risk management can reduce the degree of risk by implementing a plan for practitioners and agencies that includes the following: (1) Risk management audit (licenses, registrations in order; protocols for emergency situations; insurance coverage paid; maintenance and safeguarding client records; and other factors all in order and up to date); (2) Consultative relationship with legal counsel; (3) Specialist consultants (diagnosis and treatment; second-opinion referrals; ruling out organic pathology; psychological testing; evaluations regarding appropriateness of psychopharmalogical interventions); and (4) Continuing education (Kurzman, 1995).

There are additional means of protecting oneself from malpractice actions. One's practice can be limited to clients for whom the social worker is prepared by virtue of education, training, and experience. Other precautions are honesty and openness with clients, knowing one's limitations, and using consultation for difficult situations (Corey, Corey, & Callanan, 1998).

WHO NEEDS PROFESSIONAL ETHICS?

Do professional practitioners require special norms and ethical principles to guide their well-intentioned activities? Are not general ethical principles sufficient?

Whenever two ethical principles or two ethical rules provide contradictory directions, social workers need guidelines to help them decide which takes precedence. Professional ethics seek to provide such guidelines. Yet there are those who see no need for professional ethics. They argue that "common sense" or "practice wisdom" is all that a social worker needs in order to make the right decision. While no one should underrate the importance of sound judgment and practice wisdom, many recall the occasions when these simply were not sufficient to arrive at an ethically correct and effective practice decision.

Those who argue that professional ethics are not necessary for social workers cite one or more of the following arguments:

1. *Competence is enough.* Correct practice is based on competence and skill, not on the mastery of ethical principles. Many so-called ethical problems merely reflect poor practice. For example, good contracting will avoid many situations that are presented as ethical problems. Social workers will make more appropriate ethical decisions by becoming more competent.
2. *Uniqueness of each case.* Every case is different and every client presents unique problems. No code of ethical principles can provide adequate guidance for every unique situation that a social worker faces.
3. *Scientific social work is value-free.* Scientific social work must pay more attention to knowledge and technology than to religion and morality. An exaggerated interest in ethics will deflect prac-

titioners from developing further skill and knowledge, two areas that are most important for strengthening professional practice.

4. *No time.* Social work practitioners have no time for lengthy ethical reflections because practice demands that they act quickly. They do what they think is best for their clients. A code of abstract ethical principles will not help. If social workers were to analyze each ethical problem, they would never get anything done.

5. *Philosophers' ambiguity.* At least since Aristotle's days, philosophers have been unable to agree whether anyone can determine the truth of an ethical principle. Under these circumstances it is not possible to know the correctness of any ethical proposition. It is best not to fool ourselves into believing that professional ethics can help us know what is "right."

6. *Relativity.* What is thought to be "right" varies from country to country and even within a country at different times and for different population groups. In one society it is rude to come late for appointments, in another it is rude to come on time. Which is correct? In one culture a social worker is encouraged to recommend sexual abstinence when appropriate, while in another culture this option is taboo. Which is right? Within American society, different ethnic and cultural groups provide conflicting guidelines to what is "correct." In the social welfare field the emphasis has shifted pendulum-like between individual well-being and societal welfare. Which emphasis best reflects professional social work ethics? Those citing this reason conclude that there are no fixed ethical principles that hold over time or space. Everything is relative and there is no way of indicating which choice or option is correct.

7. *Instinct and "gut" feeling.* Practitioners usually know what is right in any given practice situation without having to turn to an authoritative ethical guide prescribed by some superior body. It is far better to trust a worker's intuition than to depend on the enforcement of bureaucratic rules.

8. *Coercion.* The adoption of a code of professional ethics will result in latent, if not overt, coercion on practitioners to act only in accordance with that document. Such coercion contradicts the basic social work and societal value of self-determination. A code also tends to stifle professional creativity because it places every social worker in the same mold and expects the same routine standard behavior from every practitioner. Personal ethics and regard for client welfare are far more important for ethical behavior than any fear of sanctions imposed by a professional organization.

9. *Virtuous persons.* There is yet another argument, already made by Aristotle, that all that is required for ethical decisions is that social workers be virtuous persons. When ethical decisions have to be made, people of good moral character will act ethically, based on their virtuous and morally schooled characters (Broadie, 1991).

10. *Wasted effort.* There are so few valid complaints about unethical behavior that a code of ethics and an enforcement machinery really are wasted efforts. The number of complaints concerning ethics violations have increased in recent decades. However, an NASW study indicates that in a 10-year period between 1982 and 1992, on the average, only 33 ethics violations occurred each year for the entire country (NASW, 1995b).

These arguments against a code of professional ethics are not entirely persuasive. Some are fallacious, others distort reality. Here a brief response to some of the arguments must suffice. The philosophical and clinical bases for these arguments will be dealt with in greater detail in the next chapter.

Anyone who practices social work knows that social workers seldom take time for drawn-out theoretical debates. Large caseloads and constant client demands for service do not leave time for calm contemplation and leisurely thinking. But ethical decisions need not take a long time. Social workers need help in making correct choices, precisely because they have so little time, and in some cases ethical choices that will need to be made can be anticipated.

Every social worker knows that each case is unique and different; yet there are commonalties. Ethical codes address these common elements. Principles and rules in a code of ethics are stated on a generalized level in order to permit adjustment to the unique features of each situation.

The voluntary acceptance of professional discipline, including a code of ethics, can hardly be viewed as a violation of the self-determination principle. A person becomes a professional social worker as a result of a voluntary decision. In Kohlberg's theory of moral development, this occupational choice could be identified as Level 5 moral behavior, which is a very high level of moral development, characteristic of a person who is a rational moral agent and a builder of a moral society—"society creating" rather than "society maintaining" (1984, p. 634).

Even though a code of professional ethics does not supply all of the answers that contemporary social workers need, there is a real demand for such a code. In time, improvements will make such a code even more useful. But no code will ever provide "all" the answers—that is not and should not be a code's function.

CODES OF PROFESSIONAL ETHICS

Every occupation that strives to achieve professional status attempts to develop a code of professional ethics. Such a code usually contains a compilation of the ethical principles relevant to the practice of that profession, principles to which the members of that profession are expected to adhere. Many codes of professional ethics also describe the sanctions that will be invoked against those who are unable or unwilling to meet these expectations.

The code of almost every contemporary profession has been written with the following functions in mind:

1. Provide practitioners with guidance when faced by practice dilemmas that include ethical issues.
2. Protect the public from charlatans and incompetent practitioners.
3. Protect the profession from governmental control; self-regulation is preferable to state regulation.
4. Enable professional colleagues to live in harmony with each other by preventing the self-destruction that results from internal bickering.
5. Protect professionals from litigation; practitioners who follow the code are offered some protection if sued for malpractice.

Since a code of professional ethics tries to provide guidance for every conceivable situation, it is written in terms of general principles, not specific rules. Yet when we compare codes written two or three decades ago with those written in more recent years, we note that the contemporary ones tend to be more specific and try to cover a greater variety of specific situations. Thus, the NASW *Code of Ethics* of 1967 had many fewer paragraphs and was written in much more general terms than the ones adopted in 1979 and reconfirmed in 1984 and 1993. The trend toward specificity continued in the *Code* approved in 1996, which more than doubled the number of standards found in the *Code* as of 1993. On the other hand, the American Medical Association's code of ethics adopted in 1980 is much briefer than its previous code, including, as of 1997, seven principles. One reason for the lack of detail in the new AMA code was the desire to prevent lengthy litigation that resulted from the detailed provisions of the previous code.

One of the possible consequences of greater specificity is the possibility of internal inconsistencies between various paragraphs of the same code. When there is greater specificity, ethical principles often conflict with one another, even though each may be valid. By avoiding any formulation of ethical principles in a hierarchical order, the task force provided the ingredients for many of the ethical dilemmas that we will examine in the following chapter (Cohen, 1980). This approach was also followed in the 1996 *Code* where the specification of a hierarchy of values, principles, and standards was avoided. Yet it should be remembered that codes of ethics "are not intended as a blueprint that would remove all need for the use of judgment or ethical reasoning" (Conte et al., 1989, p. 5). Marcuse (1976), on the other hand, suggested that codes of professional ethics fail to provide answers to many ethical dilemmas because their orientation is more likely to be system-maintenance than system-challenging.

Codes of ethics generally provide guidance only for good/bad decisions. They are far less effective in helping practitioners make decisions of the good/good and bad/bad variety. But it is precisely these types of decisions that trouble many social workers. Good/bad decisions are those where one of the two options under consideration is thought to be correct or right, while the alternative is assumed to be incorrect or wrong. In most instances, social workers have no trouble making ethical decisions of the good/bad variety. Common sense and sound ethical judgment are usually sufficient to guide the practitioner's choice. Good/good decisions, on the other hand, are those where all of the options are beneficial, while bad/bad decisions are those for which all options result in undesirable consequences (Keith-Lucas, 1977). In many of these latter situations, social workers need help to sort out the ethical aspects in order to make a correct decision.

The following exemplar illustrates a practice situation that includes an ethical dilemma that is not of the good/bad variety.

➤ 2.2 John Miller's Return to State Hospital

John Miller is mentally ill and has been so diagnosed by several psychiatrists. For the past three years this 21-year-old young adult has been living at home with his elderly parents. He can take care of his own minimal needs, but he has no interest whatsoever in any personal contact. Most of every day he sits in the living room, staring either into empty space or at TV. His parents dare not leave him home alone. They have approached you, John's social worker, requesting that you make arrangements to have him returned to the state hospital since they feel that they can no longer give him the care he needs. You appreciate their situation, but you also know that returning John to a state hospital may harm him.

You know that it is unethical to deprive anyone, even a mentally ill person, of his freedom except under certain clearly specified circumstances. What are the circumstances that would warrant a social worker's considering involuntary hospitalization? Is the parents' request sufficient? How would this social worker's dilemma differ if the psychiatric diagnosis indicated that sooner or later John would inflict serious harm on others or to himself, even though he has been entirely harmless until now?

A BRIEF HISTORY OF CODES OF PROFESSIONAL ETHICS

All modern professions have developed codes of professional ethics. These became common only in the past century, but their long and checkered history goes back to antiquity. More than two thousand years ago, Hippocrates (c. 460–c. 377 B.C.) demanded that all Greek physicians pledge themselves to a high level of professional and ethical conduct. There is no record of similar codes for theologians and lawyers, the only other professions in the ancient world. But the Hippocratic oath became a guide, informing medical doctors in many parts of the ancient and medieval world of the correct way of professional behavior.

Just as medicine was the first profession in the ancient world to develop a code of ethics, so did it lead the way in modern times. Dr. Thomas Percival of England is credited with writing the first of the modern professional codes of ethics in 1803. The first American code was promulgated by the American Medical Association in 1847 and was modeled on Percival's code. Pharmacists followed a few years later with their own code. Contemporary accounts suggest that pharmacists wrote this code because they wanted the public to know that their professional conduct differed from that of physicians, who in those days did not enjoy a very high repute.

For most American occupational groups, the development of a code of ethics coincided, more or less, with the decision to formalize the transformation of the occupation into a profession. Social workers, for example, were aware that a code of ethics was one of the prerequisites for professional recognition long before the appearance of Greenwood's important article on the attributes of a profession (1957). They tried to draft codes of professional ethics soon after Flexner (1915) told them that social work was not yet a profession. An experimental draft code of ethics for social case workers, printed in 1920, has been attributed to Mary Richmond (Pumphrey, 1959, p. II).

The prestigious *Annals of the American Society for Political and Social Sciences* devoted its entire May 1922 issue to ethical codes in the professions and in business. Contemporary observers viewed the appearance of this journal issue as crucial to the emerging interest in such codes. In the *Annals* article on social work ethics, Mary Van Kleeck and Graham R. Taylor, two veteran social workers, wrote that social work did not have a written code of professional ethics, but that social work practice was ethical because practitioners were guided by the ideal of service and not by any thought of financial gain. Several local and national groups developed draft codes during the twenties. The American Association for Organizing Family Social Work prepared, but did not adopt, a detailed draft code in 1923. Many of the 38 paragraphs of that draft still sound relevant today.

The American Association of Social Workers (AASW), the largest organization of professional social workers of that day, endorsed the need for a code of professional ethics. An editorial in the April 1924 issue of *The Compass*, the official journal of the AASW, came out in favor of a code of professional ethics and asked, "Hasn't the public a right to know how the ordinary social worker is likely to act under ordinary circumstances?" The Research Committee of the AASW tried to identify common problems of ethical practice. The AASW Executive Committee appointed a National Committee on Professional Ethics even before this study was completed. This action spurred many local chapters to discuss the need for a code. Several chapters tried to produce draft documents. The Toledo (Ohio) chapter reportedly was the first local AASW chapter to publicize a draft code. Though that draft was limited to a few general ethical principles, it inspired other chapters to try their hand at preparing their own draft code of professional ethics. However, despite much interest, the adoption of a nationwide professional code had to await further organizational developments. It was only in 1951 that the AASW Delegate Assembly adopted a code of ethics.

When the historic merger of all professional social work organizations took place in the mid-1950s, work on drafting a new code of professional ethics was started almost immediately, but the NASW Delegate Assembly adopted a code of ethics only in 1960. Seven years later this code was amended to include a nondiscrimination paragraph. The absence of such a provision from earlier codes tells much about the change in the moral climate of the country and of the profession.

Before long, many social workers called for a complete revision of the code in order to produce a document that would provide clearer guidance for practitioners and that would be more in tune with the realities of contemporary practice. A completely new code was adopted by the 1979 NASW Delegate Assembly. But soon it became evident that this code did not yet provide sufficient guidance for social work practitioners who sought help when facing difficult ethical issues. In an early discussion of the draft code, one prominent social worker noted that its usefulness was limited because of "its high level of abstraction and lack of practice utility" (McCann, 1977, p. 18).

The revised NASW *Code of Ethics* placed a much greater emphasis on the welfare of individuals than did the earlier 1967 document. This change is problematic because it tends to shift the focus away from the common welfare. One analysis of different codes of professional ethics found that all other helping professions (with the exception of medicine) placed a greater emphasis on the common welfare than did social work (Howe, 1980). Social workers affiliated with the National Association of Black Social Workers have prepared a code of ethics that gives expression to their belief that individual welfare can be served best by promoting the common welfare of all African-American people. Social workers in clinical practice have adopted a code of ethics that reflects their specific concerns. The Code of Ethics of the Canadian Association of Social Workers reflects some of the special concerns of Canadian society.

A Feminist Therapy Code of Ethics is based upon feminist philosophy, psychological theory and practice, as well as political theory. In 1996 a revised NASW *Code of Ethics* was approved by the Delegate Assembly and implemented in 1997. Earlier in 1993, new standards were included related specifically to practitioner impairment and dual/multiple relationships. All of the professional codes mentioned above can be found in Appendix B.

EXERCISES

1. Ethical principles and rules are derived from societal values. Identify the relevant social work ethical rules for the following societal values:
   cultural diversity
   equality
   freedom
   integrity
   knowledge building
   privacy
   social justice
   Note the differences in the ethical rules offered in the several Codes of Ethics that appear in Appendix B.
2. Discuss in small groups whether it is possible and desirable for a social worker to remain neutral and keep her own values from influencing clients.
3. As a social worker, if you had to choose between a child's right to confidentiality and a parent's right to know things that affect the child, how would you go about making this decision?
4. Study the Feminist Therapy Code of Ethics in Appendix B. When you compare that code or guidelines with the NASW Code, can you identify themes not emphasized in the NASW Code but that are found in the Feminist Code? Are there any standards that conflict?
5. Discuss in small groups whether it is preferable that social workers work only with clients whose values are similar to their own. Are there any potential ethical positives to such a decision? If not, what are the potential ethical negatives of such a decision?

SUGGESTIONS FOR ADDITIONAL READINGS

McGowan (1995) examines how values shape professional decision making as well as the history of shifts in social work value preferences and ethical concerns. Reamer (1998) traces the evolution of social work ethical norms, principles, and standards. Excellent introductions to the place of moral philosophy in social work practice can be found in Siporin (1982), Goldstein (1987, 1998), and Manning (1997). Conrad (1988), Walden, Wolock, and Demone (1990), Kugelman (1992), Proctor, Morrow-Howell, and Lott (1993), Dolgoff and Skolnik (1996), Regehr and Antle (1997), and Healy (1998) report on research on the ethical aspects of social work practice in various settings. Barker (1988b) raises a question that faces social workers who are members of several professional associations. Which code of ethics should they follow?

3. Guidelines for Ethical Decision Making

Social workers must make ethical choices every day. A client tells her social worker that she is planning to commit suicide. A group member who has been unemployed for the past nine months asks his social worker not to tell a prospective employer about his criminal past so that he can get the job, which he needs so desperately. Another client has been telling his worker that he has been embezzling funds from his employer in order to pay for his son's open-heart surgery. A young man threatens to harm a fellow worker who he believes has raped his fiancée. Each of these situations confronts the social worker with one or more ethical dilemmas because they involve conflicting obligations. What are a social worker's obligations toward her clients? Toward others who may be harmed or benefited by what the client did or will do? Toward society? Toward her own values?

A better understanding of the philosophical and practical components of ethical decision making is desirable in order to encourage ethical behavior among social work practitioners. An analysis of a practice situation, the case of Serena Adams, will illustrate this approach.

➤ **3.1 Serena Adams Is HIV⁺**

In the Jeanette April residential treatment center for teenagers with emotional problems, the staff has become aware that Serena Adams, an 18-year-old female who is HIV⁺, has been sending notes to Donnie, an

18-year-old male resident, suggesting dates for sex. The fact that Serena is HIV⁺ is known only to the staff members and to Serena. Both state law and the American Disabilities Act forbid exposing the fact that anyone is HIV⁺. When the treatment team was told about this development, after discussion, they asked Jackie LaMartine, Serena's social worker, to speak to her to explore the situation with her and to try to avoid any sexual liaison between Serena and Donnie, or at the least to make sure they know safe sex methods. When approached, Serena refused to cooperate, arguing that the information must be kept confidential, that she and Donnie love each other, and that how they have sex is their own business. She asked that no one tell Donnie of the facts. The team members are split as to what to do. Some argue that, as long as Serena informs Donnie, they should not interfere. Others argue the team should try to prevent any sexual relationship between them.

The facts seem fairly clear, as are several of the ethical dilemmas that face Ms. LaMartine and the team. There are many questions that arise out of the social worker's professional knowledge and experience, among them:

1. Should Ms. LaMartine and the team leave Serena and Donnie to make their own decisions despite the risks to them both? Is the duty to protect Donnie more correct ethically than the maintenance of confidentiality for Serena? If Ms. LaMartine tells Donnie the facts, she will interfere with Serena's self-determination and freedom, but if she doesn't tell him, she exposes him to potential infection. Is the social worker ethically justified to discuss the situation with Donnie without Serena's agreement?

2. Because there is a potential conflict between ethical decision making and legal responsibilities, which choice takes priority? Is it more correct to obey the law and protect neither Serena nor Donnie by maintaining confidentiality and not informing Donnie of the risks? What is the social worker's duty to protect?

3. What are the long-term potential costs for Serena and Donnie if the team accedes to Serena's request? Are the costs to the agency, to these two residents, as well as to other residents, worth an effort to prevent a sexual relationship—which may not be preventable in any case?

4. Since the social worker and team are employed by an organization that seeks to prevent sexual relations outside of marriage, what implications are there for social workers whose values are or are not consistent with the espoused values of the April residential treatment center?

Ethical decision making does not involve the automatic application of arbitrary rules. What MacIver wrote many decades ago is still relevant today: "ethics cannot be summed up in a series of inviolate rules or commandments which can be applied everywhere and always without regard to circumstances, thought of consequences, or comprehension of the ends to be attained" (1922, p. 7). If this were the situation, social workers would find it easier to deal with the ethical problems they encounter.

Social work professionals, as do other professionals, make many ethical judgments every day with confidence, not thinking these judgments difficult or controversial. The professional Code of Ethics or common sense provides sufficient guidance to cope with many of these dilemmas (Beyerstein, 1993). But social workers often do not face the "simple" choice between one good option and one bad option. Instead, they are confronted by a number of choices, each one of which contains both positive and negative features, as in the above exemplar. In such a situation, the skilled worker must assess and weigh all options and outcomes and then select the one that appears to be the most ethical. But how does a social worker know which option is "the most ethical"?

FOUNDATIONS FOR ETHICAL DECISION MAKING

Decisions about ethical questions are rarely idiosyncratic and usually follow an individual's consistent patterns. Since such decisions involve questions of right and wrong, they are deeply rooted in that value system which is most important to the decision maker. Though philosophy has had a major impact on the development of ethics, there have also been other influences. Frankena (1980) made reference to traditional, political, religious, racial, and gender influences on the development of contemporary ethics. Essentially ethical systems are derived in two ways. Those systems in which the moral rules are determined by humans are known as *autonomous ethics*. Ethical systems that derive moral rules from nonhuman sources are known as *heteronomous ethics*. For example, when religious philosophers teach that moral rules are of divine origin, they are representative of heteronomous systems.

Aristotle and other Greek philosophers sought to discover the most rational way to live. Consequently they did not pay much attention to moral choices, nor were they greatly concerned with interpersonal relations. Many contemporary philosophers, on the other hand, emphasize moral choices in their search for the best way to live together with fellow humans. While for many of the classical Greek philosophers ethics were guided by a sense of egoism, altruism has become the moral principle that guides many modern ethicists.

Contemporary philosophers have identified two major theories that encompass most approaches to ethical decision making. These two theories are known as (a) ethical relativism and (b) ethical absolutism. Some have given these two various other names or have subdivided them into many subtheories.

Ethical Relativism

Ethical relativists reject fixed moral rules. They justify ethical decisions on the basis of the context in which they are made or on the basis of the consequences that they create. An option is chosen because it will lead to desired results, or is rejected because it will lead to results that are not wanted. The amount of good that is produced or the balance of good over evil (not any absolute standard) serves as the major criterion for reaching an ethical decision.

Ethical relativists differ when it comes to identifying the target or the intended beneficiary of the planned decision. Ethical egoists believe that one should always maximize what is good for oneself, no matter what the consequences for others. Ethical utilitarians, on the other hand, argue that the most important thing is to seek the greatest good for the largest number of persons. Philosophers who base their ethical thinking on the consequences of the activity are known as *teleologists*. Ethical relativism was already known in ancient Greece, where among its followers were the Sophists and Herodotus. In more recent times, John Stuart Mill, Jeremy Bentham, and Sigmund Freud were counted among those who followed this approach. They taught that ethical decisions should be made on the basis of maximizing pleasure and avoiding pain.

Ethical relativists say that the only thing that matters is the result. But is this position always defensible? Is there really no difference between an armed robber who kills a bystander during a bank holdup, a soldier who kills an enemy in combat, and a social worker who, by following the provisions of the child welfare code and not removing a youngster from his abusive parents, contributes to the death of a child? Different motivations and differing activities lead to the "same" results, but are they really the same? There are those who are even more critical of ethical relativism, suggesting that it is essentially asocial and perhaps even amoral because it assumes that individual satisfaction is the primary value.

Ethical Absolutism

Ethical absolutism, the other theory, stresses the overriding importance of fixed moral rules. These philosophers hold that an action is inherently right or wrong, apart from any consequences that might result from it. A specific action or practice is morally right or wrong not because of its consequences or the circumstances but "because of some feature intrinsic to the act or practice itself" (Callahan, 1988, p.20). Ethical absolutists maintain that ethical rules can be formulated and that these should hold under all circumstances. For example, they will argue that the rule, "A social worker shall tell the truth to her client," is always correct and applies in every situation, no matter how much damage may be caused by telling the truth in any particular situation. Philosophers who follow this theory are known as *deontologists*. Immanuel Kant (1724–1804) was the first of modern philosophers to adopt deontological concepts. He insisted that categorical imperatives are morally necessary and obligatory under all circumstances and that people know right from wrong.

Ethical absolutism and ethical relativism represent two approaches to ethics. Each has its followers. Some contemporary moral philosophers, such as Henry Sidgwick and William Frankena, have tried to synthesize ethical relativism and ethical absolutism.

Teleologists may argue for situational ethics, but there are times when they will also follow fixed rules. Jeremy Bentham (1748–1832), one of the earliest exponents of English utilitarianism, accepted "the greatest good for the greatest number" as a binding principle that applies in every situation. Some modern-day philosophers who are committed to situation ethics argue that "love" is the principle that should guide all human behavior (Fletcher, 1966; Lyden, 1998). On the other hand, many ethical absolutists, even those who teach a heteronomous ethics, allow for situations where the fixed rules do not apply. Many theologians have accepted the argument, first proposed by the Dutch jurist, Hugo Grotius (1583–1645), that one must always tell the truth and never lie, but that it is permissible to speak falsely to thieves because no one owes them the truth. However, there is an important difference between not applying a rule in an exceptional situation and deciding each situation as if there were no rules (Diggs, 1970).

According to some persons, our era is a postmodernist age, that is "the point at which modern untying (dis-embedding, disencumbering) of tied (embedded, situated) identities reaches its completion; it is now all too easy to choose identity, but no longer possible to hold it" (Ulrich & Beck-Gernsheim, 1996, p. 24). Necessity and certainty are being replaced by contingencies. The certainties of God, nature, truth, science, technology, morality, love, and marriage are being turned into "precarious freedoms" in which "nothing that has been binds the present while the present has but a feeble hold on the future" (Bauman, 1996, p. 51).

The search for certainty, a rational and definable truth, is questioned by many persons and even discredited. Some believe there are no universal "truths" and absolute rules are unacceptable while—at the same time—various "isms" (postmodernism, deconstructionism, social constructionism) claim that situations, including those that require ethical decision making, are best viewed from their "more truthful" perspectives. Because postmodernists believe there are no universal "truths" or absolute rules, they are included here as a subset of ethical relativism.

Practitioners may not be aware of these efforts by professional philosophers. Neither do they always know which ethical theory they follow when making ethical decisions. This is especially true because the differences between the major theories frequently are not as clear in practice as they are on the printed page. The two theoretical approaches often seem to merge in practice, but it does make a difference in ethical decision making whether a social worker follows one or the other theory, as the following analysis will illustrate.

Different Approaches of Two Social Workers

We will examine how two social workers—Ruth, an ethical relativist, and Anne, an ethical absolutist—might approach the ethical aspects of Serena's situation (Exemplar 3.1). Our focus will be on learning how these differences might lead to different worker considerations and decisions.

Serena demanded that her social worker keep her HIV$^+$ state confidential. Social worker Anne believes that every person has an absolute right to make decisions about himself or herself, even if the consequences of those decisions might harm that person. She also believes that confidentiality is a first-order professional value that social workers must follow at all times. Anne therefore has no hesitation about respecting Serena's demand since violating the confidential relationship will destroy the trust that a client must have in her worker. After all, Serena is in the residence because of her serious emotional problems. But this "practical" consideration is not the crucial ethical criterion for Anne's decision. No doubt Anne would give her priority to helping Serena see the long-range advantages of either avoiding sex with Donnie or informing him of her condition. However, as far as social worker Anne is concerned, the principles of confidentiality and client autonomy are absolute, no matter who the client or what the situation.

For the time being, we have proposed that social worker Anne has elevated confidentiality and client autonomy to absolute status, regardless of situations. Later in this chapter, we will introduce an approach to setting priorities in ethical decision making. But, for now, we note that confidentiality and client autonomy are two values but—as you will see—are not the highest on our ethical principles screen. When it comes to AIDS and sex, the LIFE value may have an even higher priority, and this would lead social worker Anne to entirely different professional decisions because she would now do everything to help Donnie protect his.

Social worker Ruth views the ethical aspects of Serena's situation in another light. Being an ethical relativist, she assesses the consequences of respecting Serena's request for confidentiality against the consequences of not informing Donnie. She concludes that protecting Serena's privacy can have very serious immediate and long-term consequences for Donnie's life and, potentially, also for Serena's life and emotional health. She tells Serena that either Serena herself or the worker must without delay inform Donnie of the risks he will run for having sex with Serena. If Serena is unwilling or unable to do so, social worker Ruth will do so, waving aside client autonomy and confidentiality issues in order to prevent harmful consequences. The two decision-making scenarios just described illustrate ethical absolutist and ethical relativist decision making. The decisions made by social workers Anne and Ruth are in each case only one of many different scenarios they could choose. The scenarios presented above are to illustrate the general decision-making patterns connected to each philosophy.

The answer to what is the best course of action in this situation depends upon the social worker's philosophy of life, her values, her tendency to ethical relativism or ethical absolutism, and the issue of immediate and direct danger to Donnie's life within the context of the influences of her peer group, family, professional group, neighborhood, and society. The situation, as with all ethical dilemmas, touches on the question of priorities. What is best for Serena and what is best for Donnie? Donnie's health and, perhaps, life are at risk, whereas Serena's health is already at risk, and reducing her privacy may be considered a lesser priority than placing Donnie's health at risk.

Furthermore, the impact of any decision involving Donnie and Serena must also take into consideration other participants in the situation, including the agency, the society that pays for the care being (or to be) provided, the families of the two actors who will be affected by any negative consequences, and other persons involved.

Not all deontologists follow identical ethical rules with respect to any given problem. Identification of the relevant rules is therefore of the greatest importance. For example, some ethical systems consider abortion to be the same as murder and prohibit it altogether, no matter what the circumstances; others permit abortions under specified conditions, such as danger to the mother's life. Still other ethical systems are mute on this issue, leaving any decision to the individual involved. But social worker Anne may face other ethical dilemmas after she has identified the relevant moral rules. One dilemma arises out of a conflict between two categorical imperatives—the professional value and standard that calls for client self-determination and her own values that may value the protection of life above all. There is also another conflict between two competing professional values, confidentiality and client decision making based on full information. Here are situations where the social worker cannot honor both categorical imperatives, but must make a choice about which one to follow. The problems involved in making such a choice will be discussed later in this chapter.

CONTEMPORARY APPROACHES TO ETHICAL DECISION MAKING

Philosophers have identified ethical absolutism and ethical relativism as two major ethical theories. Yet these theories are usually presented at so generalized or abstract a level that people do not always find them helpful when coping with the ethical issues they face. In the past, conscience was often suggested as the key to ethical decision making. Some contemporary philosophers have substituted guilt feelings for the older concept, and others have added "feeling good," "democracy," and "empowerment" as current keys.

But conscience or guilt feelings are too idiosyncratic to serve social work professionals as guides for ethical decision making. One person's conscience will not be the same as another's. Professional ethics are common to the entire professional group and should therefore be relevant to every individual member of that profession. What a social worker needs are tools of analysis that will permit a more systematic and a more rational consideration of the ethical aspects of social work intervention. Such models must of course include knowledge elements, but ethical decision making cannot be based on knowledge alone because ethics deal principally with what ought to be and not with what is. Before presenting our ethical decision-making models, we will discuss various approaches that other social workers have found useful in making ethical decisions.

Clinical Pragmatism

Many social workers indicate that they are neither philosophers nor specialists in solving ethical problems. Instead, they believe that their primary responsibility is to deliver a high level of professional service. Perhaps they agree with Jim Casey, who, in John Steinbeck's *Grapes of Wrath*, said, "There ain't no sin and there ain't no virtue, there is just stuff people do." They are sure that they will not become entangled in ethical problems if they concentrate their efforts on improving practice. In addition, they suggest that the type of service provided, the nature of the problems dealt with, and the modes of intervention used are determined in the first instance by society, so that a worker's personal ethical stance is far less important than societal ethics. Social workers who follow this approach focus on implementing the values of the society that sanctions their activities. For example, one of the functions of social workers in contemporary American society is to help individuals and groups who face various kinds of emotional disturbances and crises. These social workers use societal values as the only criterion to identify the types of behavior that require professional intervention. They try to resolve any value conflicts that may arise in the practice context by considering the value priorities of the group in which they work.

While this approach seems simple, straightforward, and even supportive of scientific practice, it has a conservative tinge. Radical writers, such as Thomas Szasz and Ivan Illich, have criticized this approach as unethical because these social workers tend to act as agents of social control on behalf of dominating and exploiting societal institutions. Social workers who follow this approach rarely question society's ethics or its norms (as they understand them). Their practice supports the status quo. These social workers rarely encourage the autonomous development of alternate lifestyles, nor will they be found among those who challenge society's values in other ways. They should remember that social workers have the responsibility and ethical imperative to "not practice, condone, facilitate or collaborate with any form of discrimination on the basis of race, ethnicity, national origin, color, sex, sexual orientation, age, marital status, political belief, religion, or mental of physical disability" (NASW *Code*, 1996, 4.02). Furthermore, social workers "should advocate for living conditions conducive to the fulfillment of basic human needs . . . and . . . the realization of social justice" (NASW *Code*, 1996, 6.01). The questions are whether those who follow this approach are aware of the implications of doing so and the degree to which social workers who follow clinical pragmatism are in compliance with these ethical imperatives.

Humanistic Ethics

Many practitioners have found the humanistic ethical approach attractive because it combines a strong idealism with opportunities for individual choices. An idealistic view of human nature as essentially positive, together with an optimistic stance toward the future, provides the basis for this approach. The focus is on causal rather than on moralistic explanations of human behavior. This approach stresses the capacity, opportunity, and responsibility of every person to make choices that make sense to him or her. The individual client or group, rather than any institution or ideology, occupies the center of attention. Such an approach appears to be particularly suited to contemporary America, with its emphasis on individualism and pluralism.

Self-realization has been at the center of the humanistic theories of Abraham Maslow, Erich Fromm, and other existentialists. Human beings are believed to be innately good and to have the ability to behave ethically. The inner core of the human personality is intrinsically ethical. Individual freedom and responsibility form the basis of social life. Self-expression and self-actualization are postulated as the desired outcome of mature development. Personal identity is defined by each individual according to self-chosen values that are derived, hopefully, rationally. The priority of professional intervention at the individual level and group level will be to help people achieve self-actualization, rather than to help them to learn how to adjust to the existing social order. On the societal level, social workers following this approach will intervene to change those social institutions that inhibit the growth and self-realization of individuals.

Practitioners following this approach can be found in the forefront of many causes that promote freedom and equality. Some oppose stable social authority structures (Rogers, 1977); others emphasize hedonistic rather than traditional values (Schutz, 1967). All followers of this approach feel that they have minimized the ethical dilemmas they face. By clearly identifying value priorities, they feel that they can cope with the ethical aspects of most practice problems. More important, by emphasizing individual responsibility, the major burden for ethical decision making is shifted from the practitioner to the client.

The selection of humanistic ethics as the major approach to ethical decision making can be criticized on several grounds, primarily because such a choice does not reduce but increases the necessity for dealing with dilemmas. Not everyone comes to social workers seeking help for self-actualization, and the fact is that one person's individual self-realization may very well interfere with another person's self-realization, including the social worker's aims. Conflicts generated by individual self-realization and clashes of will can exist between the client, the practitioner, the agency, community, the profession, and society—all of which will require means of dealing with the dilemmas that arise out of the conflicts.

There is yet another criticism of this perspective. Is it better for social workers as a profession to encourage individualism and hedonism, which in many ways fragment and undermine the social work aim to build a sense of community and alter societal structures so they are more enhancing of people? Such a question raises the reality of conflicts between individuals and professions and society. After all, few, if any, clients or social worker behaviors are devoid of moral questions and considerations in their lives. The chief criticisms of self-realization are that not everyone is innately good, one person's or group's fulfillment can clash with other persons and groups, and self-realization without boundaries and responsibility can lead to destructive as well as constructive actions.

Situational Ethics

Popularized during the decade of the 1960s, an era in which authority was widely questioned, situational ethics claimed there are no ethical laws by which one should make ethical decisions other than by the norm of love. One should evaluate what is the right thing to do in every situation and choose a course of action that demonstrates the most love for all those concerned. Thus, situational ethics would allow one to lie to save a life or to prevent harm to many others. Originally promulgated as a Christian ethic, critics of situation ethics suggested that love is primary for Christian believers but is expressed in rules and laws of the Christian tradition, not just by individual intuitions of what is loving in particular situations. Situational ethics sanctioned personal judgment in an era when authority and institutions were being challenged. Other critics thought this approach to ethical decision making overly simplified (Lyden, 1998).

Nevertheless, situational ethics found a widespread audience. The secularization of modern life encouraged the abandonment of absolute rules and universal criteria. A plurality of ethical rules has emerged and no one is able or willing to say that any one rule is correct or applicable in every situation. As a result, many deal with ethical dilemmas on a case-by-case basis, preferring to use "fragmentary moral rules as a substitute for universal rules" (Carlton, 1978, p. 2).

Situation ethics has had many forerunners. The Danish philosopher Søren Kierkegaard (1813–1855) insisted that truth is subjective, while the French philosopher Jean Paul Sartre (1905–1980) taught that ethical decisions can be made only in the light of the prevailing situation, since each case is unique and unlike every other case. Different and changing situations call for different ethical criteria and different ethical decisions. As one philosopher writes, "The good differs from culture to culture, and there is no objective way . . . of verifying one [culture's good] as better than another" (Shirk, 1965, p. 58). Environment, circumstance, and context shape human behavior as well as the criteria for ethical conduct. What might be considered correct or proper in one sphere will be incorrect in another. A social worker may be ethically justified to intervene in one situation, even while a similar intervention in another situation might be ethically questionable. The activity itself is neither ethical nor unethical. It is the situation in which it occurs that defines its ethical dimension.

The critical importance of the context was experimentally demonstrated in what is known as the *simulated prison experiment*. College students who volunteered to participate in this experiment were randomly assigned roles of prisoners or guards. Those who became "guards" had little notion that within less than twenty-four hours they would behave in a very authoritarian and very punitive manner. Prior to the experiment, all of these students had utilized very different ethical criteria, but the experimental context invited ethical considerations that the participants believed to be appropriate to the prison setting. In the words of the senior experimenter, "evil acts are not necessarily the deeds of evil men, but may be attributable to the operation of powerful social sources" (Haney et al., 1973, p. 90).

Social workers who follow the situation approach do not have any fixed rules that help them make decisions about the ethical aspects of practice problems. Because of this, they need even more support systems and guides for making such decisions than do most other social workers.

Religious Ethics

Religious ethics presuppose a belief in the existence of God. While secularist philosophers teach that men and women are the creators of their own values, religious philosophers maintain that humans can only try to discover divine values, not create them. Instead of denying the existence of absolute truth and absolute ethical rules, those who follow religious ethics declare that there are eternal rules that give direction for correct behaviors at all times. Believers are convinced that religious faith and ethical morality are two sides of the same coin. They cannot conceive of the long-term effectiveness of ethical principles that come from a source other than the divine will. The ethical aspects of interpersonal relations can exist only if one accepts the authority of God. They agree with Ivan in Dostoyevsky's *The Brothers Karamazov* when he said, "If there is no God, everything is permissible."

Jacques Maritain, a Christian philosopher, argued that a secular ethics in which the individual becomes the ultimate goal does not deify the person but degrades him or her because "the greatness of man consists in the fact that his sole end is the uncreated Good" (1934, p. 269). For believers, the search for divine meaning is meaningful, while nonbelievers consider this search futile.

One of the consequences of accepting the religious approach is that ethics and law merge into one comprehensive, interrelated system.

Because ethical principles are usually stated on a very generalized and abstract level, the authorized interpreters of religious law deduce specific applications to daily problems. These deductions become precedence or law. When this occurs, law is no longer "divorced from ethics but serves as a means to implement ethical principles in the every-day life of society" (Kurzweil, 1980, p. 71). To the extent that such a conclusion is warranted, this approach provides those who follow it with a powerful tool that helps them cope with many of the ethical issues encountered in social work practice. The problem facing those who follow this approach is its application in what is essentially a secular society.

Feminist Ethics

Traditional Western approaches to ethics are criticized by feminist ethicists. These feminists raise questions about Western ethics and view traditional ethics as reflecting masculine culture and masculine ways of reasoning. According to this view, traditional ethical decision making emphasizes universality and impartiality over "culturally feminine ways of moral reasoning that emphasize relationships, particularity, and partiality" (Tong, 1998, p. 261). Much emphasis is placed by feminist ethics on an ethic of caring that views individuals as "existing and flourishing only within networks of care . . . networks of relationships, practices, values, and ways of life" (Manning, 1992, p. 163). These feminists suggest that traditional ethical decision-making patterns are faulty and the feminist perspective—differing from traditional Western ethical reasoning and ethical decision making—provides a better way of making ethical decisions.

Among the aspects of feminist theory that have importance for professional ethics are the following:

1. The critique of domination and the concomitant articulation of the value of reciprocity
2. The recognition of the distinctive individuality of the other
3. A commitment to an ideal of caring
4. A rejection of abstract universality, and a model of reasoning that is concerned with context

Because domination and oppression in any form are considered morally wrong, feminist ethics are concerned with both particularities of individual situations *and* a concern with social structural conditions such as racism, classism, and sexism. In ethical decision making, private troubles are viewed within the context of public issues. Personal situations and societal contexts should not be viewed separately (Abramson, 1996).

However, there is no one feminist approach to ethical decision making, and different models have been developed, including maternal, political, and lesbian. Furthermore, as Glassman suggests, feminists also will find that "their feminist beliefs come into serious conflict with other deeply respected social work traditions, values, and principles" (1992, p. 161). Can social workers respect the cultural values and customs of some ethnic groups without accommodating and perpetuating oppression? What should social workers do who are respectful of self-determination when clients accept patriarchal or other communal values? Is there a line between value imposition and supporting a feminist consciousness by both clients as well as by social workers, both professionally and personally?

Perhaps over time as these newly developed approaches find means of dealing with various ethical dilemmas, they may challenge and alter more traditional ethical decision-making patterns in social work practice. Just as clinical pragmatism, humanistic, situational, and religious ethics, among other perspectives, have had their particular impact on ethical decision making in social work, so feminist ethics may also contribute to contemporary ethical decision making, although it is not clear whether or in what ways it may yet impact.

PERSONAL, GROUP, SOCIETAL, AND PROFESSIONAL VALUES

Values, as noted earlier, are a key element in the ethical decision-making process. No wonder that Levy (1976b) called ethics "values in action." Before clarifying the relationship between values and ethics it may be helpful to differentiate between different levels of values:

1. *Individual* or *personal values* are values held by one person but not necessarily by others.
2. *Group values* are values held by subgroups within a society—such as religious groups, ethnic groups, and so forth.
3. *Societal values* are those values that are recognized by major portions of the entire social system or, at least, by the leading members or spokespersons of that system.
4. *Professional values* are those values proclaimed by a professional group, such as social workers.

Generally, these four value sets are complementary or reciprocal, although at times they may be in conflict. Most of the time and in most places, discord among the different value sets is infrequent, though differences in interpretation, priority, and intensity are not uncommon.

Clarifying Personal Values

Some social workers question or denigrate the importance of personal values for professional practice. They suggest that a social worker must suspend or neutralize all personal values when serving clients. Charles Levy, who chaired the NASW committee that drafted an earlier *Code of Ethics*, said: "To be a professional practitioner is to give up some of one's autonomy and to relinquish some of one's right as a freely functioning being" (1976a, p. 113). However, the conflict between personal and professional values is rarely as unambiguous as this. The desirability, as well as the possibility, of suppressing personal values is much more problematic than Levy indicates.

Others suggest that personal values have relatively little influence on ethical behaviors. They claim that social workers know instinctively or intuitively what is the right thing to do. Admittedly, feelings and instincts are important and do influence behavioral choices. However, having a strong feeling for something does not necessarily make for an ethical choice. A worker may feel that she wants to have sex with or befriend a client, but this instinctive feeling, strong as it may be, does not make this behavior ethical.

Frankena (1980) indicated that a person's cultural experiences and background, including personal values, implicitly direct the ethical decision-making process of that person. But unless these become explicit, there is danger that biases and stereotypes, rather than professional values and ethics, will shape professional behaviors. For example, Garb (1994, pp. 82–83) reports recent empirical research showing that gender biases exist for both male and female clinicians in personality assessment. Dunkel and Hatfield (1986) have shown how hidden and unconscious personal values and biases interfere with helping clients who are HIV-positive. Similar observations have been made when analyzing social work intervention with such client groups as cancer patients, gay persons, unmarried mothers, and others.

The difficulty that many social workers have when it comes to making ethical decisions has been noted by Siporin (1985b). He suggests that in today's libertarian and relativist moral climate it has become increasingly difficult for many persons to be clear about their own values. Even when personal values have been identified, making ethical choices on the basis of these values is often difficult, as Coughlin noted when he said that "in a society that is philosophically, culturally, politically, and religiously pluralistic, making value choices is no way to win friends" (1966, p. 97).

Shakespeare gave sound advice when he wrote: "This above all, to thine own self be true . . . . Thou canst not then be false to any man"

(*Hamlet*, 1, 3, 78–80). This same advice may also help social workers when they consider the personal values that are relevant in ethical decision making. No matter what approach social workers use, it is essential that they clarify and make explicit their own personal values. If personal values are only abstract principles, they will not be useful to integrate and organize a person's resources and behaviors, or her relations with others.

Those who agree with Siporin that "there is a moral and ethical imperative that social workers act as moral agents" (1985b, p. 20) know the importance of holding clear, unambiguous, and specific personal values. Only such values are effective in influencing and guiding behavior. In no other way can a social worker be true "to thine own self" and not act as a "hired gun" for a client, an agency, or even the state. It just will not do to speak in generalities. Instead, a social worker must carefully scrutinize and define her values.

It is not enough for a social worker to say that she favors (or opposes) assisted suicide. She must be able to define her values about assisted suicide clearly. Does she believe a person has a right to doctor-assisted suicide if death is expected in the next six months and the person is found by a psychiatrist not to be depressed? Or does she believe that, with palliative care, all terminally ill persons can take advantage of the dying process to search for important values, to reconcile with families, and make some valued use of the time? Does she dismiss assisted suicide under any circumstances and opt for life despite the difficulty of the last days? These questions are raised here to emphasize that social workers must first clarify their own value stance in relation to value-laden issues they meet in practice situations if they want to be true to themselves and to their profession. In the section Clarifying Professional Values, found later in this chapter, this theme of clarification, differentiation, and integration of personal, group, professional, and societal values will be further discussed.

Clarifying Group Values

Social workers as individuals and as professionals, like their clients, gain their values from families, neighborhoods, as well as professional, religious, and many other groups. Part of analyzing one's value system is clarifying those reference groups with which one identifies. Group membership and context are powerful—but not totally—decisive value forces. Like everyone else, social workers act in ways that they might not have chosen except for the influence of groups; for example, we often change values when we form families and join large organizations. When our roles change, it may be difficult to hold values different from those of the other members. Although there is much conformity to group norms, there are also many people who are able to resist various group influences (May, 1992).

Most Americans are wedded to the idea of autonomy and grow up valuing a sense of independence. But there is a growing diversity of group values and cultural standards that social workers encounter and/or hold. Some of these may be contrary to those held by many other Americans. Independent decision making is valued by Americans in general, but some groups may hold other values. For instance, persons with Pacific Island backgrounds (among other groups) attach a greater value to group-oriented values than to self-determination as understood in general American life. In contrast to those groups that place a high value on group values above individual-oriented values, the NASW *Code* (1996, 1.02) elevates self-determination among the ethical responsibilities of social workers when it up front encourages social workers to respect and promote this right among clients (Ewalt & Mokuau, 1995).

Immigrants often share their residence with relatives or other families. This group value is foreign to many Americans who are raised and live in one-family apartments and homes, valuing their privacy. Many social workers may come from groups that find fault with such arrangements on the grounds of health, legal, and other preferred values. Similarly, a professional stance may clash with immigrants who turn chiefly to kin and hometown networks rather than the organizations in which social workers are employed (Padilla, 1997; Chow, 1999).

Just as assumptions cannot be made by social workers about their own group values, it is often difficult to offer generalizations about the values of particular groups. Social workers should keep in mind that: (1) There can be a conflict between the social worker's values and client values, based on the client's membership in a particular group. (2) There are limits to the generalizations that can be made about groups. Clients may have values that differ from others in their *own* cultural group by date of immigration, whether American born, education level, geographic origin, social class, and even language (Agbayani-Siewert, 1994). Differences within a group may be greater than differences between two groups. (3) Professional social workers should not assume their clients will necessarily reflect or follow the values of their group.

Similarly, American social workers are members of groups that hold many sets of values that may conflict: individual versus family, self-reliance versus interdependence, secular versus religious, struggle versus entitlement, and so forth. A person may hold multiple value sets and different—even conflicting—values may operate in different contexts and change over time (Tropman, 1984). Social workers who understand and clarify their values and the connection of those values to the groups that impact on them have a better chance of identifying and handling value conflicts in ethical decision making.

Clarifying Societal Values

Radical changes in societal values have occurred within the lifetime of many social workers. Values that our parents or grandparents considered sacred have been swept away or have been altered so much that they are no longer recognizable. Though changes of values around lifestyles and sexual mores gain headline attention, more fundamental changes have taken place with respect to inequality and equality. Not too long ago it was self-understood that all people were not equal. An unemployed person did not enjoy the same rights as a working person. Women were considered inferior to men. Whites were thought to be better than everybody else. These views were held openly, even by the "best" people in society. Public policy was designed to reflect and support these values. It does not require any lengthy discussion to point out that major changes have occurred with respect to these values. Although racism, sexism, and ageism still exist in our society, these are no longer accorded the general respect and public recognition that they once received.

The equality value is not the only value that has changed dramatically in the last few decades. Similar changes can be observed with respect to many other values—for example, those related to sexual and gender issues, disparities between the rich and the poor, and individual responsibility. To the extent that ethical behavior in general reflects what society values, a social worker must have accurate knowledge of the current societal value stance. Knowing does not mean that a social worker must follow these values blindly, but she must take them into consideration when assessing a problem situation and when making her decisions. Societal values usually, but not always, provide guidelines for professional ethical behavior. But there may be situations when a social worker is justified, even obligated, to act in ways that are contrary to societal norms. However, in every instance the worker first has an obligation to clarify the relevant societal values.

One should be mindful that there are those today who maintain that societal values do not exist. Even those who admit there may be a statistical validity to the notion of societal values may vigorously reject the idea that—if they exist—they can serve as guidelines to ethical decision making. As with all concepts related to ethical decision making, individual social workers will have to examine the extent to which this or other concepts or approaches have implications for their decision making.

The application of societal norms may become problematic when a society accepts values that previously were disvalued, especially when the adoption of the new value occurs unevenly among different groups within society. For example, today the value to chose one's lifestyle freely is accepted by many—but not all—Americans, particularly if one's actions do not impinge on the lives of others. But there are issues such as school prayer, pornography, abortion, and assisted suicide that still divide Americans because the acceptance of these new values has not been uniform across American society.

Clarifying Professional Values

The social work profession takes its basic values from those held by the larger society, but there may be differences in emphasis, interpretation, and priorities. These differences can, at times, contribute to ethical problems. By selecting and emphasizing certain values, while attaching lesser importance to others, social workers may place themselves at risk of engaging in unpopular behaviors and of being charged with behaviors that society has declared unacceptable.

Social work professional ethics are based on "social work's core values of service, social justice, dignity and worth of the person, importance of human relationships, integrity and competence." The profession expresses its values through its primary mission "to enhance human well-being and help meet the basic human needs of all people, with particular attention to the needs and empowerment of people who are vulnerable, oppressed, and living in poverty" (NASW *Code*, 1996, Preamble). Essentially, the social work value system reflects a democratic ethos that provides for individual and group fulfillment. It calls for respect of individuals and their differences, while at the same time recognizing the need for mutual aid and societal supports so that all persons can attain their maximum potential.

Finding the correct balance between the rights of the group or community and the rights of the individual is often not an easy matter and is a challenge not unique to social work. Such choices present serious dilemmas for which there are few guidelines. But within this balance, ethical decisions clearly follow a democratic ethos.

Social work practice always involves ethical decision making. Assumptions about morals and values are basic to social workers' theories, policies, and practice decisions. Ethical dilemmas may arise when there is a conflict between the personal, group, societal, and professional values that are relevant in a given situation. In addition, clients introduce their own moral conflicts to which social workers must respond. The "absence" of conflict for the social worker may indicate either that the social worker is unconscious of the moral nature of the choices she faces or that the social worker is so clear about her values and societal priorities that the choice is prima facie correct (child abuse, suicide threats) or so routine because of habit and repeated justification that making the decision is not problematic for this worker (Fleck-Henderson, 1991). Neither case implies that decisions made in such situations will be ethically correct. When decisions become so routine that they do not cause the social worker second thoughts, the time may have arrived for taking extra care in regard to ethical decision making.

THE DECISION-MAKING PROCESS

Making a decision is seldom a split-second act. Typically it is a process or series of thoughts and activities that occur over time and that result in a person or group acting (or not acting) in a particular manner. Every decision is approached step-by-step so that one moves gradually through a series of stages until, at the end of the process, one makes the decision. It is erroneous to assume that only one person, the decision maker, participates in this process. Many different persons present information, react to assessments, introduce additional options, or make changes in the environment; these in turn change the nature of the decision or the nature of the data on which the decision is based.

In real life it is almost impossible to point to any one discrete decision. Observing decision making is like watching the ocean waves approach the shoreline. Choices are always influenced by previous decisions that in turn lead to new directions. Ethical decision making is far too complex to permit the development of a simple "how to" problem-solving model. Yet some model is necessary if we are to understand what decision making is all about. A simpler model of decision making may help social workers understand what is involved in ethical decision making. Such a model, like all models in science, will simplify reality by focusing on only one decision. A model is a permissible didactic device as long as it is understood that in real life every decision is preceded and followed by other decisions, many of which have a direct bearing on the matter under consideration.

In Figure 3.1, we present one such general model for decision making. As a general model, it is applicable to many different situations and is not limited to ethical decisions. This model is based on the assumption that social workers can plan rationally what is needed for intervention in human situations and that they want to minimize the irrational, the impulsive, and the unplanned consequences of purposeful actions.

ETHICAL ASSESSMENT SCREEN

The social worker who is alert to the ethical aspects of practice will examine and assess the available options and alternatives somewhat differ-

Figure 3.1   A General Decision-Making Model

Step 1 Identify the problem and the factors that contribute to its maintenance.

Step 2 Identify all of the persons and institutions involved in this problem, such as clients, victims, support systems, other professionals, and others.

Step 3 Determine who should be involved in decision making.

Step 4 Identify the values relevant to this problem held by the several participants identified in Step 2, including the client's and worker's personal values, as well as relevant professional, group, and societal values.

Step 5 Identify the goals and objectives whose attainment you believe may resolve (or at least reduce) the problem.

Step 6 Identify alternate intervention strategies and targets.

Step 7 Assess the effectiveness and efficiency of each alternative in terms of the identified goals.

Step 8 Select the most appropriate strategy.

Step 9 Implement the strategy selected.

Step 10 Monitor the implementation, paying particular attention to unanticipated consequences.

Step 11 Evaluate the results and identify additional problems.

ently than her colleague who is not as concerned with the ethical aspects of practice. This becomes clear in the following pages, where we consider various assessment criteria. In Figure 3.2 we present an ethical assessment screen designed to help social workers further clarify and integrate the ethical aspects of decision making in social work practice.

Protection of Clients' Rights and Welfare

The definition of rights and privileges changes over time. What is thought to be a right at one time may not be so defined in another era. These changes may create ethical problems. Social workers were once expected to protect confidentiality, no matter what the obstacles. Nowadays, because of changes in laws; the introduction of various technologies; managed care and administrative record keeping required by funding and accrediting organizations; participation and consultation with team members, including those from other disciplines; and responsibility to supervisors and courts, social workers remain concerned but have much less control over potential breaches of confidentiality.

Changing definitions of what constitutes rights may also create ethical problems for social workers. Consider the ethical problems faced by social workers in the adoption field as the right of adopted persons to information about their biological parents is becoming recognized in more and more jurisdictions. At one time, the biological parents as well as the adoptive parents were assured that such information would remain confidential and would never be shared with the adoptee. Now, when court decisions or legislative enactments in some states support the right of adopted persons to this information, social workers in these jurisdictions have little choice but to reveal it. However, is it ethical for other social workers to continue to tell biological and adoptive parents that this information will always remain confidential when they have no way of implementing this promise in the future?

Protection of Society's Interests

Sometimes it is difficult to balance society's interests with a client's interests. If a client tells his social worker that he has committed a property crime, the social worker must weigh her obligations to the client against her obligations to society. Social control is one of the functions of every social worker, but so is the maintenance of a helping relationship. To which function should the practitioner give priority if she cannot pursue both at the same time? Would the same considerations apply if the client were a part-time prostitute in a town where prostitution was prohibited by law? Can lawbreaking be overlooked when a client makes progress toward attaining identified and constructive intervention goals? Does it matter whether the law violation harms another person? Keep these questions in mind as you assess the ethical dilemmas posed in the following exemplar.

➤ 3.2 Security or Protection?

John Newton was a likable young man—22 years old, not steadily employed, but always willing to help. Even before Ray Dunkirk, the community worker, had arrived on the scene, Newton had organized a number of young adults into a club. This club was well known in the neighborhood for the many helpful services it provided. The community's elderly population was especially appreciative of the security services that the group gave them. Thefts and holdups of older people had ceased ever since this club began to operate in the community.

But Dunkirk also became aware that Newton has intimidated local store owners and has obtained regular payoffs from them in return for promising them "protection."

What was Ray Dunkirk to do? He considered various options, including the following:

1. He could overlook Newton's protection racket in view of the many positive things he was doing that were benefiting the community.

2. He could report Newton's protection racket to the police, since illegal activities should never be condoned.
3. He could strengthen his relations with Newton with the view of helping to guide him away from the illegal activity; in the meantime he would not report the law violation to the police.

What are the ethical aspects in choosing the best option? One ethical dilemma is how to balance the best interests of the various publics involved: oldsters, storekeepers, the community, the larger society, and others. Another question concerns the ethics of doing something that might result in the return of violence against the older people of this community. The following discussion is intended to help social workers cope with these conflicts and to find answers to these questions.

The "Least Harm" Principle

Sometimes social workers are confronted by problems for which there are no positive choices. Regardless of the option chosen by the client and/or the worker, some harm will come to one person or another, perhaps even to the client or to the social worker. What is the ethical choice in such situations? The "least harm" rule suggests choosing the option that will result in the least harm, the least permanent harm, or the most easily reversible harm.

Consider the options facing Morgana Elam, the social worker who has to consider the options in the Guevara family situation (Exemplar 1.1). Does the least harm principle offer guidance in choosing the most ethical alternative? How?

Some have suggested that the routine application of the least harm principle may diminish the possibility of choosing the most effective intervention technique. There may be times when it is justified to utilize an option that has great risks but which enhances the likelihood of a successful outcome. Examples of such situations include placing an emotionally disturbed person who is only marginally able to cope in a boarding home because the social worker believes that leaving the hospital is worth the risk, or placing a person with mental retardation in a completely unfamiliar rural setting when the person had known only institutional and urban life, or using a new and personally untested treatment method with a long-term and highly resistant patient. These and similar situations are examples in which it might be desirable to take risks because the potential gain is judged worthwhile and the chance of success exists. However, such a choice should be made only with the full consent and agreement of the client.

Efficiency and Effectiveness

Many people think that efficiency and effectiveness are synonyms, but there are important differences between the two terms, especially when it comes to ethical decision making. The *efficiency criterion* is concerned with the relative cost (including budget, staff time, agency and community resources) of achieving a stated objective. Whenever two options will lead to the same result, the one that requires less budget, less staff, and less time is the more efficient one. The *effectiveness criterion,* on the other hand, relates to the degree to which the desired outcome is achieved. When the implementation of one option results in halving the number of poor people in a county, while the second option reduces the poverty population by 80 percent, the latter option is the more effective one—but its cost may be so high that it is considered inefficient.

Difficult choices arise when the more efficient option is the less effective one, or vice versa. Making decisions on the basis of only efficiency and effectiveness criteria may result in unethical decisions. At times, the most efficient or the most effective option must be rejected because of its ethical implications. For example, sending poor people or people with chronic mental illness to another city or deporting them to another country may be the most effective and the most efficient way of eliminating poverty or the expense of long-term hospitalization, but such decisions must be dismissed out of hand by anyone who is concerned with the ethical implications of these proposed plans.

More often the ethical assessment of an option is not as clear as in these examples, so that a social worker may find it difficult to make a decision. For example, what are the ethical implications of forcing poor people to work? Work is highly valued in our society, but *force* means limiting a person's freedom, another important value in our society. The ethical assessment, in this case, demands that we assess *work* and *independence* against the loss of *freedom.* In the past, social work ideology rejected out of hand the various *workfare* programs that forced poor people to work. With the implementation of Temporary Assistance for Needy Families (TANF) in place of the long-standing Aid to Families with Dependent Children (AFDC) program, apparently a change in social work ideology and values may be taking place. However, there are no widely accepted assessment procedures that can help a social worker weigh the ethical aspects of each of the many state workfare options. Of course, there are assessment procedures that can be used in these cases—we are offering some in this book. What is lacking is a professional consensus on the issue.

Another kind of ethical quandary arises out of the continuing efforts to deinstitutionalize patients of mental hospitals. When this policy was first proposed some years ago, certain professionals supported and

Figure 3.2   Ethical Assessment Screen

1. Identify your own relevant personal values in relation to this ethical dilemma.
2. Identify any societal values relevant to the ethical decision to be made.
3. Identify the relevant professional values and ethics.
4. Identify alternative ethical options that you may take.
5. Which of the alternative ethical actions will protect to the greatest extent possible your client's rights and welfare as well as the rights and welfare of others?
6. Which alternative action will protect to the greatest extent possible society's rights and interests?
7. What can you do to minimize any conflicts among 1, 2, and 3? What can you do to minimize any conflicts between 5 and 6?
8. Which alternative action will result in your doing the "least harm" possible?
9. To what extent will alternative actions be efficient, effective, and ethical?
10. Have you considered and weighed both the short-term and long-term ethical consequences of alternative actions?

---

implemented the program because they thought it would right a wrong. In some instances, the option of releasing mentally ill patients from hospitals was adopted even though it was known that most communities lacked adequate resources for caring for these people. Many state governments were unable to help communities with the problem because they themselves were facing major budget cuts. How ethical was it to institute a strategy that might result in some long-range improvements, but which in the short run might harm many fragile people? Was it ethical to do so without first ensuring the availability of adequate community resources? Consider this question by using the ethical assessment screen (Figure 3.2).

RANK-ORDERING ETHICAL PRINCIPLES

In the preceding pages we discussed a number of ethical criteria that some social workers have found helpful when assessing decision alternatives. These criteria have not been arranged in any order of priority. More specific guides are needed whenever two or more of these criteria point toward different alternatives.

Even though some social workers disagree, we believe that the preferred way of resolving such conflicts among ethical principles is a lexical ordering of these principles—that is, rank-ordering them from the most important to the least important. Such ordering is necessary even though "ordering principles is not an easy task" (Christensen, 1986, p. 82).

A lexical ordering of ethical principles can provide social workers with a guide, but such a guide is not meant to be a magic formula that can be applied blindly. As Baier (1958) suggested, the *principle of priority* should be used when two or more moral rules (standards) conflict. Based on the earlier work of a number of authors (including Baier, 1958; Kitchner, 1984; Joseph, 1985; Lewis, 1984; Reamer, 1983; Siporin, 1983; and Zygmond & Boorhem, 1989) we have prepared guides for ethical decision making. Social workers rarely make direct use of theoretical knowledge or philosophical principles when making practice decisions. Instead, they have integrated knowledge and values into a set of practice principles—and these are what social workers utilize at the critical points in the decision-making process.

We have used the work of the authors mentioned, as well as additional sources and our own practice experience, to prepare the following two guides or screens that we believe will be helpful in making ethical decisions. We call these guides the ethical rules screen (ERS) and the ethical principles screen (EPS) (see Figures 3.3 and 3.4). These guides are meant to be tools; they should not be used as magic formulas to be applied blindly.

The ERS should always be used first. Only when this screen *does not provide* any satisfactory guidance should the social worker use the EPS. To be useful, a guide for rank-ordering ethical principles must clearly indicate the order of priority of such principles. Once such a priority list has been established, the operating rule is that the satisfaction of a higher-order principle takes precedence over the satisfaction of a lower-order principle. Even though there is not yet any general agreement on the rank order of professional ethical principles, we have developed the EPS on the basis of our perception of what might be the consensus among social workers. All ethical principles are important. When more than one ethical principle is relevant in the analysis of a set of practice options and each of these principles leads to a different outcome, the rank order suggested in the EPS should be utilized to make a decision. In other words, an assessment based on Ethical Principle 1 is more compelling than one using Ethical Principles 2 or 3. For example, if both confidentiality (Principle 6) and full disclosure (Principle 7) apply, the ethical principle of confidentiality should receive priority. Since the EPS is the key ethical assessment tool for resolving ethical practice dilemmas, we will comment in detail on several of these principles.

Ethical Principle 1. The protection of human life applies to all persons, both to the life of a client and to the lives of all others. This principle takes precedence over every other obligation. "The right to life is the most basic of all rights, for if one's right to life is violated one cannot enjoy any other rights" (Kuhse & Singer, 1985, p. 509).

Figure 3.3   Ethical Rules Screen (ERS)

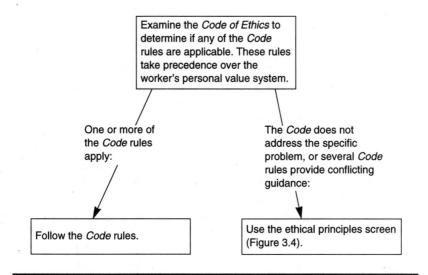

Figure 3.4   Ethical Principles Screen (EPS)

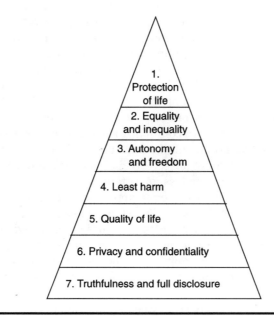

Most physicians follow this principle of saving and prolonging human life, regardless of the resulting quality of life or the economic costs involved. This life-sustaining principle received wide publicity through the case of Karen Ann Quinlan, whose physicians refused to withdraw life-support systems, even though this patient had been unconscious for many years and there was no further hope for any positive change. Today physicians keep many Americans "alive" through the use of high-tech life-sustaining instruments. Social workers, on the other hand, tend to place more emphasis on improving the quality of life for individuals, groups, and communities. Most of the time, social workers are not aware of any conflict between the biophysical principle of sustaining life and the psychosocial principle of improving life. But at times there is conflict. One example is the case of a middle-aged man with marked hypertension. The medication that brought down his life-threatening blood pressure also caused sexual impotence (Roberts, 1989). Is it ethical for a social worker to support this client's decision to stop taking the medication so that he can once again enjoy sexual relations? Such a decision may lead to an improvement in the quality of his life (Ethical Principle 5), but may also contribute to shortening his life (Ethical Principle 1).

Ethical Principle 2.   The principle of equality and inequality suggests that all persons in the same circumstances should be treated in the same way; that is, equal persons have the right to be treated equally and nonequal persons have the right to be treated differently if the inequality is relevant to the issue in question. Unequal treatment can be justified when other considerations such as beneficence outweigh the equality principle or on the ground that such unequal treatment will promote greater equality (Frankena, 1973, p. 52) This principle, as formulated by Kitchner (1984), is based on the seminal work of Rawls (1971). Kitchner specifically applied this principle to ethics. She taught that a principle can suggest an obligation, but if there are special circumstances or when there are conflicting and stronger obligations, one should act on the basis of the obligations derived from the higher principle. The ethical screen requires the choice of the more important principle, thus overriding the less important one.

Examples in which this principle applies occur in situations that involve child abuse or elder abuse. Since the abused child or elder is not in an "equal" position, the principles of confidentiality and autonomy with respect to the abusing adult are of a lower rank order than the obligation to protect the child or adult, even when it is not a question of life and death. Another situation in which this principle applies occurs when several families apply for certain resources (e.g., food, housing, health care), but one family is demonstrably nearer nutritional or other disaster;

in this situation the ethical principle permits or even requires the unequal allocation of scarce resources.

Ethical Principle 3.   A social worker should make practice decisions that foster a person's autonomy, independence, and freedom. Freedom, though highly important, does not override the right to life or survival of the person himself or of others. A person does not have the right to decide to harm himself or herself or anyone else on the grounds that the right to make such a decision is her or his autonomous right. When a person is about to make such a decision, the social worker is obligated to intervene since Ethical Principle 1 takes precedence.

The risk/benefit ratio may also help determine when the autonomy principle applies and when it is ethical to ignore a client's "decision." If the condition facing a client is life threatening and if the risk of intervention is minimal (while the potential benefit of the intervention is great), the social worker may consider proceeding even without a client's consent. In this situation, the client's refusal must be considered an indication of his lack of competency. On the other hand, if the risk is great and the potential benefit minimal, the client's refusal is logical and should be accepted.

Ethical Principle 4.   When faced with dilemmas that have the potential for causing harm, a social worker should attempt to avoid or prevent such harm. When a harm must be done to one involved party or another, a social worker should always choose the option that will cause the least harm, the least permanent harm, and/or the most easily reversible harm. If harm has been done, the social worker should attempt where possible to repair the harm done.

Ethical Principle 5.   A social worker should choose the option that promotes a better quality of life for all people, for the individual as well as for the community. Consistent with the *Code of Ethics*, "social workers should promote the general welfare of society, from local to global levels, and the development of people, their communities, and their environments" (NASW *Code*, 1996, 6.01).

Ethical Principle 6.   A social worker should make practice decisions that strengthen every person's right to privacy. Keeping confidential information inviolate is a direct derivative of this obligation. Professionals have a duty to protect the privacy of clients and groups to the greatest extent possible consistent with laws and the will and agreement of the clients. But, confidentiality is not sacrosanct when the social worker can prevent violence or harm of a serious nature to others.

Ethical Principle 7. A social worker should make practice decisions that permit her to speak the truth and to fully disclose all relevant information to her client and to others. Social and professional relationships require trust in order to function well, and trust—in turn—is based on honest dealing that minimizes surprises so that mutual expectations are generally fulfilled.

Application of Ethical Decision-Making Screens

Let us try to apply these two ethical decision-making screens to analyze several exemplars.

> ### ➤ 3.3 What Will Happen to Jimmy Prego?
>
> Jimmy Prego is a passive, deeply disturbed early adolescent who lives in a therapeutic home where he has sometimes had to be protected from other residents. He is now ready to be moved to a less restrictive environment but clearly needs a therapeutic foster home, something your supervisor originally suggested.
>
> You have contacted such a home and begun plans to move Jimmy in about two weeks. When you inform your supervisor that you have initiated the move and that everything is proceeding as usual, he tells you that space has become available in an even less restricted group home run by your agency and that it would be appropriate to move him to the group home instead of the therapeutic foster home.
>
> You tell your supervisor that you will check it out but he seems a little uncomfortable. When you check the group home out, you discover the residents are older, bigger, and more aggressive than Jimmy. You do not agree that the group home is appropriate for Jimmy who has had difficulty defending himself where he currently resides. Also, you learn that the agency has placed pressure on the supervisors to boost the group home's census, an action related to agency financial considerations. Jimmy's mother is unable to assist in making the decision because of overwhelming personal and mental health problems. Jimmy's problems and his youth make him incapable of making the decision. Mrs. Prego insists that she trusts you and that you will do what is best for Jimmy.

Several issues are involved in this exemplar. First, whose best interest takes priority—the client, agency, or worker? What is best for Jimmy and his mother? When you examine the *Code of Ethics* for applicable standards, you find that your "primary responsibility is to promote the well-being of clients" (NASW *Code*, 1996, 1.01). To whom do you owe loyalty as you make your decision about what the correct thing is to do? To Jimmy? His mother? Your supervisor? Your agency? Yourself? Some social workers might argue that EP5 is relevant because the worker wants to promote a better quality of life for Jimmy Prego and the right treatment situation will support that outcome. Will the least harm (EP4) be done by confronting your supervisor and—even in a small way—reducing the agency income when that is what the agency needs, but perhaps succeeding in obtaining the placement in the therapeutic home? Or, by not confronting your supervisor, placing Jimmy in the group home, and increasing agency income? If you don't go along with the supervisor, harm may come to you, your supervisor, and the agency.

Second, who is competent to make decisions? When clients lack "the capacity to provide informed consent, social workers should protect clients' interests by seeking permission from an appropriate third party" (NASW *Code*, 1996, 1.03c). Jimmy is not capable of making an informed choice. Mrs. Prego trusts the social worker and wants her to make the best decision for her son. Is your supervisor an appropriate third party? He is placing the agency needs before those of Jimmy. In addition, "social workers should not allow an employing organization's policies, procedures, regulations, or administrative orders to interfere with their ethical practice of social work" (NASW *Code*, 1996, 3.09d).

You, the social worker, are the only one in this situation who is competent to make decisions for the best interest and protection of Jimmy and to advocate for the right treatment plan. Jimmy's needs take priority over the supervisor's, the agency's, and your own needs.

Let's look again at the ethical dilemma that the social worker for Serena Adams (Exemplar 3.1) faced. This social worker, you may recall, had to decide whether or not to inform Donnie that Serena is HIV+, even though Serena demanded that confidentiality be respected and she has the law on her side. Several *Code of Ethics* standards are directly applicable to this dilemma. "Social workers should respect clients' right to privacy" (NASW *Code*, 1996, 1.07a); "Social workers should protect the confidentiality of all information obtained in the course of professional service, except for compelling professional reasons. The general expectation that social workers will keep information confidential does not apply when disclosure is necessary to prevent serious, foreseeable, and imminent harm to a client . . ." (NASW *Code*, 1996, 1.07c).

Because the *Code* standards conflict, we will use the EPS. Ethical Principle 6 indicates that a social worker should not invade a person's privacy by involving others without that person's consent. Ethical Principle 3 stresses the ethical requirement to foster a person's autonomy. Both of these ethical principles direct the social worker to respect Serena's demand to refrain from informing Donnie. But Ethical Principle 1 requires decisions that protect a person's life and survival. This social worker felt that Serena will find ways to have sex with Donnie, placing his health, life, and welfare in danger. Since EP 1 has the highest priority, overriding any decisions required by lower-ranked principles, she decides that she must inform Donnie, regardless of the legal implications. Do you agree with this worker's decision? If not, what would you do and on what basis would you decide?

A third example is the following.

➤ 3.4 Starting in Private Practice

Cliff Baxter is an experienced social worker who recently resigned his agency job in order to devote all of his time to private practice. Before Cliff left the agency, Dennis Norton, a colleague in the agency, told him that he would be willing to refer clients to him for a "finder's fee." As in many beginnings, Cliff is having a difficult time making ends meet. His income last month was not even sufficient to pay the rent for the office. Should he give Dennis a call?

We will use the ERS and examine the NASW *Code of Ethics* to determine if there are any rules relevant to this situation. The NASW *Code* (2.06c) states: "Social workers are prohibited from giving or receiving payment for a referral when no professional service is provided by the referring social worker." This rule provides such clear and unambiguous guidance that no further screening seems necessary. Cliff should not call Dennis to take advantage of his offer.

In the next example we will apply the EPS.

➤ 3.5 The Wrong Man Sits in Prison

Raul Lovaas has been enrolled in a drug rehabilitation program in order to break his cocaine addiction. The program's treatment routine includes pharmacological treatment, group therapy, and individual therapy. You are his social worker. You have succeeded in establishing a positive and meaningful relationship with Raul in the daily treatment sessions. One morning Raul tells you that, some years ago, he accidentally injured a bank guard during a holdup. He was never caught by the police, but another man was convicted for this crime and now sits in prison on a lengthy sentence. For several days you have been trying to convince Raul that he should talk to the police in order to free an innocent man from prison. Raul not only refused to listen to your suggestion but has told you that he expects you to keep in complete confidence what he has told you. What should you do?

These are some of the thoughts that you have:

1. Raul has neither a legal nor a moral right to have another man serve a lengthy sentence for a crime that Raul committed.
2. The "wrong" that you may cause by breaking confidentiality is hardly of the same importance as the wrong inflicted on an innocent person who is now imprisoned.

3. On the other hand, the effectiveness of the entire program may be compromised if it becomes known that social workers do not always keep confidential the information they receive from clients.

We will focus our analysis on the latter two considerations since the first point, though obvious, does not relate directly to what you, the social worker, should do, but rather to what the client is ethically required to do.

At least two ethical principles are involved in the second consideration: Ethical Principle 3, principle of autonomy and freedom, specifically the freedom of an innocent man who is now imprisoned; and Ethical Principle 6, principle of confidentiality, specifically respecting the confidence of the information that your client, Raul Lovaas, gave you.

Some may also base their decision on Ethical Principle 2, the principle of equality and inequality. An innocent man in prison is obviously not in an equal situation and requires additional resources in order to regain access to equal opportunities.

Since EP 6 (principle of confidentiality) is of a lower order than both EP 3 and EP 2, the second consideration leads to the decision that this social worker is ethically justified to break confidence and report to the police what she has learned from Raul.

From a practice point of view, the third consideration may be especially important since in most situations we would hesitate to do anything that might impede the effectiveness of an intervention. It might be argued that a program that can improve the quality of life (EP 5) of many addicts should receive preference over the quality of life of one individual, even if that person is falsely imprisoned. But it is likely that such reasoning involves a number of fallacies, including:

1. We have no information on the effectiveness of this rehabilitation program. How effective is it in improving the quality of life of all/most/some participants?
2. We do not know what impact, if any, breaking confidentiality will have on the effectiveness of the program. It may well be that other participants will be happy that the worker was instrumental in freeing an innocent person from prison.
3. Statistical probabilities are never a permissible substitute for ethical screening.

In other words, the quality of life principle (EP 5) is not relevant in this situation, but even if it were, it would be of a lower order than EP 3 and EP 2. Consideration 3 is therefore not relevant and should be ignored in making an ethical decision. We would, therefore, conclude that the social worker is obligated to inform the police if she is unable to convince Raul to do so himself.

In this chapter, we have examined a series of guidelines and decision-making processes that social workers can use when making ethical decisions. We noted that every social worker is confronted by ethical dilemmas and that these always require choices that must be made before action can be taken. Iserson (1986) suggested that we ask three questions as a final "check out" before moving to the action phase of ethical decision making.

1. *Impartiality*   Would you be willing to act the way you have chosen if you were in the other person's place? This question asks the social worker to consider the effect her action would have if she or a member of her family or other loved ones were the recipients of the action. The purpose of this question is to correct for partiality and self-interest and to minimize or prevent the possibility they will play too dominant a part in the decision.

2. *Generalization*   Are you willing to undertake this action in similar circumstances? Generalizing a particular decision may reduce bias and partiality but also may blind one to the unique qualities of a situation that demands a unique response, one that would not generally be used in many other situations. When one evaluates a particular action in light of its general applicability to similar situations, one is concerned with both the breadth and range of effects and the short- and long-range consequences. The purpose of this question is to make the social worker think of the consequences of an action beyond the short term and to consider it not as a particular instance but as a justified general practice in similar circumstances.

3. *Justifiability*   Can you explain and justify your decision to others? The purpose of this question is to make certain that you have, in the available time, consciously and planfully considered the options and have made certain the client's rights and best interests are served by your professional actions in the context of the values and standards of the profession.

EXERCISES

1. The legislature of your state has been alarmed by a sharp rise in the number of children born to young adults with mental retardation. Even when these infants are healthy, many of the parents with retardation are not able to give their children the care that they need. As a result, most of these children must be placed in foster homes at great expense to the public. A bill has been introduced by a group of powerful state senators calling for mandatory sterilization of all men and women with mental retardation. The senators

argue that this is an effective, efficient, and painless way of taking care of this problem. You have been asked by your local NASW chapter to prepare testimony in opposition to this bill. In your testimony you should be mindful that considerations of efficiency and effectiveness cannot be dismissed out of hand in these days of tight welfare budgets. Yet you might argue that ethical considerations are sometimes even more important. Remember, however, that you are trying to convince legislators, not social workers.

2. Organize a class debate on the proposition: "A true professional must be willing to give up some of his autonomy and some of his rights as a freely functioning individual, especially when there is a conflict between personal and professional values."

3. Tonight's forecast is for below-freezing temperatures. The mayor has ordered the police to pick up all homeless persons and to deliver them to the city shelter. The police have asked the shelter social workers to help them to locate the homeless and to persuade them to come to the shelter. You are one of the shelter social workers and know that many homeless persons will refuse to go to the shelter. What are the ethical implications of the police's request? What should you do as a professional social worker?

4. Ruth and Anne, social workers, approached Serena Adams's demand for confidentiality from different perspectives. The discussion of their approaches illustrated some of the differences that arise when a social worker follows one or the other ethical approach. These are not the only differences. Can you identify others that result from the two different approaches?

5. Examine the ethical principles screen (EPS). Would you order the principles in the same way? What, if any, principles would you add or delete?

SUGGESTIONS FOR ADDITIONAL READINGS

Fleck-Henderson (1991) draws on social psychological research on moral reasoning and behavior and applies it to moral reasoning in clinical practice. In "Religious Denominational Policies on Sexuality," Bullis and Harrigan (1992) describe how the religious values and beliefs of clients and social workers in relation to sexuality can impact on the therapeutic process. Loewenberg (1992) illustrates some potential conflicts between personal and professional values. Reamer (1993) in *The Philosophical Foundations of Social Work* provides a chapter on moral philosophy and social work. Glassman (1992) presents a series of personal and professional dilemmas that emerge when social workers attempt to implement feminist values in a practice setting.

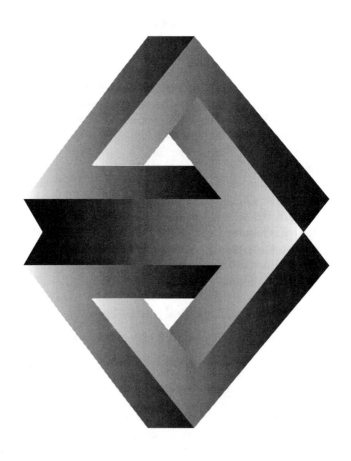

PART TWO

Ethical Dilemmas
in Professional Practice

4. Confidentiality and Informed Consent

A person's right to privacy is a first-order value in our culture. Every person has a right to determine *when*, *how*, and to *what extent* he or she wants to share (or have shared) personal information with others. Even though the Constitution does not explicitly mention a right to privacy, Chief Justice Richard B. Hughes of the New Jersey Supreme Court wrote that "Supreme Court decisions have recognized that a right of personal privacy exists and that certain areas of privacy are guaranteed under the Constitution" (*In re Quinlan*, 170 NJ 10, 1976).

The professional ethical principle of confidentiality is derived from this societal value. This principle is not a modern invention but was already recognized in ancient times by Hippocrates. The physician's oath that is attributed to him states, "What I may see or hear in the course of treatment . . . I will keep to myself, holding such things shameful to be spoken about" (Van Hoose & Kottler, 1985, p. 7). In the NASW *Code of Ethics* this principle appears as a major standard:

> Social workers should respect the client's right to privacy. Social workers should not solicit private information from clients unless it is essential to providing services or conducting social work evaluation or research. Once private information is shared, standards of confidentiality apply (NASW *Code*, 1996, 1.07a).

Seventeen other paragraphs provide additional explanations and limitations. Valid consent is required before social workers can disclose confidential information (1.07b), and clients must be informed of disclosure of confidential information and the possible consequences of such disclosure (1.07d). However, if compelling professional reasons exist, such as imminent harm to a client or when laws require disclosure, then confidentiality may be broken (1.07c). Social workers should also "protect the confidentiality of clients during legal proceedings to the extent permitted by law" (1.07j). Social workers should discuss with clients the nature and limitations of their right to confidentiality (1.07e).

In addition, social workers providing services to couples, families, or other groups "should seek agreement among the parties involved concerning each individual's right to confidentiality and obligation to preserve the confidentiality of information shared by others" (1.07f); they should also inform client of policies "concerning . . . disclosure of confidential information among the parties involved in the counseling" (1.07g).

Social workers should not discuss confidential information for teaching or training purposes (1.07p), with consultants (1.07q), or with third-party payers (1.07h) without the client's consent. Confidential information should not be discussed in public areas (1.07i) and should be protected "when responding to requests from members of the media" (1.07k). Client records should be stored in a secure location (1.07l), should be transferred or disposed of "in a manner that protects clients' confidentiality" (1.07n), and "reasonable precautions [should be taken] to protect client confidentiality in the event of the social worker's termination of practice, incapacitation, or death" (1.07o).

Social workers should ensure the confidentiality of information transmitted through electronic or computer technology (1.07m). Finally, "social workers should protect the confidentiality of deceased clients consistent with the preceding standards" (1.07r). The professional relationship between practitioner and client is based on the social worker's acceptance of these standards and their derivatives.

PRIVACY AND CONFIDENTIALITY

Confidentiality means that a social worker will not reveal to anyone information that she has received from a client who expects that the information will not be shared with others. However, it is not always easy or possible for a social worker to implement this rule. The *Code* itself recognizes the possibility that "compelling professional reasons" (NASW *Code*, 1.07c) may require a social worker to reveal information received in confidence "when disclosure is necessary to prevent serious, foreseeable, and imminent harm to a client or other identifiable person or when laws or regulations require disclosure without a client's consent" (1.07c). The nature of some of these compelling reasons will be discussed later in this chapter under the section on Duty to Warn. Even for those who are committed to practicing in an ethical manner and who want to observe confidentiality, this has become a major ethical problem because no social worker can guarantee that information received by her will always remain confidential.

Confidentiality is an ethical principle rather than a legal one. It affirms "an explicit promise or contract to reveal nothing about an individual except under conditions agreed to by the source or subject" (Siegel, 1979, p. 251). An ethical dilemma occurs whenever a practitioner has to find the correct balance between a client's right to privacy and the right of other people and of society to certain information.

It is generally assumed that a client's reliance on confidentiality promotes trust in the social worker. Many think that this relationship with the professional would be harmed if clients were aware that there are limits to confidentiality. They believe that the confidentiality principle is crucial for maintaining an effective professional relationship (Edward, 1999). Without observing confidentiality, there is a risk that:

1. People who need professional help may be deterred from requesting this help.
2. People who have already begun a relationship with a social worker may not fully engage.
3. The trust relationship that has already been developed may be destroyed; clients who have disclosed confidential information may feel betrayed by the professional whom they trusted.

In this spirit, one New York family court judge ruled that "it cannot be seriously controverted that essential attributes of the [social worker–client] relationship include confidentiality, trust and reliance" (*Hector M. v. Commissioner of Social Services of City of New York et al.*, 102 Misc. 2d 676, 1980). However an empirical study by Muehleman and colleagues (1985) does not support the assumption that limiting confidentiality necessarily endangers the client–social worker relationship. In addition, Steinberg and colleagues found that retention in treatment was higher when the informed consent procedure was more explicit (Steinberg et al., 1997).

In considering confidentiality and its limits, we must consider the difference between information received directly from a client and information received about the client from others, such as a hospital, an employer, or another social worker. In both cases, the person who supplied the information wants to restrict its dissemination. In the first case, the client does not want others to receive the information; in the second case, the party supplying the information does not want the client to have knowledge of it. The question in the latter case is whether the client who has a direct interest in (and perhaps a right to) this information should have access to it. Another problem occurs when the client is aware of what information is being transmitted about him from a third party, but does not want it to go further, even if the transmitting agency has no objections. The question is who has the *rights* to information about the person—that person or the agency that "owns" the information. For example, a client does not want a prospective employer to know that he has had a history of mental illness, but the hospital where he was hospitalized has provided the worker with a full record specifically for the purpose of alerting every relevant person of the patient's condition. Is this information confidential? Who has the right to release it?

The *Code of Ethics* (1996) contains the following standards for providing clients with access to their records:

(a) Social workers should provide clients with reasonable access to records concerning the clients. Social workers who are concerned that clients' access to their records could cause serious misunderstanding or harm to the client should provide assistance in interpreting the records and consultation with the client regarding the records. Social workers should limit clients' access to their records, or portions of their records, only in exceptional circumstances when there is compelling evidence that such access would cause serious harm to the client. Both clients' requests and the rationale for withholding some or all of the records should be documented in clients' files.

(b) When providing clients with access to their records, social workers should take steps to protect the confidentiality of other individuals identified or discussed in such records (1996, 1.08).

Confidentiality is an especially problematic issue because this ethical principle is based on an oversimplified practice model that includes only the social worker and the client. If this simple model fully reflected reality, observance of this ethical principle would depend almost entirely on the intentions of the worker (assuming that the client does not inform the worker of activities that she would be mandated by law to report, such as child maltreatment). The reality, however, is much more complex because most often there are many participants in the social work action system, with each of the participants making conflicting demands for confidential information. These participants may include other social workers, colleagues from other fields, administrative personnel, insurance companies and third-party payers, law enforcement agencies, relatives, and the client. The ethical considerations for sharing confidential information with each of these participants may differ.

Other Social Workers

Often we do not give sufficient thought to the ethical implications of sharing confidential information with other social workers. We are not referring here to small talk at a cocktail party (which is clearly against the ethical rule of confidentiality), but to formal or informal consultations with colleagues or supervisors, as well as to the transmission of such information to other social workers who have a professional interest in the information (such as a social worker who is working with other members of the same family, the social worker who will take over the case while the worker is on vacation, and so on). This type of information transmission is for the client's benefit because it is intended to assure more effective service, but is it ethical to provide this information to others without the client's specific consent?

The 1996 *Code of Ethics* provides some guidance on this issue. In addition to discussing the limitations of confidentiality with clients (1.07e), "social workers should take reasonable steps to ensure . . . that clients' records are not available to others who are not authorized to have access" (1.07l). Further, "social workers should take reasonable precautions to protect client confidentiality in the event of the social worker's termination of practice, incapacitation, or death" (1.07o). Social workers should not disclose "identifying information when discussing clients for teaching or training purposes unless the client has consented to disclosure of confidential information" (1.07p). Finally, "if a new client has been served by another agency or colleague, social workers should discuss with the client whether consultation with the previous service provider is in the client's best interest" (3.06b). These sections of the *Code* suggest that it is generally not ethical to share information about the client with other social workers without the client's prior consent.

However, the social worker should also consider the possible harm that may be caused by not providing vital information to colleagues who are in a position to be helpful to the client. It is this consideration that led Taylor and Adelman (1989) to conclude that "keeping information confidential can seriously hamper an intervener's efforts to help" (p. 80).

Colleagues from Other Fields

Many social workers practice on multidisciplinary teams or in settings where information must be shared with colleagues from other professions whose confidentiality practices may differ from those of social workers. To what extent is it ethical for hospital social workers to reveal confidential information to physicians or nurses? Is it ethical for a school social worker to share with a teacher confidential information about a child and his family, knowing that this information may be entered into the child's permanent school record and thus shared with many others?

Some types of social work positions, such as providing case management services, inherently require that the social worker share client information with others. However, the client must consent to what information will be shared with which agencies before the social worker shares confidential information. According to Galambos (1997), "information provided to the client should include the essentials of when, where, why, and how information will be shared with others" (p. 63).

Administrative Records

Social agencies and other employing organizations need information about clients and client contacts for administrative and accountability reasons. The initial request to supply these data may be entirely proper, but once the requested data have been transmitted the practitioner is no longer able to protect their confidentiality. According to Davidson and Davidson (1996), "it appears that information, once passed from the social worker to a managed care service and logged into the medical database of a third-party insurance payer, may be as accessible as credit card information or mortgage payment records" (p. 209). As the use of computerized records becomes more common in social agencies, this aspect of the confidentiality issue has become even more crucial. For example, a California court has ruled that social workers have no legal grounds to refuse to enter confidential information about welfare recipients into the agency's computerized record system (*Belmont v. California State Personnel Board*, 35 Ca. App. 3d 518, 1974).

The 1996 *Code of Ethics* specifically addresses these issues, requiring social workers to "protect the confidentiality of clients' written and electronic records and other sensitive information . . . [and to ensure] that clients' records are not available to others who are not authorized to have access" (1.07l). In addition, "social workers should take precautions to ensure and maintain the confidentiality of information transmitted to other parties through the use of computers, electronic mail, facsimile machines, telephones and telephone answering machines, and other electronic or computer technology. Disclosure of identifying information should be avoided whenever possible" (1.07m). Unfortunately, once the social worker transmits the information, she may not be able to control further dissemination of the data. Davidson and Davidson (1996) recommend that "social workers, individually and in consortium, need to negotiate with managed care policymakers and government regulators to develop new mechanisms to protect client information" (p. 208).

Insurance Companies and Third-Party Payers

New dimensions have been added to the problem of confidentiality as more and more social workers are required to report diagnoses to insurance companies or other third-party payers in order to qualify clients for reimbursement. While clients may consent to sharing this information because they are interested in having a third party pay for part or all of the services they receive from a social worker, they are not always aware of the diagnosis reported. Many social workers do not report the actual diagnosis; for example, many social workers routinely report "adjustment disorder," no matter what the problem. But at other times the severity of the diagnosis is overstated in order to qualify clients for reimbursement (Kutchins & Kirk, 1987). This problem will be discussed in greater length in Chapter 10.

Social workers must also be aware of the possibility that information shared with a third-party payer may then be shared with others, such as the client's employer; "under some managed care contracts with employers, part of the agreement is to report which employees seek services" (Watt & Kallmann, 1998, p. 44). "Anecdotal accounts indicate that armed with full information on the vagaries of information privacy, clients may elect to pay out of pocket rather than run the risk that information may be shared with their employers or future service providers" (Strom-Gottfried, 1998a, p. 30). The 1996 *Code of Ethics* specifically states that "social workers should not discuss confidential information with third-party payers unless clients have authorized such disclosure" (1.07h).

Police

In many states the law requires that social workers, as well as other professional practitioners, inform the police whenever they acquire information about criminal activities that have taken place or that are being planned. For example, a social worker who is present when an adolescent street gang plans a holdup should have no ethical qualms about reporting the gang's intentions to the police. But when a third party (such as a parent or neighbor) tells her about such a plan, she must ask herself several questions: How reliable is the report? Can the information be used without revealing the source? How might such revelation affect the helping relationship? All of these and other questions have factual, professional, and ethical implications. Often it is difficult to separate these aspects.

Many social workers are perplexed by ethical dilemmas arising out of various other kinds of law violations, particularly delinquent acts that do not seem to harm others. The following exemplar describes one such situation that raises a number of ethical questions.

➤ **4.1 Suspected Fraud**

Social worker Jean Fisher is a marriage counselor and family therapist in the Old Town Family Consultation Center, a nonsectarian United Way agency. Sue and Dean Kern have been coming to her for marital therapy once a week for the past two months. Though their problem is not critical, they came to seek help while their marriage was still salvageable. They have made good progress toward reaching their goal.

During today's session Dean Kern mentioned that he has continued to receive supplemental security income (SSI) support payments for his aged mother, who lived with them until she moved overseas two years ago. She now makes her home with his sister, who lives in England.

Should Ms. Fisher report this case for possible fraud? Or does client/worker confidentiality cover this communication? According to the *Code*, disclosure required by law or regulations is a compelling reason to break confidentiality (1996, 1.07c); therefore, it is important for social workers to know what the reporting regulations are in their jurisdiction and to act accordingly.

If Ms. Fisher is not required by law to report this case, then several other issues should be addressed. For example, what will happen to the client/therapist relationship if Ms. Fisher does reveal what she learned today? Should she consider the possible consequences to the treatment before she decides what to do? What other criteria should she use to resolve the ethical issues posed here?

What would be Ms. Fisher's obligation if she had learned that Dean Kern had escaped from prison several years ago? Or that Sue Kern was pushing drugs? Does the seriousness of the offense change the ethical considerations? Does the degree of harm (to the client or someone else) the offense may cause make a difference?

Relatives

Are the relatives of a client entitled to confidential information that might affect them? For example, if a terminally ill man asks that his relatives not be told how ill he is, what should the social worker do if the man's son asks her whether his father is dying? How does the social worker decide whether to keep the confidence or tell the truth? Do the relatives of a person living with HIV have the right to know about the person's HIV status? Does the type of relationship matter (e.g., a spouse as opposed to a sibling)? This is a type of ethical dilemma that may be especially acute for social workers who are engaged in genetic counseling and who are privy to genetic information that may be relevant to the health of other relatives (Sammons, 1978; Schild & Black, 1984).

Are parents entitled to confidential information about their children? Does the age of the child make a difference? Does it make a difference whether the information came from the child or another source? Should parents be told about their daughter's pregnancy as described in the following exemplar?

➤ **4.2 Debbie Roberts Is Pregnant**

Debbie Roberts is a 12-year-old sixth grader who is 10 weeks pregnant. She has been a good student and her teacher reports that she has never had any problems with Debbie. The school nurse referred Debbie to the school social worker because Debbie refused to discuss her condition with the nurse. At first, Debbie also refused to speak to the social worker, but later she told her that she did not want to have an abortion. Debbie asked the social worker to make arrangements so that she could carry to full term; she repeatedly emphasized that she did not want her parents to know that she was pregnant.

Clients

What are a social worker's obligations when a client wants information about himself, such as wanting to read his own case record? According to the *Code of Ethics*, "social workers should provide clients with reasonable access to records concerning the clients. . . Social workers should limit clients' access to their records, or portions of their records, only in exceptional circumstances when there is compelling evidence that such access would cause serious harm to the client" (1996, 1.08a). However, questions may still remain about what constitutes "reasonable access," "exceptional circumstances," or "serious harm."

There are several possible arguments against sharing confidential information with the client, especially against granting him access to his own record:

1. The case record may contain information supplied on a confidential basis by a third party, such as another social worker, teacher, neighbor, or relative. According to the *Code of Ethics*, "when providing clients with access to their records, social workers should take steps to protect the confidentiality of other individuals identified or discussed in such records" (1996, 1.08b). This suggests that while the social worker needs to protect the confidentiality of others mentioned in the client's record, it is not sufficient reason to deny the client access to his records.
2. The case record may contain "raw data" that have not yet been checked or evaluated, or test results or other data that may be misinterpreted by a lay person. The *Code of Ethics* requires social

workers to "provide assistance in interpreting the records and . . . consultation with the client regarding the records" (1996, 1.08a). Therefore, this may not be a sufficient argument for denying access to client records.

3. The social worker may use the case record to explore various options or to ask herself questions that need further clarification; when the client reads such material, his trust in the worker may be impaired. In this situation, the social worker will need to assess the potential for serious harm to be caused by reading the record; if such potential exists, then access may be denied (*Code of Ethics*, 1996, 1.08a).

4. Reading or hearing negative information about himself may hurt the client. Again, if the potential for serious harm exists, then access may be denied. Whenever the social worker denies access to the record, "the rationale for withholding some or all of the records should be documented in clients' files" (*Code of Ethics*, 1996, 1.08b).

5. The client may use these data for purposes for which they were not intended, including making legal claims against the worker and the agency.

There are also several arguments in favor of giving clients access to their own case records:

1. Reading the information gives the client an opportunity to correct mistakes.

2. A client can give informed consent to share information with others only if he knows what this information is.

3. Knowledge of information may lead to change, while ignorance will result in only maintaining the present unsatisfactory situation.

4. Opening the case record will demonstrate the efficacy of client/worker cooperation and may be followed by even greater client participation in the social work process.

We have presented several arguments for and against opening case records to clients in order to help social workers arrive at an ethical decision. Admittedly, this is a decision that few social workers have to make alone because, generally, agency policy and directives on this point are specific and clear. However, if you were asked to present to an agency board of directors on the issue of client access to records, what would your recommendation(s) be?

Clearly there are limits to confidentiality. It is recommended that these limits be explained to the client "as soon as possible in the social worker–client relationship and as needed throughout the course of the relationship" (NASW *Code of Ethics*, 1996, 1.07e). However, in what level of detail should these limits be discussed? Some explanation is important in view of the fact that most clients assume that everything they tell their social worker will remain confidential. Miller and Thelen (1986) report that 69 percent of the respondents in their study of clients thought that confidentiality was complete and permanent. It is important to consider that stressing the limits of confidentiality too early in the developing client-worker relationship may be harmful rather than helpful.

CHILD ABUSE AND CONFIDENTIALITY

Social workers and other professionals are required by law to report all cases of suspected child abuse and neglect to the child protective services agency or other designated authority. Although details vary from state to state, such reporting is required in every jurisdiction in the United States and in many other countries. There is somewhat less concern with the ethics of breaking confidentiality in cases of child abuse and neglect; instead the ethical concerns focus on ways to assure the safety of the maltreated child. However, in the Third National Incidence Study of Child Abuse and Neglect (NIS-III, Sedlak & Broadhurst, 1996), Child Protective Services (CPS) had investigated less than one-half of children identified as maltreated, suggesting that many children who were identified as experiencing child abuse and/or neglect were not reported to CPS. When a report is made to CPS, a child protective services worker is required to investigate the reported maltreatment and is supposed to take any necessary action to protect the child.

In Barksdale's (1989) study of child abuse reporting, eight out of ten social workers responded that they would report suspected child abuse, one indicated that he would persuade the client to file a report himself, and the tenth social worker indicated that he had never reported a case of child abuse. Few of these social workers were concerned that their reporting might have an impact on their relationship with the client. In another study of 202 family therapists (including many social workers), 68.3 percent responded that they would report to the authorities a father of a family in treatment who had physically abused his children several times during the past year, even though he now promised never to do so again. An additional 12 therapists reported that they would make sure that the family itself reported the abuse (Green & Hansen, 1989).

Social workers who continue to be uneasy about the ethical and practice implications of reporting suspected child abuse that involves one of their clients might want to consider the following when the need to report arises:

1. Working with the client to help him make the report himself; the social worker should follow up with the client to make sure that the report was made.
2. Discussing with the family why a report needs to be made, what the potential benefits and risks to the family are, what procedures will be followed during the investigation, and, if the report is substantiated or indicated, what some of the treatment options are likely to be. The social worker should be aware of the procedures followed in her area so that she can accurately inform clients about what to expect.
3. Making an anonymous report and not informing the client that the report has been made. Although this may initially seem like the easiest option and perhaps the least likely to potentially harm the client-worker relationship, there are at least two potential problems. First, some agencies are less likely to investigate reports made anonymously; if you really think the child is at risk of harm, you would want to ensure that the report will be investigated. Second, if at some point the client finds out that you made the report anonymously, the client may feel more betrayed and/or alienated than if you had discussed it with him in advance of making the report.

PRIVILEGED COMMUNICATIONS

Privileged communication is a legal right granted by legislative statute. It guarantees that certain information will not be revealed in court without the consent of the person who originated the communication. The rules of evidence define this "privilege" as follows:

> Where persons occupy toward each other certain confidential relations, the law, on the ground of public policy, will not compel, or even allow one of them to violate the confidence reposed in him by the other, by testifying, without the consent of the other, as to communications made to him by such other, in the confidence which the relation has inspired . . . (97 C.J.S. Witnesses, Section 252, cited in Albert, 1986, pp. 172–73).

Privileged communication is a rule of evidence that allows one party in a legal proceeding (in this case, the client) to limit the admissibility of statements originally communicated in confidence, thus rendering the witness (that is, the social worker) "incompetent" to testify regarding a particular matter.

The common law principle that the public has a right to every person's evidence is followed in the absence of a statute of privilege. No person can refuse to testify in court, when called to do so. Persons reluctant to testify can be subpoenaed or commanded to testify by the court; failure to appear and testify in response to a subpoena can result in a citation for contempt of court. Historically, privileged relationships have been limited to husband/wife, attorney/client, and priest-confessor/worshipper. Any other relationship is privileged only when so defined by a statute enacted by a state legislature.

Wigmore's (1961, vol. 8, p. 52) criteria for privileged communications are generally used to determine whether the privilege should apply. Wigmore believed that a privilege status exists only when all four of the following criteria are met:

1. The communication must originate in the belief that it will not be disclosed.
2. The inviolability of the confidence must be essential to achieve the purpose of the relationship.
3. The relationship must be one that society should foster.
4. The expected injury to the relationship through disclosure of the confidential information must be greater than the expected benefit to justice if the witness were forced to testify.

The physician/patient relationship, according to Wigmore, does not qualify because it does not meet the fourth criterion. Social workers who practice psychotherapy appear to meet all four of Wigmore's criteria for privileged communications, but it is doubtful whether social workers practicing in other areas, such as community organization, do so. However, statutes generally cover an entire profession, no matter what specific activities any one practitioner performs (VandeCreek et al., 1988).

The U.S. Supreme Court ruling in *Jaffee v. Redmond* (1995, cited in Alexander, 1997) recognized privileged communication between social workers and clients; "now, all federal courts must recognize the absoluteness of social workers' right to privileged communication" (Alexander, 1997, p. 388). The *Jaffee* decision does not apply to state courts and "most states do not provide absolute confidentiality for social workers or other mental health professionals" (Alexander, 1997, p. 389). However, "every U.S. jurisdiction has recognized some form of evidentiary privilege for statements made by a patient to a psychotherapist for the purpose of obtaining treatment" (Harris, 1999).

The privilege belongs to the client, not to the social worker. When a client waives the privilege, the social worker must testify in court even if the client does not know or is not certain what information is included in his case record and even if this testimony may harm him. Other interested persons do not control the privilege. For example, a father or husband cannot suppress or waive testimony of a social worker who is treating his child or wife, even when he pays for the treatment (Vande-Creek et al., 1988).

The privilege is not applicable and ceases to exist in a number of situations, including the following (this list is not exhaustive and may differ from state to state):

1. When the client is dangerous and plans to harm another person or himself.
2. When there is a serious risk of suicide or other danger to the client's life.
3. When there is serious suspicion of child abuse or neglect.
4. When information is mandated by court.
5. When a social worker is appointed by a court to make an assessment (however, if one of the attorneys requests a pretrial examination by a social worker, then that social worker is covered by attorney/client privilege).
6. When the client plans to commit a crime.
7. When the social worker determines the client is in need of hospitalization for a mental or psychological disorder.
8. When the client sues the social worker for malpractice.
9. In child custody cases, because the interest of the child is considered paramount.
10. When the client has already introduced privileged material into the litigation.
11. When the client threatens to harm the social worker.
12. When a social worker needs a court order to collect fees for professional services rendered.

In many states, the privilege ceases to exist if a third party was present at the time that the client communicated the confidential information to the social worker. However, some state laws specifically extend the privilege of communications to situations that involve group, marital, and family therapy—that is, to situations where third parties are present. These states include California, Idaho, Kansas, Louisiana, Maryland, New York, Oklahoma, and Virginia (VandeCreek et al., 1988). In several other states, the courts decide whether the rule of privilege applies. The Minnesota Superior Court addressed this question in *Minnesota v. Andring* (10 FLR 1206, 1984) and ruled:

> The participants in group psychotherapy sessions are not casual persons who are strangers . . . Rather, every participant has such a relationship with the attending professional, and in the group setting, the participants actually become part of the diagnostic and therapeutic process for coparticipants.
>
> An interpretation which excluded group therapy from the scope of the psychotherapist-patient [privileged communication rule] would seriously

limit the effectiveness of group psychotherapy as a therapeutic device . . . [T]he confidentiality of communications made during group therapy is essential in maintaining its effectiveness as a therapeutic tool . . . .

In the absence of a privilege statute, a social worker who is forced to testify in court about confidential information that she has received from a client may face a double bind—if she testifies, she may be sued by the client for revealing confidential information; if she refuses to testify, she may be cited for contempt of court.

In summary, privileged communication is a legal and not an ethical concept. Questions arising out of privileged communications require legal consultation, while questions about confidentiality require ethical resolution. Admittedly, the line between these two areas is often blurred.

INFORMED CONSENT

The professional ethics rule of informed consent is derived from the moral principle of autonomy. Informed consent means that a social worker or another professional will not intervene in a client's life or release confidential information about him unless the client has consented. Informed consent involves issues of *disclosure of information,* *voluntariness,* and *competence* (Grisso & Appelbaum, 1998). Problems involving any one or all of these issues make for difficult ethical dilemmas in social work practice.

It is generally agreed that confidential information should be released only with the consent of the person who supplied the information. The problem arises most often when another agency needs information originally supplied (directly or indirectly) by the client. Generally social work agencies require the client's written consent before they will release such information. In order not to delay the transmission of vital information, some agencies routinely ask clients to sign a release form at intake. While observing the technicalities of consent, such a routine does violence to the concept of informed consent. Often clients do not understand what they are signing, nor is their signature always voluntary, because they are left with the impression that signing the form is a condition for receiving service. Moreover, many of the routine forms used by social agencies require a college reading level in order to understand them (Wagner, Davis, & Handelsman, 1998). Wagner and colleagues (1998) found that personalizing informed consent forms and making them easier to read increased participants' perception of the helpfulness of the forms.

The problem may be that many forms in use today were designed primarily to protect the agency and the worker from malpractice suits rather than to guarantee the client's informed consent. While some social workers believe they are legally protected by formal consent agreements, ethical problems cannot be avoided in this manner (Davidson & Davidson, 1996). The challenge facing ethical social workers is to develop forms that are both readable and sufficiently specific, but do not scare the client. In addition, informed consent needs to be viewed as a *process* in which adequate information is provided in an ongoing manner as the client's needs and/or treatment progresses (Manning & Gaul, 1997; Wineburgh, 1998). Consent needs to be obtained at the time of treatment, and it cannot be assumed that because the client consented to the same treatment in the past he will again consent in the present (Manning & Gaul, 1997).

According to the NASW *Code of Ethics*, "social workers should provide services to clients only in the context of a professional relationship based, when appropriate, on valid informed consent. Social workers should use clear and understandable language to inform clients of the purpose of the services, risks related to the services, limits to services because of requirements of a third-party payer, relevant costs, reasonable alternatives, clients' right to refuse or withdraw consent, and the time frame covered by the consent. Social workers should provide clients with an opportunity to ask questions" (1996, 1.03a). If a client is not capable of providing informed consent, then permission should be sought from an appropriate third party (1.03c). If a social worker is serving involuntary clients, then she "should provide information about the nature and extent of services and about the extent of clients' right to refuse service" (1.03d).

Ethical problems around informed consent are often difficult to resolve, as will become evident when we consider the following exemplar.

➤ 4.3 Archie Walker's Golden Years

Muriel Palmieri is an outreach worker for the Downtown Elderly Program (DEP). She has organized a group of volunteers who regularly visit with homebound older people. These volunteers have been trained to identify older people who need additional help, so that they can report their names to the DEP. One of the volunteers recently told Ms. Palmieri that she had discovered a bedridden older man in a cold and dirty fourth-floor walk-up apartment.

Archie Walker was probably not as old or as feeble as he appeared, but the volunteer thought that he required more care than the occasional help provided by his 79-year-old neighbor, who brought him food whenever he thought of it. When this neighbor forgot to come, as happened not infrequently, Mr. Walker subsisted for days on cold water and bread. It had been years since Mr. Walker last saw a doctor. He seemed delighted with the volunteer's visit and begged her to come again soon.

Ms. Palmieri told the volunteer that she would see what could be done to make Mr. Walker more comfortable. When Ms. Palmieri visited Mr. Walker, he welcomed her warmly and she was able to verify the volunteer's observations. Mr. Walker seemed relatively alert. Ms. Palmieri thought that his dissatisfaction with his present condition was realistic and a hopeful sign, indicative of a capacity to participate in developing plans for the future. Mr. Walker explained that his only income came from Social Security. He had never heard of the federal Supplemental Security Income (SSI) program; Ms. Palmieri suspected that he would qualify for SSI. Mr. Walker said that he could not afford to move to another apartment, but he insisted that he did not want to go to an old folks' home.

Ms. Palmieri explained to Mr. Walker about many of the programs that were available to help persons in his situation. She listed the advantages and disadvantages of each and indicated the time it might take before each program or service would start for him. She also noted how she could help him qualify. Among the programs they discussed were SSI, Meals-on-Wheels, health visitors, homemakers, Title 8 housing, and the Manor Apartments.

Mr. Walker seemed bewildered by the many programs from which he could choose and by the many decisions he had to make. He asked Ms. Palmieri to do whatever was best for him.

If you were in Ms. Palmieri's place, what would you have done? Here are some of the ethical issues that may arise in trying to help Mr. Walker:

1. What did Mr. Walker mean when he told her to do whatever was best for him? Does this mean that he gave his consent for her to make arrangements on his behalf? Is this a satisfactory way of giving informed consent? If not, in what ways does it fall short?

2. Instead of overwhelming Mr. Walker with so many choices, should Ms. Palmieri have simplified the decisions he has to make by presenting only a few options at a time? Perhaps it would have been better to have Mr. Walker decide first whether he really wanted to stay in his present apartment or move somewhere else. But can he make this decision without having a full knowledge of all options? Do social work ethics require that a client have *full* knowledge of *all* the relevant options?

3. Ms. Palmieri tried to present all of the advantages of every option. But did she really know *all* of the consequences? And does Mr. Walker really care about *all* of the consequences? Is he not much more interested in what will happen to him in the next few months? How much knowledge must a client have before the social worker can be sure that she has met the demands of the *Code of Ethics?*

4. Would it be ethical for Ms. Palmieri to design a package of relevant services on the basis of her assessment and on the basis of Mr. Walker's wishes—and then ask Mr. Walker whether this package was acceptable?

Additional questions could be asked, but it is already clear that in social work practice informed consent is beset with many difficulties and that these difficulties often lead to ethical dilemmas.

Disclosure of Information, Voluntariness, and Competence

The three issues of informed consent, as noted already, are (1) disclosure of information, (2) voluntariness, and (3) competency (Grisso & Appelbaum, 1998). We will discuss briefly the ethical aspects of each of these issues.

Disclosure of information.   A person can be considered sufficiently informed to give consent only if he knows what will occur during the intervention or treatment, what the results of the intervention will be, and what will happen if consent to the intervention is not given. He should know how much better (or worse) he will be if he agrees to the intervention than he will be if he does not agree. He should also have full knowledge about alternate options and their associated risks and benefits. In situations in which the client is being asked to consent to the disclosure of confidential information to a third party, he should know what information will be released, to whom, for what purposes, and with what consequences. Finally, the disclosure of information must be done in a clear and understandable manner (Grisso & Appelbaum, 1998).

Much of this information can be provided by the social worker, but even she may not be cognizant of many of the outcomes. In fact, the nature and consequences of any option are never entirely clear and may be interpreted differently by different experts. Ms. Palmieri might explain to Mr. Walker how Meals-on-Wheels operates, the type of food this program provides, and how much it costs. However, she does not know whether Mr. Walker's stomach will tolerate warm food, how long the present cook will stay, or whether this program will survive the next budget cuts. In fact, Mr. Walker may lose the help of his neighbor (inadequate as it is) if he joins Meals-on-Wheels and be in a worse position if that program is terminated. Ms. Palmieri might point out all the benefits and risks, but there are always secondary and unanticipated consequences which, though unpredictable, may be equally if not more important.

There is also evidence that people often do not pay attention to information presented to them. Whether this is a case of selective listening or of suppressing unpleasant information is not always clear. In one study it was found that most patients were unable to recall accurately what they had been told by their surgeon 24 hours earlier, no matter how carefully the details of surgery and the possible risks had been explained to them. Lest it be thought that the patients in this study were not given adequate information before signing the consent for surgery form, the informed consent explanations were videotaped and later reviewed by independent judges. Many of the participating physicians told the researchers that they had provided their patients with all available information, but they gained the impression that most patients simply did not want to know what might go wrong in surgery (*Los Angeles Times*, June 8, 1980).

Social workers differ in many ways from surgeons, but many social workers also report that their clients really do not want to know all the details. They have a problem and want help from an expert whom they trust. Yet, the social worker is ethically committed to the principle of informed consent. One of the dilemmas around informed consent that has ethical implications occurs because a social worker does not want to overwhelm the client with too much information, but does want to provide sufficient information so that the client can make a meaningful decision. Should the worker proceed when the client gives permission, even though the social worker knows that this client's consent is less than informed? Or should the social worker delay help in order to give the client additional information (which the client may not even want)?

Voluntariness.   Consent is meaningful only when it is given freely. Though there is wide agreement with this ethical rule, some social workers practice in settings where the client has little or no freedom. Prisoners and hospitalized persons with mental illnesses are classic examples of involuntary clients. When working with court-mandated clients, there are three barriers to informed consent. First, the risks and benefits of the court-ordered assessment cannot be fully anticipated. Second, the power imbalance results in client vulnerability that undermines voluntariness of consent. Third, while the "ability to form a therapeutic alliance and obtain relevant information is valued by the court, the therapeutic alliance may not always serve the best interest of the client, who may not be aware of the complexity of the relationship" (Regehr & Antle, 1997, p. 301).

In the *Kaimowitz* decision (42 USLA 2063, 1973) the court ruled that persons whose privileges and eventual discharge depended on their cooperating with the custodial staff cannot give legally adequate voluntary consent. Is it ethical for a social worker to practice in prisons or mental hospitals—settings where consent cannot be given voluntarily? A social worker who accepts employment in such settings faces serious ethical problems almost constantly. The usual practice, giving as much choice as possible under the circumstances (see NASW *Code of Ethics*s, 1996, 1.03d), may be the only feasible option, but this does not completely resolve the ethical dilemma facing the social worker who practices in an involuntary setting.

Consent may also be less than voluntary in other settings. Voluntariness is often presented as a dichotomous value—a decision either is or is not voluntary. However, closer inspection will suggest that there is a wide range of possibilities between the two absolutes. For example, how voluntary will be the consent of a "voluntary" client who believes it is important to gain the worker's goodwill? A destitute single mother may agree with almost everything her social worker suggests because she desperately wants to qualify for assistance. The man who is eager for a reconciliation with his estranged wife may agree with everything his social worker mentions because he believes that in this way he may be able to salvage his marriage. These people are not forced to come to a social agency or to agree with the social worker, but is their consent fully voluntary?

Another ethical dilemma facing social workers arises out of the desirability of client trust. Research has shown that trust or faith in the practitioner is a key component in effecting change. Yet frequently, faith or trust results in a surrender of decision-making participation. Instead of giving voluntary consent, the client who has blind faith will agree to everything his worker says. Developing and encouraging trust, while strengthening voluntary consent, is a challenge for every social worker. Grisso and Appelbaum (1998) comment that "encouraging patients to pursue a particular option is not coercion, unless unfair threats are involved. Clinicians need not simply lay out the alternatives for patients. They can distinguish among the options they consider more or less viable" (p. 9).

The problem of involuntary consent takes on special significance when a client wants to harm himself, either by wishing to commit suicide or by wanting to engage in other self-destructive behaviors. There are those who have argued that a social worker has no right to interfere with a person who really wants to harm himself. Every person has a right to make decisions that affect only himself or herself. But there are others who have suggested that intervention, at least temporary intervention, may be justified in order to determine whether the contemplated action is fully voluntary and whether the decision maker is indeed knowledgeable and competent. Gewirth held that "the conditions of voluntary consent are never fulfilled in such cases [because] only abysmal ignorance or deep emotional trauma can lead persons to extreme measures like these" (1978, p. 264). He no doubt would suggest that a social worker must always intervene in cases of threatened suicide or other self-destructive behavior in order to protect that person's welfare.

There is still another aspect to voluntary consent. Social workers often work in settings in which clients are served by using authority and where their participation is nonvoluntary. Such settings include corrections, juvenile justice, child protection, involuntary commitments for mental health treatment, and court-ordered treatment for substance abuse. There may also be subtle coercion for employees to obtain specific services. In addition to issues of voluntariness, other issues that may arise include those of trust, privacy, relationship, and the efficacy of treatment.

The Group for the Advancement of Psychiatry (1994) reported on the findings of research that suggest that forced treatment can be successful, perhaps even more successful than voluntary treatment. Social workers have reported mixed effectiveness for individual interventions with those involved in the criminal justice system (Ivanoff, Blythe, & Tripodi, 1994). Another review of the literature on the effectiveness of social work with legally mandated clients found that clients can have more successful results than had earlier been thought to be the case. These positive results, however, also found that coerced intervention often produces *time-limited* benefits that do not last beyond the use of external pressure (Rooney, 1992). In addition to the long-standing belief that successful mental health treatment must be voluntary and uncoerced, the use of involuntary treatment modalities also raises many ethical questions that social workers must face.

Competence.   Informed consent presupposes that the person who gives consent is competent to do so. However, many social work clients are less than fully competent. Young children, persons with dementia or mental retardation, and the seriously emotionally disturbed may not be competent to give informed consent for some or all decisions. However, Robertson (1985) notes that even though "competence appears to be a binary process, . . . on closer examination its binariness dissolves and vanishes" (p. 555). In other words, it is not a question of classifying clients as those who are competent and those who are not. Instead, persons will be located along a continuum, ranging from those completely competent, to others who are somewhat competent, to still others who are barely competent or not at all competent. This conceptualization has many implications when we consider professional ethics and practice.

Only a court of law can declare a person incompetent, but there are many situations in which a social worker must make an informal assessment of a person's competency to participate in decision making. The ethical problem is complicated because ostensibly the issue of competency is raised only when a client disagrees with his social worker's recommendation. Rarely do we consider him incompetent if he agrees.

Ethical problems arising out of the issue of competence are well known to social workers in many fields of practice, especially those who are working with adoption, foster placement, custody, abortion, contraception, and end-of-life decisions.

The social worker's dilemma may become a difficult one, especially when young children are involved. While there isn't agreement about how old a child must be before he or she is considered competent, everyone agrees that an infant is never competent. Children, like adults, may not always mean what they say or say what they mean. Stated preferences may not reflect actual preferences. One social worker reported, "Children always want to stay [with their families]. No matter how badly they have been abused, they feel they belong to mom and her habit or her boyfriend who brings her the stuff and hits them or rapes them" (*Boston Globe Magazine*, February 5, 1989, p. 33). Can such a request by an abused child be considered a competent or informed decision?

The decision to intervene in a person's life must never be taken lightly. To limit a person's freedom by removing him from his home and placing him in an institution is a very serious decision, which ordinarily should not be made without the person's consent. What are some important criteria that are relevant for waving aside the need for informed consent?

At the same time, it may be a mistake to always accept a client's consent or refusal at face value. A client may be temporarily depressed, may change his mind upon further reflection, or may be reacting to a situational fear or misunderstanding. Robertson (1985) warned "the alacrity [to accept the first response] may stem from a superficial sense of legal and ethical duty" (p. 569).

The issue of informed consent takes on a special significance when the client is a community or neighborhood. A social worker involved in a neighborhood renewal program must consider whether the elected representatives really represent all residents. Does their informed consent suffice, or must every resident consent? What is the situation when the initiative for intervention comes from the outside? It will not be possible to obtain informed consent if the social worker's first objective is to raise the residents' consciousness to the fact that there is a problem. Requiring every person's consent in this latter situation may be tantamount to ruling out any intervention activity, yet intervening without informed consent is a violation of professional ethics. What should a social worker do in these circumstances?

Ways of Consenting

Oliver Goldsmith (1764) wrote that "silence gives consent," but social workers have learned that silence and other nonverbal signals, such as a nod or even a verbal yes, may be deceptive and may indicate something other than consent. Clients may be ashamed to withhold consent or simply not understand what they have been asked to agree to. Though clients often do not seem to listen, a social worker is still obligated to offer a full explanation of what the intervention involves, what the projected benefits and risks will be, what other options may be available, and what might happen if the client does not consent. All this must be presented in a language that the client can understand.

Aside from questions of disclosure of information, voluntariness, and competency, the various forms of consent also make for ethical problems. Consider the following possibilities:

1. *Direct or tacit.* "Direct" refers to the client's verbal response, while "tacit" means that the client remained silent. But when can not saying no be interpreted as consent?

2. *Oral or written.* Written consent is often preferred, but is the use of oral consent necessarily unethical? Does using written consent forms automatically eliminate all unethical behavior? Should services typically provided via telephone (e.g., suicide hotlines) be withheld until written consent can be obtained?

3. *Past/present.* Does current dissent invalidate all past consents? Is this a case of change of mind, of diminished competence, of situational fear, or of something else? To state this dilemma differently, how much credence should a social worker give to a person's present consent when she knows that in the past he consistently expressed a contrary view?

4. *Present/future.* Can a social worker assume that the client would (or will) agree with her decision if he were (or when he becomes) more aware of what is involved?

5. *Forced consent.* One way to obtain a client's consent is to frame options in a way that the client will consent, no matter what the response. For example, the social worker may ask: Do you want to move to the nursing home this week or next? Is this an ethical way of obtaining consent?

As we have already said, each of these forms of consent presents ethical problems and dilemmas that require resolution. However, one thing is certain: Involving the client in providing informed consent is not a one-time activity but an ongoing process.

Some have suggested that good clinical practice will resolve all of the problems around informed consent. If a client is fully involved in the decision-making process, questions of consent will not arise. Yet it is a fact that even formal contracting does not resolve all the problems involved in obtaining informed consent. The power gap between client and worker often results in contract negotiations between unequals. Some unintended coercion may be brought into play, and this may lead the client to agree to choices that are not entirely of his choosing.

DUTY TO WARN

One legal case that received wide publicity concerned a young man who told his therapist that he intended to kill his former girlfriend just as soon as she returned from an out-of-town trip. When the girl was killed shortly thereafter, the girl's family charged the therapist with neglect. The therapist argued that he was not guilty because his relationship with the client/killer was confidential. However, the judge held that:

> Public policy favoring protection of the confidential character of patient-psychotherapist relationship must yield in instances in which disclosure is essential to avert danger to others; the protective privilege ends where the public peril begins.
>
> When a therapist determines, or . . . should determine, that his patient presents a serious danger of violence to another, *he incurs an obligation to use reasonable care to protect the intended victim* against such danger. [This duty] may call for him (1) to warn the intended victim or (2) [to inform] others likely to apprise the victim of the danger, (3) to notify the police, or (4) to take whatever other steps are reasonably necessary under the circumstances (*Tarasoff v. Regents of the University of California*, 1976, 551 P 2d 334 at 340; emphasis added).

We have cited at length from the *Tarasoff* ruling because it has had such a wide impact on social workers. A subsequent court decision explained that under the *Tarasoff* doctrine, a social worker or other professional (1) must be able to predict "pursuant to the standards of his profession" that the client is violently dangerous and (2) must be able to specify one or more clearly identifiable victims (*Brady v. Hopper*, 1983, 751 F 2d 329).

In another decision, the California Supreme Court extended the *Tarasoff* doctrine beyond the identified intended victim to others who also might be in danger. In this case, the victim's minor children were murdered and their father successfully sued. In the same decision, the court ruled that a therapist's failure to use reasonable care to protect a third party from harm constituted "professional negligence," rather than "ordinary negligence." This definition allows suits to be initiated for as long as three years after the injury occurred, rather than the usual one-year limitation (Butz, 1985, p. 87, citing *Hedlund v. Superior Court*, 1983, 669, P 2d 41).

The *Tarasoff* doctrine, however, has had a wide impact on all helping professionals. Conte and colleagues (1989) report that 70 percent of their respondents believe that failure to warn a potential victim is grounds for a malpractice suit. Pope and colleagues (1987) found that 88 percent of their respondents consider it "unquestionably ethical" to break confidence when a homicidal client threatens to injure another person. But it must be noted that the California court did *not* establish an absolute duty to warn an intended victim. Warning is only one possible option, as a careful reading of the decision (cited above) suggests. Yet 90 percent of the psychiatrists surveyed by Givelber and colleagues (1984) thought that they had no choice and that it was their legal duty to do so. So do most social workers.

In recent years, the duty to warn has been further explicated, but its practice applications still are not entirely clear. More psychiatrists consult the American Psychiatric Association legal consultation service about the *Tarasoff* duty than any other issue (Egley, 1992). New decisions by various courts clarify some questions. For example, a 1994 "California appellate court case, *Gross v. Allen* expands the *Tarasoff* duty to include suicide threats. It also makes explicit that a psychotherapist's 'duty to warn' includes informing a subsequent therapist about a patient's known dangerousness" (Meyers, 1997, p. 365).

Yet other important issues remain open, undecided, or ambiguous (Almason, 1997). Social workers must become aware of and remain up to date on the current laws in their states. In *Rost v. State Board of Psychology,* a Pennsylvania court held that ignorance of the law is not a sufficient defense for not protecting confidential records. The court stated that "a psychologist cannot claim ignorance of the ethical obligations of her profession, and if there was a conflict between her ethical duty to maintain confidentiality and the subpoena, she should have sought legal advice" (Beck, 1998, p. 378). Although this case deals with confidentiality, rather than duty to warn, it suggests that ignorance of ethical or legal responsibilities is not a defense for unethical or illegal behavior.

The duty to warn varies from state to state (Beck, 1998) and may be ill defined in states where laws regulating professions do not define the *Tarasoff* duty. Some professions may receive the benefit of immunity from liability for breaches of confidentiality while others do not. Some state laws create legal confidentiality as a right of the client but do not provide liability waivers for mental health practitioners who warn a potential victim. There is no wide agreement on what is meant by "serious threat of physical violence," nor on the meaning of "intended" or "capable of being carried out." However, "most state statutes require an actual or serious threat; thus therapists in these jurisdictions no longer have to attempt to predict dangerousness" (Almason, 1997, p. 481).

Different states also vary in their requirements in regard to how the warning duty may be discharged: warning the potential victim or someone close to the victim, notifying the police, starting commitment proceedings, or informing mental health evaluators of the nature of the threat. But each of the alternatives may present new ethical dilemmas. Reporting to the police, for example, may fulfill the duty to warn, but the police may have different values in regard to the uses of this information (Egley, 1992).

Admittedly, the prediction of violence is not a hard science. While some characteristics have been found to be related to a higher probability of violent behavior, potential violence cannot be predicted; in some cases, short-term hospitalization or other interventions seem justified based on assessments of potential dangerousness (Newhill, 1992). Beck (1998) comments on the difficulty of predicting violent behavior, especially for clients who are likely to be impulsive, such as those with certain mental disorders. So far, "when violence appears to be impulsive for whatever reason, courts are reluctant to find the defendants negligent" for not warning a potential victim (Beck, p. 381).

Certain ethical problems arise in regard to the *Tarasoff* duty, the answers to which are not readily found in the NASW *Code of Ethics.* A social worker should reveal a confidence only "for compelling professional reasons. The general expectation that social workers will keep information confidential does not apply when disclosure is necessary to prevent serious, foreseeable, and imminent harm to a client or other identifiable person" (1996, 1.07c). However, there remains much ambiguity about the definition of threats to injure.

The *Tarasoff* decision has not only produced new ethical dilemmas but has also led to changes in practice and to new ways in which professional organizations deal with clients. Clients are now routinely informed about the limits of confidentiality and of informed consent in situations necessitating the prevention of violence. Some practitioners and agencies may avoid accepting potentially dangerous clients because of the possible liability problems that may arise. Some may not explore sufficiently issues of dangerous intent so that charges of negligence can be avoided when no stated specific threat was actually heard. Others have used mental hospitals for preventive detention, at times appropriately and at others inappropriately. Such defensive practices may be considered safe because they may help the social worker avoid legal problems, but are such practices ethical? Are there more appropriate ways to comply with the *Tarasoff* decision?

Egley (1992), as a result of his review of the *Tarasoff* decision and subsequent court rulings and legislation, concluded that legislatures offer a better opportunity to define the duty to warn than do the courts. However, according to Almason (1997, p. 471), "statutes and case law have added to, rather than reduced, the concerns and uncertainties in this area of the law." Currently, there exists no statute or model law that provides a complete definition of all the components. The major question is whether social workers have a duty to protect the victims. Because there is so much activity in this area of the law, even social workers who practice in states where there is no clear precedent would be well advised to proceed as if they have such a duty (Egley, 1992; Kopels & Kagle, 1993).

But there are those who hold that the *Tarasoff* doctrine should not present social workers with any new ethical problems because the requirement to break confidentiality and warn the intended victim applies only in specific instances. Beck (1998, p. 375) suggests that the legal and ethical issues surrounding the duty to warn are "remarkably congruent with good clinical practice." When the duty to warn does apply, the ethical decision screens provide clear guidance because saving human life from direct and immediate danger is a higher-order ethical principle than confidentiality. The ethical issue becomes problematic only when the risk to life is ambiguous. An example of this dilemma will be raised later, in Chapter 12, on social work with clients who have AIDS.

EXERCISES

1. Investigate the laws in your state (or of neighboring states or of your home state) concerning confidentiality, privileged communication, and the duty to warn, as they apply to social workers.
2. Prepare a brief to be presented to your state legislature, urging that the privileged communication rule be extended to the client/social worker relationship and that it include group, couple, and family therapy.
3. Divide the class into groups of two. In each small group, have one person assume the role of the social worker and the other the role of an applicant who is seeking help for coping with an alcoholic and physically abusive significant other. The specific task is for the social worker to inform the applicant/client of the limits of confidentiality. Students should try several different approaches and report to the class the one that they think is most effective and best meets the demands of the *Code of Ethics*.
4. Divide the class into groups of two. In each small group, have one person assume the role of the social worker and the other the role of an applicant who is seeking help with parenting issues. The specific task is for the social worker to inform the applicant/client of the limits of confidentiality, especially given the possibility of the need to report child maltreatment to the appropriate agency. Students should try several different approaches and

report to the class the one that they think is most effective and best meets the demands of the *Code of Ethics*.

5. Your agency is reviewing its policy on giving clients access to their case records. Almost all staff members agree to abide by the *Code of Ethics*, but there is a difference of opinion on how to define "reasonable access" and "exceptional circumstances when there is compelling evidence that such access would cause serious harm to the client" (1.08a). Try to define these in ways that are congruent with both professional ethics and clients' rights. If there are differences of opinion in your class, organize a discussion to examine the strengths and weaknesses of each position. Can the class reach consensus on how to best define these issues?

SUGGESTIONS FOR ADDITIONAL READINGS

Roberts, Battaglia, and Epstein (1999) discuss the unique ethical issues related to mental health care in rural communities. Abramson (1989) reports on her research on ethical problems faced by social workers in protective services with the aged, especially on ethical dilemmas arising out of the conflict between autonomy and beneficence. Royce and colleagues (1999) discuss confidentiality and other legal and ethical considerations for field instruction of social work students. Conte, Fisher, Callahan, and Roffman (1996) describe a procedure for obtaining informed consent via telephone.

Schlossberger and Hecker (1996) discuss the *Tarasoff* ruling as it relates to family therapists working with clients who are HIV-positive. Beck (1998) discusses the *Tarasoff* duty as it relates to work with impulsively violent clients, and Meyers (1997) discusses the *Tarasoff* duty to subsequent caregivers. Harris (1999) discusses the *Tarasoff* duty and the *Jaffee* decision on psychotherapist-client privilege.

5. Client Rights and Professional Expertise

Social workers believe that every person has a right to make his or her own decisions. Veteran social worker Charlotte Towle noted that "the client's right to self-determination was one of the first, if not the first, of our beliefs to become a banner around which we rallied" (1965, p. 18). Similarly, the NASW *Code of Ethics* states, "Social workers respect and promote the right of clients to self-determination and assist clients in their efforts to identify and clarify their goals." (NASW *Code*, 1996, 1.02). This rule seems clear and unambiguous. But there is also an ethical rule that requires that social work practice be based on professional knowledge, professional values, and professional skills. Social workers are obligated to utilize these when asked to provide professional help. The *Code of Ethics* states, "Social workers practice within their areas of competence and develop and enhance their professional expertise. Social workers continually strive to increase their professional knowledge and skills and to apply them in practice" (NASW *Code*, 1996, Ethical Principles). It is assumed that the social worker should serve clients with the maximum application of professional skill and competence. These two ethical statements may at times conflict and thus create a serious ethical dilemma for the social worker who tries to abide by both.

At one time this ethical problem was less severe because there was a great deal of uncertainty about the adequacy of social work knowledge and about the effectiveness of social work intervention. In more recent years, studies by Videka-Sherman (1988), deSmidt and Gorey (1997), Reid (1997), Gorey, Thyer, and Pawluck (1998) and others have shown that the application of professional knowledge and appropriate professional skills can result in positive client outcomes. The practice problem with potentially critical ethical implications is how to combine client self-determination with the use of professional knowledge and skill. Is it ethical for a social worker to refrain from using professional knowledge if the client chooses an option with which the social worker cannot concur?

The issue is not so much that the social worker does not concur but rather that the social worker *knows* that the client's choice will result in harm to others. The practitioner's ability to help will be severely limited when the client makes decisions that are contrary to the strategy suggested on the basis of professional knowledge. The social worker may know what strategy will best achieve the objectives that the client has chosen, but is it ethical for the social worker to implement this more effective strategy when the client prefers another? Or the social worker may understand what it is that the client needs or wants even before the client is aware of this. Again, the ethical question arises: May the social worker follow the strategy suggested by her knowledge and insight when the client has made another, less beneficial decision, based on ignorance or partial knowledge?

Some social workers do not hesitate to give priority to their professional knowledge and skill even when this means ignoring a client's input. Halmos observed that a therapist cannot be helpful "unless we mean therapy to be therapeutic and, therefore, determining and directing in important ways" (1965, p. 92). This view follows the tradition that professionals "profess to know better than . . . their clients what ails them . . . " (Hughes, 1965, p. 2). But others hold that a social worker should never make decisions for a client, even if the client's decision does not seem as congruent with the worker's knowledge. This position is based on a number of principles, including (1) the primacy of the client self-determination rule, (2) the philosophical principle that no one but that person himself or herself can change a person, and (3) the practice principle that change efforts without the participation of the person to be changed will not be effective.

Often a social worker can follow the best of practice knowledge and professional skills and still respect a client's right to self-determination. One of the reasons for this is that social workers believe not only in the right but also in the therapeutic effectiveness of client participation in all phases of the social work process. Almost all professionals have moved a long way from the traditionally negative attitude toward clients, such as the one expressed by the 1847 *Code of Ethics* of the American Medical Association, which declared that professionals have "a right to expect and require that their patients should entertain a just sense of duties which they owe to their medical attendants." Early social workers may not have been as blatant in their public statements, but they too expected that clients follow their good advice without asking too many questions.

The conflict between client self-determination and the worker's use of her professional knowledge and skills need not result from any Machiavellian desires. Even when a social worker cares about her client's interests and rights, this ethical problem becomes a critical one in many practice situations. Connected to the issues of client self-determination and the worker's use of knowledge and skills, however, is the question as to who is the client for whom knowledge and skills will be applied. We will turn now to consider this question.

WHO IS THE CLIENT?

The question "Who is the client?" may be the source of several ethical dilemmas. Traditionally, a client was defined as the person(s) who engaged the practitioner and paid her a fee. Alternately, the client is the person (or the system) whose behavior is to be modified or changed by the professional's intervention. However, these definitions may not be entirely appropriate for most social workers, especially for those who are employed by an organization, such as a social agency, a department of government, or an institution. According to the first definition, the organization that pays the social worker's salary should be considered the client. But is the school really the client of the school social worker? Is the prison the client of the correctional social worker? Nowadays the traditional definition may be too narrow, since it was originally devised for clients of "free" professional practitioners in private practice.

The alternate definition also is problematic because it is not always correct to say that the client is the person or system whose behavior needs to be changed. Often social work intervention involves changes in systems other than the client system. When a social worker helps a recently widowed woman complete an application for Social Security benefits, the worker does not intend to change the widow, but instead helps the client to gain access to resources in her environment. Until not too long ago, a physician was certain that the sick person who came to his office was his patient, just as the social worker automatically considered the person(s) who applied for help as her client(s). Today, neither physician nor social worker is certain that the answer to the question "Who is the client?" is quite so simple, as the following exemplars illustrate.

➤ 5.1 Arlene Johnson's Abortion

Arlene Johnson, 18 years old and single, is nearly six months pregnant. Yesterday she came to the Women's Counseling Center to request help in getting an abortion. Because of the advanced phase of pregnancy, she was rushed through intake and was referred almost immediately to Community Hospital.

The procedure was initiated within 24 hours after Ms. Johnson contacted the Center. At the time of delivery the fetus was considered viable and was placed in the neonatal intensive care unit as a high-risk premature baby.

Arlene was most upset when she learned that the "abortion" had resulted in a live infant. She refused to look at the baby or take care of it. Instead, she threatened to sue the doctor and the hospital if the infant survived despite her expressed wish for an abortion.

Arlene asked Robin Osborn, the hospital social worker, to make sure that the baby not be given intensive care, but rather be left alone so that it would die quickly.

Who is Robin Osborn's client? Arlene Johnson? The premature infant? Or who? Whose interests should be accorded priority? The next exemplar is entirely different, but raises similar questions.

➤ 5.2 Mrs. Linden's Classroom

Mrs. Linden is a fifth-grade teacher in the Abraham Lincoln Elementary School. The school is located in a neighborhood into which a large number of Central American families moved recently. Mrs. Joan Ramirez is the social worker assigned to this school.

Yesterday, Mrs. Linden asked Mrs. Ramirez for help in keeping her pupils quietly in their seats. She told Mrs. Ramirez that never in her 20 years as a teacher has she had as much trouble as this year. She thought that her troubles were caused by the many children who recently transferred from foreign schools. Surely Mrs. Ramirez could advise her how to handle these children so that they would be quiet and stay in their seats.

Again, who is the client? Mrs. Linden? The pupils? Their parents? The school? Whose interests should be accorded priority? The two problem situations seem quite different, but in each case the request made by the applicant for service creates for the social worker a dilemma that has ethical implications. Arlene Johnson does not want to have a baby, but once a live infant had been born, her expectations of the obstetrician (and request she made to the social worker) conflict sharply with the rights of the infant and with what society expects from these professionals. Similarly, Mrs. Linden's expectations are different from those of her students. Both teacher and students (and their parents) have different expectations from those of Mrs. Ramirez. The social worker is not at

Figure 5.1   Some Participants in the Social Work Process

APPLICANT	The person(s) or system that requests help with a defined or felt problem.
CLIENT	The applicant who enters into a formal, contractual, goal-focused relationship with the social worker.
TARGET	The person(s) or system(s) that must be modified in order to achieve the desired outcome to which client and worker have agreed.
BENEFICIARY	The person(s) or system(s) that will benefit from success-ful goal achievement.

all sure that the problem is with the pupils; perhaps the teacher is the real problem.

One of the reasons why the "Who is the client?" question causes so many ethical dilemmas is that the question itself is based on an over-simplified and not entirely accurate model of the professional relation-ship. The traditional model included only the practitioner and the client. But an updated model should include the applicant, client, target, bene-ficiary, practitioner, agency, community, and others. Each of the four positions noted in Figure 5.1 can be occupied by one or more persons or institutions. Sometimes one person is the applicant as well as the client, target, and beneficiary. At other times or in other situations, different persons occupy each of these positions. The applicant may not be the client and the client need not be the target, nor is the client necessarily the beneficiary of the intervention. When these positions or roles are occupied by different persons, we can be almost certain that each one will have a slightly different expectation of the social worker. Often these differing expectations are in conflict with each other, thus creating an ethical dilemma for the social worker. When there is a conflict of expec-tations, whose expectations should receive priority attention? Arlene Johnson and Mrs. Linden are the applicants, and their requests are impor-tant. However, both Robin Osborn, the hospital social worker, and Joan Ramirez, the school social worker, must deal with the question of iden-tifying the primary client, target, and beneficiary. Here are the seeds for ethical dilemmas. Similar questions arise in the Pomer case, which we shall soon consider (Exemplar 5.3). Who is the applicant and who the client? Is the "welfare" of Eleanor's brothers and sisters less important (or more important) than Eleanor's welfare? To whom does each of these social workers have a primary ethical obligation? These are practice dilemmas that also involve ethical issues because they are based on con-flicting value assumptions.

Social workers who engage in genetic counseling are constantly faced by difficult problems that involve ethical issues. Modern medical procedures, such as amniocentesis and chorionic villus sampling make it possible to detect hundreds of different genetic disorders, in some cases as early as the tenth to thirteenth week of pregnancy. When there are positive findings, the social worker must help parents think through all of the implications so that they can make a wise decision. However, some physicians expect the social worker to persuade the pregnant mother to abort whenever there are indications of a genetically defective fetus. Should the best interest of the as-yet-unborn child play a part in the decision? What is the best interest? Should the social worker stress arguments in favor of abortion, even if it is evident that the parents do not want to terminate this pregnancy? What is the ethical stance that the social worker should adopt?

Social workers in the criminal justice system face similar ethical issues. In the probation service, social workers regularly prepare reports for the juvenile court judge. The judge takes these reports into consideration when making a final disposition of the case. The ethical dilemma here is that the social worker is both helper and judicial fact finder. The client/worker helping relationship starts during the very first contact with the juvenile, long before the social worker has completed her evaluative assessment or presented her report to the judge. To whom does the social worker owe priority consideration—to the juvenile detainee or to the judge? Who is her client? Note that in the criminal justice system social workers will often face situations in which the resolution of the ethical issues may not fully coincide with the legal requirements.

SELF-DETERMINATION

Immanuel Kant, one of the early giants of modern philosophy, insisted that a person's right to determine his or her own destiny is an unconditional right. He taught that persons are always ends in themselves and should never be treated as means. Self-determination is also a first-order principle in American society. Though not specifically mentioned in the Constitution, the Supreme Court, in a series of due-process cases, equal protection cases, and privacy cases, developed the position that self-determination is a fundamental right that is protected by the Ninth and Fourteenth Amendments. Supreme Court Justice Brandeis (Brandeis & Warren, 1890, p. 1) many years ago suggested that the fundamental right is "the right to be left alone." In recent years, this view has been somewhat curtailed by several Supreme Court rulings (*Bowers v. Hardwick*, 1986; Greenhouse, 1998, 1999a, 1999b; Holmes, 1998; *Rust v.*

Sullivan, 1992; *Planned Parenthood of Southeastern Pa. v. Casey*, 1992) concerning consenting homosexual sex in a private home, car searches, passenger and driver searches, abortion rights, use of government funds to provide abortion information, and abortion and parental consent.

A person's right to make his or her own decisions is the source for the social work value of self-determination. Self-determination is an absolute right, yet most social workers would agree with Rothman (1989) that when used as a practice principle, its application is limited. Bernstein (1960) writes that self-determination is "not supreme, but supremely important," while Perlman (1965) suggests that self-determination, though important, is nine-tenths illusion. No wonder that Rothman states "self-determination is accorded utmost esteem in the profession [but] its meaning and application are clouded" (1989, p. 598). The right of self-determination has become the source for "one of the most common and most perplexing dilemmas for social workers" (Abramson, 1985, p. 387). How can a practitioner respect and uphold client self-determination when working with a client whose conception of what is good for him or her differs from that of the social worker? Or differs from the conception of those who will be affected by the client's decision?

These ethical dilemmas become more frequent and increasingly perplexing as more and more major decisions about life involve highly technical and specialized considerations that often are beyond the comprehension of lay people. Reliance on professionals who have the necessary expertise has become increasingly common. Under these circumstances, directiveness as a helping technique seems to have become more acceptable. As social workers respond to new mandates and demands concerning persons with disabilities and those who are especially vulnerable, a need to reexamine issues of self-determination and autonomy has arisen (Murdach, 1996). In some cases, clients are unable to fend for themselves, causing social workers to intervene protectively, despite the client's objections. But the use of directive methods raises many ethical questions, such as whether the results achieved by a social worker are more important than the methods used. Should a client be pressured into doing things he does not want to do even when his worker is certain that this will contribute to solving or reducing his problem? Is it ethical for a social worker to deceive a client in order to have him participate in a technique that he would reject if he knew all the facts?

The ethical dilemma arises out of a conflict between two guides: (1) the self-determination or autonomy guide, which states that the person most affected by a decision should make that decision, and (2) the benefit guide, which posits that the professional social worker has the knowledge and skill necessary to best assure a positive outcome and is, therefore, responsible for making the decision that will secure the optimum benefit for the client.

Some professionals do not hesitate to use their superior knowledge and power to move the client in the "right" direction. Thus Gillis writes that "all modern psychotherapists, whether they know it or not, engage in maneuvers and manipulations that add to their power over the patient" (1974, p. 91). Dworkin (1985) adds that control of the client by the worker occurs in all professional relationships, no matter what theoretical framework is utilized. Usually this control is not manifest but occurs in an implicit or unconscious way; Dworkin suggests that it would be better if this control were acknowledged and exercised on a systematic and explicit basis.

Control and *manipulation* are concepts that social workers once avoided but which in recent years have entered into the professional vocabulary. This has forced social workers to reassess the meaning and practice of client self-determination. What are the ethical considerations that should guide a social worker who is convinced that an older adult client (who can no longer cope alone at home) should enter a home for the aged very soon, but who knows from past experience with this client that every worker suggestion elicits a "no" response? If this client has close relatives, should they be asked to make the decision? If there are no close relatives, should the worker make the decision without fully involving the client? To do so limits the client's freedom of choice. Such interventions in the life of the client can range from limited to extensive involvement and must be related to the degree of rational impairment or incapacity for decision making demonstrated by the client, as well as the amount of risk or danger present in the situation.

Or is it more ethical to involve the client, but frame the choice in such a way that there is no opportunity to say "no"? For example, the client might be asked whether he prefers to enter the East Side Home or the West Side Home. Or he might be asked whether he wants the intake worker from the Home to come to his apartment or prefers that the social worker drive him to the Home for the intake interview. Or is there no alternative but for the social worker to respect the client's "no," even though she knows that this client can no longer live alone?

Stereotypes should never be used to limit client self-determination. There is some evidence that class-related or age-related criteria are sometimes used to assess the capacity of different client groups to make autonomous decisions. Those who work with aged clients are very much aware of this problem, but this ethical quandary is not limited to the aged. Freedberg (1989) cites as an example an "expert's opinion" that a majority of lower-class unmarried mothers "are incapable of making their own decisions" and therefore should not be expected to make autonomous decisions.

A somewhat different situation, involving both the problem of "Who is the client?" and the problem of self-determination is illustrated in the following case situation.

➤ 5.3 Should Eleanor Pomer Come Home?

Eleanor Pomer is eight years old, the youngest of six siblings. She has been a resident in a special school for the last three years because of a diagnosis of Down's syndrome. According to her cottage parents, psychologist, teacher, and social worker, she functions on a moderately retarded level.

Both of Eleanor's parents are employed. They rent the downstairs apartment of a two-family home in a working-class neighborhood, about one hour's drive from Eleanor's school. The Pomers visit Eleanor once a month. For the past year, Eleanor has also spent one weekend a month at home. Eleanor's home visits have been successful. Both Eleanor and her family look forward to these monthly visits.

The school's staff feels that Eleanor now is ready to leave the school and live again at home. The social worker has acquainted Eleanor's parents with this staff assessment, has told them about the community resources that are available in their city, and has urged them to take Eleanor home. However, the Pomers do not agree with this recommendation. They are satisfied with the present arrangement; they feel that it would be too much of a strain on their other children if Eleanor again lived at home.

The social worker is convinced that it would be best for Eleanor to leave the school and resume a more normal home life. Eleanor is excited about the possibility of again living with her parents and brothers and sisters. The ethical problem in this situation arises out of the conflict between applying professional knowledge and respecting the client's right to make decisions. How much weight must the social worker give to the Pomers' wishes? To Eleanor's wish? Should the most important criterion in reaching a decision be what is best for Eleanor? Who decides what is best for Eleanor? What about the welfare of the other Pomer children? Does the social worker have an ethical right to manipulate the environment (for example, by raising the tuition fee) in order to "help" the Pomers reach the decision that staff thinks is best for Eleanor?

Another basic ethical dilemma in social work practice arises out of two—at times contradictory—professional principles that all social workers have accepted. These are (1) the principle to provide professional help when needed or requested by a client in order to assure or improve that person's welfare, and (2) the principle not to interfere with a person's freedom. These two professional principles are almost identical with Gewirth's basic or generic rights of "well-being" and "freedom" (1978, p. 64). Ideally, a social worker should not experience any conflict between these two rights (or principles). But what if a person's well-being can be achieved only at the expense of his or her freedom? Who defines well-being? Who defines the need for professional help? Who can legitimately request professional help for another person?

Unless there are serious indications to the contrary, no social worker will want to interfere with another person's freedom, even if that person is her client. Some even argue that "the right of self-determination includes the right to fail" (Soyer, 1963, p. 78) and that every person should have "the freedom to make a shamble of his life" (Miller, 1968, p. 30). But it is generally agreed that there are occasions when intervention becomes necessary, even if it is at the expense of freedom. Most people agree that a person's right to self-determination should be limited when its exercise will result in harm to another person, but what if the harm is only to the person himself or herself? This is why Abramson suggests that "paternalism takes precedence over autonomy" whenever the value of client autonomy comes into conflict with the value of securing a client's safety (1989, p. 105).

Though the conditions which justify intervention may seem clear, a social worker will discover many ambiguities. What is *clear and present danger?* How can it be demonstrated? When is harm sufficiently grave to warrant coercion? Who may coerce? How certain must the social worker be that her intervention will prevent the harm before she is justified in curtailing a person's freedom? Consider the following situation.

➤ **5.4 How Immediate Is the Danger?**

Social worker Maria Espinosa has been working for one month with Allison Bode, an extremely thin, almost gaunt, reserved 17-year-old college freshman. Allison was referred to the Family Counseling Center by her pastor after she told him of her loneliness and obsessive thoughts. She came for help with the agreement and support of her parents. Allison is doing passing work academically but has been unsuccessful making friends at school. This afternoon, Allison told Ms. Espinosa that her menstrual cycle stopped. When Ms. Espinosa explored the situation, she learned that Allison is on a diet and exercises two to three hours a day to lose weight. She is slightly depressed but still able to concentrate on her school work and reports she is seldom irritable. Based on all of this information, Ms. Espinosa is quite certain that Allison has anorexia and suggests she go to the college health service to consult with a physician. As soon as Allison heard the suggestion, she rejected it. Is this a case of clear and present danger that requires immediate action? What harm would be done if a few more weekly sessions are used to help Allison act to protect her health and her visit to a physician delayed? What is the ethical correct choice?

More crucial than the type of problem or the chances of rehabilitation or recovery is the question of the client's capacity to make decisions.

As long as he can make informed decisions, the social worker has no mandate to interfere, unless it is question of life, the duty to warn because of danger to self or others. The social worker's mandate is to enable the client, to the maximum extent possible, to make an informed decision.

An additional dimension of this ethical problem arises from the social worker's obligation to do more than merely observe the negative injunction of not interfering with a person's freedom. This obligation demands positive action designed to strengthen or promote the client's freedom. If promoting and not interfering with a client's freedom is to be more than empty rhetoric, social workers must understand that a person is truly autonomous only when all of the following conditions prevail:

1. The environment provides more than one option from which a person can make choices.
2. There is no coercion on the person from any source to choose one or another option.
3. The person is aware of all the available options.
4. The person has accurate information about the cost and consequences of each option so that he can assess them realistically.
5. The person has the capacity and/or initiative to make a decision on the basis of this assessment.
6. The person has an opportunity to act on the basis of his or her choice.

No extensive research is needed to discover that the freedom of most social work clients is quite limited. Though these limitations usually do not result from practitioner activities, social workers must be concerned when anybody's freedom is limited. Americans enjoy more freedom than the citizens of many other countries, but the structural conditions of most contemporary societies limit some of the freedom of most people. This is especially blatant with respect to those conditions that reinforce inequality, racism, sexism, and ageism. As Stevens reminds us, the freedom to choose and the right to make decisions are profoundly cherished rights. However, "self-determination is grievously restrained when opportunities for social mobility are blocked" (1998, p. 294).

Social workers are committed to use their professional skill and know-how to help all people gain full freedom. This ethical commitment may explain why many social workers have been in the forefront of those struggling for more freedom and greater equality for all people. But this ethical concern for greater autonomy must also find expression in the day-by-day practice of social workers.

Access to self-determination also varies with the dependency of the client on the benefits he receives from his social worker. The more essential and valuable the goods or services received, the greater the client's feelings of dependency on the worker and the less likely it is that he will choose an option that he believes his social worker will disapprove. Among those receiving public assistance, those persons who believed themselves to be personally responsible for being on "welfare" were less assertive about their rights as public assistance clients and were least likely to have disagreed with a caseworker or appealed a decision. Stigma, loss of self-esteem, psychological and economic hardship, and a lack of options undermine the ability to be self-determining (Goodban, 1985). Another study found that clients who received only "talking" goods (such as advice and discussion) felt relatively free to reject their workers' advice, while others who had received cards from their workers that made them eligible for medical treatment felt much more dependent on their workers and no longer felt free to reject their advice (Handler & Hollingsworth, 1971).

The limited knowledge and/or capacity of many clients to engage in autonomous decision making places a particular ethical obligation on the social worker to help them make reasoned choices so that they can maximize their benefits, even with unrealistic goals. Yet, in the final analysis, the center of gravity in the helping process remains with the professional. Or as Rothman stated, "The prime responsibility for making professional decisions about means of helping the client falls to the practitioners" (1989, p. 608).

AMBIGUITY AND UNCERTAINTY

The degree of ambiguity and uncertainty in practice situations influences how social workers make professional decisions to ignore or countermand client rights in order to assure a higher value, such as the protection of life. The more clear and relevant information available, the better for the decision-making process. Three types of ambiguity and uncertainty make for ethical problems in social work practice. These are (1) uncertainty about values and goals, (2) uncertainty about scientific knowledge and about the facts relevant to any specific situation, and (3) uncertainty about the consequences of the intervention.

These uncertainties occur in a world characterized by a general disillusionment with authority. The infallible guides and granite virtues of yesteryear have been discarded like last season's fashions. Even faith in science and progress, characteristic of the belief system of previous generations, has moved from center stage and has been replaced by a pervasive sense of uncertainty. For many, the pursuit of personal happiness and individual fulfillment has become more important than following any established ethical imperatives. It has become more and more difficult to know what is right. As a result, some have suggested that right is whatever one thinks is good. But even those who accept this approach find that they must cope with ambiguity and uncertainty, just as their colleagues have to do who are still searching for ethical imperatives relevant to modern society.

Ambiguity may be more critical a problem for social workers than for many other professional practitioners. The reasons for this include the following:

1. The issues with which social workers deal are often nonspecific and vague.
2. Social work does not offer its practitioners the same comprehensive knowledge base that many of the more established professions have been able to provide.
3. Social workers generally have less control over the outcome of their intervention than do practitioners in many other professional fields.

So many different factors impinge simultaneously on a person that it is often difficult for a social worker to assess the specific impact of her intervention. An unsuccessful outcome may be (but need not be) due to something that the social worker did or did not do. The same intervention activity in two seemingly identical problem situations may lead to two entirely different outcomes because of factors over which the social worker has no control. Nor will a social worker ever know what might have happened had she not intervened or had she utilized a different strategy.

For example, in a case of suspected child abuse, a social worker cannot predict with certainty what will happen if the child continues to stay with his parents, nor will the worker know for certain what might happen if the child is forcibly removed. Similarly, no social worker can predict with any accuracy whether helping a neighborhood council obtain a grant for restoring dilapidated houses is the best or the worst help that she can offer.

One such situation with many ambiguities is explored in the next exemplar.

➤ 5.5 A Victim of Child Abuse

Several months ago, Ms. Gillis told her public welfare social worker that she suspected that an upstairs neighbor, Mr. Hill, regularly and brutally beat his two-year-old son, Leroy. She heard the most frightful noises several evenings each week. When she saw the boy at rare intervals, he always wore bandages and looked so sad. The worker noted these remarks in her case report, but took no further action.

Last month Mrs. Hill brought Leroy to Lakeside General Hospital emergency room. Leroy suffered from multiple fractures which, according to his mother, occurred when he fell down the front stairs. The attending physician did not believe her story since the X ray revealed a large number of previous fractures in addition to the current ones. As required by law, he notified the public welfare department that he suspected child abuse.

Andre Conti, an experienced child protection social worker, was sent to the Hill home to investigate. He talked at length with both parents. They admitted beating Leroy occasionally when he misbehaved. This, they explained, was their way of disciplining him. Mr. Conti suggested that there were other ways to teach a boy to behave properly. But he concluded that the boy was in no immediate danger. Two weeks later, another social worker made a follow-up visit to the Hill home. This worker, Millie Walker, agreed with Mr. Conti's assessment that for the time being there was no need to remove Leroy from his home.

Ten days after Ms. Walker's visit, Mrs. Hill called for an emergency ambulance, saying that her son was having difficulty breathing. When the ambulance crew arrived, they found Leroy unconscious. Twelve hours after he was brought to the hospital, he was pronounced dead. He had not recovered consciousness. The postmortem confirmed that death was caused by a severe beating with a blunt instrument.

This exemplar gives rise to a number of questions with ethical implications, including the following: Did Ms. Gillis's social worker pay sufficient attention to the report of child abuse? Are a neighbor's suspicions sufficient cause to warrant interfering in the Hill family? How can Mr. Conti or any social worker know for certain that "a clear and present danger" exists for Leroy's life? When does parental discipline become child abuse? Under what conditions is the removal of a child from his family justified? How certain must a social worker be of the consequences before deciding to leave an endangered child with his family?

It should be noted that there are three sets of ambiguities in the Leroy Hill exemplar: (1) ambiguities resulting from a lack of clarity of societal norms (e.g., What are the limits of parental discipline?), (2) ambiguities resulting from a lack of knowledge (e.g., What evidence is sufficient to warrant intervention?), and (3) ambiguities resulting from an inability to know what the future will bring (e.g., What will be the consequences of intervention?). The social workers involved in this case made professional judgments that Leroy was not "at risk." As a consequence of their mistaken judgment, Leroy is now dead. But the mistake could also have gone the other way—identifying a risk when there is no danger to the child's welfare and thus removing the boy from his home needlessly. Every social worker in this situation faces a critical ethical dilemma because both types of mistakes cannot be avoided at the same time. Ambiguities and uncertainties are endemic conditions in social work practice. Neither the social worker, nor anyone else, can know for certain that a given parental behavior will lead to the child's death. The test of an effective social worker is that she should retain the ability to function even while coping with the ethical dilemmas that result from ambiguity and uncertainty.

EXERCISES

1. Role-play the situation described earlier in this chapter where the social worker has determined that her older adult client is no longer able to live alone in his home. We know that this client responds negatively to every worker suggestion. Try various approaches to this problem situation. Keep in mind the ethical aspects!
2. Rothman (1989) and others have stated that the primary responsibility for making professional decisions falls on the social work practitioner. On the other hand, many social workers argue that the client has the exclusive right to make decisions about his life. Organize a debate around these two professional positions.
3. Assume that you are the child protection social worker sent to investigate the report of Leroy Hill's abuse (Exemplar 5.5). What criteria would you use to arrive at a decision to remove or not to remove Leroy from his parental home? Keep in mind the ethical aspects!

SUGGESTIONS FOR ADDITIONAL READINGS

Abramson (1985, 1989) analyzes the dilemma of social workers who face at one and the same time both the autonomy rule and the beneficence rule—How can a social worker encourage self-determination and at the same time take full responsibility for delivering the professional services that the client needs? Freedberg (1989) and Rothman (1989) review the development of the self-determination principle in social work practice and its impact on practitioners. Weick and Pope (1988) also raise important questions about the self-determination rule. Murdach (1996) reexamines issues of autonomy and self-determination raised by new mandates concerning disabled persons and vulnerable individuals. Bernstein (1993) explores self-determination in group practice. Jayaratne et al. (1997) report on advice-giving behavior by social workers.

6. Value Neutrality and Imposing Values

In today's world, many scientists try to avoid all questions of values and morals because they attempt to derive knowledge only from empirical facts. One of the traditional expectations of professional social workers is that they not impose their personal values on clients and that they suspend judgment about clients' behavior and actions even when their own values or societal values demand a judgment. But in the real world of social work practice, things are not always so simple. The *Code of Ethics* (NASW, 1996, Purpose) recognizes that social workers "should be aware of the impact on ethical decision making of their clients' and their own personal values and cultural and religious beliefs and practices. They should be aware of any conflicts between personal and professional values and deal with them responsibly." Crucial professional decisions always involve value choices—if not worker values, then values of clients or of society. Professional decisions "are not simple choices of technical means to ends, and even choices of means have a value component" (Bayles, 1981, p. 67).

VALUE NEUTRALITY

For many years, the practice principle of value neutrality found wide acceptance among social workers. In an attempt to gain scientific credibility, psychotherapy "has moved towards being 'value free'"(Parrott, 1999, p. 1). Even today, some clinicians view the duty of neutrality as a fundamental clinical and ethical principle (Simon R. Gutheil, 1997). Several writers, for example, urged social workers who work with pregnant teenagers to maintain a neutral position about the girls' behavior if the workers want to be really helpful (Cain, 1979; Cervera, 1993). One reason for suspending value judgments, according to many, is that in our pluralistic society there is no longer any absolute *right or wrong*. What might seem wrong to me will seem right to the next person. What is right today may be wrong tomorrow.

Yet there are critical questions about this value-neutral stance that must be considered. Many have asked whether value neutrality or value suspension is a realistic option for social workers. They point out that social workers are human beings, not robots. What are they to do with the values they hold when working with clients who hold contrary values? Can they really avoid imposing their own values by either subtle or nonverbal communications?

There are no easy answers to these questions, yet they need to be considered by every practitioner. *Suspension of judgment*, a basic concept in social work, has in the opinion of many been so misinterpreted that it has caused rather than prevented much unethical professional behavior. Siporin writes that "in being of help to people, there is need to make moral ethical judgments, and to help clients do so as well" (1985a, p. 202). Goldstein (1998) suggested that social work should not be concerned only with what works (without a moral orientation) and ignore what is good. Manning (1997) also views social workers' ethical practice as best guided by a framework of moral citizenship. Value neutrality may actually be causing damage. Rhodes suggests that "the idea of value-free counseling is impossible and dangerous" (1986, p. 87). Social workers have to make moral judgments. Sometimes these difficulties are present when social workers have to distinguish between what is functional or dysfunctional, normative or pathological behavior. There is no escaping moral and ethical issues at each step of social work processes. Maslow indicates that a science that is "morally neutral, value free, value neutral is not only wrong, but extremely dangerous" (1969, p. 724). When a social worker does not challenge a client's behavior, that client may think that she approves of what he does. The worker may intend her silence to be an expression of value neutrality, but in fact her silence may be interpreted as a signal of acceptance of that behavior!

Value neutrality is itself a value. Sometimes social workers do not acknowledge their own moral judgments. The contemporary social worker who bases her practice on value neutrality may be evading moral dilemmas through a more complete acceptance of client self-determination or judge a compulsively conscientious but constructive client (emotionally driven) in psychologically critical terms, as her colleague a hundred years earlier morally judged a "lazy" one.

Value suspension became a professional response to the moralistic paternalism of the Friendly Visitors, the volunteers who preceded professional social workers in the last decades of the nineteenth century. Originally suspension of judgment meant that the social worker related to the whole person and to his strengths, instead of only to his weaknesses and problems. It meant trying to understand this person in terms of his personal history, environment, culture, and community. If the client's behavior was problematic, then the social worker was ready to help him change that behavior without condemning him. This was often expressed by, "I accept you, but not your behavior." More recently this stance has been changed so that now many social workers seem to say, "I love you and your behavior, no matter what you have done." But can we honestly say that we do not care what a client does? Can we accept child molestation, neglect, violence, cheating, stealing, or lying? Dare social workers not condemn physical and sexual abuse, rape and beatings, irresponsible sexual activities, and similar antisocial behaviors?

In today's practice context, social workers have to balance the notion of the client's right to self-determination against social workers being directive. There is more clarity about directiveness or paternalism when clients do not have the capacity to make informed decisions and in the face of potential harm and danger to the client and others. However, managed care and other accountability factors can encourage more directiveness by social work practitioners. A study by Rothman, Smith et al., (1996) found that social workers, including those utilizing psychodynamic as well as cognitive-behavioral, task-centered, and brief treatment focuses, used a broad range of directiveness modes in their practices. The directiveness modalities used were influenced by specific contextual factors, but also confirmed was the fact that social workers were directive in their practice. However, they avoided either extreme—paternalism or client self-determination—as their one confirmed practice pattern. This flexibility and consistency reflects one of the practical limitations to social worker neutrality, the fact that neutrality ignores "the therapist's ethical and legal responsibility to protect the welfare of clients" (Woody, 1990, p. 291).

IMPOSING VALUES

Much of what social workers do involves helping people choose between available options; ethical principles are one important consideration in this choice. How can a social worker provide this help without imposing her values? This question takes on special urgency because social workers often grapple with strategies that are designed to modify or change the beliefs and values of clients.

Some approaches to helping people with problems hold that it is desirable to systematically change their values and thought patterns and substitute for these more sensible and more rational thoughts and values, such as those held by social workers. The rational/emotive therapy developed by Ellis is one school of therapy that urges this view. The therapist's values always influence client values. Those following this school suggest that these values be used in a conscious and controlled manner (Ellis, 1973; Frank, 1991). But many others disagree with this approach.

A social worker may actually impose her own values when she tries to "suspend" value judgments and offer instead a range of value choices. Covert value messages are often more powerful than overt ones. A social worker may define the goals and outcomes of the treatment without once saying what it is that she deems appropriate. How can one ethically justify such unilateral worker control? Some have suggested that an explicit communication of the social worker's values would safeguard the client against any potential misuse of power by the worker (Lewis & Walsh, 1980). Such self-disclosure of the worker's values may enhance the client's comfort with and sense of trust in the practitioner. But value self-disclosure may also be harmful when used inappropriately or at the wrong time (Anderson & Mandell, 1989). Spero (1990) concluded that any short-term advantages of a worker's value disclosure may be cancelled by long-term harmful effects.

The problem facing the social worker of Bess and Todd Moore illustrates the range of ethical dilemmas around the issue of imposing values.

➤ 6.1 Saving a Marriage

Bess and Todd Moore have agreed to seek help to "rescue" their marriage. Bess recently discovered that Todd has been having sex with several women over the past few years. Todd has told the social worker that his sexual relations with other women are only physical. Since he has greater sexual needs than Bess, he cannot give up these relations. Yet he loves his wife and wants to continue this marriage.

Bess is ready to forgive the past, but cannot bring herself to live with Todd, knowing that at the same time he has sex with other women.

Different social workers hold different values about marriage and extramarital relations. Should the social worker keep her own values to herself so that she will not influence the decision of the Moores? Is this possible? Or should the social worker openly state her own values and then let Bess and Todd work on a solution of their problem? Which is the more ethical approach?

Do social workers have a responsibility to examine together with the client the ethical nature and quality of the problems that people bring to them? Or is it more helpful to overlook the moral aspects of the situation? The following exemplar raises these ethical questions.

➤ **6.2 A Smoking Lounge for High School Students**

Kate Collins is a school social worker. She is a member of the student-faculty council that recommends policy in the local high school. At a recent meeting, several student members proposed setting up a "smoking lounge" to eliminate the safety hazard of students' smoking illegally in the bathrooms and in the locker rooms.

Kate is convinced that smoking is extremely dangerous to one's health. Her reading on the subject has led her to the conclusion that it is most important to discourage young people from smoking. But she also knows that as a professional she must not impose her values on others.

How can she be a party to a recommendation that she considers harmful? But how can she let her values interfere with democratic and autonomous decision making? What if the student council voted to establish a racist or sexist club?

Some think that smoking, although potentially injurious, is not immoral, yet they condemn suicide because they believe it to be highly immoral. What are the ethical implications for a social worker who believes suicide to be immoral when she is assigned to a committee charged with preparing a guide to help people commit suicide? Would it make an ethical difference if the distribution of this pamphlet were to be limited to persons with a terminal illness?

Society, with near unanimity, condemns child sexual abuse and incest. Yet the number of incidents of child sexual abuse relationships that come to the attention of social workers rose dramatically from the early 1970s through the early 1990s, when a dramatic reversal followed (National Research Council, 1993; Finkelhor, 1998). Earlier increased reporting might have been a result of child maltreatment publicity and reporting mandates, as well as people feeling freer to talk more openly about all types of sexual activities. The more recent decline may reflect a new caution or even intimidation by professionals and the public because of publicity about false reports, misguided prosecutions, and civil law suits, or it may be a result of a real abatement of cases.

Many ethical questions face a social worker who receives information about intrafamilial child sexual abuse by stepfathers and mothers' boyfriends, as well as incest by siblings and biological fathers. Should she assume a value-free stance and listen to her client's report of what could be incestuous behavior with the same equanimity as she would to any other problem he may raise? Should she communicate the community's valuation of incest? Does it make a difference whether the abuser or the victim is the worker's client? Are there cultural factors that might make a difference in assessing the ethical implications of this type of behavior? What if the client's ethnic culture does not proscribe father/daughter relations that do not involve penetration? What if the incestuous relations occur between consenting adults?

The three types of "deviant" behavior that have been discussed in this section form a matrix of ethical intensity. The discussion suggests that beyond a certain point most social workers will abandon any attempt to maintain a value-free stance. But the ethical dilemma is more serious than these "unusual" examples suggest because, in fact, ethical quandaries involving the social worker's judgment occur at every step of the social work process. The social worker who "suspends" her judgment when a client relates a promiscuous episode or an aggressive behavior incident may be as judgmental as her colleague who does not hesitate to indicate disapproval. When a client feels guilty about a certain behavior but the worker addresses only the problem of guilt, the client may conclude that the worker considers such behavior acceptable.

It has been suggested that in these and similar situations a social worker can avoid making judgments by letting the client decide what he wants—whether he wants help with his "guilt" or with the "deviant" behavior. At first glance this appeal to the principle of client self-determination seems to solve all ethical problems. But on second thought it may turn out that this is an irresponsible and perhaps even an unethical response to a client who desperately seeks help. Even when the client's request for help is specific, the worker may have a societal responsibility that she dare not shirk. Should a social worker help a client reduce his guilt so he can continue to enjoy an incestuous relationship with his teenage daughter?

As the population of the United States grows more diverse through changing patterns of immigration, social workers are faced more frequently with behaviors that generally lie outside the experiences of American-born and-raised social workers. Consider the following case situation.

➤ 6.3 Loyalty to Self or Family?

Mrs. Arriga, a social worker at a Family Service agency, has seen Ms. Salima, a recent immigrant, for three sessions because she has been depressed and experiencing much conflict at home with her parents and other relatives and much anxiety on her job as a packer. All family members, including Ms. Salima, must work because everyone's paycheck is necessary to maintain a marginal existence. Her supervisor, who likes her, referred her to the agency for help. Ms. Salima told Mrs. Arriga with some ambivalence that her family will not allow her to have a normal American social life. Her parents want to arrange a marriage for her and do not allow her to date. She cannot leave home because her earnings are insufficient to support herself, and her English and other skills are not developed enough for a better job.

Ms. Salima vascillates between love for her family, pride at doing what is expected in her family's culture, and becoming more Americanized by dating and deciding for herself whom she should marry.

What should Mrs. Arriga do? Should she support loyalty to Ms. Salima's family? After all, they are all dependent on each other and they are her only relatives in the United States. Should she support Ms. Salima's struggle toward more independent values? Is a social life possible other than through dating? If Ms. Salima has the possibility of living with extended family members or friends she knows from her past, should she be encouraged to leave home and live with them? How should a social worker who is a feminist respond to this situation? What if Mrs. Arriga is from the same culture as Ms. Salima's family and is known in their community? Will that make a difference? Mrs. Arriga must respond to Ms. Salima now.

It seems that suspension of judgment is an impossible demand. The *Code of Ethics* and social work practice stress self-determination, but doesn't Ms. Salima have some obligation to her family and group? Some try to avoid the ethical dilemma by suggesting to a client that they approve or disapprove only of a specific behavior, but not of the client. This is a fine, almost legalistic distinction that may seem to avoid the ethical issues posed here. But such a solution creates other practice problems and does not really avoid the ethical issues raised. Perhaps a more realistic way of phrasing this ethical obligation is to demand that the social worker's own value judgment, probably reflective of her own American value system, never become the sole criterion for making a decision. There is no relationship that is free of values. At the same time we must remember that in the final analysis, it is the client's responsibility to identify the values that will guide his behavioral choices; the social worker can never assume this responsibility (Frankl, 1968).

CLIENT-WORKER VALUE GAP

A significant gap between worker values and those of a large proportion of social work clients is characteristic of many settings in which social work is practiced. This gap is another potential source for several ethical problems and dilemmas. A major discrepancy between the religious beliefs and practices of many clients and the nonreligious values held by many mental health professionals has been noted by Siporin and Glasser (1986) and Loewenberg (1988). Practitioners need information about their clients' participation in any religious group. The degree of religiosity and strength of a client's knowledge of, and commitment to, specific religious values can influence the worker's choice of interventions. When sexuality (abortion, adultery, homosexuality, premarital sex) issues arise in therapy, there may be value conflicts between the worker's values and those of the client (Bullis & Harrigan, 1992). This gap in religious values is only one area of value discrepancy, reflective of the discrepancies that exist in many other value areas.

Shared values may optimize the chances for successful outcomes. Goldstein writes that "the initiation of any substantial relationship (including the helping relationship) depends on the extent to which its members can share, complement, or otherwise resolve their moral differences" (1987, p. 181). Though matching of client and worker values may be desirable, this is not always possible in the world of practice. Various problems can arise when there is a significant client-worker gap, but here our concern will be limited to the ethical aspects of these problems. These relate primarily to the possibility of value imposition when there is a major difference between client and worker values. Because of the power imbalance between client and worker, this ethical problem is often very real.

Typical of the client-worker gap is the following exemplar.

➤ 6.4 A Drug Addict Has a Baby

Jeff Butz, public welfare worker, received a call from the Community Hospital social worker. Mona Koss, a single mother with a drug addiction, gave birth to a baby girl two days ago. Mother and baby are due to be discharged tomorrow, but the hospital social worker does not think that the infant will be safe if she goes "home" with her mother. As far as is known, Mona Koss has no permanent home. Currently she shares a bed with a drug pusher who has been involved in the past in physical and sexual abuse situations.

The world of Jeff Butz is as far from Mona Koss's world as the North Pole is from the South Pole. Their values are diametrically opposed. This, incidentally, is a situation in which value matching is neither possible nor desirable! One way for social worker Butz to respond to the telephone call he received is to initiate legal proceedings designed to remove the infant from her mother. This may seem congruent with his own personal values and with what he believes to be societal expectations. But

Mona Koss, though a drug addict, is also a human being with her own personal values. Can these be ignored? And what is best for the newborn infant? Jeff Butz feels that he should explore these questions with Mona Koss before making any decision.

In this case, as in many others, a client-worker value gap is often unavoidable. Social workers must, therefore, develop ways to deal with these value differences. Some have found the following approach useful:

1. During the intake/assessment/diagnostic stage the social worker should determine if there is a relationship between the value differences and the presenting problem. The marital problem for which Bess and Todd Moore sought help (Exemplar 6.1) may very well be related to value differences between themselves and their social worker.

2. The social worker should discuss her finding with the clients if they are able to participate in determining whether these differences might complicate the social work process. No prior assumption should be made that a client is not ready and able to participate in such joint decision making. Though Mona Koss holds values that are quite different, Butz must not assume that she cannot participate in making decisions for herself and her newborn baby.

3. A joint decision should be made whether to continue the social work process or whether to refer the client to another social worker with more congruent values, if such a worker is available.

Some have suggested that the social worker should always disclose her own values during the first session so that the client can protect himself against overt and covert value imposition. Raines (1996) considered therapist self-disclosure appropriate at the beginning of the treatment process because the therapist should have an underlying ethic of selfless love devoted to the welfare of the client. Yet routine disclosure of the worker's values too early in the social work process may actually harm clients since they may feel that the worker is challenging their own values even before a working relationship has been established between them (Anderson & Mandell, 1989; Beit-Hallahmi, 1975; Spero, 1990). Strean concluded that such questions should not be answered but turned back to the client to explore underlying anxieties because the problem "in answering personal questions at the beginning of treatment is that the client then has the 'right to know' encores" (1997, p. 366). Goldstein defended the right of therapists to "feel free to not self-disclose to patients. Therapists and those close to them personally do have rights to their privacy and therapists can have limitations about what they can deal with in the therapeutic process at certain times" (Goldstein, 1997, p. 56). In certain instances, the social worker's right to privacy has ethical implications when a serious illness or impending death may be involved.

THE INEVITABILITY OF VALUES

In this chapter, we have included sections on value neutrality, the imposition of values, and client-worker value gaps. One must remember that practice should reflect the value principles of the social work profession expressed in the *Code of Ethics*, albeit at a high level of generality, including service, social justice, dignity and worth of the person, importance of human relationships, integrity, and competence (NASW *Code*, 1996, Ethical Principles).

Social workers and their clients sometimes act unethically, sometimes without meaning to do so. Some clients fall into circumstances that lead them to act unethically and, thus, violate norms for right and correct conduct in interpersonal relationships. Many social work clients abuse each other, break the law, ignore or harm their children, cheat, and behave irresponsibly. Clients, as Siporin (1983, p.16) suggests "bring many moral problems for help, as in choosing between family obligations and their own need for freedom; choosing between undesirable alternatives of a divorce or an unhappy marriage; revealing unfaithfulness to a spouse." However, they may not conceive of these choices in moral and ethical terms. Siporin further suggests that "a basic social work job is to help people see that they have choices and control; that they can make moral decisions and behave responsibly, properly, and rightly; and that they can resolve the moral/ethical difficulties and predicaments in which they are involved" (Siporin, 1983, p. 20).

Similarly, Goldstein (1998, p. 246) describes the ethically grounded social worker as "alert and responsive to questions of moral choice, social justice, prevailing moral codes of conduct, and, not the least, personal accountability whether she is doing research, applying theory, planning, or engaging in practice—any professional activity, that impinges on the life and well-being of others." If one accepts that value neutrality is very difficult, if not impossible to achieve, and possibly harmful in some circumstances, then it is important for social workers to identify their own personal values that are related to social work practice. For example, would it be ethical for a social worker who believes that abortion is ethically wrong in all circumstances to accept a position with a family planning clinic that offers abortions to clients?

Ethical decisions by social workers have importance at every level from individual case to social and political action. One means of selecting

Figure 6.1   Continuum of Worker Values

| Ethical behaviors—those that the worker believes are *ethically right* (e.g., protecting human life): The worker may find it difficult to work with clients or an agency with opposing values (e.g., an agency that provides adults with information on assisted suicide) | Behaviors that the worker believes are neither inherently right or wrong—those that the worker does not have strong personal values about: The worker could support agency or client values as long as they are not in conflict | Unethical behaviors— those that the worker believes are *ethically wrong* (e.g., abortion): The worker may find it difficult to work with clients or an agency with opposing values (e.g., a family planning or pro-choice clinic) |

from the multitude of ethical issues for clients and oneself in practice is through a screening device. Behavior can be considered along a continuum (see Figure 6.1).

Situations as described in this chapter may present painful dilemmas for both clients and social workers but—for example—neglect, abuse, and violence also raise questions as to who the social worker represents, whose welfare is at stake, and social work's role as moral agents. The *Code of Ethics* states that "social workers should promote the general welfare of society . . ." (NASW *Code*, 1996, 6.01) and "social workers should act to expand choice and opportunity for all people, with special regard for vulnerable, disadvantaged, oppressed, and exploited people and groups" (NASW *Code*, 1996, 6.04b). Is it ethical then to be value neutral at one level but not at another? Or, are social workers, according to major theorists and the *Code*, obliged to be moral agents at all levels?

EXERCISES

1. It has been said that even when a social worker does not declare her values publicly, her lifestyle and her nonverbal communications will usually indicate the values that she holds. Identify ways in which your own lifestyle and nonverbal messages will inform a client of the values you hold. What problems might this create for maintaining a professional relationship?

2. The risk of being HIV+ and contracting AIDS from sexual activities has been compared with the risk of fatal automobile accidents (Gochros, 1988). Does such a comparison communicate a value or is it an example of value neutrality? Defend your answer.

3. Your client feels very guilty about engaging in certain behavior. Assume that this behavior is not illegal. He asks your help, but does not specify whether he wants help (1) in dealing with his guilt, or (2) in extinguishing the behavior. Discuss the ethical implications of choosing either approach. Will the specific behavior make a difference in your ethical assessment? Try to assess the two approaches with the following types of behavior: overeating, smoking, gambling, masturbation, eating foods his physician suggested he avoid for medical reasons, having an extramarital affair, or taking the time to work out for an hour five times a week.

4. How would you respond to the telephone call that Jeff Butz received (Exemplar 6.4)?

5. There are social workers who support a person's right to commit suicide, or to commit adultery. There may even be others on the "fringe" of the profession who support the right to incest under certain circumstances, use of drugs, and other behaviors. Some persons believe these positions are derived from a value-free approach. Others believe they prove the impossibility of a value-free approach. In the first case, the question becomes: What values and whose values will prevail? In group discussions, decide which view is right and identify the implications of each approach for ethical decision making.

SUGGESTIONS FOR ADDITIONAL READINGS

Siporin (1985b) and Goldstein (1998) suggest that the place of values in social work practice is crucial and social workers have to be moral agents. Simon and Gutheil (1997) defend the duty of neutrality for therapists. Rothman, Smith et al (1996) report on the directiveness of social workers in practice. Jayaratne, Croxton, and Mattison (1997) also describe social workers' advice giving. Raines (1996), Strean (1997), and Goldstein (1997) approach therapist self-disclosure from different perspectives and place quite different limits on it.

7. Equality, Inequality, Limited Resources, and Advocacy

Every person has an equal right to obtain social benefits and an equal duty to carry social burdens. This principle is based on the first-order societal value of equity (Frankena, 1973; Rawls, 1971). From this societal value, social workers have derived the professional rule that obligates them to distribute available resources on an equal basis to all clients.

COMMITMENT TO EQUALITY

An ethical problem occurs when available resources are so limited that an equal distribution is not possible. For example, when a county has only 20 beds for the chronically ill aged, these cannot be distributed on an equal basis to 30 clients who need this service. The equity value may create ethical problems even with respect to goods and services that lend themselves to an equal division (such as the social worker's time or the department's budget), because another rule obligates a practitioner to meet the specific needs of each client.

Time

Time is a very limited and precious resource in the social work process. For example, a social worker in a family agency may be available 30 hours a week for direct service to clients. Is each of her 30 clients entitled to a one-hour interview every week? For some clients, an hour a week may be more than they need, while for others it may not be sufficient. Client Peter Barr needs many hours of counseling this week to help him cope with an unexpected and sudden family crisis, but his social worker can meet this need only if she allots less time to other clients. Is such an unequal division of time ethical?

Many treatment strategies are ruled out because sufficient staff time to implement them is not available. Many social workers recall situations when a client could have received more effective service if only there had been more time available. The attempt to observe equity in the allocation of time to clients results in several ethical dilemmas, one of which is illustrated in the next exemplar.

> ### 7.1 Incest in the Schild Family

Doreen Schild is a cute 13-year-old with a history of school truancy, alcohol and drug experimentation, and several attempts at running away from home. Her parents appear warm and accepting, but the family agency worker who has been meeting with Doreen for the past four weeks suspects that the real problem is Doreen's home.

Today was the fifth session with Doreen. The conversation was routine, and little of significance was said until three minutes before the next client was scheduled to appear. Suddenly Doreen started to relate some very important and emotionally charged material. Both her father and older brother have tried repeatedly to have sexual relations with her, but thus far she has not let them go all the way. When she told her mother about this, she was told to forget it had ever happened. As Doreen related this information, she became noticeably more upset.

The social worker realized that this interview could not be terminated just because time was up now. But how long could she keep the next client waiting? Doreen could easily use all of the next client's hour. But that would not be fair to the other clients scheduled for today. Furthermore, if Doreen was not exaggerating, immediate arrangements would have to be made to remove her from her home. This might take many additional hours of the worker's time, hours already scheduled for other urgent assignments.

What would you do? What other ethical issues, in addition to the equity issue, does this worker face? What are the social worker's obligations to Doreen? To her parents? To the community?

Inequality

Americans have accepted as a self-evident truth that all persons are created equal (even though the signers of the Constitution claimed this right only for white men). From this first-order value, social workers have derived the ethical rules of "equal distribution of resources" and "equal access to opportunities."

Equality is popularly equated with democracy. Those raised in this tradition often find it difficult to understand how some people can raise questions about it. They are upset when it is suggested that an equal distribution of resources is not always ethical and may lead to injustices. Some have asked whether it is right that medical resources, especially scarce and expensive life-extending technologies and instruments, are distributed equally, regardless of a patient's age. Daniel Callahan, a philosopher and medical ethicist, does not seem to think that such an approach is ethical. He writes that medicine should "resist the tendency to provide to the aged life-extending capabilities developed primarily to help younger people avoid premature and untimely death" (1987, p. 24). He suggests that age be used as a decision criterion for allocating life-extending therapies. What does this mean? Does this mean that open-heart surgery should be available only to people under a given age, such as 80? But is not the life of an 84-year-old person as important and valuable as that of a 74-year-old? Some would argue that the chances of a successful operation decrease rapidly as people grow older. Others avoid this statistical argument by noting that it is preferable to use limited resources to add 20 years of life rather than one or two years. This is particularly so when the younger person can still make a contribution to society, while the aging person may be entirely dependent on the efforts of others.

Deciding for and against the allocation of societal resources on the basis of possible returns gives rise to other serious ethical problems. The social contribution of high-intelligence people may be more valuable than that of people with a lower intelligence and perhaps more significant than that of persons with mental retardation. Does this give society the ethical right to limit open-heart surgery to people whose IQ is above 150? Or above 98? Or to people with a college degree? Or with a certain income? This diabolic argument can be pushed even further by arguing for the "elimination" of all undesirables, a policy implemented by Nazi Germany in the 1940s. While few will maintain that the "final solution" was ethical or moral, the implication of this approach for the unequal distribution of resources demands further careful thought.

It is a fact that many social work resources are not distributed equally. Lower-class and minority persons are less likely to be accepted for psychotherapy and, if accepted, are often seen for briefer periods of time or treated by less qualified personnel. This differential allocation of resources is often justified by alleging insufficient motivation, lack of readiness, and verbalization difficulties by these clients (Rabkin & Struening, 1976). It is urgent that, wherever such unequal distribution of resources exists, this issue be reexamined and, if necessary, corrected.

But as noted in Chapter 3, "Guidelines for Ethical Decision Making," there is another side to inequality. Those who are not equal should receive special (and therefore "unequal") help (both services and resources) in order to gain equal access to life opportunities. It is this consideration that often justifies the unequal allocation of resources. Children with disabilities, for example, will receive more attention and greater resources than other children in order to compensate for disabilities. A blind child will not have the same access to education as a sighted child unless we provide the blind child with extra resources, including talking books and/or a reader.

RACISM

Despite the efforts of many social workers and other citizens, racism continues to exist in America. In what has become increasingly a multiracial, multiethnic society, intergroup competition for various resources undoubtedly exacerbates conflicts between groups, especially during times of recession, economic changes, and increased international economic competition.

For social workers, racism is a societal problem that impacts directly on their practice, on the availability of resources, and on the delivery of social services. One study found that few social workers in Massachusetts were aware of such problems as racism in their work settings, and that even when they did become aware of it, they did not act ("National Association of Social Workers, People in the News," *NASW News*, 1990a, p. 17). A content analysis of social work articles on Asian Americans, African Americans, Latinos, and Native Americans published in the 1980s found that most of the literature on social work practice and minorities "portrays the social work profession as naïve and superficial in its antiracist practice" (McMahon and Allen-Meares, 1992, p. 537). According to the authors, minority clients are viewed out of the racist context in which they live, proposed changes have to do with changes in the awareness of social workers, and the literature seems to accept the status quo by focusing on individual change. These trends have continued (Courtney et al.,1996).

Social workers must do more than they are doing now to prevent and oppose racism. Racism is inconsistent with the ethical standards of the profession, and social workers cannot achieve their aims where racism interferes. The Ethical Principles enunciated in the NASW *Code of Ethics* (1996) call on social workers "to help people in need and to address social problems," to "challenge social injustice," to be "mindful of individual differences and cultural and ethnic diversity," and to "promote, restore, maintain, and enhance the well-being of individuals, families, social groups, organizations, and communities." There is a whole range of activities that are necessary, ranging from individual interactions to confrontation of institutional and societal racism. Indicative of such efforts are those of the Council on Social Work Education over several decades to fight racism and sexism in Schools of Social Work (Trolander, 1997) and the efforts of all schools to become antiracist institutions.

Some have suggested that one must differentiate between the individual social worker's obligation to fight racism and the obligation of the profession to fight racism. These two aspects are interrelated, but they are not the same (Bayles, 1981). *The Code of Ethics* makes explicit the ethical stance toward racism when it states "Social workers are sensitive to cultural and ethnic diversity and strive to end discrimination . . . " (Preamble) and that "Social workers should act to prevent and eliminate . . . discrimination against any person, group, or class on the basis of race, ethnicity, national origin, color, sex, sexual orientation, age, marital status, political belief, religion, or mental or physical disability" (NASW *Code*, 1996, 6.04d).

Individual social workers have an ethical responsibility to work toward the elimination of discrimination in their practice, employment, and in society. Also, the National Association of Social Workers and other social work professional organizations have responsibilities to eliminate racial and other discriminations through advocacy, social action, legal, and other efforts within their organizations and in society. Racism in the society and when found in the profession makes difficult the achievement of social work's goals and ethical aims of equal access—equitable services and resources—for the fulfillment of individuals and the society.

The situations described below suggest some of the ways in which racism expresses itself in situations in which social workers may be involved. A review of child welfare research found that "children of color and their families experience poorer outcomes and receive fewer services than their Caucasian counterparts" (Courtney, Barth et al., 1996, p. 99). Children of color are overrepresented in child maltreatment reports, particularly physical abuse. African-American children are less likely to exit out-of-home care, therefore have longer spells in out-of-home care than Caucasian children, and have a dramatically lower likelihood of leaving such care and being adopted. A pattern of discrimination exists, based on race and ethnicity, in the provision of child welfare services whereby Caucasian families and children receive more services than families and children of color.

To the extent that these conclusions are warranted, there is the suggestion that some social workers have been guilty of serious ethical breaches. Even though they did not necessarily engage in deliberate unethical activities, their behavior was unethical when they remained silent in the face of systematic institutional racism. The single child welfare worker may not have been able to change the entire system, but this is hardly an acceptable excuse to avoid attempts to change as much of one's local system as possible. What are the ethical obligations of social workers who encounter such ethics violations by systems or institutions? As background, see the NASW *Code* (1996, 3.07b, 3.09d, 4.02, and 6.04).

Dilemmas about race and racism occur in different situations, not always as serious as the system problems in child welfare noted above. For example, what do you suggest the social worker do in the following situation?

➤ **7.2 Al Tabrizzi Is Fragile but Makes a Racist Comment**

You are a clinical social worker seeing Al Tabrizzi, an elderly, somewhat irrational, and very depressed client in a family service agency. This client has been making progress on dealing with a number of tasks—getting out of the apartment, seeking social life, improving his eating habits, and taking care of his affairs—but he has much further to go. Often he has spoken to you about how comfortable he feels with you as his worker and how he has been growing more trustful of your relationship because you have been so fully accepting of him and not judging him. In today's session, he has spoken slurs about Latinos.

Mr. Tabrizzi is "somewhat" irrational and clinically depressed. Is this the first time he has made such comments? How much control does he have over his remarks at this point? Are these slurs related to situational events or a sign of his failing health? If he is aware of his comments, he may be reflecting the culture in which he has lived his entire life, or he may be testing you. In that case, should you confront him about his slurs directed at another group? Or, if his remarks are the result of physical problems, should you ignore them? Does the *Code of Ethics* require questioning racism in all circumstances? How much change is Mr. Tabrizzi able to make in his values and behaviors? What is the ethical thing to do?

What do you do if you are on the staff of a training program for young adults whose funding will be cut unless the program serves both white and black persons? At present few whites are enrolled. In order to meet the demands of the funding agency, the staff is making strenuous efforts to recruit qualified white applicants, even though there is a waiting list of qualified black candidates. In these circumstances, should you condone giving a preference to whites? Is this ethical? Weigh the alternatives. If you report the situation publicly, the program will lose its major funding base. If you do not serve more white young adults, funding will stop, and no one—neither white nor black young adults—will receive the service they now receive. If you do comply and recruit more white participants, the result will be that the program will serve fewer black young adults. What is the ethical thing to do?

LIMITED RESOURCES

The ethical problems resulting from the equality-and-inequality rule are often aggravated by the fact that available resources are always limited. If they were unlimited, there would be no problem in providing all persons with the help they need. But in the real world there is never enough for everything that should be done. Life is like a zero-sum game. Allocating a scarce resource to one person means that another will not receive it. But the concept of limited resources may be a manipulation of language used to conceal certain decisions. Often it merely means that available resources have been allocated elsewhere or that commitments or priorities have been shifted. For example, at the beginning of the 1960s, decision makers in Washington decided to give highest priority to landing a person on the moon by 1970, no matter what the cost. While there undoubtedly was a great deal of waste and even loss of life in pursuing this goal, the first astronaut did land on the moon in the summer of 1969. But this success was made possible only by assigning a lower priority and by making fewer resources available to other important programs, including social programs, such as eradicating poverty, eliminating discrimination, battling illiteracy, and so on. In other words, even while overall societal resources are limited, it is possible to assign almost unlimited resources to one particular program if such a policy decision is made at the highest level and if there is a wide consensus that this program deserves the very highest priority, even at the expense of limiting allocations for other important projects.

If this is the meaning of limited resources, the focus of ethical decision making shifts from the micro to the macro, from the specific case to societal allocations. On one level the ethical problem facing the social worker practitioner will be how to allocate the resources she controls. But on another level the profession as an organized group, as well as individual social workers as citizens, has an ethical responsibility to become involved in the societal allocation process, that is, the political process. For example, home health care, a major segment of community-based long-term care, is especially important for frail elderly persons. When budgets for this program are cut back because of soaring costs, many of these elderly people are pushed into nursing homes and hospitals, even though this type of care creates unnecessary dependency and is more costly. Social workers have a responsibility on ethical and other grounds to advocate for continued home health care services (Beder, 1998).

Much of what social workers can and cannot do is determined by political decision makers. When the legislature passes budgets, it determines to a large extent the resources available both for public and voluntary agencies and institutions. Other political decisions have a major impact on the nation's economic health, rate of economic growth, availability of jobs, and so forth. Are social workers merely passive observers of these political processes? Or is there an "ethic of responsibility" that obligates social workers to take an active part in these societal processes?

We agree with Siporin (1985b) and Goldstein (1998) that social workers are moral agents who have a responsibility to influence organizations and communities. Priorities and commitments determine resource allocations. Significant resources have been allocated to drug rehabilitation programs, while considerably less monies have been allocated to solve the problems of the homeless. What are the ethical implications of such decisions?

Ethical Problems in Allocating Limited Resources

Many allocations are made at the highest political level in Washington or at a state capitol, settings in which most social workers do not feel at home. However, at other times such decisions are made much closer to home. Consider the decision facing the social workers of the Centro Latino, a United Way agency in Westport, a community that has always had a large concentration of Spanish-speaking immigrants. Centro Latino was started as an indigenous self-help group in the 1960s by immigrants from Latin America. Nowadays its budget is met largely by the United Way and supplemented at times by specific state and federal grants. Though volunteers are still used, most assignments are now handled by professional staff members. The decision-making powers are vested in the agency's board of directors, made up largely of veteran Spanish-speaking residents of the community. At a recent staff meeting the staff discussed an issue that many felt had ethical implications.

➤ **7.3 Refugees in Westport**

Early last year, more than 400 new Central American refugee families arrived in Westport. Centro Latino was able to generate a special onetime $100,000 grant to help in the adjustment of these refugees. The board of directors decided after lengthy discussion to allocate 20 percent of this grant to employ two more part-time social workers and to distribute the remaining funds directly to families to help them in their adjustment. The detailed rules for distributing these funds were to be developed by the agency's staff.

The current staff meeting was devoted to developing criteria for distributing the funds. The agency's director, Sandra Lopez, argued that equity demanded that each of the families receive an equal cash grant of approximately $190, which each family could use as it wished. Several staff members agreed with Ms. Lopez. But others urged that the limited funds be used where they could do the most good. Since the basic needs of these families were already met, the new monies should be earmarked for special needs where an intensive use of resources could best achieve the desired objective. Each staff group believed that its proposal was supported by the professional ethics code.

If you had been participating in this staff meeting, which position would you have supported? Look at the NASW *Code of Ethics.* Do you find guidance there for your proposal? Following your review of the *Code,* look at the ethical principles screen in Chapter 3. What ethical considerations should be weighed before making a decision? What would you say is the ethically correct decision? Why?

ETHICAL DILEMMAS IN ADVOCACY

In 1969, the NASW Ad Hoc Committee on Advocacy suggested that a social worker " is ethically bound to take on the advocacy role if he is to fulfill his professional responsibilities" (1969, p. 16). The NASW *Code of Ethics* supports this obligation of social workers to "promote the general welfare of society . . . advocate for living conditions conducive to the fulfillment of basic human needs and . . . promote social, economic, political, and cultural values and institutions that are compatible with the realization of social justice" (NASW *Code,* 6.01). A social work advocate "identifies with the plight of the disadvantaged. He sees as his primary responsibility the tough-minded and partisan representation of their interests, and this supersedes his fealty to others" (Brager, 1968, p. 6). The objective on a case level is to intervene to obtain a needed resource or service for individuals, or on a class level to alter the environment through social policy change or concessions from resistant or unresponsive systems (Mickelson, 1995).

The Ethical Principle of Equality and Inequality provides the ethical justification for engaging in the advocacy role. Empowerment techniques are necessary in order to give deprived groups and individuals a chance for equal access to life opportunities. However, this ethical justification does not mean that social worker advocates can avoid all ethical dilemmas.

Suppose there is but one bed available in the only home for the aged in your community. Your client needs to enter this institution because he no longer can cope at home. You also know that there are other elderly people (not your clients) whose situation is even more desperate. Should you become an aggressive partisan on behalf of your client, knowing that, if you are successful, his admission will be at the expense of other oldsters who need this service? Should you advocate his admission even if you are fairly sure that your success will cause irreversible harm to others? What might be other ways in which you can meet your ethical obligation to all the older persons who need this service?

Another ethical dilemma a social worker advocate may encounter is illustrated by the following exemplar.

➤ 7.4 No Winter Clothing

Three children in a family receiving public aid are sent home from school because they are not adequately dressed. There is no money available at home because their mother has used every last cent she has to pay off more pressing bills. You, the family's social worker, have no emergency funds available for such purposes.

What should you do? Should you become an advocate to press for institutional changes, such as more adequate public welfare allowances or special clothing allowances? Or should you mobilize your volunteer network to locate suitable clothing donations so that the children can return to school as quickly as possible?

What are the ethical implications of causing short-run harm to your client (by ignoring a client's request for immediate help) in order to gain an ultimate benefit? The use of a cost-benefit analysis in this instance (as in so many others) is complicated by the fact that in one strategy the cost is certain (not attending school), while the benefit is uncertain (modification of policy). The immediate strategy may result in early benefits for your clients, but other children most probably will face the same problem sooner or later.

Social worker advocates will encounter many ethical problems when their practice role is not fully supported by the employing agency. The case of the Apple Hill Young Adult Social Club (Exemplar 9.6) provides one example of this problem. The following exemplar provides another illustration.

➤ 7.5 Traffic in Shady Hill

Shady Hill was a quiet residential neighborhood until last year, when a new expressway exit brought a great amount of nonlocal traffic into its streets. As a result, there are now several very dangerous intersections. Last month, three children on their way to school were seriously injured crossing one of these intersections.

Parents and neighborhood residents are enraged and have demanded that the city close the exit or put up traffic lights. A meeting with the mayor has led to no results.

Lou Seward is the neighborhood worker who for the past two years has been staffing the Shady Hill Neighborhood Council. Since his arrival, the council has undertaken several projects to improve the quality of life in the neighborhood. Everyone has been happy with what these projects have achieved. Since the current problem has become acute, Seward has helped council officers organize a coalition of all neighborhood groups interested in the problem, including the PTA, churches, and fraternal organizations.

At last night's meeting of the coalition it was agreed that ways must be found to put additional pressure on City Hall. It was decided to call a news conference tomorrow morning in order to announce that a protest rally would be held across the street from City Hall next Monday afternoon. If no positive response is received, the exit will be blockaded by residents for a week following. Seward participated in last night's meeting by raising a number of questions and by providing technical information and advice.

In this morning's conference with his supervisor, Seward reviewed the Shady Hill situation to see if there were additional ways in which he could be helpful. His supervisor thought that Seward had not done enough to calm the neighborhood. Though the problem demanded attention, his supervisor did not think that an aggressive conflict strategy was helpful. He and the agency expected Seward to use his influence to keep the neighborhood quiet. That, after all, was the major reason why the city allocated monies to this department. The message was clear—and so was the problem.

To whom does Lou Seward owe loyalty? To the Neighborhood Council that has successfully improved life in the neighborhood? To his supervisor and the agency? (After all, they have been in the neighborhood and accomplished much good and will still be there after he leaves.) To himself as a professional who wants to place service to clients as his highest priority or to himself as a social worker who wants to retain his job?

EXERCISES

1. What would you do if you were the neighborhood worker in Shady Hill (Exemplar 7.5)? What are the ethical problems this neighborhood worker faces? How would you resolve them? Do you think that the supervisor's comments are in accord with the *Code of Ethics?* What are the supervisor's ethical dilemmas?

2. The director of a drug addiction rehabilitation program faces a difficult budget allocation decision. He has sufficient budget to mount only one of the two programs his agency would like to offer.

Program A is geared to elementary school students. It will serve five hundred children from some of the city's most troubled neighborhoods. Past experience has shown that, without such a program, two hundred children will be addicted by the time they are sixteen years old. With such a program, it is expected that no more than fifty will become addicted.

Program B focuses on the rehabilitation of adolescent drug addicts. Fifty teens can be served each year. The success rate of this program is 60 percent.

What ethical considerations should the director examine? What ethical rules and ethical principles can he use to help him make a decision?

3. The East Side Neighborhood Council has received a small grant to mount an educational program for Central American refugees now settling in large numbers on the East Side. The board is considering two projects—one calls for funding supplementary classes in local schools, the other for establishing English classes for adult refugees. There is a need for both projects, but there is barely enough money to mount one. What ethical considerations should the board members keep in mind? Does the social worker who staffs the board have a responsibility to acquaint board members with the relevant professional ethics? Suggest ways that can be employed by this social worker to reach an ethically correct decision.

4. The racist situations described earlier in this chapter in the research on social workers in Massachusetts, in Exemplar 7.2—Al Tabrizzi, and by Courtney, Barth et al. (1996) are situated at different levels in social work practice (organizational, direct service, and general institutional). What would you do in each of these cases?

SUGGESTIONS FOR ADDITIONAL READINGS

Schools of Social Work and the Council on Social Work Education (Trolander, 1997) have made strenuous efforts to eradicate racism in individual schools and in social work education. See Basham, Donner et al. (1997) who describe the efforts and process by which the Smith College School of Social Work moved to become an antiracist institution. McMahon and Allen-Meares (1992) use publication as an advocacy technique in regard to antiracist practice. Courtney, Barth et al. (1996) report on discrimination in child welfare and its effects. Robert Sunley (1997) describes advocacy required of social workers in an era of managed care.

8. The Professional Relationship: Limits, Dilemmas, and Problems

THE PROFESSIONAL RELATIONSHIP AND TRUST

Social work practice is based on the relationships between social workers and clients, and these relationships—in turn—require trust, an essential element. Trust is an interactional phenomenon, and helping relationships require that the client be able to trust the social worker and, often, that the social worker trust the clients. For the client, as Pellegrino (1991, p. 69) suggests, "to trust is to become vulnerable and dependent on the good will and motivations of those we trust." Going to a social worker or other professional for help requires an act of faith that the professional will act morally, will perform professional functions competently, and will be concerned about the problems the client brings to the situation. The problem that Pelligrino raises is not limited to clients but is inherent in the trust relationship. This means that the recipient of the trust (in our case, the social worker) must repeatedly, perhaps continuously, earn this trust—by demonstrating concretely that she is worthy of this trust relationship.

The client is dependent upon the prudence of the professional. There is often a requirement that, for the client to receive the service, he remove his protective cover and privacy used normally in day-to-day life. The client does so with the expectation that the professional will use her good judgment and skill for the client's good.

The "relationship between the professional and the client is a professional relationship. The client trusts the professional and entrusts himself or herself—not just his or her possessions to the professional" (Sokolowski, 1991, p. 31). The professional presents herself as trustworthy because she is certified as a professional and she is obligated both to the client and to the profession. In turn, clients actually place their trust in the certifying system. For example, we don't check out personally every airplane pilot or railroad engineer with whom we travel. Similarly, we trust that our vulnerability will not be exploited by the professional for her own purposes such as power, profit, or pleasure.

The social work professional's relationship with the client assumes special duties that arise because of the trust or confidence the client places in the social worker. The professional also has special knowledge and powers that can dominate and influence the client as a result of the relationship; and, as a result, the social worker must act in the best interest of the client and not take advantage of the client to promote her own best interests. Several important concepts derive from the professional relationship. The professional role introduces a power imbalance—a relationship in which the client has certain needs and the social worker has various powers. The confidentiality and informed consent obligations are intended to prevent the abuse of power by the professional agent. Social worker honesty is required to build trust, which is integral to the relationship. It is important for social workers to recognize the legal nature of the professional relationship and the limits it places on social workers in their dealings with clients—legal duties that are reflected in the *Code of Ethics* and can lead to conflicts of interest (Kutchins, 1991).

Although, many social workers assume clients trust them and the agencies that employ them, today there is an ethos of distrust of professionals and of many social agencies. Many people are cautious about placing their trust in professionals, including social workers. Trust, while necessary, is not enforceable. Clients cannot be made to trust a worker or a social agency even when they have no choice about the service they need. Reciprocally, social workers cannot be forced to trust clients, even when practice theory demands they do so.

Until recently, the lack of trust in clients was an individual worker's ethical problem, just as the client's lack of trust in a worker was that worker's problem alone. As indicated in Chapter 2, there has been a rise in the number of malpractice suits against social workers. This multiplication of legal relationships between clients and social workers may be related to the *general* distrust of professionals and others in an increasingly litigious society. The caution of clients may reflect not only their own individual questions but also the skepticism and climate of distrust found throughout society. However, distrust of social workers predates the first malpractice suit and cannot be attributed only to recent societal attitudes. More probable is the historic distrust of social workers by those who had to tolerate social workers because they had no choice.

Several "viruses" have attacked the trust relationship, including deprofessionalization, democratization and the rights revolution, and the information deluge.

Deprofessionalization

Deprofessionalization began with the introduction several decades ago of the employment of paraprofessionals. The use of paraprofessionals was instituted and promoted precisely to increase the trust of clients by employing persons from the same background as the clients.

More recently, where specialized skills are required, managed care and the privatization of health services have tended to deprofessionalize clinicians and others by limiting their control over treatment choices, creating pay schemes that compel clinicians to think in terms of billable hours, instituting productivity reporting systems that intrude themselves into professional decision making, and skewing treatment choices and options (Dumont, 1996). Clients do not know who is making decisions— the clinician or someone at the insurance company.

Democratization and the Rights Revolution

The consumer rights revolution grew out of the civil rights movement and legislation, the development of self-help organizations, demedicalization and self-care, deinstitutionalization of the mentally ill population, and the independent living movement of physically disabled people (Tower, 1994). These consumer movements often criticized professionals. Two aspects of these criticisms are (1) a desire by consumers to affect the quality of services they receive and (2) their desire to participate in gaining some control over standards by exerting political power. Previously, human service systems and professionals were less accountable to clients and could more easily hide errors. As a result of the rights revolution, professionals are now charged to explain to clients how they can help, how long it will take, and what the expected outcomes will be of their services. Decisions and notes previously unshared with clients are now open to inspection by clients and others. These changes served to empower clients and democratize to a greater extent the delivery of services.

But, for every change there is a cost. The question is whether the cost is to the client or to the worker or to the effectiveness of the helping system. These accountability systems are interpreted by many professionals as indicating a lack of trust in their judgment, while the social worker's caution about what to place in a record and hesitation about opening records may be viewed by clients as a lack of trust. Furthermore, because of managed care, social workers often cannot make decisions about what services they can provide, thus conveying to the client the existence of a hidden, unapproachable, and unaccountable presence impacting on his life.

Information Deluge

Service providers must communicate information to insurance companies and governmental agencies. This information is not always completely protected. No one can ensure with confidence that information provided will indeed remain confidential, the historically necessary building block for the trust relationship.

LIMITS OF THE PROFESSIONAL RELATIONSHIP

The client–social worker relationship is not a primary relationship. Primary relationships, especially those within the family or between friends, have few limits. The professional relationship, on the other hand, is focused on a problem for which help is sought. The professional assumes responsibility for helping the client with his problem(s) and traditionally the relationship terminates once these objectives have been achieved. It is a limited relationship in contrast to the broad primary relations most people treasure.

We will not explore here the practice problems that occur because many clients misunderstand the friendliness and informality that characterize their contacts with a social worker; these practice problems arise because most people have become accustomed to a greater degree of formality, impersonality, and even indifference from their previous contacts with other professional practitioners. We will focus instead on the ethical problems and dilemmas that social workers face because of their commitment to certain values within the professional relationship.

One of the major causes for ethical problems in this area arises whenever a social worker determines that the help a client needs requires a relationship that goes beyond what the traditional definition of the limited professional relationship allows. But as the discussion in this chapter will show, this is only one cause; there are others that create equally perplexing ethical dilemmas.

Anomie is a core problem in the contemporary world. Many people have become rootless; they have lost all connections with their sources, as well as with their fellow human beings. The psychosocial symptoms reflecting anomie are well known and need not be repeated here. Practitioners realize that often they treat only these symptoms without resolving the core problem. In order to strike at the roots of the problem, it is necessary to establish or reestablish more meaningful interpersonal relationships. Some have suggested that the social worker provide a model for this more meaningful relationship. But how can a client learn a new interaction pattern if the limited professional connection does not permit the social worker to fully invest in this relationship?

Some social workers hide behind the limited professional relationship because they are uncomfortable with their clients' lifestyles and cultures. But many more social workers want to identify with their clients by expressing empathy with their fate. Without wanting to imitate a lifestyle not authentic for them, they want to learn about and participate more fully in their clients' lives. They know that they cannot be effective and helpful without such knowledge. But this type of relationship cannot be limited to the 9 A.M.-to-5 P.M., Monday-through-Friday workweek. Yet the conscientious social worker often is not entirely clear about what the correct professional conduct is. Is it ethical for a social worker to accept an invitation for Sunday dinner in the client's home? Or to join the client on Friday evening in the local bar? May a social worker reciprocate and invite a client for supper at her home or in a restaurant? Is it appropriate for a social worker—who wants to learn about a particular culture—to accept an invitation from a client to explore the client's ethnic neighborhood with him so as to understand better the culture from which he has come? Practice wisdom has given fairly clear and generally negative answers to all of these questions, but increasingly social workers express discomfort with the barriers erected between them and their clients.

Though the relationship is supposed to be a limited one, social workers often have an emotional reaction to their clients. Such feelings may be natural, but the consequent worker behavior may cause ethical problems. When a worker's own needs become entangled with the professional relationship, emotional feelings may become destructive. In such situations, the social worker may lose her sense of objectivity; instead of helping the client, she may cause harm.

CLIENT INTERESTS VERSUS WORKER INTERESTS

Giving priority to a client's interests is one of the cornerstones of every professional code of ethics. The *Code of Ethics* expresses this professional obligation as follows: "Commitment to Clients: Social workers' primary responsibility is to promote the well-being of clients. In general, clients' interests are primary. However, social workers' responsibility to the larger society or specific legal obligations may on limited occasions supersede the loyalty owed clients . . . " (NASW *Code*, 1996, 1.01).

This ethical rule is meant to safeguard the client from exploitation, since most clients can neither control nor evaluate practitioner activities. Unnecessary treatment is one widely known violation of this ethical principle, but in fact some members of every profession have at one time or another ignored this rule by placing their own self-interests ahead of those of their clients. Some years ago, when school populations were dwindling, teachers were charged with failing students in order to assure full classrooms and in this way prevent threatened personnel cutbacks. This charge is no different from the accusations that some social workers failed to recommend the discharge of institutionalized children in order to assure continued state supplementation and thus guarantee their own jobs. Some hold that this is hardly an ethical problem for the vast majority of social workers who are employed by social agencies since they do not gain any economic advantage by ignoring this ethical rule. Perhaps an occasional social worker in private practice may be tempted to place financial gain above client interests, but do agency-employed social workers face this dilemma? However, this problem touches every social worker when the issue is self-preservation and survival, rather than financial gain. Must a social worker give priority to client interests, even when this may result in physical injury to the worker? Or in severe retribution and harm to her children? Do considerations of self-preservation and survival legitimize actions which ordinarily might be considered unethical?

There are other ethical dilemmas of this kind that do not involve a threat to life. A social worker is in the middle of preparing supper for her family when she receives an emergency call for help from one of her clients. Should she drop everything and rush out to help her client, even if this means that her family will once again have a cold supper? Another social worker has a very important date whom she is to meet within the hour when she is notified that one of "her" foster children has run away. What should she do? What is the ethical thing to do?

Gewirth's Principle of Generic Consistency may be helpful when considering these problems. He stated, "Act in accord with the generic right of your recipients (that is your clients) *as well as yourself*" (1978, p. 135, emphasis added). Gewirth seems to suggest that there is no need for the worker to abdicate the right to her own welfare, even when this right conflicts with another person's right to professional services. Since Gewirth's principle was not developed to guide professional activities, some people argue that it does not apply to professional practitioners. Instead, they hold that a professional should always be guided by the ethical obligation to give priority to a client's interests, no matter what the consequences.

Those who would follow Gewirth's lead must consider whether ethics are relative. Do ethical obligations change according to their consequences? What must be the degree of potential harm before it is permissible to disregard the ethical rule that demands giving priority to a client's interests? Must social workers serve their clients' interests at all times, regardless of the consequences? Or is it ethical for them to declare that under certain unusual circumstances the professional obligation to serve their clients' interests is no longer primary? Consider Diggs's observation that "there is an important difference between interpreting a rule, or violating it in *special circumstances*, and deciding each individual case just as if there were no rules" (1970, p. 267). This formulation permits retention of the client-priority ethical rule except in special circumstances, such as when the life of the worker is threatened.

Social workers involved in a strike situation also may face ethical dilemmas of this type. On the one hand, the *Code of Ethics* mandates that the "social workers' primary responsibility is to promote the well-being of clients" (NASW *Code*, 1996, 1.01), and that "social workers generally should adhere to commitments made to employers and employing organizations" (NASW *Code*, 1996, 3.09). On the other hand, the *Code* states "social workers may engage in organized action, including the formation of and participation in labor unions to improve services to clients and working conditions" (NASW *Code*, 1996, 3.10a).

But, as Fisher (1987) notes, there are no ready ethical guidelines for social workers involved in strikes. The *Code of Ethics* mandates the primacy of the worker's service obligation to clients and her commitment to the employing organization; there also are severe sanctions against the abrupt withdrawal of professional services. At the same time, the NASW Personnel Standards support the collective bargaining process and oppose any laws or policies that limit the right of social workers to strike (NASW Standards for Social Work Personnel Practices, 1990b, Standard 4, Interpretation). This conflict in obligations creates immediate ethical problems. The *Code* does not provide clear guidance on this issue when it states "Reasonable differences of opinion exist among social workers concerning their primary obligation as professionals during an actual or threatened labor strike or job action. Social workers should carefully examine relevant issues and their possible impact on clients before deciding on a course of action" (NASW *Code* 1996, 3.10b). If you had to participate in such a discussion with colleagues, what do you think are sufficient grounds for you to join a strike? Should social workers cross a picket line when the institution in which they are employed is struck by a labor union that does not include social workers as members?

DUAL ROLES WITHIN THE PROFESSIONAL RELATIONSHIP

Professionals may fill more than one role concurrently or in serial fashion with clients. It is possible that a social worker, because of the nature of the community in which she resides and practices, may have social, business, financial, religious, or other roles in addition to her professional role with a client. While this possibility may be minimized in large urban areas, those who practice in rural areas may encounter the problem more frequently, as may those in particular smaller subcommunities such as religious, political, sexual orientation, and new immigrant groups.

Here are some examples of dual role relationships:

1. You discover that your client Bertha Martins is your dentist's mother.
2. Ms. Olds, your daughter's new teacher, is the mother of Tom Olds, a troubled teenager whom you have been treating for the last year.
3. Mrs. Simkins, the wife of Al Simkins, stockbroker, is your client and inadvertently discloses insider information about local businesses in which you own stock.

In such dual role situations, it is always possible for a client to be confused by the circumstances, for the professional to exploit or harm the client in some manner, or for the additional role to interfere with the professional relationship. The *Code of Ethics* states "social workers should not engage in dual or multiple relationships with clients or former clients in which there is a risk of exploitation or potential harm to the client. In instances when dual or multiple relationships are unavoidable, social workers should take steps to protect clients and are responsible for setting clear, appropriate, and culturally sensitive boundaries" (NASW *Code*, 1996, 1.06c). "Social workers who provide supervision or consultation are responsible for setting clear, appropriate, and culturally sensitive boundaries" (NASW *Code*, 1996, 3.01c), and "Social workers should not engage in any dual or multiple relationships with supervisees in which there is a risk or exploitation of or potential harm to the supervisee" (NASW, *Code*, 1996, 3.01c). Also, "Social workers who function as educators or field instructors for students should not engage in any dual or multiple relationships with students in which there is a risk of exploitation or potential harm to the students" (NASW *Code*, 1996, 3.01d).

These standards highlight the issue of dual role relationships so that social workers may take steps to set limits on such relationships or to avoid them wherever possible and in this way avoid actions detrimental to clients, supervisees, and students. The avoidance of exploitation of or of harm to clients, former clients, supervisees, and students, among others, is the major focus of these standards.

Must dual role relationships necessarily interfere with professional relationships or be conflictual? In modern society, everyone fills multiple roles, and there are many opportunities for social workers and clients to participate in dual or multiple relationships. Both may be members of the same political party, or church or synagogue, or their children may attend the same schools or be classmates. There is no reason for a social worker to withdraw from these activities simply because the client also engages in them. The issue is to separate the professional relationship from other relationships. On the other hand, a social worker must avoid situations that have the potential for exploitation or harm. Included among these relationships with clients are dating, bartering services, buying, investing work or money in businesses, and endorsing or recommending a client's business to potential buyers. For example, the used car salesman who is a client may offer to sell you a car at a discount. Don't accept!

Questions have been raised about social workers in health care settings who receive gifts from representatives of insurance companies, medical equipment companies, and nursing homes. The vendors expect "gratitude" for their gifts. A number of issues are raised by the gifts. The cost of the gifts is passed on to patients and others. The best interests of some patients become less than paramount. The acceptance of the gift creates a dual role relationship between the social worker and the donor, a relationship that suggests an obligation for reciprocity. Social workers are in a position to reciprocate through referral of patients who pay either personally or through insurance. As a result, social workers can become enmeshed in a dual role relationship that is not known to patients but which has the power to influence what happens to the client. Is there a difference between the acceptance of gifts for oneself or for patients? Are gifts given to the social work department different from those provided to individual social workers? Do all gifts carry "attached strings" deserving of reciprocation? Since patients are unaware of these relationships, is the acceptance of gifts consistent with fully informed consent (Ross, 1992)?

SEXUAL RELATIONS WITH CLIENTS

There are many "gray" areas in regard to social workers and their social, nonsexual relationships with clients. Undoubtedly, there are many qualifications, contextual factors, and motivations which need to be considered for many such relationships. But the *Code* is quite clear that "social workers should under no circumstances engage in sexual activities or sexual contact with current clients, whether such contact is consensual or forced" (NASW *Code*, 1996, 1.09a). This ethical rule is found in the codes of ethics of most professions. In addition, similar standards are stated for such activities "with clients' relatives or other individuals with whom clients maintain a close personal relationship when there is a risk of exploitation or potential harm to the client" (NASW *Code*, 1996, 1.09b), "with former clients because of the potential for harm to the client" (NASW *Code*, 1996, 1.09c), and "should not provide clinical services to individuals with whom they have had a prior sexual relationship" (NASW *Code*, 1996, 1.09d).

Kagle and Giebelhausen (1994) reviewed research and publications concerning sexual and nonsexual dual role relationships and professionals. Sexual intimacy is not simply an ethical breach, but such intimacy with clients is also grounds for legal action in fifty states—where the social worker may be sued for battery, malpractice, intentional and negligent infliction of emotional distress, and sexual abuse. Some states have defined sexual exploitation of a client a crime.

In some states, potential legal action against the practitioner is not avoided by the formal termination of the treatment relationship. In a number of states, sexual contact following the termination of client status is illegal for one-, two-, or three-year periods (Perry & Kuruk, 1993). Current as well as past clients are dependent on the social worker; exploiting this dependency for personal gain, sexual or nonsexual, is unethical, illegal, and unprofessional, regardless of whether the social worker's action affects the therapeutic or other outcome. In all cases, the burden to prevent harm rests with the social worker.

To be sure, some social workers have questioned these rules, pointing out that nowadays many problems brought to their attention involve problems of sexual dysfunction (Schultz, 1975; Moser, 1980). The professional intervention, they argue, might include sexual techniques and activities unthinkable only a few decades ago. There are therapists who believe and practice the notion that sexual involvement with a client is beneficial. They suggest that this is not a new helping technique; Freud's colleague Sandor Ferenczi already "helped" his clients express their physical affections toward him as a way of compensating for their childhood deprivations (Van Hoose & Kottler, 1985). One finding of a study of a sample of NASW members in direct service positions found only a small 1.1 percent acknowledging having sex with a former client. (No questions were asked about current intimate relationships.) However, almost 5 percent saw nothing professionally inappropriate in such behavior (Jayaratne, Croxton, & Mattison, 1997). But those who say there is no problem regarding sex between social work professionals and their clients are underestimating the impact of such behavior on professional relationships and on the lives of their clients. Although this problem does not occur frequently, it is quite serious because of the consequences for the persons involved. Pope and Bouthoutsos (1986) reported that 90 percent of the 559 clients they studied, all of whom were sexually involved with their therapists, had adverse effects and suffered some kind of damage. In 34 percent of the cases, the client's personality was negatively affected. Other consequences included problems of identity and self-esteem, mistrust, anger, tension, apprehension, dissociation, fatigue, lassitude, lack of motivation, depression, anxiety, pessimism, deterioration of familial relationships, inability to work, self-blame, self-hate, and even suicide.

There is some evidence that those most vulnerable to sexual exploitation by their therapists are those who have been sexually abused in the past (Coleman & Schaefer, 1986). Far from being helpful, sexual relations with clients are in fact destructive. Sexual relationships with students also injure and have the potential for imitative behavior by the student. Such sexual relationships can be replicated and reinforced in subsequent work with clients. A national study of 481 psychologists found that a student's engagement in a sexual relationship with a supervisor is statistically linked to the likelihood that this pattern will repeat itself with future clients. One in ten of the psychologists reported sexual contact with a teacher or supervisor. Of those, almost one in four (23 percent) reported subsequent engagement in sex with a client (Pope, Levenson, & Schover, 1979; Bonosky, 1995).

How frequently does this problem occur in social work practice? A review of seven national surveys of mental health practitioners, including social workers, found that 3.8 to 12.0 percent of male practitioners and 0.2 to 3.0 percent of female practitioners reported having had sexual contact with a current or former client (Kagle & Giebelhausen, 1994). A survey of licensed social workers in Texas revealed that during the previous year, 17 percent had worked with at least one victim of sexual exploitation by a psychotherapist (Sloan, Edmond et al., 1998).

Sexual behavior with clients is the most frequently reported ethical violation in the social work profession. Although it is probable that some inappropriate sexual behavior goes unreported, malpractice suits for sexual misconduct are increasing despite the prohibition in licensing laws, professional standards, and the *Code of Ethics* (Houston-Vega et al., 1997, p. 72). Furthermore, incorrect treatment and sexual misconduct together accounted for the largest percentage of malpractice suits (NASW, 1995b).

Attitudes of almost all practitioners about having sex with clients are changing. Among psychologists it was reported in 1977 that 5.5 percent of male psychologists and 0.6 percent of female psychologists had

Table 8.1 **Frequency and Percentages of Incidents and Perceived Appropriateness of Behavior**

Behavior	Done		Appropriate	
	N	%	N	%
Go on date with former client	7	0.8	53	6.4
Have sex with a former client	9	1.1	37	4.6
Develop a friendship with a client	174	21.2	170	21.0
Have clients with whom you had another relationship	185	22.5	270	33.5
Serve on community boards or committees with clients	187	22.6	471	58.7
Use massage	15	1.8	107	13.7
Touch a client as a regular part of therapy process	253	31.2	319	39.9
Give financial investment advice	37	4.5	64	7.7
Advise clients to do something that may be illegal	25	3.1	30	3.7

Source: Adapted from S. Jayaratne, T. Croxton, and D. Mattison (1997), "Social Work Professional Standards: An Exploratory Study," *Social Work 42* (2), 187–98.

sexual intercourse with patients (Holroyd & Brodsky, 1977). A decade later, Borys and Pope (1989) reported that only 1.3 percent of therapists reported sexual involvements with clients. (One should be aware that all studies of sexual relations between social workers and clients find that male social workers are many times more likely to have such relations than female social workers.) It may be that this marked drop in sexual activity reflects a broad acceptance of the ethical rule prohibiting sexual relations with clients. What is not entirely clear from the data is whether therapists now refrain from having sex with their clients or whether they are less willing to admit that they behave in unethical ways!

Jayaratne, Croxton, and Mattison (1997) studied six domains of social work practice: intimate relationships, dual role relationships, mixed modalities, advice giving, boundary behaviors, and financial transactions. The study was based on a large sample of the membership of the Michigan Chapter of NASW. In Table 8.1 are presented some of their findings. While only a small number of practitioners report they have dated a former client, over 6 percent think it appropriate to do so. Similarly, a small number report they have had sex with a former client, while almost 5 percent believe that such behavior is appropriate. Very large percentages report they have dual role relationships with clients (friendship, persons with whom they had another relationship, service on the same boards or committees). Only a few social workers use massage in their practices, however, more than one in eight believe to do so is appropriate; almost 40 percent believe it is appropriate to touch a client as a regular part of the therapy process. One can also note the numbers and percentages of those who believe it is appropriate to give financial advice and to advise clients to do something that might be illegal.

The following exemplar raises a number of ethical issues to which all social workers must pay attention.

➤ 8.1 Treatment of an Inferiority Complex

Jill Jordan, a 35-year-old divorcee, has been a client of the Family Consultation Center for a number of months. Her presenting problem was that she feels inadequate, unattractive, and stymied in her job career. She feels her negative self-image contributed to her divorce and has become a barrier to advancement on the job. She feels that her career and more fulfilling relationships depend on her being more positive about herself and being more optimistic.

Bob Temple, an experienced social worker, was assigned as her therapist. A contract was established with the presenting problem as the focus. During the course of treatment, Temple was very understanding and warmly responsive to Jordan. His objective was to restore Jill's faith in herself. As treatment proceeded, Jill became more and more openly admiring of Temple. At the end of one session, she spontaneously hugged him and said how appreciative she was for all his help. As she experienced more successes in her life, she would ask for a hug as a sign of his support for her. Still later she made it evident that she was attracted to Bob and would not reject his interest in her. Bob was also attracted to Jill. He very much wanted to express further his feelings toward her and have sexual relations with her, but he knew that the professional ethics demanded that he not do so. What is the most ethical way of handling this problem?

1. It is best that he deny his feelings and continue treatment but discontinue the hugs. Chances are that these emotions, if controlled, will not interfere with the treatment.
2. He can maintain a professional relationship in the office and join her church, where there will be opportunities for them to meet after hours, outside the office.
3. He can accept his emotional attraction to Jill, but at the same time realize that a professional social worker cannot have a personal relationship with a client. Next time Jill breaches the subject, he should tell her that he likes her and that if he were not her social worker he might become involved with her. But since he is her social worker, his task is to help her professionally; no other relationship is possible.

4. He realizes that he cannot control his emotions. Therefore, it is best to terminate the relationship and refer Jill to another social worker.

5. He realizes that he cannot control his emotions. Therefore, it is best not to deny his attraction for Jill and instead do what comes naturally, that is, have sex with her; at the same time he can continue to be her social worker.

Option 5 is clearly not acceptable. In most jurisdictions this behavior is judged as illegal, even criminal. The NASW *Code of Ethics* prohibits it, as do the ethical codes of all other professions. Though there is no ethical or professional justification for this choice, we mention it because we are aware that a small number of our colleagues do engage in such behavior, a behavior that is blatantly unprofessional and unethical. Obviously some of the other options are unethical and go against the code. Use the two ethical decision screens to determine which might be the preferred approach in the situation facing Bob Temple.

TOUCHING

What about erotic behaviors that do not involve genital relations? Touching became a popular practice technique during the late sixties and early seventies as a result of the popularity of the encounter movement. Clients "touched" by their therapist evaluated counseling more positively than those not touched, particularly if the touching was done by a therapist of the opposite sex (Algana et al., 1979). Some have questioned the ethical propriety of touching, believing that such behavior is only a first step that will inevitably lead to full sexual relations. Others reject this assumption. The available research evidence is contradictory and does not provide an unambiguous answer (Bogodanoff & Elbaum, 1978; Borenzweig, 1983; DeYoung, 1988; Willis, 1987). Nevertheless, the *Code* provides for physical contact but "Social workers who engage in appropriate physical contact with clients are responsible for setting clear, appropriate, and culturally sensitive boundaries that govern such contact" but "should not engage in physical contact with clients when there is a possibility of psychological harm to the client as a result of the contact" (NASW, *Code*, 1996, 1.10).

NONSEXUAL SOCIAL RELATIONS

While almost all social workers agree that it is unethical to engage in sexual activities with clients, there is less agreement about the ethical propriety of engaging in different social relations. One can note in Table 8.1 the lack of agreement that exists among professional social workers as to what are appropriate professional behaviors. Some of the results highlight the lack of consensus about which social relations are deemed unethical. Although not identified in the table, large percentages think it appropriate to hug or embrace a client (see NASW *Code*, 1996, 1.10), pray with a client, recommend a religious form of healing, comment to clients about their physical attractiveness, discuss one's religious beliefs, accept goods or services from clients instead of money (see NASW *Code*, 1996, 1.14), and terminate clients who no longer have benefits or the ability to pay (see NASW *Code*, 1996, 1.16a, b).

Social workers who do not practice psychotherapy may have somewhat different views about the ethical implications of some of the behaviors studied by Jayaratne, Croxton, and Mattison. Group workers and community workers may have no compunctions about going to the local deli or coffeehouse with a group of clients after a session, but may (or may not) draw the line when it comes to doing the same with an individual client. (See Chapter 12 for a discussion of ethics and social work with groups and macrosocial work.) Some social work administrators report that their most important contacts with board members occur in social settings. Obviously, the definition of who is a client and the purpose of the professional relationship are two factors that affect the ethical assessment of such professional behaviors.

As long as social workers think that there is no conflict between agency interests and client interests, dual role relationship (client/agency) ethical problems do not exist for them. Usually it is suggested that the agency is committed to what is best for the client. But if we examine this proposition objectively, we must realize that this is only the social work version of "What is good for General Motors is good for the country!" In fact, organizational survival interests often do not coincide with what is best for the client.

The ethical issue of the dual role relationship dilemma arises out of a social worker's attempt to serve at the same time both the best interest of the client and the best interest of the employing agency or institution. This ethical problem is familiar to hospital social workers. Hospital policy (often as a result of requirements by the government or insurance companies that reimburse hospitalization expenses) is to send patients home at the earliest possible time, even if this is not in a particular patient's best interest. In this instance, a social worker who is the "agent" of both the hospital and the patient cannot meet the best interests of both. Such pressures can result in social workers rushing the caretakers of those to be discharged from hospitals. A study of perceptions by discharge planners in an urban hospital and family caregivers found that planners overrated the amount and adequacy of information provided about posthospital care, the choice of discharge to home or nursing home, and the need for decision-making time by the caregivers (Clemens, 1995). Similar problems are faced by social workers in the armed forces, police, prisons, mental hospitals, and schools. Increasingly this problem is faced also by social workers employed in industrial settings and in social agencies. (See Exemplar 1.2, "Blanca Gabelli Costs Too Much," for another example of this problem.)

A somewhat different version of this ethical dilemma is faced by social workers who employ various group strategies: How can they simultaneously serve the best interest of every participant? If the focus is on strengthening the group or family, one or the other participant may not receive the maximum benefit. On the other hand, if the group is the vehicle to help one or more group members with their problems, there may be other group participants who will not obtain any significant benefit. Dolgoff and Skolnik (1996) found when they studied ethical decision making by social workers with groups that the social workers, when asked to make group records available to a court so that one member could obtain child visitation rights, sided in 84 percent of the cases with the group members that did not want to release the records.

TRUTH TELLING AND MISREPRESENTATION

The NASW *Code of Ethics* states that "social workers should not participate in, condone, or be associated with dishonesty, fraud, or deception" (NASW *Code*, 1996, 4.04). Telling the truth and avoiding deceptions are basic ethical obligations. Every human interaction is based on the premise that each side in the interaction intends to tell the truth. Deceiving—that is, deliberately misrepresenting facts in order to make another person believe what is not true—violates the respect to which every person is entitled. Telling the truth to a client is an even stronger professional obligation than the generalized obligation of truth telling. This professional ethic is anchored in the specialized client/practitioner relationship and in the obligations that a practitioner owes to her clients. Practitioners may believe that dishonesty that serves the client is ethical. A social worker may assign the wrong diagnosis so as to provide service that otherwise would be unavailable, or otherwise be dishonest to the benefit of the client.

Bayles concluded that the obligation to be honest with clients does not require honesty toward others when acting on a client's behalf (1981, p. 71). Honesty may not always be the best policy for a social worker. Expressing such a view is, of course, a little bit like attacking home and mother. But Haley raises a number of questions about the efficacy of always being honest (1976, p. 208). These include:

1. The therapeutic situation itself is not an honest human experience, but a paid relationship. Does the therapist have an ethical obligation to be honest in such a relationship?
2. Can any therapist, no matter what her orientation, claim that she is willing to share with a client all of her observations and understandings?
3. Must a therapist answer all questions that a client has about the therapy that will be used? Will this patient be better able to achieve autonomy when he fully understands the theory used by the therapist?
4. Will an "honest sharing" of understanding solve the problems for which the patient is paying his money to get help?

Haley presents one point of view, but not everyone agrees. In addition to Haley's questions, there are other ethical dilemmas that may arise out of the attempt to tell the truth. Consider the ethical problems facing Gail's social worker in the following exemplar.

➤ **8.2 Gail Finds a Job**

Gail Silva is a single parent; she is raising two daughters, ages seven and six. She has been trying to find a part-time job to supplement her meager child support income ever since her younger daughter started kindergarten. She has been repeatedly refused a job because she has had no prior employed work experience. By now she has become very frustrated and has developed a very negative self-image. She believes that nobody wants her—neither as a spouse nor as a worker. This morning she told you excitedly that she thinks she has found a job. As she describes the job, you realize that she is telling you about an employer who is known to exploit his workers and who pays below the minimum wage, when he pays at all. Should you tell Gail the truth about her prospective employer? Or should you share her enthusiasm, hoping that things will work out? What is the ethical thing to do?

Deception has become so common in our world that we hardly pay attention to the little lies and half-truths that everyone uses and knows how to justify. Nyberg (1996, p. 187) suggested that deception is a necessary part of our world: " . . . deception is not merely to be tolerated as an occasionally prudent aberration in a world of truthtelling; it is rather an essential component of our ability to organize and shape the world, to resolve problems of coordination among individuals who differ, to cope with uncertainty and pain, to be civil and to achieve privacy as needed, to survive as a species, and to flourish as persons." Or, as he suggests: "to live decently with one another we do not need moral purity, we need discretion—which means tact in regard to truth" (p. 202).

But what are the ethical implications for a social worker who uses "lies"? What is the ethical question involved in telling another person a bit less than the full truth? When a social worker decides to withhold the truth from a client or to deceive him, she usually thinks that she is doing so for the client's benefit. Whether this is really so is subject to empirical assessment. But whether her decision was ethically justified cannot be assessed empirically.

There are many reasons why a social worker might deceive her client or not tell him the full truth, including the following:

1. To make a client-selected goal less desirable.
2. To create new goals.
3. To obscure options.
4. To increase options.
5. To change the cost/benefit estimate for one or more options.
6. To increase or decrease client uncertainty.
7. To increase or decrease client anxiety.
8. To protect the client from "damaging" truth.
9. To protect the effectiveness of the current intervention strategy.
10. To obtain the client's "informed" consent.
11. To protect confidential information received from a third party.
12. To strengthen the relationship with a client by lying at his request to a third party.
13. To increase the worker's power over a client by withholding information.
14. To make the worker look good by "papering over" mistakes she has made.

Which of these reasons are applicable in the following exemplars?

➤ 8.3 A Growth on the Foot

Art Elder, age 34, is a high school teacher. At present he is a patient in University Hospital because he has "a growth on his foot." His physician told him that there are two ways of treating this problem. Both involve some risks. When Art asked what he would advise, he suggested surgery.

Sally Brown is the social worker in the surgical department. From her discussion with the resident she learned that Dr. Kutner, the physician, did not tell the patient all the available choices and that he withheld information about the option with the least risk. Evidently he weighted his presentation in favor of the experimental treatment method that he is just now developing.

Here we are not concerned with Dr. Kutner, but with Sally Brown. Should she tell Mr. Elder the truth? Or should she mind her own business and leave the giving of medical information to the medical staff? Truth telling requires us to note that the ethical problem presented in this exemplar is undoubtedly less common among physicians than it once was. But Sally Brown still faces a dilemma. On what basis can she decide what the ethical course of action is?

Truth telling is not a problem that only social caseworkers face. An exemplar from the field of social work administration also raises questions about the ethics of truth telling.

➤ 8.4 The Frans Music Appreciation Room

The Frans family contributed a considerable sum of money to the Uptown Community Center to furnish and equip a music appreciation room in memory of their late mother. An appropriate plaque marks the room. Since the center accepted the contribution the neighborhood has experienced a large influx of immigrants from Southeast Asia. Because of their needs, the room is now used for purposes other than those designated by the donors.

You are the center's associate director. You know how important the music appreciation room is to the family. There is a good possibility of obtaining additional donations for other projects from this family, but if the family discovers that "their" room is no longer used for music appreciation activities they may lose interest in Uptown Community Center. At the monthly meeting of the United Way Board of Directors you meet Mr. Frans. He asks you how the music appreciation room is doing. How should you reply? Do you tell the truth? Do you try to avoid the issue by shifting the conversation to another area? Do you tell a little untruth, such as "the immigrants love music"? Or what? What is the ethically correct response? How do you decide?

Social workers at every level sometimes have to choose between loyalty to a friend or colleague and telling the truth. In the following situation, a supervisor has to make a choice concerning truthfulness.

➤ 8.5 A Supervisor Decides

Karl Samil is a supervisor in a large Department of Social Services where it is difficult for anyone to know all members of the staff because of their large number and the fact that many work at satellite locations. Roger Lewis, a colleague, applied for promotion. Samil is one of those asked for his opinion. Samil is aware of earlier instances when Lewis acted in ways that were harmful to the agency. He inappropriately criticized the agency at several interagency committee meetings, and these remarks seem to have injured the reputation of the agency's elder-abuse team. For over a year, Samil has noted that Lewis has been distracted and jumpy about his cur-

Table 8.2 Intentions and Facts

The statement is factually:	The speaker intends to be truthful	The speaker intends to deceive
True	The speaker intended to tell the truth and did so.	The speaker intended to deceive, but unknowingly spoke the truth. While her intentions were not ethical, her actual behavior does not raise any ethical issues.
False	The speaker intended to tell the truth, but failed to do so because she did not have the correct information. The problem here may be lack of competence or lack of skill, or both, which although unintentional, *may be unethical.*	The speaker intended to deceive and did lie. *This situation involves questions of unethical behavior.*

rent job responsibilities. Most of his local colleagues have been aware of his behavior but out of loyalty have kept quiet and have often "covered" for him. To confuse matters further, Samil and Lewis have played cards together in a weekly game since they graduated college. Even there, Lewis's behavior has been somewhat erratic. When Samil spoke to Lewis to say he seemed unusually upset and distracted, Lewis brushed it off. If promoted, Lewis will move to another part of the agency.

Should Samil because of personal loyalty give a positive reference, thereby passing Roger Lewis on to another setting without letting them know of his limitations? Should he risk his own reputation if the promotion is gained but Roger does poorly at the job? What about loyalty to himself and family? Should he turn his back on the agency and the profession? Or, should he speak to Roger again and suggest that Roger defer promotion and take care of his own problems? This approach seems not to have worked but if Roger agrees this time, it would finesse the problem for everyone but himself.

The question of truth or deception involves the intention of the speaker and not the factual accuracy of the statement. Knowing the truth does not necessarily result in telling the truth, while not knowing the truth does not always result in a deception. The relations between the objective situation and a speaker's intentions are summarized in Table 8.2.

Some practitioners who abhor lying have suggested that it is possible to deceive without lying by exaggerating or manipulating. One social worker, for example, wanted to dissuade a client from placing his daughter with mental retardation in an institution. She arranged for the father to visit the worst possible institution, but did not mention the availability of other alternatives. This social worker would never lie, but did she tell the truth? A social work administrator exaggerates the benefits that may result from a new program so that the agency will receive a larger budget allocation next year. Are these social workers acting ethically? Or is this yet another version of the ends-justifying-the-means quandary?

PRACTITIONER IMPAIRMENT

The personal and professional abilities of a social worker can be damaged, diminished, and impaired by extreme mental or physical health difficulties, overwhelming personal/familial problems, psychosocial distress, or substance abuse. These problems can affect an individual social worker, her family and friends, and colleagues, and may result in a social worker's inability to provide professionally competent services. Social workers are thought to have about the same rates of alcohol and substance abuse problems as members of other health professions and as the general public. The New York City Chapter of NASW reported that 43 percent of the respondents to a study knew at least one social worker with a drug or alcohol problem. A survey of all Indiana Chapter members reported that 53 percent knew a social worker whose performance was affected by emotional or mental health problems, substance abuse, burnout, or sexual misconduct (Hiratsuka, 1994).

Among the ethical issues for the profession is the assurance that all professional social workers are able to provide quality professional services and that such a standard is maintained while respecting all other ethical norms, including confidentiality. Impaired social workers may act in undisciplined, insensitive, erratic, unprofessional, and unethical ways. Sometimes they use inappropriate language or behavior with clients and colleagues, pay haphazard attention to job requirements, fail to follow through on assignments, or engage in excessive absenteeism. Impairments can lead to inadequate and even unethical behaviors, which can lower the public's estimate and trust of the profession, result in actions detrimental to clients and others, and present ethical problems for other social workers.

The *Code of Ethics* includes four standards directly related to the impairment of professional social workers, referred to as colleagues. Those who have direct knowledge of such impairment should consult with the colleague and, where the colleague has not taken adequate steps to address the impairment, are expected to take action through appropriate channels (NASW *Code*, 1996, 2.09a, b). Similarly, where social workers have direct knowledge of a colleague's incompetence, they are expected to consult with the practitioner. Where the practitioner does not take adequate steps to address the incompetence, action should be taken through appropriate channels (NASW *Code*, 1996, 2.10a, b).

But clarification of the responsibility does not provide answers for all the dilemmas that exist in this area. Consider the following situation.

➤ **8.6 My Friend, Mentor, Supervisor, and Alcohol**

You are a social worker assigned to a satellite unit of a family service agency with Davis Jones, your supervisor, the only other social worker who works in that office. Your relationship with Davis goes back at least fifteen years, and he has been very important in your life at several junctions. He helped you get into social work school; he recommended you for an advanced treatment institute; and once when your child was ill, he helped you obtain medical care from the best specialist in town. Recently, however, Davis—who also evaluates you for pay and possible promotions—has been late arriving for work and has missed some meetings. You have had to cover for him more than a few times with his clients. You are still somewhat in awe of Davis and owe him a lot. He has helped you out of many a difficult situation. You feel that his current erratic behavior is related to alcohol and family difficulties.

What is the most ethical way of handling this problem?

1. Encourage one of his clients for whom you have had to replace him for several sessions to register a complaint with the agency.
2. Call in sick one day and ask for a substitute to cover cases so that another social worker discovers the problem.
3. Ignore the situation. Wait for someone else to "blow the whistle." Meanwhile, cover his cases.
4. Ask a mutual friend to call him and say that he has heard about his behavior on the job and suggest that it is important that he do something about his problems.
5. Report the situation to a higher-level agency administrator.
6. Speak to Davis Jones directly. State that you will keep quiet about the situation but he must go for help.

So far Davis has done little if any harm. At what point must you act? Earlier or later? What about loyalty to a mentor, friend, and colleague from whom you have learned much? What about loyalty to yourself, your career, and your family? What about the risks you expose yourself to by acting? What should you do?

Options 1, 2, and 4 are unethical because you are asking others to serve as your surrogate and placing your self-interest over the interest of clients and friends. Option 3 has the value of playing for time but changes nothing. If you have not spoken previously to Davis Jones about the problem, then only Option 5 is an ethical choice. Even in this case, however, one must consider whether one can give a deadline for action to a supervisor and at what personal cost. Also how much improvement is enough? Would there be an alternative choice if you had previously discussed the problem with Mr. Jones?

PSYCHOLOGICAL INDIFFERENCE AS AN ETHICAL LIMITATION

Today, almost everyone experiences sensory overload. Information comes at us constantly by word of mouth, but also through technological devices such as pagers, cellular phones, computers, television, radio, and other technologies. We live in an era of "soundbites," brief messages intended to convey complex information. Social workers, along with other human service workers, also experience stress on the job, stress in their personal lives, and pressures to be productive, along with a myriad of other stressors. In many cases, "burnout"—both as personal alienation and as a coping mechanism in response to stress—serves as a defense against the invasion of our personal and professional spaces. Social workers upon occasion can "tune out," deal with the surface of things, experience a sense of impotence, and distance themselves from clients, colleagues, and their work (Powell, 1994; Soderfeldt, Soderfeldt, & Warg, 1995).

One possible result of psychological distancing is paying less attention to the ethical dilemmas that one encounters in practice. Hannah Arendt in *Eichmann in Jerusalem* characterized this human ability as leading to "the banality of evil." Americans learned about the potential insidious impact of this kind of banality at My Lai in Viet Nam, as well as in Stanley Milgram's prison experiment discussed in Chapter 3. Such psychological distancing can lead a social worker through acts of commission to avoid responsibility by distancing herself from clients, by treating clients with less individualization and dignity, by serving the organization or society when the right action is to serve the individual, and by acts of omission that avoid doing the right thing in professional service.

➤ **8.7 An Administrator Decides What to Do**

Joseph Parocha is the overworked and stressed-out executive director of a Meals-on-Wheels program. Drivers recently have begun reporting seeing longer and longer lines at several soup kitchens as they travel to deliver meals to shut-in aging persons. Also, drivers have discovered mothers with young children without sufficient food at several of the houses where they deliver meals. In speaking to the president of the board, Haakon Query, Mr. Parocha suggested that the agency has a responsibility to also try to help these other people. After all, their job is helping feed people who are hungry. Mr. Query responded sharply that the agency has trouble enough maintaining itself and that he and others on the board would oppose any attempt to assist either the soup kitchens or the young families. The homeless and the young parents are the responsibility of other agencies. The agency should focus on its primary mission. Mr. Parocha was torn by his feeling that something should be done, and he knew that the staff could be doing more, although he personally didn't need any more pressures. When he talked it over with his wife, she reminded him his health is also important, their son is to start college this fall, and their daughter needs braces. Mr. Parocha was upset but eventually decided that it was better not to confuse the mission of the agency by trying to move it in new directions and that there was little else he could do.

Is Mr. Parocha's decision a result of self- and family protection, burnout and having reached his personal emotional and energy limits, or a pragmatic decision? What should Mr. Parocha have done? After all, he doesn't know the people whose problems are being reported to him by staff members and volunteers, nor is it his responsibility to help support all other social agencies. In fact, he understood his situation in terms of his role as executive director and told himself: "Anyone in my position would do the same thing." Was his decision correct?

Mr. Parocha was confronted with a situation in which he decided to tolerate inadequate situations for young women and their families and the homeless while working hard to maintain the Meals-on-Wheels program and to protect his family. To whom does he owe loyalty? His agency? The president and board members? The soup kitchens? The homeless? The young women and their families? Himself? His family?

EXERCISSES

1. If there is an NASW chapter in your area, invite the chair of the Chapter Committee on Inquiry to discuss with your class how complaints about ethical misconduct are handled. You might want to examine with the chair how effective these procedures are.
2. Sexual activities with clients are prohibited by the NASW *Code of Ethics* (1996, 1.09). Some social workers have argued that there is no scientific evidence that such activities are necessarily harmful. They say that a rule of this kind is no longer relevant in a society that permits a wide variety of lifestyles. Present arguments both for changing and for keeping this rule.

3. The "limited professional relationship" characteristic of the client–social worker relationship baffles many clients. It is a relationship that is quite unlike the formal, bureaucratic relationships with which they are familiar, yet it is also different from the informal relations they maintain with friends and relatives. How important is this principle from an ethical point of view?
4. In teams of two, develop two lists: (1) social relations with clients that are ethical and permissible, and (2) social relations with clients that are definitely unethical and therefore prohibited. Compare your lists with those of other teams. Discuss those areas where you find disagreement.

SUGGESTIONS FOR ADDITIONAL READINGS

The conflict between workers' and clients' interests in a hospital strike situation is examined by Fisher (1987). Kagle and Giebelhausen (1994) examine sexual and nonsexual dual role relationships between social workers and their clients, including ethical, legal, and practice issues. Clemens (1995) illustrates a dual role dilemma for a hospital social worker. Sloan et al. (1998) report findings of a survey of licensed social workers in Texas of their knowledge of and experience with sexual exploitation by psychotherapists. Jayaratne et al. (1997) report on research on dual role and intimate relationships and on boundary behaviors.

9. Bureaucratic and Work Relationships

So far, our discussion has focused on ethical problems and ethical dilemmas occurring in the professional relationship between social workers and clients. In this chapter, our attention will be directed to ethical issues arising out of the relationship among social work colleagues and between social workers and their employers.

We noted earlier in Chapter 2 that one of the functions of professional codes of ethics is to permit colleagues to work together in harmony. The *Code* "informs other professionals with whom the professional must work about the kind of cooperation they have a right to expect from the professional and the limits to the cooperation that a professional ought to give" (Beyerstein, 1993, p. 420). This information serves to reduce bickering and infighting that might lead to professional self-destruction. One section of the NASW *Code of Ethics* deals with the social worker's ethical responsibilities toward colleagues, and another section with her ethical responsibilities to employers, employing organizations, and practice settings. Several additional ethical rules dealing with relationships with colleagues are found in the section devoted to ethical responsibilities toward the profession.

Twenty-nine percent of the sustained ethical complaints received by NASW Chapter Committees on Inquiry during the years 1979 to 1985 dealt with unethical behaviors toward colleagues (Berliner, 1989). However, the total number of sustained complaints during this six-year period was only 96, or 16 sustained complaints per year for the entire United States! An NASW study of a random sample of 300 adjudicated cases filed between 1982 and 1992 found that of the 300 cases, 10 percent concerned colleagues. A more recent study reports the findings of ethics cases concerning collegial complaints filed with NASW for the years from 1986 to 1997. Of 894 ethics complaints, 34.3 percent (306) were filed by colleagues, employers, or supervisors. Of those, 56 percent (173) were filed by employees against their supervisor or administrator, or an average of 14.5 such complaints annually. The most commonly occurring violation concerned poor supervision—involving failure to maintain or share performance standards with workers, using insufficient investigation and documentation in performance review processes, not holding regular supervisory sessions, or holding sessions that were unclear and ineffective. The second most common violations involved employee dismissals that were judged to have been based on insufficient or absent personnel policies, or which diverged from accepted processes of progressive discipline (Strom-Gottfried, 1999). The findings of the 1993 and 1997 studies are very similar. The small number of complaints may represent only the tip of the proverbial iceberg because many unethical behaviors of this type are not brought to the local NASW committee but are handled in other ways, as will be discussed later in this chapter.

RELATIONS WITH PROFESSIONAL COLLEAGUES

What is a social worker to do when she discovers that a colleague engages in unethical or unprofessional conduct? How should she respond when she realizes that a fellow worker provides client services of a poor quality? What are her obligations when she believes that another social worker harms a client? What is her responsibility when she discovers that another worker engages in activities prohibited by their agency? What are her responsibilities when she learns that a colleague has violated the *Code of Ethics?*

The ethical rule obligating social workers to treat colleagues with respect (NASW, *Code*, 1996, 2.01a) is one of those rules that ordinarily do not create an ethical quandary. Most people understand that the members of a club do not "wash their dirty linen" in public. Goffman wrote about the backstage area, access to which is restricted to colleagues (1959, pp. 106–40). Whatever happens in this area may not be revealed to those who are not members of the profession. It should remain forever a secret among those who work backstage.

Social workers faced relatively few ethical problems as long as the rules governing relations with professional colleagues was unambiguous and not challenged by other ethical rules. But as accountability to clients and others became more important, the rule to "protect your own" became increasingly problematic. Some examples of unethical behavior are: (a) having sexual relations with a client; (b) terminating treatment because the worker wants to go on vacation; and (c) encouraging clients to buy a product or service that happens to be provided by a family member.

Today, most social workers are no longer willing to overlook their colleagues' unethical behavior. Yet what to do is not always clear. On learning that a colleague has engaged in unethical behavior, a social worker can choose one of the following options:

Option A. The violating behavior can be ignored. Reporting it may be too troublesome. Or past experience suggests that nothing will be done about it, even if it is reported. Or the conduct thought to be in violation of the *Code* may be so widespread that it is unlikely that anyone will take the complaint seriously.

Option B. An informal approach to the colleague may resolve the problematic behavior, especially if the violation is of a minor or technical nature or appears to be the result of lack of experience or lack of knowledge.

Option C. If the alleged unethical conduct also violates agency rules, it may be brought to the attention of one's supervisor or it may be raised formally by utilizing agency procedures established for this purpose.

Option D. The alleged unethical behavior may be brought to the attention of the local NASW Chapter Committee on Inquiry. In order to utilize this procedure, the colleague who allegedly engaged in the unethical behavior must have been an NASW member at the time of the alleged violation, the complaint must charge a specific violation of the *Code of Ethics*, the complainant must have personal knowledge about the alleged behavior, and the complainant must be able and willing to provide the Committee on Inquiry with relevant and reliable testimony (NASW Procedures for the Adjudication of Grievances, 1994b). Prior to 1998, local chapters acted on all complaints received. During 1998, NASW promulgated a new first step in the process. Before accepting disputes for the adjudication process, NASW chapters must first examine the facts of the alleged violations to determine whether the complaint meets the criteria for acceptance into the adjudication process before designating it as a complaint (NASW, 1998).

Option E. In states where a state licensing board regulates social work practice, unethical conduct harmful to clients can be reported to the board, which may be in a position to take effective remedial action within a relatively short time.

Option F. The unethical conduct may be brought to the attention of the general public (whistle-blowing), with the expectation that an aroused public will demand appropriate action to bring an end to the violation.

There are a number of possible alternatives within each option. Options B, C, D, and E are sanctioned by the *Code of Ethics*, while option F may be itself in violation of this code. Yet undoubtedly there are times and occasions when "going public" is the only way to proceed. However, the decision to "go public" should never be a routine one and should be taken only after careful consideration of all possibilities.

Before resolving ethical dilemmas of this type, the social worker should attempt to clarify what she hopes to achieve by the action she intends to initiate. Elsewhere Loewenberg (1987) suggests the following as possible objectives:

1. Discontinuance of the unethical behavior.
2. Punishment for the offending social worker.
3. Identifying the unethical practitioner so that potential clients and/or employers will avoid this person and turn to another, more ethical practitioner.
4. Preventing others from engaging in this behavior by warning them that it is unethical and will result in sanctions against the practitioner.
5. Protecting the "good name" of the profession by declaring publicly that the unethical behavior is not approved by the profession.

Several exemplars will highlight some of the problems involved in this ethical issue.

➤ 9.1 Sex with Clients

Your colleague Mitchell Moore has been hospitalized quite suddenly. While he is on sick leave, you have been assigned to cover some of his cases. You learn from one of his clients that Mitch has been having sexual relations with her. She says that she was uncomfortable but felt something bad would happen if she had objected. She also asks you to protect her confidentiality and that she will handle the situation when he returns. You do not question Mitch's intentions since you know him to be a conscientious social worker, and this is one unverified report by one person. If true, this behavior is clearly in violation of the *Code* which states, "Social workers should under no circumstances engage in sexual activities or sexual contact with current clients, whether such contact is consensual or forced" (NASW, 1996, 1.09a).

The violation of the *Code of Ethics* as reported is obvious, but what you should do is not clear because many conflicting claims are made on you. Your most serious consideration is: How trustworthy is this client's report? Can you/should you act if you have questions about what happened? However, assuming you believe the client's report, let us examine these claims, one by one, but not in any order of priority. The references are to the relevant paragraphs of the *Code of Ethics* (NASW, 1996).

1. Your obligation to uphold the code of ethics of the profession (NASW *Code*, 1996, 5.01b).
2. Your obligation to "take adequate measures to discourage, prevent, expose, and correct the unethical conduct of colleagues" (NASW *Code*, 1996, 2.11a).
3. Your obligation to protect clients from exploitation, even from exploitation by another social worker (NASW *Code*, 1996, 1.01, 1.06a, b).
4. Your obligation to respect confidential material received in the course of the professional relationship (NASW *Code*, 1996, 1.07a).

   The foregoing obligations are derived directly from the professional *Code of Ethics*. But there are also other considerations, some related to the *Code*:

5. Rumor has it that a number of other social workers also engage in this type of behavior. Making a fuss about it will only result in making yourself look ridiculous.
6. Sex and touch therapy may be modes of practice, but social workers are cautioned by the *Code* that they "should not engage in physical contact with clients when there is a possibility of psychological harm to the client as a result of the contact . . ." and if they do so they "are responsible for setting clear, appropriate, and culturally sensitive boundaries that govern such physical contact" (NASW *Code*, 1996, 1.10). Further, "social workers should base practice on recognized knowledge, including empirically based knowledge, relevant to social work and social work ethics" (NASW *Code*, 1996, 4.01). In regard to the utility of therapeutic touch, experienced therapeutic touch practitioners who claimed to treat conditions by using their hands to manipulate a "human energy field" perceptible above the patient's skin were unable to detect "energy fields" (Rosa et al., 1998, p. 1005), casting doubt on this type of treatment.

These latter considerations argue against your taking any action (Option A), while the earlier considerations suggest a more active response (perhaps Option B, C, or even D). How can a social worker order these considerations into the more and less important? Does the ethical principles screen (EPS) help you in unraveling this conundrum? Which is the priority ethical obligation?

Let us consider another situation that presents the social worker with ethical quandaries in her relation to colleagues.

➤ **9.2 Failure to Report a Case of Child Abuse**

Jake Dember, a frail five-year-old, was brought to the Emergency Room of Mt. Ebal Hospital unconscious, covered with blood from head to toe, obviously with serious internal injuries. His father, Hiram, said that Jake fell from their second-floor apartment and landed headfirst on the cement sidewalk. The medical team was able to save Jake's life, though serious brain damage could not be reversed. Now, two weeks later, Jake is still in the hospital's critical care unit. The attending physicians are determined to report this as a case of child abuse. Before doing so, they have asked the hospital social worker, Josie Perry, to appraise the general home environment.

Erica Dember, Jake's mother, did not want to talk to Josie. She said that she and her husband were already in family therapy at the Family Service Agency. If Josie wanted to know anything about them, she should talk to their therapist, Ed Custer.

Josie arranged to meet with Ed Custer on the following afternoon. Ed was willing to share his assessment of the Dember family since both parents had signed the customary consent forms when Jake was admitted to the hospital. In the course of their conversation, Ed acknowledged that he had been aware of ongoing child abuse in this family, but since he thought that it was not too serious, he did not file a report as required by law. He feared that such a report would have interfered with the therapeutic relationship that he was trying to develop with this family.

There are similarities and differences between this exemplar and the previous one. In both cases, one social worker became aware that another social worker may have violated ethical standards. In the first case, continuation of the unethical behavior (sexual relations with a client) might result in further harm to the client. In the present case, the harm to Jake had already been done and perhaps will not be repeated with Jake, but Ed Custer's criminal conduct and his failure to report other cases of child abuse may cause harm to other clients. Are the conflicting claims on Josie Perry similar to those that faced Mitch Moore's colleague? How valid is Custer's fear that reporting a client's child abuse may interfere with the therapeutic relationship, especially when there are data suggesting that such fears may be overstated.

Research findings do *not* support the claim that reporting child abuse interferes with maintaining a therapeutic relationship. A national survey of psychologists who are psychotherapists and who had filed at least one mandated child abuse report found that clients remained in treatment when such reports were made, especially when certain factors were present. Important for maintaining this relationship was the explicit involvement of the client in the informed consent procedures. It was also important that the limits of confidentiality were fully discussed with the client. Moreover, clients were more likely to continue when there were positive therapeutic relationships prior to the report and when the perpetrator was a third party (someone not engaged directly in the treatment). Most surprising, clients reacted more positively when sexual abuse—rather than other forms of abuse—was reported (Steinberg et al., 1997). How should Josie Perry resolve the ethical dilemma facing her? Should she report Ed's negligence to the NASW chapter? Ignore it? Choose another action?

So far, our consideration of the ethical quandaries arising out of this issue have focused on relations with social work colleagues. But social workers also interact with practitioners from other professions and with nonprofessional human service workers. Although the nature of these relations may be different, the NASW *Code of Ethics* states that the same respect and cooperation that is extended to social work colleagues should also be extended to colleagues of other professions (NASW *Code*, 1996, 2.01a). In one sense, the ethical problems arising out of these relationships will be the same as those that occur in relationships with social work colleagues. But in other ways the ethical dilemma may be more critical because these non–social work colleagues are not subject to the provisions of the NASW *Code of Ethics*. They may follow other norms of confidentiality or may routinely engage in behaviors that professional social workers define as unethical. For example, what should social workers do if their values and ethics are in conflict with the values and ethics of other team members?

If a social worker learns of the incompetence of a team member from another discipline, what is one's ethical responsibility? What if social workers are working in cooperation with lawyers in a legal organization and become aware of child abuse? The ethical and legal expectations of lawyers and social workers can conflict. Lawyers are not required to report the abuse. Social workers are. If the professional team includes both social workers and lawyers, what is the ethical responsibility of the social worker who is from an ancillary profession, in a legal organization, when the social worker is ethically responsible to report the abuse and the lawyer is not? Is the ethical responsibility of the social worker always the same in whatever setting concerning abuse, confidentiality, sexual impropriety, inadequate professional performance, conflicts of interest, and the like? In face of the conflicts and obligations, to whom does the social worker owe responsibility—the client or patient, the team, herself, the social work profession, the other involved professions, or society (Abramson, 1984)?

ADHERENCE TO AGENCY POLICIES AND REGULATIONS

The fact that most social workers are employed by bureaucratic organizations makes for another set of ethical dilemmas. Every organization has rules and policies. Those individuals who accept employment voluntarily agree to abide by these regulations. The NASW *Code of*

Ethics considers this commitment to the employing organization a basic ethical obligation: "Social workers generally should adhere to commitments made to employers and employing organizations" (NASW *Code*, 1996, 3.09a). But the goals and objectives of some organizations, even of some social service agencies, are not always congruent with the values of the social work profession. Organization maintenance and survival demands may result in rules that contradict the primary obligation of social workers to give priority to their clients' interests. Efficiency measures may limit intervention options so that the most effective option for a given client may not be available. Budgetary considerations may result in service cutbacks that will not necessarily be in the clients' best interest. In these and similar situations, a social worker, and especially a social work administrator, must resolve a critical ethical dilemma—whether to give priority to adherence to agency rules or to service to clients.

One response to these situations is collusion with clients to violate agency policies. This approach is often rationalized by the social worker by defining her activities as promoting the client's welfare or contributing toward social justice. But is it ever ethical to violate agency policies? Levy holds that such activities are always unethical (1982, p. 52). But are there no exceptions? For example, what should a social worker do upon learning that a client has an occasional additional income, which she is supposed to report to her public assistance worker so that part of this income can be deducted from the following month's welfare check? Or, a Social Security beneficiary is working "off the books" and not reporting the extra income, which is above the legal limits either for Social Security or income tax purposes? If the social worker does not report this income, all of the extra money will be available to the clients. In the first case, the additional cash may help her to return to employment and independence and, in the second case, enable the Social Security beneficiary to live at a minimal subsistence level. Keeping quiet may be in the best interest of both clients. But in each case, what about the worker's obligations to the laws, her employer, and society?

A particularly difficult ethical dilemma is faced by social workers when they discover that their agency's policies or regulations are unethical. A hospital social worker discovers soon after employment that it is hospital policy to pressure social workers to coerce mentally competent patients into nursing homes. Intended to counter excessive concern by the hospital staff about patient safety following discharge, these actions override patients' rights to autonomy and self-determination (Clemens, 1995). The administrator of a child protective agency hires inadequately trained paraprofessional workers to investigate complaints of child abuse since insufficient budgets have made it impossible for him to hire professionally trained workers, even though this assignment requires a particularly high skill level.

In a community organization, there are those social workers who advocate that only African-American professionals should work with African-American groups and neighborhoods. In another community organization, there are social workers who advocate that only lesbian and gay persons can be successful in working with lesbian and gay communities (Shillington et al., 1994; Tully et al., 1994). The *Code* requires that social workers should understand cultures, have a knowledge base of their client's cultures, and obtain education about the nature of social diversity (NASW *Code of Ethics*, 1996, 1.05a, b, c). However, the *Code* states "social workers should not practice, condone, facilitate, or collaborate with any form of discrimination on the basis of race, ethnicity, national origin, color, sex, sexual orientation, age, marital status, political belief, religion, or mental or physical disability" (NASW *Code*, 1996, 4.02). How can an agency executive in either of these organizations resolve these ethical dilemmas?

A different aspect of the conflict between agency interests and client interests that results in ethical quandaries is illustrated by the following exemplar.

➤ **9.3 Case of a Hyperactive Boy**

David is a hyperactive child in a residential institution. In the last few weeks he has become very disruptive. He frequently tosses food during meals with other children, "shortsheets" other childrens' beds, turns on fire alarms, arrives late wherever he is expected, throws pencils in class, and other such behaviors. Although he is not physically harmful to himself or others, he has been highly disruptive of the institution's daily routine. The consulting physician has prescribed large doses of a tranquilizer to calm the child and manage him better, but the cottage social worker has refused on ethical grounds to administer this medicine to David. She feels strongly that such pharmaceutical control will interfere with the child's welfare and freedom and will be counterproductive in any therapy attempted. Her social work supervisor has supported this decision. The physician insists the medication prescribed be given to David. The institution's director, a psychologist, supports the doctor against the decision of the social worker.

The agency executive requires an institution that runs smoothly. He also needs a physician who is willing to cooperate with the institution's staff. The social workers in this case argue that David has engaged in some asocial behavior—behavior they believe can be controlled more productively in other ways. Is their responsibility to the executive, the physician, and the agency or to David and their own treatment plans?

Non–Social Work Employers

When a social worker is employed by an organization outside the human services field, she may face even more perplexing ethical problems. Nowadays, social workers are employed by hospitals, industry, police, prisons, the military, colleges, long-term care facilities, and a variety of other organizations that are not social work–oriented. To whom do these social workers owe their *primary* loyalty? Who is the "client" of these social workers? For example, the employees of a large manufacturer may consult about personal problems with the social worker whom their employer has hired. Should the employer be informed when a worker's problems may affect the production schedule of a factory? Or that may have security implications? Should detectives have access to confidential information that a prison social worker has obtained from her contacts with prisoners?

That such social workers face very real ethical dilemmas became clear from the findings of one study of social workers employed by various Illinois police departments. Seventy percent of these social worker respondents said that they considered themselves most responsible to their clients, while only 7.5 percent said that their first loyalty was to the police department that employed them. Yet 39 percent of these same social workers occasionally shared confidential information about their clients with police officers; 5 percent indicated that they did so often or frequently (Curtis & Lutkus, 1985). School social workers are employed in institutions where students have few rights. On many issues, power is transferred from parents to school personnel. Schools assume a protective stance in regard to children, often to the detriment of the childrens' right to self-determination and autonomy. Social workers cannot function without the cooperation of the school personnel with whom they are in close daily contact. The institutional expectation is that all material relevant to understanding the child will be shared with team members. Not to do so is to alienate other staff members. Too rigid insistence on confidentiality can isolate the child, as well as the social worker. As a result, "confidentiality and informed consent rarely are applied evenhandedly to children" (Berman-Rossi & Rossi, 1990, p. 205). Social workers in such settings frequently have to deal with the basic ethical question—who is the client?

From a practical point of view, this problem may be especially difficult for social workers in military service. Consider the following exemplar.

➤ **9.4 A Colonel Outranks a Captain**

Pfc. Richard Mozart recently discussed some personal difficulties with Capt. Emilio Pacifico, a social worker on an air force base. Mozart is very concerned about his aged parents, who live in a distant state and who find it increasingly difficult to cope by themselves. He has been so worried about this situation that he has started to use drugs intermittently. He told Capt. Pacifico about this in confidence.

Recently, because of some physical complaints, Mozart took a number of tests at the base hospital, including a urinalysis. The results of this test confirmed his use of drugs, but Pfc. Mozart is not aware of this finding.

On this base, the commander does not have access to the medical files of servicemen, but social workers, psychologists, nurses, and physicians have ready access. Yesterday, the base commander, Col. Benjamin Brown, discussed with Capt. Pacifico his concerns about Pfc. Mozart. His work has been less than satisfactory; his behavior suggests that he has serious problems and that he may be on drugs. Col. Brown asked Capt. Pacifico to check out the situation and let him know whether Mozart uses drugs.

Capt. Pacifico is troubled by this request. Must he comply with the order issued by his commanding officer and disclose the results of the medical test or information that he has received on a confidential basis from his client? Or should he refuse and claim privileged communications? What is the ethical behavior expected of him?

The following exemplar describes an ethical dilemma that a social worker involved in international service may encounter, but it has implications for service anywhere.

➤ **9.5 Serving Only the Good People or . . . ?**

Amanda Frankel is a social worker for an international aid organization in a war zone. The forces of one side of the conflict are particularly cruel, attacking civilians, raping young girls and older women, and murdering groups of men and burying their bodies to do away with evidence. Until yesterday, Ms. Frankel was happy and proud to serve those in need who were being attacked. But then her supervisor sent a message that she was going to be transferred to the other side to serve the people there. Just as here, she would serve all people, including military and paramilitary personnel. She was awake all night considering what she should do. What is the ethically correct choice in this situation?

In what way is Ethical Principle 2 (equality and inequality) relevant to Ms. Frankel's situation and dilemma? In what ways do her personal values conflict with her employing agency's values and requirements? Does the *Code of Ethics* suggest there is a correct choice for Ms. Frankel? Can you identify in your local community situations in which social workers might have their personal values challenged by similar decisions by the agencies for whom they work?

Ethical problems arising out of adherence to agency policies occur in all settings. Some of our illustrations are taken from non–social work settings because there the ethical dilemmas may be more evident. But social workers employed by social agencies should not think that these problems cannot happen to them, as the following exemplar illustrates.

➤ 9.6 Apple Hill Young Adult Social Club

The Apple Hill Community Center is a group service and recreation agency in a "changing neighborhood." When it was established almost 50 years ago, it served an immigrant population and was instrumental in the Americanization of many thousands of newcomers. It now sees "character building" and "strengthening democratic decision making" as its major contribution to the community. As a matter of policy it avoids all political activities. Neither staff nor groups affiliated with the center are allowed to take a public stand on controversial issues.

Otto Zupan, a social group worker, staffs the Young Adult Social Club. This group is composed of 25 young men, ages 18 to 21, almost all of whom are high school graduates. They spend much time at the community center because most of them are unemployed. Lately they have talked a lot about why there are no jobs for them. Some thought that the recession was to blame, others felt it was because they were black. Otto urged them to do some research and see if they could come up with the real answer to their question. The results of their field study left little doubt that they were the victims of discriminatory hiring practices. Otto urged them to go public because discrimination in hiring was against the law. Letting the public know about their findings might help them get a better break when applying for the next job. They thought that Otto's idea was great and decided to call a news conference. They asked Otto to arrange for a room at the center for the news conference.

When Otto talked over their plan with the center's director, he was rebuffed flatly. Not only could they not have a room for the news conference, but as a center social club they could not engage at all in this type of action program. Furthermore, Otto must do everything to bring the group back to its original objectives as a social club. The center director added that if he could not do this, he should ask for another assignment.

Loyalty to agency rules or meeting client needs—these are two conflicting professional obligations that create a serious ethical problem for social worker Otto Zupan. Is it ethical for him to abide by the agency's directives and thus abandon the young adults at this critical point in their development? Or should he ignore his obligations to his employer and help group members organize outside the center? What is the ethical stance demanded of a social worker who faces this situation?

Another type of ethical dilemma occurs when an agency channels clients into programs that are not beneficial for them. For example, what are the ethical issues faced by social workers when a large number of unskilled men and women are directed into job-training programs that lead only to dead-end or nonexistent jobs? Should social workers act against agency policy and tell their clients all that they know about these programs? Or is it more ethical to follow organizational directives and keep quiet? How does a social worker make ethical decisions of this type?

What are the ethical implications when a social agency engages in discriminatory practices? There was a time when such practices were blatant and open; nowadays they are less obvious but may be equally damaging. One child welfare agency places white children in adoptive homes and minority children in institutions "because there are no adoptive homes for them." In another agency, homosexual AIDS patients receive one type of service, while heterosexual AIDS patients, another. Whatever the reason, discriminatory practices never benefit the client who is being discriminated against. The *Code of Ethics* clearly states that "Social workers should not practice, condone, facilitate, or collaborate with any form of discrimination on the basis of race, ethnicity, national origin, color, sex, sexual orientation, age, marital status, political belief, religion, or mental or physical disability" (NASW *Code*, 1996, 4.02). What does this mean in practice? Should a social worker refuse to accept employment in an agency that practices discrimination? Must she resign when she discovers such practices? Should she ignore such agency policies and, whenever possible, not follow them? Or should she accept a job with the intention to change the agency? What would you do if you had Dale Jenkins's job?

➤ **9.7 Social Work in a Bank**

Social worker Dale Jenkins is employed by a large bank as a community representative in a minority neighborhood. Jenkins is black. Part of his assignment is to be visible and become accepted in the community. He has been very successful in meeting this objective. He is accepted by the neighborhood's residents and is liked by nearly everyone. In the past year he has been able to help a number of residents qualify for business loans and mortgages. Mr. Stamos, vice president of the bank to whom he reports, recently told Jenkins that the bank has decided to direct less money and services to this neighborhood, but his job is "safe." Stamos implied that in a few years the bank might again direct monies to this neighborhood. In the meantime, Jenkins should be more "selective" in referring residents to the bank for loans and mortgages.

Jenkins understood this message as meaning that the bank no longer would give mortgages to minority group applicants.

He considered the options he had, including the following:

1. Try to persuade Mr. Stamos and other bank officials to change the new and discriminating policy.
2. Ignore the new policy and operate as he had in the past.
3. Tell community leaders about the new policy and encourage them to apply political pressure on the bank to change its policy.

What are the ethical implications of each of the options that Jenkins is considering?

ETHICAL DILEMMAS IN SOCIAL WORK ADMINISTRATION AND SUPERVISION

Social work administrators and supervisors have an ethical responsibility to protect clients' rights and to foster an atmosphere in which workers will do the same. At the same time, they are accountable to the agency's sponsors for productivity and for operating within the authorized budget. With diminishing budgets and rising demands, this can be a most difficult task. In addition to ethical obligations toward the agency, an administrator also has responsibilities toward his or her employees.

For many administrators, the line between ethical and unethical behavior is crossed only when their activities result in personal gain. They feel that it is ethical to do whatever is necessary as long as their activities benefit clients or the agency. If a government contract provides budget for staff training but not for staff supervision, they have no hesitation to "redefine" supervision as training. Or recreation services are renamed "respite services" if government funding for recreation is dropped (Bernstein, 1990). In such cases, an illusion of compliance is achieved by playing semantic games, but is this ethical?

The adoption of the success model by many administrators has created another set of ethical dilemmas. Although in earlier generations business was always depicted as the antithesis to civilized values, in recent decades the world of Big Business has been presented as the Good Thing. The overriding message is that bigger is better and that profitability is the most important objective, even for social programs. The success model directs social work administrators to do whatever needs to be done to increase the agency's share of the "market." Emphasis is placed on growth. Everything is reduced to time, money, and quantitative outputs. Efficiency becomes the bottom line and at times overrides human considerations (Miller, 1990). Administrators who follow this success model may not even be aware of the many ethical questions they encounter.

Another ethical dilemma that some administrators face occurs when there is a conflict between their responsibility for organizational maintenance, on the one hand, and professional or communal responsibility, on the other hand. Take the case of the director of a children's home that for decades has provided institutional care for infants aged three days to one year. From a professional point of view, there is no longer any justification for continuing this service, yet the director has responsibilities to the sponsors, to staff, and to others for ensuring that the agency continues to function. How would you respond to the ethical dilemma facing this social work administrator?

A dilemma of a different nature is presented in the following exemplar.

➤ 9.8 The Good of the Agency, Community, or the Staff?

John Meenaghan is a social planner in a United Way community fund-raising and social planning agency. Over lunch with Melissa Bridgewater, a longtime friend and a member of the executive staff, she told him that the executive director—who is not a social worker—and several favored members of his personal staff have been living lavishly on their expense accounts and padding their expenses. All information she provided in the past has been completely accurate. The executive director is tyrannical and punitive but has been extremely creative and improved productivity many times over. The fund drive has reached new heights. Later, in his office, Meenaghan spent almost an hour contemplating why Ms. Bridgewater shared this information with him. Why doesn't she go public herself? What should he *do,* if anything?

John Meenaghan understands that "whistle-blowing" can do good as well as harm. If he goes public with the information about agency corruption, he could do much harm to the agency and undermine its fundraising capacity for some time into the future. Alternately, if he goes public with the information (for which he has no direct evidence), he could perform a public service, protecting the community's resources while ensuring that funds will be spent on the problems for which they were intended. At the same time, the element of trust that generally exists in the agency will be destroyed. The authority structure of the agency will be damaged, at least for a time, thus potentially creating havoc in the administration. If he reports the problem to his supervisor or to a member of the board of directors, he might further his good relations with some superiors and colleagues, and perhaps with members of the board, but the executive director and others will be angry and will be liable to legal actions. Finding successful executive directors is not an easy task.

A number of standards in the *Code* are relevant in this situation: "Social workers' primary responsibility is to promote the well-being of clients" (NASW, 1996, 1.01); "Social workers should treat colleagues with respect and should represent accurately and fairly the qualifications, views, and obligations of colleagues" (NASW, 1996, 2.01a, c). In addition, "social workers should take adequate measures to discourage, prevent, expose, and correct the unethical conduct of colleagues" (NASW, 1996, 2.11a, b, c, d); "social work administrators should take reasonable steps to eliminate any conditions in their organizations that violate, interfere with, or discourage compliance with the *Code*" (NASW, 1996, 3.07d); and "social workers should be diligent stewards of the resources of their employing organizations, wisely conserving funds where appropriate and never misappropriating funds or using them for unintended purposes" (NASW, 1996, 3.09g).

Who is the client or what is the priority in this situation? Ms. Bridgewater, who shared the information? The executive director, who has done an outstanding job for the agency? Maintaining the viability of the United Way? The community agencies that benefit from the United Way? Those being served by communal agencies? What does John Meenaghan owe to Melissa Bridgewater? Lacking detailed information about the improprieties, would he be treating any of his colleagues with respect if he were to move forward? Does he have the right to correct a non–social worker, someone who is not bound by the *Code?* What do you advise John Meenaghan to do?

More generally, both supervisors and administrators have a responsibility to support workers' ethical behaviors and to stop workers' unethical behaviors. But they must remember that workers (as well as clients) are human beings, not robots.

Dual Role Relations

Supervisors and agency administrators are powerful persons because they have considerable influence over the social workers and students whom they employ or supervise. They make assignments, evaluate their work, decide on promotions, and at times terminate their employment. They are obligated to use this power in ethical ways. This rule has a number of implications.

To engage in any relation with employees or students in which an administrator/supervisor takes advantage, exploits, or harms persons with less power is unethical, even if the initiative comes from the employee (supervisees). This holds for sexual relations, as well as for other types of relations that create bonds that may negatively affect the professional relationship. Among the standards in the code are several introduced to provide clearer guidance for social workers in regard to dual/multiple relationships. This area of unethical behavior has received increased attention in recent years. Here we wish to highlight the need for social workers to consider seriously the ethical problems that may arise in work settings among persons with different degrees of power.

When you consider the following supervisory situations, how would you assess each of the following situations:

- Your supervisee's husband is an insurance broker. She tells you that her husband will give you a large discount on your automobile insurance. Will you avoid the dual relationship problem if you place your insurance with him but pay the full insurance rate?

- Your supervisee, a BSW social worker, just enrolled in a graduate school of social work. The school is ready to appoint you as a field instructor and have you supervise your employee's field instruction.
- Your agency is employing your wife as a caseworker and assigns you to work on a team with her.
- Your supervisee has a summer home in the mountains. She invites you and your children to use it this summer while she and her husband are vacationing elsewhere.

In each of these situations there is a potential for an ethical difficulty. Do the standards give clear answers to these problems?

Other Conflicting Obligations

Social work supervisors are often in the position of the person "in between" with multiple pressures and obligations, as the next three case situations will illustrate.

Supervisors have many roles and obligations in social agencies. In addition to their primary responsibility to ensure the delivery of services of high quality, their middle-management responsibilities are often joined with direct service to clients. In addition, there are committee meetings, assignments representing the agency in the community, phone calls, emergencies, and other demands on their time and energy.

➤ **9.9 Friend, Self, Family, Agency—Loyalty to Whom?**

Thomas Kinane recently was promoted to supervisor, a job that pays much more than his prior position. His teenage daughter has been in therapy for dysthymia, and he feels lucky because the money is arriving just when the family needs it. He is responsible for supervision of 12 workers who are on a task force to implement a new service in Gordonsville, a satellite location. He has an enormous amount of record keeping and report writing to do. Because of demands of the job on his time, both in Gordonsville and central headquarters, he frequently has to cancel supervisory sessions with individual workers, yet he does not feel ready to use group supervision—which would help him to better control his time.

Thomas Kinane's situation is not unusual. Kadushin (1992) found that both supervisors and supervisees identified a lack of time for supervision as a significant shortcoming among supervisors. Thomas Kinane wants to succeed in his job, needs the money, and has a responsibility to his employer. But he also has a responsibility to his supervisees' clients, to his family, and to his supervisees. How would you choose among these conflicting obligations? What would you choose to do?

➤ 9.10 The Ethics of Moonlighting

The employment contract of the Bay City Department of Human Services (DHS) states: Social workers may not work for another employer in their professional social work capacity, even outside of their regular working hours. Every new social work employee in the department Is made aware of this provision and acknowledges her agreement to it in writing. The other evening, Ellen and Bill Stock had to rush their infant daughter Sharon to the hospital because she had a very high fever. While Ellen stayed with the baby in the emergency room, Bill handled the admission routines.

Later on, Bill told Ellen that among the people with whom he had to speak in the admissions office was a social worker. He had been very impressed by her warm and sympathetic interest in their sick child. Ellen asked Bill if he recalled the worker's name and was surprised to learn that it was Joan Gilligan, one of the social workers she supervises at DHS.

On the way out of the hospital, Ellen peeked into the admissions office to make sure that this was the same social worker she supervises. It was she. Since Ellen did not use her husband's name at work, she was sure that Joan did not realize that she had been helping her supervisor's husband.

Ellen did not know what she should do about her discovery. On the one hand, Joan's moonlighting was in violation of the commitment that she, like all DHS social workers, had made to the agency. The *Code of Ethics* states clearly, "Social workers generally should adhere to commitments made to employers and employing organizations" (NASW, 1996, 3.09a). On the other hand, Joan's moonlighting did not harm anyone. As a matter of fact, her presence in the hospital admissions office benefits many patients at a time when they are in a state of crisis. Yet what about Ellen's obligations to her employer? To her colleague? To the profession?

The next exemplar will deal with yet another aspect of this issue.

➤ 9.11 A Caribbean Cruise

Wilma Stevens supervises a unit of six social workers, of whom Carla Bick is the most qualified and most effective. Last week Carla was not at work. Her boyfriend called in to say that Carla had a bad case of the flu and would probably be out all week. Today she returned to work, bringing a note from her doctor stating that she had been sick all week. Aside from the note, there was no evidence of her having been sick. She explained that yesterday she went to the beach; this accounted for her suntan.

Wilma's cousin had been on a Caribbean cruise all of last week. When they had supper together, the cousin told Wilma all about the trip and about the many interesting people she had met on board the cruise ship. One of those people had been a young social worker, Carla Bick. The cousin wondered whether Wilma happened to know her.

As Wilma thought about Carla's absence from work last week, she noted the following points:

1. Carla's absence was not authorized and was in violation of agency policy.
2. Carla's behavior was unethical and unprofessional.
3. Carla harmed her clients by failing to provide them with regular service.
4. Carla had not told the truth when she claimed that she had been sick.
5. But Carla was her best worker and Wilma did not want to lose her.

Other workers probably also had misused sick leave, but were not caught. Would making an example of Carla persuade others to desist from this unethical behavior? If Wilma does so, what will be the cost? Would making an example of Carla be unethical since her privacy and respect would be violated?

It will be difficult to differentiate between Wilma's administrative/supervisory responsibilities and her professional social work responsibilities. Any decision that she will reach will necessarily include both aspects. But whatever her decision, it will have ethical implications.

One of the assignments of an agency director is to "staff" the board of directors, the agency's policy-making group. Establishing a good working relationship with board members is essential for every successful agency director. But at times the agency director will encounter ethical dilemmas because of conflicting ethical principles. Consider the following exemplar.

➤ **9.12 The Board of Directors of the Alzheimer's Association**

The Alzheimer's Association is a local, voluntary United Fund agency established about ten years ago to provide a wide range of community services to families of Alzheimer's patients. At last night's meeting, the board of directors voted to eliminate all homemaker services because the insurance carrier had again raised the premium for liability insurance that homemakers must carry.

You, the agency director, know that the demand for homemaker services has always exceeded the staff available. It is not only a popular service, but a resource that has enabled many families to keep their Alzheimer's patient at home instead of placing him or her in an institutional facility.

You know that the agency provides other services for which there are fewer demands; reducing these services could pay for the higher insurance premiums. But these other services are of special interest to several board members; they will do everything to protect "their" services.

What are the ethical problems that this exemplar raises? How can you resolve them?

ADVERTISEMENTS AND SOLICITATION

In 1988, NASW entered into a consent order agreement with the Federal Trade Commission that resulted in several changes being introduced into the *Code of Ethics* having to do with solicitation of clients, advertisements, and payments for referrals. These changes illustrate the power of the state and law in relation to the nature of a profession's code of ethics. As of 1988, NASW members were free to truthfully and nondeceptively advertise and market their services. Payment to a referral service was allowed. Prospective clients could be solicited among prospective clients receiving similar services from another professional.

NASW was allowed to formulate and enforce reasonable principles or ethical guidelines to prevent deceptive advertising and solicitation practices, as well as guidelines with respect to solicitation of business or testimonials. NASW was not prohibited from issuing reasonable principles or guidelines requiring that factual disclosures be made to clients or other consumers regarding fees paid by any social worker to any patient referral service. Other changes focused on providing services for a private fee to clients who are entitled to such services through the social worker's employing agency, not accepting anything of value for referrals, and not exploiting relationships with clients for personal advantage.

In regard to deceptive advertising and solicitation practices, the NASW *Code* of 1996 requires that "social workers should ensure that their representations to clients, agencies, and the public of professional qualifications, credentials, education, competence, affiliations, services provided, or results to be achieved are accurate. Social workers should claim only those relevant professional credentials they actually possess and take steps to correct any inaccuracies or misrepresentations of their credentials by others" (NASW *Code*, 1996, 4.06c).

Social workers also may not "engage in uninvited solicitation of potential clients who, because of their circumstances, are vulnerable to undue influence, manipulation, or coercion" (NASW *Code*, 1996, 4.07a) and may "not engage in solicitations of testimonial endorsements (including solicitation of consent to use a client's prior statement as a testimonial endorsement) from current clients or from other people who, because of their particular circumstances, are vulnerable to undue influence" (NASW *Code*, 1996, 4.07b).

The changes in the *Code* make some things clearer, and others remain ambiguous. What is truthful, nondeceptive advertising and marketing? How much training, education, and experience entitle one to claim expertise in a particular therapeutic method? Who is vulnerable to undue influence, manipulation, or coercion? What is unwarranted solicitation of potential clients? Aren't most social work clients under stress? How much real choice does a potential client under stress actually possess? Do such stressful situations allow for truly informed consent in which the liberty and autonomy of the potential client are assured?

Social workers are not to give or receive payment for a referral when no professional service is provided by the referring social worker (NASW *Code*, 1996, 2.06c). Is referral itself a professional service, entitling the referring social worker to receive a payment? Are personal gifts—donations to organizations or political campaigns supported by a social worker who refers cases to you— "payments"? At what point would a "gift" clearly be a payment? What about the payment or receipt of referral fees by organizations? Is there a double standard? What is the ethical difference between payment for receiving referrals and payment for directing referrals to certain services?

➤ **9.13 Payment for Referrals in an Employee Assistance Program**

Libby Rudo is a social worker in the employee assistance program (EAP) of the Colonel Electric Company. The company administration worked out an arrangement with one agency—the Central City Services Group—so that they will pay the Colonel Electric Company a fee for every case referred to them. They also established a policy that the employee assistance program staff will refer employees to Central City Services only when longer-term treatment is needed by employees than is provided by the EAP. Ms. Rudo is certain that Mrs. Quarles, who is in her office consulting her about a family problem, requires a kind of treatment that is not available at Central City Services. What is the ethical thing for Ms. Rudo to do?

May a social worker solicit payments for referrals so that they are paid not to her directly but to a nonprofit agency or department? If a social worker is a member of a for-profit group, may the group receive payment for referrals and include the payments in the overall income of the group to be distributed to the members as part of their earnings? Does it make a difference if business suppliers provide honoraria, conference expenses, luggage, lunches, or other gifts to an individual social worker? What if the gifts are provided to the agency and the agency distributes them? When a business firm provides free or discounted service for one of your poor clients because of other referrals you have sent to the firm, is this "payment" a fee for referrals in the same way that it would be if you received it directly?

EXERCISES

1. Consider the ethical dilemmas facing social worker Timothy Land (Exemplar A.5 in Appendix A). How would you resolve the ethical problems that he faces?

2. Some employment situations make demands that may force social workers to violate professional ethics (if they do not want to look for another job). Exemplar A.1 (in Appendix A) presents such a dilemma. How would you respond to this ethical challenge?

3. Prepare a list of unethical professional behaviors that you think should be actionable by your state social work licensing authority. What are the unethical professional behaviors on the authority's promulgated list? What sanctions or punishments are available to this authority?

4. Review the employee handbook for the agency where you are employed or in field instruction. Are any of the agency policies inconsistent with the *Code of Ethics?* If you were to choose to do so, how would you address these inconsistencies?

SUGGESTIONS FOR ADDITIONAL READINGS

See Berman-Rossi and Rossi (1990) for an exploration of problems facing social workers in schools in regard to childrens' self-determination and autonomy. Verschelden (1993) argues that social work values and ethics suggest social workers should be pacifists. Do you join Verschelden in the belief that social work ethics require a social worker to be a pacifist? Loewenberg (1987) analyzes how a social worker might respond to a colleague's unethical behavior. Ethical decision making by social work supervisors is examined by Congress (1992). Steinberg, Levine, and Doueck (1997) report on the effects of legally mandated child-abuse reports on therapeutic relationships.

10. Private Practice Social Work

A number of ethical problems and dilemmas faced by private practitioners will be discussed in this chapter. Some of these problems (such as misdiagnosis) are also encountered by social workers in agency practice, but are discussed here because practitioners in private practice come upon these problems and dilemmas more often and more acutely than their colleagues who practice in social work agencies. Many of the ethical problems discussed in this chapter are problems faced not only by social workers but by all private practitioners, regardless of their professional affiliation.

In 1995, of the employed NASW members surveyed, 14 percent of the respondents indicated private solo practices as their primary practice setting. Another 31.9 percent indicated private solo practices as their secondary practice setting. Thus, a large number and percentage of employed NASW members in 1995 were in private practice, either on a full-time or part-time basis (Gibelman & Schervish, 1997).

When the NASW Delegate Assembly officially recognized private practice in 1964, few thought that so many social workers would choose to practice outside the traditional agency setting. The thinking of the delegates on this question emerges clearly from the 1964 decision, which states specifically that "practice within socially sponsored organization structures must remain the primary avenue for the implementation of goals of the profession" (Golton, 1971, p. 950). The recognition of private practice by the professional association, along with their view that socially sponsored, organization-based social work would remain the predominant emphasis, must be viewed within a historical context. The creation of private practice social work reversed the evolutionary pattern of the development of professions in general. Toren makes the point that the classic professions (medicine, law, clergy) grew out of individual, solo practice. Social work reversed this evolutionary pattern by first being organization-based, a factor that influences social work's commitments, professional conduct, degree of public recognition, theoretical study and technical skills, and its focus on supervision (Toren, 1972).

As more and more social workers engage in private practice, moving away from nonprofit and governmental auspices, there is concern about changing attitudes and behaviors that may no longer be in consonance with the profession's ethics. This concern was expressed by Specht and Courtney (1994), as well as others, who suggested that one consequence of such a shift is a diminishment of social work's historic mission to help the poor and oppressed, those who are the most vulnerable in our society. This charge has been made of the profession as a whole, and particularly of social agencies. The problem is especially critical when social workers opt for private practice in order to gain status, prestige, and higher incomes. Gibelman and Schervish (1997, p. 164) ask: "How do private practitioners honor a professional code of ethics that not only requires services to individuals but delineates social workers' responsibility to make larger social systems more responsive to the needs of individuals?" One conclusion of a national survey of the NASW Register of Clinical Social Workers was that "private practitioners concentrate their work on the 'haves' of society, rather than the 'have nots'" (Strom, 1994, p. 87). Many practitioners were found to have a "bottom line" orientation as reflected in the level of fees and the limited amount of free care provided. When this happens, some professional ethics concerns (e.g., social responsibility) may become secondary considerations.

Private practice is consistent with the capitalist and free enterprise system. Furthermore, American values stress freedom and autonomy. The freedom of social workers as private entrepreneurs to enter into contractual relationships with those persons who seek assistance is consistent with American values. But is there an ethical problem when some people do go without services while others who are able to pay receive the assistance they need? Does the *Code* or the ethical principles screen (Chapter 3) provide sufficient guidance for social workers who want to decide whether to engage in full-time or part-time private practice? Whether to serve clients who are unable to pay?

FEES

Social workers must make sure that the fees they charge "are fair, reasonable, and commensurate with the services performed. Consideration should be given to clients' ability to pay" (NASW *Code*, 1996, 1.13). Some private practitioners do not know what "due regard for the client's ability to pay" means. Does it require a sliding scale? Does it mean that varying rates should be charged for the same service, depending on the financial resources of the client? Or is a "reasonable fee" the fee that most private practice social workers in this locality charge? This is one ethical question, but there are other questions concerning fees that also have ethical implications. For example, one of the ethical principles of the NASW *Code of Ethics* states that "Social workers are encouraged to volunteer some portion of their professional skills with no expectation of significant financial return (pro bono service)" (NASW *Code*, 1996, Ethical Principles).

Client Dumping

What is the ethical thing to do when, during the course of treatment, a client's situation changes and he can no longer pay the agreed-to fee? Consider the situation of Larry Firth.

> ➤ **10.1 A Difficult Family Situation**
> Larry Firth came to consult with you about a "difficult family situation." His wife has left him and their two sons in order to live with her boyfriend. He himself has formed a satisfactory relationship with a married neighbor. However, he is concerned what his teenage sons will say and do when they find out the truth about their parents.
> You are making good progress in helping Larry Firth come to grips with his problem. But today Larry tells you that he has lost his job and that he can no longer afford your fee. You are not yet sufficiently well established to carry "free" cases. What should you do?

"Dumping the client" is one way that some practitioners have responded to clients who can no longer pay the fee. There are various ways to dump a client. A worker may tell a client that his problem has been solved successfully (when it has not yet been solved) or that no more can be done for him (when, in fact, the worker could still be helpful). Or the worker may cancel appointments so frequently that the client loses interest. Or the worker may refer a client who no longer can afford his services to a public or private not-for-profit agency. No matter what technique is used, in *some cases*, the worker's objective is to get rid of the client who can no longer pay. In other cases, referral to an agency may not be "dumping" but the most helpful thing to do. Barker (1992, p. 110) suggests that private practitioners "are far more likely to engage in the unethical behavior of premature or precipitous termination than are agency-based professionals." But what can an ethical practitioner do when this situation arises?

A national survey of experienced and well-established psychotherapists (psychologists) found that most continued care when insurance coverage ended. They chose the following options in descending order: (1) advocate for more benefits; (2) patient pays out of his or her own pocket; (3) reduce the fee for patient who continues on a self-paying basis; (4) treat the person on a pro bono basis; (5) make a proper referral to an agency for continued treatment; (6) terminate treatment; and (7) alter the diagnosis so treatment would be covered (Murphy et al., 1998). Another available option a social worker should consider is that the client will pay when his financial situation improves. None of these options is without problems, but each—with the exception of termination—may be viewed as ethical. In the case of termination, much would depend on the state of the person, the nature of the problem, how close the client is to attainment of the goals of treatment, the number of persons being seen by the social worker, and other such variables.

Double Billing

Double billing occurs when a service provider bills a third party, such as an insurance company or a governmental program, for services not provided or for services already billed to another party. This practice usually occurs without the client's knowledge. It is both unethical and illegal. If detected, the practitioner is liable to criminal prosecution and to malpractice litigation.

DIAGNOSIS AND MISDIAGNOSIS

The controversy about the place of diagnosis in social work practice, which will be discussed below, has a number of ethical aspects. Many social workers believe that diagnosis is an essential element in every professional intervention, but others reject its use because they consider it an inappropriate application of the medical model to social work practice. Some point to psychologist Carl Rogers, who consistently argued against the use of any psychodiagnosis because he thought that such a procedure interfered with a client's need to experience himself subjectively. Diagnosis, according to Rogers (1951), substitutes an external definition about the problem at a time when it is most crucial that the client gain greater subjective clarity about his situation. Psychiatrist R. D. Laing (1967) also criticized traditional diagnostics because it often leads to a self-fulfilling prophecy. If certain behaviors are expected, chances are that the client will perform them and/or that the worker will detect them.

For many, the problem of diagnostics has become even more critical in recent years as use of the *Diagnostic and Statistical Manual of Mental Disorders*, 4th ed. (DSM-IV) of the American Psychiatric Association (APA, 1994) has spread rapidly among social workers. Many social workers are required to use DSM-IV even though they do not think that it is an appropriate diagnostic instrument for social work practice. They are required to use it by many government programs (which authorize service or reimburse for service rendered only on the basis of an appropriate DSM-IV diagnosis) and by insurance companies (which require such a diagnosis before they will authorize third-party payments) (Schamess, 1996). "Diagnosis increasingly provides a mechanism for clinicians to be reimbursed and for clients who cannot afford treatment to get the services they need," according to Kirk and Kutchins (1988, p. 226). Often authorization and reimbursements are limited to certain diagnostic categories; in other instances the amount of reimbursement (or the length of treatment authorized) depends on the diagnosis submitted. All of these requirements put pressure on social workers to use this diagnostic instrument. Some engage in deliberate misdiagnosis in order to meet the stated requirements for reimbursable social work treatment. The following exemplar illustrates one of the ethical problems that this creates.

➤ **10.2 Let the Insurance Company Pay the Bill**

When Christine Sales saw her private practice social worker last week at their initial session, she mentioned that she hoped her insurance company would reimburse her for these sessions. Today Christine brought in the insurance company forms and asked her social worker to complete them. The social worker, who was familiar with the requirements of this insurance company, realized right away that she would have to report a more "serious" diagnosis than was clinically indicated if she were to qualify the client for insurance reimbursement.

Under what circumstances is it ethical for a social worker to lie about a diagnosis? What are the potential risks for both the client and the social worker? What is the ethical thing to do if the only way the person will receive services is for the social worker to "fudge" the diagnosis?

Another problem with ethical implications occurs when using the DSM-IV scale/instrument, which attempts to codify available scientific information about mental disorders and specify objective criteria for diagnosis. It provides an atheoretical (theory-free) descriptive approach to the classification of mental disorders along five axes or dimensions. Axis III, for example, involves a medical decision on the physical condition of the individual client. Axis I is based on identifying a range of psychiatric conditions (including organic and neurological disorders). Whether social workers have the legal authority or sufficient psychiatric and medical knowledge to use DSM-IV and similar diagnostic instruments are questions that are important, but beyond the scope of this discussion (see Kutchins & Kirk, 1987).

Kirk and Kutchins (1988) studied a random sample of NASW's Register of Clinical Social Workers and found that, at that time, four out of five of the respondents used the DSM-III. Many indicated that they had questions or misgivings about using this instrument, but that they felt that they had no choice but to use it. Today the number and percentage using DSM-IV may be higher.

Most justify the practice of misdiagnosis because they think that it is harmless or in the client's best interest. Generally social workers use "the least noxious diagnosis" (also known as the mercy diagnosis). Reasons for deliberate misdiagnosis include the following:

1. It minimizes the communication of damaging and confidential information to nonsocial workers, especially to insurance companies and others.
2. It avoids the labeling effects of a more severe diagnosis.
3. It limits the adverse impact on a client's self-esteem if the client should become aware of the diagnosis.
4. It can protect the future employment prospects for the client as well as the potential for future insurance coverage.

The above reasons are used to justify underdiagnosis by suggesting that this is in the client's interest. Eighty-seven percent of respondents admit to deliberate underdiagnosis at some time. Most use the category adjustment disorders when a more serious diagnosis would have been more accurate. But 59 percent of respondents also report the use of overdiagnosis, that is, they report a more severe diagnosis than the actual diagnosis. They may use an Axis I diagnosis when this is not warranted in order to qualify a client for insurance reimbursement. Though claiming that overdiagnosis is done for the client's benefit, the real beneficiary may be the social worker whose payments are now guaranteed by a third party.

Misdiagnosis of any type is one result of managed care and third-party payers and their intrusion into the professional relationship. While managed care may provoke such responses in some cases, the misdiagnoses are caused by the social workers who do so. However, not all misdiagnoses are the result of a tactic to gain benefits for the client; some misdiagnoses are the result of practitioner incompetence, the ambiguity of some diagnostic categories, failure to consider biological and physical factors, or failure to ensure medical review when indicated. Competency in all aspects of the social worker's practice is an expected ethical norm.

Another ethical problem arises when a social worker reports a diagnosis for one individual when the primary problem is located in the family system. Since DSM-IV allows only the diagnosis of problems of an individual, this deliberate misdiagnosis is usually utilized to facilitate insurance reimbursement.

Even under the best of circumstances, social workers, like many other professionals, will make mistakes and err in their diagnosis. Mistakes are unfortunate and regrettable, but probably inevitable. Among the mistakes in diagnostics that have ethical implications are:

1. Lack of sufficient knowledge in using diagnostic instruments such as DSM-IV.
2. Poor professional judgment.
3. Deliberate misdiagnosis, often in connection with third-party insurance reimbursement claims and/or reimbursement by government programs.

Mistakes such as these may involve both illegal and unethical behaviors. Even though diagnosis and assessment are often viewed as professional techniques that are based solely on skill and knowledge, they always involve ethical considerations. Examine the following exemplar and consider the ethical aspects involved in arriving at a diagnosis.

➤ **10.3 Barry Has a Learning Problem**

Barry is a first-grader. He has two older brothers, ages eight and ten. His oldest brother is doing very well in school, but his middle brother has been identified as a "slow learner" and is in a special education class. Barry's teacher reports that Barry also has some learning problems and finds it difficult to keep up with the rest of his class.

The school social worker and the educational psychologist have been discussing what to do with Barry. His tests indicate a relatively low score but within the "normal" range. The social worker knows that Barry would benefit from special attention that his regular teacher cannot give him. However, sending Barry to an ungraded class might label him for the rest of his life.

In this situation, as in many others, the "simple" technical task of diagnosis has a number of ethical aspects that every thoughtful social worker must consider seriously before arriving at a decision.

OTHER ETHICAL ISSUES

Fitting Diagnosis to Treatment

An ethical problem occurs whenever a social worker tries to fit the diagnosis to the treatment she plans to use, rather than select a treatment that is appropriate for the identified problem. This ethical problem occurs in various guises. One such version is illustrated by the following exemplar.

➤ **10.4 Casework or Family Therapy**

The parents and adolescent children in the Martin family have been having their problems. There has been a series of incidents in which everyone involved has been shouting at each other, calling each other names, or not talking to each other for days.

Ms. Martin feels that she has failed as a mother. She has asked Ms. Aberdeen, a private social worker, to help her cope with her feelings. After talking with Ms. Martin, the worker felt that the problem went beyond Ms. Martin's feelings, and that family therapy was indicated. Even though Ms. Aberdeen is a competent caseworker, she has had no experience in providing family therapy. However, there are no family therapists in this rural county. Ms. Aberdeen, therefore, diagnoses the problem in such a way that casework intervention is appropriate.

Is it ethical for Ms. Aberdeen to define the problem in a way that makes it possible for her to help Ms. Martin? From an ethical point of view, would it make a difference if this situation had occurred in a city where there were a number of family therapists? There are other ethical aspects to this issue. Professional ethics demand that the intervention method be selected on the basis of the social worker's best professional judgment. Using other criteria may be unethical. For example, long-term therapy may be indicated for a given case, but social workers may be required to indicate short-term treatment to comply with the presumed preferences of a third-party payer. This may be done to maintain one's position on the insurer's professional panel of approved therapists. Kutchins and Kirk (1997) suggest that clinicians routinely try to fit their clinical diagnoses to the complexities of DSM and to the requirements of managed care corporations. They refer to this as "an ethically challenged game of cat and mouse among therapists, clients, and payers" (p. 256).

Social workers in both private and agency-sponsored practice often have to utilize the DSM-IV. Kutchins and Kirk (1997) raise additional questions about the ethics of its use. According to these authors, DSM "sweeps increasing numbers of human problems into the realm of psychiatric disorder and medical jurisdiction" (p. 16) on the basis of fragile scientific evidence, political advocacy, and pathologizing "those in our society who are undesirable and powerless" (p. 16). No claim is made that DSM is a valid classification system and, according to these authors, evidence is lacking for reliability claims.

There is another ethical conundrum for social workers related to DSM use. The use of DSM requires a medicalization of human or social situations. Trouble at school becomes oppositional defiant behavior. Other human problems are translated into medical and stigmatizing terms such as not sleeping (major depressive disorder), bearing grudges (paranoid personality disorder), and others. Developed under a grant from the National Association of Social Workers, the PIE (person-in-environment) system describes, classifies, and codes the problems of clients. But, it does so in such a way that it clarifies aspects of the client's problems that are in the domain of social work and facilitates work with clients (Karis & Wandrei, 1992). Is the use of DSM-IV instead of PIE ethical? Does the NASW *Code* provide guidance on these issues? Or, are these simply practical issues for those engaged in private practice? Is this an issue of pragmatism that requires an advocacy agenda by the profession of social work, or patience until the reimbursement system is less oriented toward the disease and medical model?

Supervision and Consultation

While social workers hold various views about the need for traditional supervision, there is a general consensus that an ethical social worker does not practice without availing herself of consultation. But consultation costs money; skipping supervision may be one way to "cut corners" in private or agency practice. Does the NASW *Code*, 1996 (2.05a,b,c), suggest implications for private practitioners?

Misrepresentation

The NASW *Code of Ethics* specifically states: "Social workers should ensure that their representations to clients, agencies, and the public of professional qualification, credentials, education, competence, affiliations, services provided, or results to be achieved are accurate" (NASW, 1996, 4.06c). What seems like a simple ethical rule gives rise to a number of questions, including the following:

1. Is it ethical for a social worker to identify herself as something other than a social worker (such as a marriage counselor or psychotherapist)?

2. Is it ethical for a social worker to call herself "Doctor" when she has not yet earned this degree?

3. Must a student social worker always identify herself as a student in field instruction placements? Or can she present herself as "your social worker"?

Those who engage in one of these practices claim that they do so to give clients greater confidence in their worker and thus increase the chances for a successful outcome. But is this ethical?

Promises

Reamer (1995) studied 634 malpractice claims against social workers filed between 1969 and 1990, a period in which malpractice claims were increasingly frequent. The largest percentage filed were for incorrect treatment, including failure to introduce appropriate therapeutic interventions or to apply treatment techniques appropriately.

Myers and Thyer (1997) argue that social work clients have a right to receive effective, empirically validated treatment. The *Code of Ethics*, they suggest, should place an emphasis on the client's right to effective treatment but currently only requires a social worker to "strive to become and remain proficient in professional practice and the performance of professional functions" (NASW *Code*, 1996, 4.01b). Myers and Thyer call on NASW to include in the *Code* requirements (1) that encourage ever more responsible professional behavior by social workers and (2) that empirically proven interventions become the *first* treatment choices by practitioners. Reflecting this point of view, Howard and Jenson (1999) advocate for guidelines to direct practice in the most effective and proven ways, faulting the professional association for failing to implement practice guidelines. Others argue that solving human problems through the use of an "approved list" of techniques would violate the richness and dignity of human struggles and triumphs. Social workers "deal with enormously complex and difficult issues. To do this well, they must be analytical, reflective, and compassionate in their approach to human suffering. They must recognize that they often know very little about the lives of those they serve and that therefore, they must listen and learn from them" (Witkin, 1998, pp. 79–80).

Does the *Code* provide guidance for a social worker in regard to the promise to be helpful in regard to the presenting problem? Are both of the two perspectives (guidelines regarding effective practice, including interventive choices, should be empirically proven when possible *or* complexity of life situations argues against practice guidelines) presented above ethically correct? In an attempt to convince potential clients to enter treatment, a social worker may claim (promise) that she can help the client (perhaps even obtain a cure), when she only hopes that she can do so. Is this ethical? What do you think?

EXERCISES

1. Some social workers have argued against the use of diagnosis, but most believe that diagnosis is an essential and necessary step in the treatment process. Have every student in the class select a partner. In each group of two, have one student role-play the pro diagnosis position and the other, the antidiagnosis position. Try to convince each other of the ethical problems that the other's position causes.
2. Consider the case of Barry (Exemplar 10.3). What ethical aspects does this case present? How would you resolve them? Use the ethical decision screens to answer these questions.
3. Did Ms. Aberdeen, the social worker of Ms. Martin (Exemplar 10.4), conduct herself in an ethical way? What other options could she have employed?
4. Consider the ethical questions raised in the Misrepresentation section of this chapter. Instead of simply saying that such behavior is unethical or ethical, note arguments that may be offered by a social worker who does present herself in one of these ways. Then answer these arguments.

SUGGESTIONS FOR ADDITIONAL READINGS

Kutchins and Kirk (1995, 1997) critically examine the utility, scientific evidence, and ethical and other problems related to the use of DSM-IV. A reasoned condemnation of client dumping by private practice practitioners can be found in an editorial in the *Journal of Independent Social Work*, written by the editor and one of the leading academic experts on private practice (Barker, 1988a). Myers and Thyer (1997) advocate that the NASW *Code* include a standard that requires empirically proven interventions to become the first intervention choice by practitioners. Howard and Jenson (1999) argue that formal guidelines for practice should be formed and that the use of guidelines be included as a provision in the *Code*.

11. Changing World/ Changing Problems

DOMESTIC VIOLENCE

Domestic violence is sometimes referred to as partner abuse, spousal assault, or spouse abuse. We use the term to refer to violence between adults who are intimates, regardless of their marital status, living arrangements, or sexual orientations. Domestic violence comes in several forms: physical, sexual, psychological, economic, social isolation, stalking, and coercive control (Austin & Dankwort, 1999). Females are more often the targets of violence. There are estimates that nonfatal assaults occur in one of every six American homes, with 2 million females severely injured annually. Almost 9 percent of homicides in the United States are spousal homicides (Lystad, Rice, & Kaplan, 1996).

The *Tarasoff* principle referred to in Chapter 4 requires social workers to inform those who are the targets of potential violence. But this guideline can lead to an ethical quandary in the case of women who are HIV+. Many women who are HIV+ became so through transmission by intravenous drug use and sexual contact with persons infected with the virus. From a public health perspective, the general assumption is that it makes sense for the patient to notify her sexual partners of her HIV+ status in order to protect uninfected partners from future infection, and to inform those persons who have already been exposed so they may be tested and—if positive—seek appropriate medical care.

Promoting the use of condoms is the main strategy for reducing risk of sexual transmission and is also linked to increased risk of violence. Many women are at risk of harm from their partners if the partners are informed of their HIV⁺ status. They can be injured or abandoned. Is the ethical action to promote the public health strategy by informing those involved and promoting condom use? Furthermore, which is more ethical: to attempt to get the female to warn her partner, which risks her being abused, or not to warn her partner, which risks his illness (North, 1993)?

Over two-thirds of clients in family therapy clinics engage in some form of physical violence against their partners within the year prior to the initiation of therapy. Family therapists are aware of only a small proportion of these cases. One study by the American Association of Marriage and Family Therapy members found that 60 percent did not consider family violence to be a significant clinical problem in their practice. Another study in a family therapy clinic found that more than half of all cases involving physical violence are not detected during routine interviews (Aldarondo & Straus, 1994).

Physical violence hinders therapy and harms the quality of family life and welfare of clients. Even minor violence can escalate. The choice of treatment depends on whether violence is present in the relationship. The most important reasons given for not knowing of violence in relationships were simply not asking, using unclear language, and not asking both partners specifically and separately. There are instruments developed to obtain information about violence, such as the Conflict Tactics Scale (Aldarondo & Straus, 1994). Given the prevalence of domestic violence, is it ethical for a family social worker not to ask all couples who come for help about it? What if the social worker believes her relationship with the couple prohibits such interference early in the treatment process?

Studies on the efficacy of conjoint (couple) therapy for intimate partner violence confirm that therapy results in temporary decreases in violence, but there is generally no long-term cessation following termination (Jory, Anderson, & Greer, 1997). Since many agencies are understaffed, frequently have waiting lists, and are preoccupied with those who are in treatment, is it ethical for an agency serving those involved in domestic violence not to provide frequent follow-up to persons, including those who successfully completed treatment? What if to do so means that some on the waiting list will not be seen at all?

There are other dilemmas that face social workers dealing with domestic violence. Consider the following exemplar.

➤ **11.1 Ambiguity and Predicting Violence**

Wrangley Basemore is being considered by the treatment team for discharge from a psychiatric facility. He has a history of violence prior to hospitalization—verbal and infrequent physical assaults—but in the hospital he has done neither. His wife has begun divorce proceedings against him and he has mumbled some comments that seem to convey mild threats but has done nothing overt. The situation is ambiguous and one is supposed to respect his confidentiality, but Mrs. Basemore needs protection also. If there were clear threats, you—as a social worker—could inform Mrs. Basemore. Under these unclear circumstances, should you? Does the NASW *Code of Ethics* or the discussion in Chapter 4 on Duty to Warn provide any guidance?

From the perspective of assessment and treatment models, there are other issues with ethical dimensions that confront a social worker dealing with domestic violence situations. There are hundreds of diverse therapies used in practice that have not been subjected to scientific scrutiny. Iatrogenic effects (negative effects induced by the treatment) do occur as a result of couples consulting therapists. If the prescription, strength, frequency, and duration of required treatment are unknown, under what circumstances is treatment ethical? Should informed consent by clients include information about what is unknown in regard to treatment? The NASW *Code* (1996, 1.03a) states that the social worker should "inform clients of the purpose of the services, the risks related to the services," and "limits to services because of the requirements of a third-party payer . . . ." But the *Code* does not require the social worker to explain the limits of the treatment models to be used. Wilson, Alexander, & Turner (1996) raise additional questions. The ways in which family therapy works are unknown. Family therapists "know" that family therapy works but do not know how it works. How then do family therapists know if the outcome of the therapy is negative or positive?

MANAGED CARE AND MENTAL HEALTH

Since the early 1980s, health care costs have escalated beyond the rate of inflation. In the 1990s, approximately 15 percent of the gross domestic product was being spent on health care. As a result, there has been an increasing demand to control expenditures and to utilize managed health and mental health care systems wherever possible (Davis, 1997).

Managed care is one major strategy developed in an attempt to control health and mental health costs by monitoring access to, and the type of, health care patients receive from health care practitioners or health maintenance organizations (HMOs). Costs are reduced by placing controls on health practitioners and by fostering competition among HMOs. Managed care plans attempt to reduce these costs through controlling the type of health practitioners utilized, limiting access to service, and prescribing the type and length of service provided.

Practitioners from several disciplines have objected to the ways in which cost-conscious managed care plans are limiting patient service. Some have even argued that managed care is unethical (Strom-Gottfried, 1998b). The professional autonomy of practitioners is threatened by the controls exerted by the managed care organization. There is concern that practitioners are selected not because of their excellence but because they are willing to accept lower fees and more controls over their practice. They agree to these limitations, it is argued, in exchange for an assurance of a high volume of patients and guaranteed payments. Those not selected fear the loss of income. Further, there is concern that the various controls instituted will result in poorer-quality service and less ability by practitioners to provide what they consider to be high-quality professional service. Social workers are forced to choose between giving priority to needs of the client and the interests of the insurer and/or society. On the other hand it must be remembered that clients will not receive any services unless health care organizations remain viable.

Managed care not only has an impact on professional persons in private solo or group practice but also on social agencies as these become ever more dependent on third-party payments. Carpenter and Platt (1997) found that managed care produced a greater sense of strain between personal and professional values among social workers in agency settings than it did social workers in private practice. The impact of managed care creates a number of ethical dilemmas for social work practitioners, whether in private or agency-based practice. Among the ethical dilemmas arising from managed care are those concerning confidentiality and informed consent (see Chapter 4 for discussion of these two issues), duty to assist and access, honesty, participation in treatment decisions, quality of care, and professional autonomy. Finally, the mission of social work and the mission of managed care organizations are often in conflict. Social workers are committed to service, and managed care organizations, although committed to service, have a mission of remaining financially viable.

The *Code of Ethics* has at least *eight* standards that are of special relevance in these situations. (1) "Social workers should use clear and understandable language to inform clients of the purpose of the services, risks related to the services, limits to services because of the requirements of a third-party payer, relevant costs, reasonable alternatives, clients' right to refuse or withdraw consent, and the time frame covered by the consent . . ." (NASW, 1996, 1.03a). (2) "Social workers should obtain clients' informed consent before audiotaping or videotaping clients or permitting observation of clients by a third party" (1.03f). (3) "Social workers should protect the confidentiality of all information obtained in the course of professional service, except for compelling professional reasons" (1.07c). (4) "Social workers should not disclose confidential information to third-party payers unless clients have authorized such disclosure" (1.07h). (5) "Social workers should take precautions to ensure and maintain the confidentiality of information transmitted to other parties through the use of computers, electronic mail, facsimile machines, telephones and telephone answering machines, and other electronic or computer technology. Disclosure of identifying information should be avoided whenever possible" (1.07m). (6) "Social workers should terminate services to clients and professional relationships with them when such services and relationships are no longer required or no longer serve the clients' needs or interests" (1.16a). (7) "Social workers should take reasonable steps to avoid abandoning clients who are still in need of services" (1.16b). (8) "Social workers should not participate in, condone, or be associated with dishonesty, fraud, or deception" (4.04).

Managed care programs may place the social worker in situations in which their compliance with standard 4.04 may become questionable. For example, in order to provide a "reimbursable service" for a client, the practitioner may have to consider fudging the diagnosis in some way, as was discussed in Chapter 10.

Certain ethical dilemmas arise from the requirement to continue treatment if it is needed (NASW, 1996, 1.16b) or terminate treatment once it is no longer needed (NASW, 1.16a). In a hospital setting, the managed care provider might declare that the patient should be released at the end of two weeks or a patient has no insurance coverage and cannot afford hospitalization. Because social workers do not have primary roles in the medical setting, is a social worker limited to advocacy alone or are there other roles and interventions that can be undertaken?

➤ **11.2 Suicide Threat and Managed Care Says No Hospitalization**

You have been treating Ms. Adele Lang, a 24-year-old college student who has been seriously depressed because of school failures and difficulties with her family. She has been threatening suicide and, in your professional judgment, should be hospitalized. However, the third-party provider does not agree that she should be hospitalized. You are told that the decision to refuse hospitalization is based on recent research findings.

Since the cost of hospital care is great, the payer prefers any other type of in-patient treatment. Who will be responsible for the decision not to hospitalize this suicidal patient and for what happens to Ms. Lang? A court case found that "clinicians remain ultimately responsible for decisions affecting patients" (Strom, 1992, p. 401). Social workers are bound by the *Code of Ethics* to practice with the maximum application of professional skill and competence. Under the circumstances, the social worker could agree and seek an alternative treatment, which may be less effective, but better than the alternative of no treatment. On the other hand, the social worker has a responsibility to practice consistently with her best professional judgment and to give priority to her client's welfare. Finally, the social worker needs to recognize that she is the person who will be responsible if any harm comes to her client. She may even be liable to malpractice damages.

Similarly, social workers have been confronted with pressures from managed care organizations to provide more group therapy for their clients because group service is time- and cost-efficient. The insurance companies stress that outpatient services in time-limited groups have been found to be very effective. For example, persons with panic disorder who received cognitive-behavioral group therapy in addition to medication "had lower posttest anxiety scores than those who received medication alone" (Mitchell, 1999, p. 188). It has also been found that, when clients were allowed to choose between individual and group treatment in a managed care setting, they were equally satisfied with the two types of treatment and perceived the clinicians as equally empathetic (Mitchell, 1998).

Practitioners may also be tempted to agree because group treatment can result in greater income—even when professional judgment counterindicates this mode of treatment. Here the social worker faces another ethical dilemma: how to juggle the demands of her own professional judgments, of the insurance company, and of her desire for economic security. This dilemma is not limited to workers in private practice, but occurs also in agency practice, as the following exemplar shows.

➤ **11.3 What the Pine Tree Insurance Company Wants**

Dr. Felicia Montivedeo, director of social work clinical services for Family and Children's Services of Pleasant City, was surprised when she received a letter from the Pine Tree Insurance Company (Managed Care Division) and later a phone call, both of which subtly suggested that more of the agency's treatment services be offered in time-limited groups. When she raised the issue with the agency's administrative executive committee, some argued in favor of complying because the money received from the insurance company made up a substantial part of the agency's income. Others were concerned that such a change in operating procedures would upset the staff. Still others argued that compliance would mean yielding their professional judgment to the Pine Tree Insurance Company.

Among the options suggested by committee members are the following: (1) to ignore the suggestion because it had not been explicitly stated; (2) to comply as soon as possible with the suggestion; (3) to refuse to comply and to begin to advocate with Pine Tree Insurance for the current mix of service modalities; (4) to begin research as to the relative effectiveness of various treatment methods; and (5) to meet with Pine Tree representatives to explore ways to slowly phase in more group treatment. What are the ethical implications of each option?

Other ethical issues related to the financial concerns of managed care have focused on the provision of services to African Americans and other historically medically underserved groups. Davis (1997) discusses the need to ensure the availability of culturally competent standards of care and diagnostic and treatment services. In addition, managed care organizations need to provide accessible services "located within reasonable geographic distance to Black neighborhoods" (Davis, 1997, p. 636). What should the social worker do in the following situation?

➤ **11.4 Where Are the Services?**

Ms. Anita Dee is a social worker in a state psychiatric hospital that primarily serves low-income people of color. The Medicaid recipients are served through a managed care system that is privately operated. Generally, administrators and supervisors in the public hospital seek harmonious relationships with the managed care organization, which is located in another state. Ms. Dee recently realized that when chronically ill psychiatric patients are discharged, the managed care company refers them to outpatient sites that are seldom near where they reside; transportation to the treatment sites is not provided. Consequently, the discharged persons are not receiving the help they need.

TECHNOLOGY

Social work, like many other professions, has been affected by the impact of the computer and other modern technologies. Many persons, including social workers, hold the belief that things, unlike people, are value-free. However, technology exists within a human context; it reflects and shapes human choices. Human choices go beyond questions of technological feasibility and efficiency, since they always involve value choices and ethical priorities.

At first, social workers were concerned that the introduction of information technologies into social agencies and social work practice would result in more critical ethical dilemmas because these technologies were thought to be insensitive to variations in human needs and individual differential values and cultures. Additional problems were expected in the areas of confidentiality and of protecting the ownership of personal data (Fodor, 1999). It was believed that it would be more difficult to protect information from inappropriate prying and from inappropriate control.

One study of 48 microcomputer-using private nonprofit agencies in North Carolina found that three-fourths of the agencies maintained computerized client data. The agencies in the study successfully transferred appropriate confidentiality safeguards from paper records to electronic records. No agency in this study reported that clients reviewed records for accuracy. Nor is there any indication that clients were aware that at times this information is shared with others (Finn, 1990).

As coordinating agencies, grant-funding agencies, third-party payers, and others seek to obtain detailed data that can be obtained easily from computerized data banks, improved methods for guaranteeing the confidentiality of records will be needed (Davidson & Davidson, 1996). When multiple agencies become linked in networks in order to promote collaborative case management, new problems arise. Is client permission needed for one agency/worker to share or receive the information held by another agency about a common client? To what extent can agencies successfully limit the client data they have computerized, and how can clients actually be sufficiently informed so as to be able to limit the information transferred to another agency? Another question is whether clients or patients understand the realities of the information networks to which agencies and their personal records are tied. To whom do these data belong? How can clients be assured privacy? (Relevant sections of the *Code of Ethics* (1996) are discussed in Chapter 4.) These problems are not entirely new and they also occurred in the pre-computer era. However, the ease and quickness of information transfer make these ethical issues ever more critical in social work practice.

Caputo (1991) set forth an ethical framework for information systems, which asserts the primacy of clients as citizens. The ethical framework fulfills the following functions:

1. It provides a way to inform clients about the existence of a computerized client-information system;
2. It enables clients to give an informed consent in regard to the uses of information about themselves;
3. It offers an opportunity for individuals to inspect, correct, or add information about themselves, allowing them to expunge all or parts of their records, except where such records are legally required;
4. It develops an information-needs matrix to guide unit allocation decisions on the basis of critical success factors; and

5. It holds professionals to a professional practice that is mindful of ethical standards, including respect for clients' autonomy, their right to information and privacy, the need to weigh the efficacy of demands for efficiency against the principle of human dignity, and adherence to confidentiality regarding the use of routinely collected information about clients.

Clearly, the ethical issues around the use of information technology extend beyond the early concerns for protecting confidentiality. In recent years, additional technologies have entered the practice arena; many of them have resulted in new ethical dilemmas. These may occur when social workers practice in situations that use genetic counseling; psychotropic medications; various forms of blood, alcohol, and drug testing; DNA tests; various contraceptive, fertility, and abortion means; life-support systems, and other technologies.

Other ethical issues arise out of still newer developments. We are already beginning to see the impact of "secondwave" information technologies on practice (Cwikel & Cnaan, 1991). Among these are data bases that can be used for screening and assessment; the selection of practice and service recommendations; expert systems for evaluating various risks such as foster care, parole, and suicide; and interactive treatment games and various forms of therapy. Conceptual models for the use of technology-based groups have recently become available (Schopler, Abell, & Galinsky, 1998). Galinsky, Schopler, and Abell (1997) surveyed group practitioners about their use of technology. The 213 respondents had limited knowledge of and experience with telephone groups: 29 percent had read about, 1 percent had training in, 13 percent were members of, and 7 percent were leaders of. The respondents were slightly less knowledgeable about and experienced with computer groups: 20 percent had read about, 2 percent had training in, 6 percent were members of, and 3 percent were leaders of. Respondents identified several benefits of using these technologies, including "increased accessibility, convenience, and anonymity" (Galinsky et al., 1997, p. 181).

Among the ethical dilemmas that have developed as a result of these are questions of beneficence (autonomy versus paternalism), equity of access to scarce resources (ensuring equality of opportunity), and the promotion of the common good (ensuring that the maximum number of individuals benefit from the introduction of information technology). The assumption of many advanced software and expert systems is that there is always one "right" decision that should be followed. As a result, problems concerning client autonomy and worker flexibility have become more critical. How is it possible for the worker simultaneously to defend the autonomy of the client, meet the expectations of the agency, and avoid paternalism and control of clients?

The introduction of information systems into social agencies with very tight budgets means that scarce resources must be deployed to pay for the new technology and for staff with specific expertise even while other agency programs and client supports will be reduced or eliminated. Work patterns and organizational structure will change and some resources will not be available for some kinds of client services.

Consider the common dilemma that confronts the social worker in the exemplar described below.

➤ 11.5 Computerized Information System or Services for Teens?

Miri Neidig is a member of the board of directors of a Neighborhood Service Center that provides counseling and other services, including services for low-income minority teens at a local shopping mall. This service has recently been instituted and is highly valued by community members concerned about sexually transmitted diseases and by teenagers because of the privacy afforded by the location and the likeable staff. The local United Way has been pressuring the agency to computerize its operation and has provided funds specifically for this purpose. Other funding agencies have also been pressuring the agency to implement a computerized information system. However, now the funding situation has become precarious and expenses must be reduced. The board will meet tonight to review the agency budget; the budget committee indicates that they will have to choose between eliminating services for teens at the mall or discontinuing the computerization program.

Ms. Neidig, a social worker and board member, is faced with a difficult choice. If she votes in favor of continuing services for teenagers, she will deny the agency the possibility of attaining more resources from the funding agency. If she votes for computerization, she denies the community and teens services that they desperately need. How is she to choose? Do the ethical assessment screen (Figure 3.2) and ethical principles screen (Figure 3.4) help her decide what to do when faced with this ethical dilemma?

The increasing use of electronic mail makes available unsought information that may confront a practitioner with critical ethical dilemmas. Note the following exemplar.

➤ 11.6 E-mail from Europe and Suicidal Thoughts

A university student used an electronic mail discussion group to inquire about a drug that could be used for a painless suicide. A professor in Europe who read this request communicated his concern to the sender's university, which forwarded this message to the university's counseling department. The counselor assigned to this case decided to obtain more information before deciding what to do. She contacted the director of the Computer Center, who broke into the student's account where additional messages on suicide were discovered. At this point, the counselor decided to contact the student's parents. (This situation was described on a Social Work electronic discussion list and is used with permission of Steve Marson of Pembroke University. The counselor was not a social worker.)

This exemplar has been presented because it reflects the rapidly expanding use of electronic mail and because it raises some issues that social workers must consider. One issue facing the counselor is whether to act on the basis of third-party information from someone unknown to her. Because the situation was potentially life threatening, this counselor decided to take the information conveyed by the third party seriously, but she also wanted to obtain verification of the facts, if possible. Here the worker decided that intervention was justified. But, more generally, questions can be raised regarding the circumstances under which a social worker should seek entry into a confidential electronic file. Is there any issue short of life-threatening situations that might support such an action? Under what circumstances does the Computer Center or a social agency have a right to examine someone's personal computer account? What should the counselor have done if the Computer Center (or agency) stated such an invasion was illegal or against the rules? Although the counselor felt justified in asking the Computer Center for verification because of the potential life-threatening nature of the situation, was it ethical for her to enter the student's computer account without obtaining his permission?

Because the student is at the university and the counselor is a university employee, she has some responsibility for his welfare, especially after she gained information about what was in his file. What should she have done if the student's account did not include life-threatening materials?

We do not know the counselor's reasons for contacting the student's parents rather than the student himself. Is telling the parents about their son's behavior an improper invasion of the student's right to privacy and confidentiality? What should the counselor do if, instead of contacting the student's parents, she spoke to the student, and he simply stated that he has an intellectual interest in painless suicide as a chemical problem? Which standards in the *Code of Ethics* provide guidance in this type of situation?

GENETICS

Ethical dilemmas confront social workers as a result of electronic technologies, but those who practice in health settings are more and more compelled also to deal with ethical dilemmas that arise from medical and scientific technologies. Researchers, including those at the National Center for Genome Research of the National Institutes of Health, are decoding the human blueprint. For example, it is now possible to detect a person's susceptibility for the development of certain cancers and other diseases, including breast and ovarian cancers.

The results of genetic testing are based on probability, and those involved with testing and genetic counseling express concerns that people will take irrevocable actions or make decisions based on hope or fear and not facts. Freedman (1998) studied those seeking susceptibility testing through participant observation of counseling sessions and in-depth interviews of women who sought susceptibility testing. The vast majority of those who request such testing are white, middle class, educated, and not deprived economically.

Genetic susceptibility testing is a family event. Multigenerational information is learned with implications for one's past (family of origin), present, and future health possibilities and status. If one is tested—for example—for breast or ovarian cancer, there are several possibilities. (1) If an altered gene is found, the person can be at increased probability risk of developing cancer; (2) the results might not reveal susceptibility because no altered gene is found or the test was inaccurate; or (3) the gene that causes the cancer is not yet known. A negative result does not necessarily mean the person will not eventually develop cancer. It may be that the specific gene mutation was not found. In this case, the person tested has the same risk for developing cancer as the general population.

Some of the persons who have susceptibility testing done feel guilt and concern about the children they have reared. Some also want to bring their children for testing. In these cases, there is a potential for conflict because the child—who may be a young adult—may not wish to be tested but to live without the burden of the potential knowledge.

Some ethical issues regarding susceptibility testing relate to confidentiality and privacy. Can the information learned be kept confidential and private? What rights do family members or significant others have to the information learned through the testing? To what use will employers and insurance companies put the information? What are the potential future liabilities for social workers? After all, pledges of privacy in adoptions have been overturned through new legislation.

Dilemmas of a socioeconomic character also arise. Those who are middle class or wealthy can benefit more because they have the economic means to take advantage of medical and other care that can arise from the new knowledge. Others may risk more when they learn test results. Poor persons may be at greater risk where money matters play a part in decision making.

An ethical dilemma occurs when relatives want access to genetic information that may be of importance to their health or to the future of their children. What ethical issues does the following request by Roberta Jackson pose?

➤ **11.7 The Dilemma of Huntington's Disease**

Roberta Jackson is eager to have a baby and has just asked you as her social worker not to tell her husband or family members that she has a genetic marker that identifies her as a carrier of Huntington's disease, a disease for which there is no cure but which will not show up until 20 to 30 years from now when she hopes a cure will have been discovered. This is an inherited condition that potentially affects all family members and inflicts premature senility on those affected. She is afraid that her husband will not be willing to have a child if he knows about her genetic condition. When the welfare of other people is at risk, does their right to such information take precedence over your client's right to privacy?

Confidentiality is only one of the several ethical issues present in this situation. There are others. What is the best interest of the as-yet-unborn child? And who is the person or are the persons entitled to make such decisions? What are the religious implications for all concerned (if any) of playing God? Who speaks for the fetus? What are the statistical relationships between a genetic marker and the actual occurrence of the genetic defect, and what bearing do they have on making a decision? Does Ms. Jackson's husband have a right to know and make *his* decision on the basis of complete information? What is society's best interest in this situation?

The social worker in the exemplar above has to consider several ethical issues, including client self-determination and protection of human life, confidentiality and privacy and who has a right to information, honesty, and priorities of values. A social worker involved with susceptibility testing also will face such dilemmas. In some susceptibility test facilities, the staff—including social workers—concerned that employers and insurance companies will misuse the information gained through the testing, create "shadow charts." These charts contain correct information (record of counseling, family history, clinical exams, and the test results of genetic tests) but are kept separate from official charts. Is this a correct ethical choice when the social workers cannot assure their case records will be confidential and secure?

END-OF-LIFE DECISIONS

In 1993, the NASW Delegate Assembly approved a new policy statement on "Client Self-determination in End-of-Life Decisions." Social workers have been involved in the clarification of the legal, ethical, and other issues and policies concerning the conditions under which life may be ended, but this was the first time that NASW issued a policy statement to guide social workers. NASW's position was based on the principle that client self-determination should apply to all aspects of life and death.

The policy statement contains the following ideas:

- The social work profession strives to enhance the quality of life; to encourage the exploration of life options; and to advocate for access to options, including providing all information to make appropriate choices.
- Social workers have an important role in helping individuals identify the end-of-life options available to them.
- Competent individuals should have the opportunity to make their own choices but only after being informed of all options and consequences. Choices should be made without coercion.
- Social workers should not promote any particular means to end one's life but should be open to full discussion of the issues and care options.
- Social workers should be free to participate or not participate in assisted-suicide matters or other discussions concerning end-of-life decisions depending on their own beliefs, attitudes, and value systems. If a social worker is unable to help with decisions about assisted suicide or other end-of-life choices, he or she has a professional obligation to refer patients and their families to competent professionals who are available to address end-of-life issues.
- It is inappropriate for social workers to deliver, supply, or personally participate in the commission of an act of assisted suicide when acting in their professional role.
- If legally permissible, it is not inappropriate for a social worker to be present during an assisted suicide if the client requests the social worker's presence.
- The involvement of social workers in assisted suicide cases should not depend on race or ethnicity, religion, age, gender, economic factors, sexual orientation, or disability.

Though NASW's policy statement is based on the principle of self-determination, many doubt whether meaningful self-determination and voluntary consent prevail in situations in which a person wishes to harm himself or commit suicide because "only abysmal ignorance or deep emotional trauma can lead persons to extreme measures like these" (Gewirth, 1978, p. 264).

The policy statement raises many questions, among which are the following: Whose quality of life is supported by assisted suicide? Whose life is harmed? What is competence in such a situation? How does one judge competency? Is coercion entirely absent when people are considering suicide? What should one do if the option chosen creates issues for other family members, significant others, friends, other professionals? What should one do if there are conflicts among those involved—some wanting to maintain life at all costs, others supporting the person's decision? What does it mean to be present but not participate? Is this just another form of approval of the act?

The definition of terminal illness is not always clear. Sometimes even the best of practitioners makes a mistake, and persons judged to be terminally ill live beyond the projected time. Can "comfort care" and the control of pain offset the desire to end one's life? Sometimes "lethal doses" of medications prove not to be lethal, adding to the agony of the patient.

If you look at Figure 3.4, the ethical principles screen, the principles of autonomy and freedom as well as quality of life are listed below the principle of protection of life. Was NASW correct in approving such a policy? Or should it have opened the discussion to a more extensive exploration of the issues, including ethical issues integral to the policy? What would you do? Would you base your decision on your personal values, the *Code of Ethics*, the ethical principles screen, or the NASW policy statement?

EXERCISES

1. In a group, discuss the ways in which technologies present ethical dilemmas for your agencies and for social workers. Identify ways in which these ethical dilemmas could be avoided and/or dealt with ethically.

2. You are on a committee to consider the fate of a severely disabled infant whose survival is questionable. Identify standards in the *Code of Ethics* that help you to weigh the welfare of the parents versus the welfare of the child.

3. You are serving on the committee in Exemplar 11.3, "What the Pine Tree Insurance Company Wants." Which of the options sug-

gested by committee members would you choose? What standards in the *Code of Ethics* support your choice?

4. If you were confronted as a social worker with the issue of assisted suicide, what would be your position? What justification would you provide for your decision?

5. A claim has been made that the mission of social work is the attainment of social justice, and that mental health services are outside the social worker's realm (Wakefield, 1988). Are the only goods associated with social justice economic and social goods? Is providing help for internal psychological states that are impediments to attaining economic and social goods connected to the ethical commitment to social justice? Is the search for meaning and self-respect through social worker services contributory to social justice (Dean, 1998)? Would it be unethical for social workers to desist from delivering mental health services?

SUGGESTIONS FOR ADDITIONAL READINGS

Rubin, Cardena et al. (1998) in "Outdated Practitioner Views about Family Culpability and Severe Mental Disorders" present findings of a study that illustrate how concepts influence practice models, in this case in questionable ways. Hughes (1993a, b) presents a guiding ethical paradigm for use in child welfare settings in relation to catastrophically ill newborns. Social Work Speaks (NASW, 1994a) includes "Client Self-Determination in End-of-Life Decisions," the NASW policy statement on this issue. Callahan (1994) presents arguments in opposition to the NASW policy position on end-of-life decisions.

12. Social Work with Selected Client Groups

THE ILL

Changes in health care that result from new technologies, new disease entities, and reorganization of the health care system cause social workers to face difficult ethical choices. The following situations illustrate some of the difficult ethical choices that confront health care social workers employed in these services.

➤ **12.1 To Treat or Not to Treat—At What Costs?**

Jorge Gaudi, an HIV-positive person, has contracted a strain of TB that is virulent and drug-resistant. He is extremely infectious. If he is successfully treated, he will no longer be able to infect others and his life will be extended. Successful treatment depends on his consistent compliance with the treatment regimen, but he does not comply with his treatment regimen while in the hospital and wanders the hallways where he "bothers" staff and others. He has had to be restrained. He is homeless, lacks family support, and is drug-addicted. Any possible cure depends on his complying with a difficult regimen, which is unlikely in his current life pattern.

The patient's inability to comply with the demands of treatment create a number of ethical dilemmas for the health team. When the team meets they discuss his situation, including what should be done following discharge so the social worker can begin preparations. Among the options are to (1) arrange a special comprehensive discharge plan that will require coordination among many agencies and persons and motivate Mr. Gaudi through special incentives for compliance—that is, provide housing, drug treatment, and psychiatric treatment *while others wait* for such resources; (2) provide monetary incentives, and pay him to comply; (3) involuntarily confine him and/or let him live in the community but put him on directly observed therapy, having him and all others in a similar situation mandatorily observed while taking their medications, but this is not done for middle-class patients with similar problems; (4) discharge him and leave him to make his own decisions; and (5) provide a specialized foster home placement.

He is drug-addicted, homeless, and will never regain full health. Is it ethical to single out poor and minority persons for confinement and mandatory programs? Is it fair to deprive other hospital patients of resources they need in order to help Mr. Gaudi? Which is the higher priority? If you were the social work member of the hospital team considering what to do, what would you suggest? Why?

Technological advances in neonatology have made it possible to sustain the lives of many newborn infants who in the past would not have survived. But survival for some will mean chronic disabilities, perhaps lifelong institutionalization; keeping some extremely low birth weight infants alive raises questions about the immediate and future quality of life of the child, the parents, and other family members.

There are three ethical issues that are generally involved in these situations: the welfare of the parents versus the welfare of the child; the freedom of choice of the parents versus the rights of the child; and the costs to society versus the life of the child. Embedded in these issues is one background issue: Under what circumstances should extraordinary actions be taken to enable the birth of a live fetus or to sustain a newborn child with multiple life-threatening problems?

➤ **12.2 One Baby and Two Parents Who Want Guidance**

Dr. Jane Newhouse just informed Mr. and Mrs. Lanier that their newborn son has kidney failure, gastrointestinal obstructions, brain damage, and recurrent seizures. A bowel operation, dialysis, and a kidney transplant will be needed. Dr. Newhouse was extremely pessimistic about the immediate survival possibilities and even more certain that if the infant lives, he will face survival crisis after survival crisis. The ultimate prognosis will be a child who will require institutionalization very early in life. Mr. and Mrs. Lanier, who must authorize any surgery, ask to meet with you, their social worker, because they trust you.

> Mr. and Mrs. Lanier ask you to confirm that their infant is hopelessly ill, and they tell you that they do not have funds—estimated at $200,000—to save the life of the infant by taking extraordinary measures, nor funds to support the infant at home if he leaves the hospital. They are confused, anxious, and unsure what they should do.

How should you respond when the Laniers ask your advice? (1) Should you tell them that, for many health conditions, it is very difficult to predict with any certainty what will occur in the future but that Dr. Newhouse was very clear about the prognosis? You can encourage them to stop treatment. (2) Should you tell them that miracles do happen and encourage them to continue the infant's treatment? (3) Should you tell them that you can listen and help them think the problem through but that you cannot give them guidance about what they should decide? (4) Should you encourage them to speak again to Dr. Newhouse and get her opinion? Where in the *Code* will you find guidance so you can make the correct decision? In the ethical principles screen (Chapter 3), the highest value is the principle of the protection of life. Does this mean any life, even the life of a severely disabled person?

Following the "Baby Doe" case, Congress passed the Child Abuse Amendments of 1985 and assigned public child welfare agencies the responsibility of policing decision making concerning catastrophically ill neonates. Public child welfare agencies became responsible for assuring that decisions regarding medical treatment that would either end or sustain life would be in the newborn's interest and not be neglectful or abusive. Thousands of disabled children are born each year with life-threatening medical complications.

State and county departments of social services have moved to protect children from abuse and neglect, guided by the child's best interests. One result is that child welfare agencies sometimes find themselves responsible for making such life-and-death decisions when the Department of Social Services has legal guardianship over the child for the following reasons: (1) the mother is dying or has already died; (2) the mother is incompetent; or (3) the infant is born HIV-positive, has been abandoned, or otherwise has become the ward of the agency. When social workers are faced with making recommendations in such cases, where in the *Code of Ethics* will they find guidance?

Hughes (1993a, b) concluded that in our pluralistic society there is no consensus that can provide guiding principles for child welfare workers and agencies. Nevertheless, he suggested a "guiding ethical paradigm" that can serve child welfare agencies faced with these critical and difficult decisions. This guiding ethical paradigm consists of two principles for those with responsibility for treatment and case management for catastrophically ill newborns: (1) The quality-of-life principle can be described as the need to assess and consider the future quality of a person's life as an important variable in deciding whether to intervene to prolong life; this principle suggests that some lives are worse than death; and (2) The principle of social transcendence can be defined as the requirement that decisions not be based upon the potential relative social utility of a person's life. It requires that treatment not be withheld on the basis of an assessment of a child's future potential to contribute to society or upon the priorities of social utility. Hughes believes that quality of life and social transcendence are consistent with the intent of the historical child welfare principle of best interests of the child. Suppose you are the child welfare social worker assigned to the Lanier infant (Exemplar 12.2). Apply these principles to the situation. Do they help you in making a decision? Would they do so in another and different case situation? Do the two principles form a sufficient base for decision making? What limitations can you identify for each of these principles separately and for the two in combination? Do you see any conflicts with the NASW *Code of Ethics?* Does the ethical principles screen suggest a different course of action?

Both the person with serious health problems and family caretakers risk a great deal when ill persons receive health care at home rather than moving to assisted living, nursing centers, or other health care facilities. Conflicts often arise between the autonomy of the client and the helping activities of caretakers and social workers. During their time at home, an erosion of abilities often ensues, either as a result of the progress of the disease, because of aging, or both. Difficulties arise when physical deterioration occurs at a faster rate than mental. In these cases, clients become more dependent physically but remain alert intellectually. Under what circumstances should a social worker act on her own when it appears that her client receiving home health care is not impaired cognitively and has been exploited or neglected? Is such intervention by the social worker ethical if she does not involve the client in making choices for himself?

The following exemplar also raises questions about the role of the social worker and involves several ethical dilemmas.

➤ 12.3 Our Daughter or Our Lives?

Irma Bream, a social worker at Heartland Children's Hospital, is meeting with Albert and Sorelle Clayton about the forthcoming discharge of their disabled 18-year-old daughter, Alice. The options upon discharge are: a nursing home that accepts very young persons; a specialized foster care placement; or home care. The latter option would require that her parents commit 24 hours per day to care for their daughter without hope of respite time or any other help. As the parents see it, their only real choice is whether to give up their lives for the care of Alice or to give up Alice to foster care. Despite long discussion and after several meetings with their social worker, Albert and Sorelle can't come to a decision. Now they ask Ms. Bream what she thinks is the right thing to do.

What should Irma Bream say in answer to this question? Can you identify the ethical dilemmas facing the social worker in this situation? Where in the NASW *Code of Ethics* would this social worker find guidance?

CLIENTS WITH HIV AND AIDS

As of June 1996, almost 550,000 cases of AIDS had been reported in the United States. Following the initial discovery in 1981, it took eight years for the first 100,000 cases to be reported, but it took only two years to identify the next 100,000. New incidents continue to be reported, but the rate of increase has declined (Ward & Drotman, 1998). Death rates from AIDS in the United States slowed in 1998, but the rates are not falling as rapidly as they did during the middle of the 1990s. The rate of infection with HIV is no longer declining and has stabilized recently at approximately 40,000 persons per year. The death rate has been improved for those who respond favorably to new combinations of drug treatments. However, many people are unable to follow through on the very demanding drug regimen or have HIV infections that are resistant to the drug combinations (Altman, 1999). All social workers, even those who are practicing with populations—or in areas of the country—that have so far had a low incidence of human immunodeficiency virus (HIV/AIDS), may sooner or later confront on their caseloads clients who have AIDS or who test HIV-positive. When this happens, they will face many ethical problems. Some of these will be quite different from those they faced in the past.

AIDS is not an "ordinary" disease. People who have AIDS or who test HIV-positive cannot be discussed in quite the same way as people who suffer other kinds of diseases. AIDS is a life-threatening disease; and people with HIV/AIDS have to come to terms with their own potential mortality, frequently at an early age. Although there are other diseases that are also life-threatening at early ages, there is a very high degree of stigma associated with AIDS, more stigma than is true for almost any other illness. This is because AIDS was first discovered among groups that are traditionally labeled as deviants—gay people, drug users, and prostitutes. Because of this stigma, many people with AIDS do not want others to know that they have the disease. They often go to considerable lengths to conceal the illness, even from those who are closest to them. They need support to ask for the help that they desperately need.

Social workers' concern for persons with acquired immunodeficiency syndrome (AIDS) is not new, but goes back to the very beginning of the public recognition of this epidemic. In 1984, the NASW Delegate Assembly had already adopted a policy statement on AIDS (NASW, 1985, pp. 2–4). This statement acknowledged the role social workers must play in alleviating the plight of the victims. The 1987 NASW Delegate Assembly adopted a further policy statement, *AIDS: A Social Work Response.* When social workers from 16 countries and 30 states met at the First International Conference on Social Work and AIDS in 1989, they resolved that

> social workers and social work agencies are ethically obligated to provide appropriate services to all people affected by HIV/AIDS. These agencies and social workers are further obligated to ensure that direct care providers, supervisors and administrators have necessary training, education and support to maintain high standards of service provided with full protection of civil liberties and without discrimination or fear of working with people affected by HIV/AIDS. . . .

Adopting policy statements is only a beginning, but an important beginning. Much work needs to be done to make social work intervention with this population effective. Social work with such clients requires a great deal of knowledge and expertise; this places a special responsibility on social workers to gain training and direction for work with HIV/AIDS-infected clients.

People who are infected by HIV/AIDS require a great many services, including medical, legal, employment, housing, and social services. Social workers are particularly well equipped to meet several of the special needs of this population, including:

1. Mental health, housing, entitlements, education, case management services.
2. Advocacy to protect these clients against discrimination and to ensure that they will receive all the services they need.
3. AIDS education for the general public, for the families of infected persons, and even for those with HIV/AIDS themselves.
4. Bereavement counseling for the families and loved ones of those who have died from AIDS.

Biases About AIDS

Some social workers want to avoid working with HIV/AIDS-infected persons because they are worried that they might "catch" the disease. Is it unethical to avoid serving such clients when this fear is unfounded? Medical sources agree that HIV/AIDS is not spread by casual contact. Social workers can be certain that they are not at risk of HIV infection when serving clients who have AIDS. Yet these fears, false as they are, exist and must be overcome if social workers are to provide service to people with HIV/AIDS.

There are other stereotypes and biases that interfere in establishing an effective helping relationship between social workers and HIV/AIDS-infected persons. These clients may have been infected as a result of having sex with an HIV-infected partner or because they shared a needle with such a partner. Many social workers disapprove of sexual relations outside of marriage, and most disapprove of the use of drugs. But social workers must be aware that there are many other causes for HIV infection, including blood donations from infected donors. When working with any client, whether he or she is HIV infected, a social worker is not asked to approve the behavior that resulted in the problem situation. She is expected to provide vital services to a person who needs them. The ethical social worker will always do everything to work through her own biases that may interfere with the professional relationship.

The AIDS epidemic has become widespread. Many persons have become infected, including spouses and significant others of infected persons, recipients of infected blood, newborn babies of infected parents, persons who shared needles, and others. Some of these persons may share the general public's biases about AIDS, and the stigma associated with AIDS may keep them from asking for the help they need when they know they are HIV-positive. Social workers must find ways to open communication channels with all of these people, both those who are diagnosed as HIV-positive and those who have developed AIDS.

Confidentiality and the Rights of Partners

A study by Abramson (1990) suggests that the issue of secrecy is a major ethical problem for social workers who have people with AIDS or people who are HIV-positive on their caseload. The ethical dilemmas facing these social workers arise out of (1) the obligation or duty to warn a third party that he or she is endangered by unprotected sex (this will require breaking confidence), and (2) helping infected persons to work through the problems that keep them from informing partners. Often HIV-positive clients fear rejection, abandonment, and/or loneliness if their partners find out that they are infected. The following exemplar illustrates one aspect of this dilemma.

➤ **12.4 Gary Has Unsafe Sex**

You staff a support group for HIV-positive adults. During one of the group meetings, Gary Damian relates that he continues to engage in unprotected sexual relations with his wife. When challenged by a group member, he admitted that he was not being fair to his wife but that he was afraid she would leave him if she found out that he was HIV-positive.

What is your responsibility? If you cannot help Gary talk to his wife and/or convince him that he should change his behavior, should you break confidentiality? Does the *Tarasoff* ruling require you to notify his wife of the danger she faces? Whether a social worker is required by law to warn a third party when there is a threat of HIV infection differs from state to state. Among the legal arguments bearing on this question is the proposition that harm from a gunshot is virtually certain, but that there is somewhat less certainty with regard to harm from unprotected sex with an HIV-infected partner. Not every person who has sex with an infected partner will become infected. Yet legal arguments aside, from an ethical point of view, the risk faced by the partner of an HIV-infected person may be sufficiently great to require breaking confidentiality and warning the potential victim (Girardi et al., 1988; Melton, 1988).

In the language of our ethical principles screen (EPS), this ethical dilemma can be resolved by determining whether or not Ethical Principle 1 (preserving life) is involved. If the danger to the partner's life is direct and immediate (as most social workers think it is), this principle takes precedence over Ethical Principle 6 (privacy and confidentiality). The medical profession has dealt with this ethical dilemma in a similar way. The Council on Ethical and Judicial Affairs of the American Medical Association (AMA) suggests that if a physician fails to persuade the HIV-infected person to inform a third party, the physician should inform public health officials. Only if public health officials refused or were unwilling to take on the responsibility of warning does the physician have an obligation to act directly. The notion that physicians should have the right to breach confidentiality in order to warn the unsuspecting persons was endorsed by the Presidential Commission on the HIV Epidemic. The commission held that the decision about whether to breach confidentiality remained with the physician and was not imposed as a matter of law. Instead of a duty to warn, there was a "privilege to disclose"(Bayer, 1998).

A particularly difficult ethical problem occurs when a client has AIDS but has not been told about it, either because his physician feels uncomfortable to do so or because it is felt that a child or elderly person is better off if he or she does not know. The social worker who does know the diagnosis often does not know what professional ethics expect of her in this situation. If the social worker is asked for the information directly and the patient gives an informed consent, do NASW *Code* standards 1.01 and 4.04 have implications for the social worker's response?

Where will the social worker find guidance in the *Code*, if the patient does not ask directly?

Other Ethical Problems

There are many other ethical dilemmas and problems that social workers face when working with these clients. For instance, Reamer (1988) asks whether social workers can be morally neutral when a client who has AIDS wants to commit suicide, knowing that such a person faces prolonged suffering and certain death. What do you think?

"Rationing" medical care presents another set of ethical problems in dealing with which a social worker's advocacy services may be necessary. There are numerous reports of HIV/AIDS-infected persons who have not been offered cardiopulmonary resuscitation (CPR) or ventilator support because physicians presumably think that such "heroic" measures are futile for those patients. Does a social worker have an ethical obligation to protect the rights of these clients?

As we shall see later in this chapter, ethical dilemmas may be encountered at the direct service level or at policy levels. The following exemplar presents such issues at several levels.

> ### ➤ 12.5 School Policy, Condoms, and Parental Permission
>
> You are a social worker in a high school, assigned to the school's health team. HIV and AIDS are threatening teenagers, many of whom ignore "safe sex" practices. The school system recently adopted a policy that condoms can be distributed only to students whose parent(s) have given written permission. Because of this rule, the team members can no longer provide condoms, even when students who are known to be sexually active request them. This morning such an active student asked you for condoms. How do you respond? Later in the day there will be a team meeting at which the new condom policy will be discussed. What can the team do about it?

This social worker is faced with the ethical dilemma of choosing between agency policy and protection of life in this specific instance. What about other sexually active students? At another level, what are the ethical dilemmas that face the team as they consider the school system's policy? Does the *Code of Ethics* provide direction for this social worker and for the team?

THE AGING

The "graying" of America continues to increase at a moderate rate as the elderly population increases numerically and as a percentage of the population. In the not too far future, this growth will become rapid. In 1900, only one in every 25 Americans was over 65. By 1994, one in eight persons was in this age group. According to Census Bureau projections, the elderly population is expected to double to 80 million persons by 2050, which means that one in five Americans will be over 65 (U.S. Census Bureau, 1999 a, b).

As the size of the aging population increases in the coming decades, communities must prepare for an increase in the size of the disabled population. But it must be remembered that socioeconomic status influences the pattern of disabilities. The patterns of morbidity and the incidence of disease that are reported among middle-aged people (45 to 64) in the two lower socioeconomic levels are not reported for the higher socioeconomic levels until the age group of 75 and above (Smyer, 1993).

As the number of aging persons increases and the number of such persons with cognitive and/or physical disabilities grows, one can anticipate an increase in the number of ethical dilemmas. Many of these dilemmas will focus on complex decision making in regard to autonomy, informed consent, self-determination (Dickson, 1997), and rationing of limited resources.

Informed consent is an ethical issue when working with people of any age, but it becomes critical when working with the aged. Informed consent implies a rational process. The person has a right to understand the situation, the choices, and the projected results of the decision to be made. In the case of aging persons who are clearly incompetent, courts may appoint a guardian. But there are many aged persons who have a limited capacity for understanding and decision making, yet who are legally competent and have a right to make their own decisions. Should the social worker do what she thinks is best for such clients? After all, they are aged and there are real limits to the possibility of independent decision making and functioning. Since such persons may have limited understanding and the social workers have limited time, is it fair to use more of available time to help them understand more completely the implications of their decisions? What is the necessary degree of informed consent required in such a situation?

Proctor et al. (1993) found when they studied ethical dilemmas in hospital social work that most involved conflicts between client self-determination and client best interest; dilemmas were more likely when a patient's mental status was impaired and decision making was problematic. They found that these dilemmas related to delayed discharge, in-hospital mortality, and less than adequate postdischarge care. A large proportion of these conflicts were connected to decisions about discharge destinations—that is, going home or going to a nursing home. When there were disputes among various parties, four out of five disputes were over the discharge plan or medical care. Families were in conflict with medical teams or specific physicians; there were conflicts between patients and staff members; between social workers and medical staff persons; between patients and everyone else; or among family members. Ethical dilemmas were found to be more likely when patients were physically dependent and mentally confused.

Conflicts may arise from other factors. Aside from mental impairment and mental confusion, the societal definition of aging may produce ethical problems. Social workers must remain sensitive to situations in which the aging person may hold different values, choose different lifestyles, and have different expectations than those customary in the younger-generation social workers. When such conflicts exist, this does not make the older person "incompetent," but the social worker is faced with a value clash with ethical implications.

One of the fastest growing segments of health care is home health care. One hundred and eighteen social workers employed by both proprietary and nonprofit agencies participated in the first study of social workers' professional functions and ethical concerns in home health care. Patient autonomy and self-determination were found to be major ethical issues (Egan, 1999).

Knowledge about the potential effects of one choice or another also can play a part in ethical decision making. A study of depression and mortality among nursing home residents showed a significant difference in the mortality rates of residents with depressive disorder and those without (Wicclair, 1993). Given this information, the choice facing Rosalind Lippe and her social worker, Teresa Richards, is difficult.

> ### 12.6 Depression, Day Treatment, or the Nursing Home

Rosalind Lippe, 70 years of age, has been depressed for some time, Teresa Richards has been visiting her at home and helping her in a number of ways, but Ms. Lippe's depression has only slightly lifted, even with medication. A psychiatrist has recommended a day treatment program, but Ms. Lippe cannot afford payment for this service. However, Ms. Richards knows that treatment would be available for Ms. Lippe if she were to enter a local nursing home. Medicaid will pay the nursing home because of Ms. Lippe's low income.

Nursing home placement tends to be irreversible, yet in this case placement may be the best option. Ms. Lippe is a younger old person but she is in difficulty. Right now a bed is available in the nursing home, something that does not occur often. A decision will have to be made very quickly; if a mistake is made, it will probably not be possible to correct it. Many ethical issues need to be considered. How can Ms. Richards ensure informed consent by Ms. Lippe? Very few people want to enter a nursing home. Torn among her need for help, her ambivalence, and her depression, how can Ms. Lippe make a fully voluntary decision? Given what is known about mortality rates among nursing home residents, what factors must Ms. Richards balance? On the one hand, Ms. Lippe needs help for her depression; on the other hand, there will be a loss of freedom and possible health risks if Ms. Lippe enters the nursing home. In what ways can Ms. Richards resolve these ethical dilemmas?

SOCIAL WORK WITH GROUPS

Social workers are involved with groups in many different kinds of settings. No matter what type of setting they practice in, they will encounter many of the ethical dilemmas met with in other direct service roles. One ethical issue which social workers with groups have to deal with occurs when they have to choose between group members.

➤ **12.7 Charlie's Special**

When Charlie, an emotionally disturbed youngster of ten, joined the group, Emo Wilkommen, the social worker, took an immediate liking to him. Charlie's mother died some years ago, and his father is imprisoned. In order to ease Charlie's way into the therapy group, Emo set firm limits on two rambunctious group members and also set up several opportunities for Charlie to shine. Group members claimed that the worker is favoring Charlie.

To what extent is Charlie entitled to unequal treatment in the group in order to make up for past deprivations and difficulties? Should Emo be entirely honest with the group members? What approach would do the most good and the least harm? Is it ever ethical for a social worker to be manipulative with a group?

In some situations, social workers serve as coleaders of therapy groups. In the following exemplar, a social worker is faced with an ethical dilemma resulting from the group coleadership model.

➤ **12.8 Concern for Group? Self? Colleague?**

Andrea Miller and Pat Stoner are social workers who are coleaders of a therapy and support group for psychiatric patients. They have worked together on many groups during the past few years. Recently, tensions have escalated between them because Ms. Stoner has shown up late for sessions, contradicts Ms. Miller during group sessions in front of the patients, disagrees on how to run the group, and has occasionally left the group early. One result has been that group members pay attention to the split instead of their own problems and Ms. Miller has heard two group members commenting outside the sessions about the tensions they observed. Ms. Miller attempted to solve the problem outside the group setting, but the tension and the behavior have continued. As a long-term colleague of Ms. Stoner, Ms. Miller is not sure what she should do. Obviously, Ms. Stoner has some personal problems, but it is unclear whether they will pass by quickly or continue. What is the ethical choice? Discussion has not worked. Ms. Miller can ignore the behavior. She can ask to be relieved of the assignment. If asked why, she can choose not to tell or say she is tired of the assignment. Or, she can tell their supervisor and put the problem "on the table."

Ms. Miller is torn between loyalty to group members, to herself, and to her colleague. Is there any guidance about these issues in the *Code of Ethics?* From an ethical point of view, how would you handle this situation?

Social workers often work with task groups in the community. Some of the ethical dilemmas that arise concern confidentiality, self-determination of the group and individual members, inclusion or exclusion of members, and conflicts of interest (Congress & Lynn, 1997). What is the ethically correct choice in the following dilemma? You are a social worker employed by a city housing authority and you are working with a group of mothers toward an improved playground for their children. One resident brings a friend with her to the meeting. During the meeting you discover the friend is living with the group member's family in the same apartment. This is unknown to both the housing authority and your employer, and is against the law. What should you do? Or, you are a social worker assigned to work with a community group concerned about trash pickup, speeding traffic that endangers neighborhood children, and public transportation accessibility. Your values and those of the group have been congruent concerning every concern so far. At this evening's meeting, a highly influential group member introduced the news that the state mental health department intends to establish a community residence in the neighborhood. When she took the leadership on this issue, the entire group agreed to make their opposition to the proposed residence their highest priority item. You know there is a great need for such residences. If, however, you oppose their actions, you are concerned that it will undermine your effectiveness with all the other issues. To whom do you owe loyalty? The group? Yourself? The neighborhood? Those who need such residences? Society in general?

MACRO PRACTICE

Some professional social workers hold stereotyped views of their colleagues who engage in macro practice. They believe that practitioners who engage in agencywide change efforts, social planning, neighborhood and community organization and development, social action, and social policy efforts are operating in a highly politicized arena. They think that this practice area is grounded on techniques and methods based on pragmatism rather than on ethical decisions. This perception is fostered not only by the nature of the settings in which macro practitioners practice but also by the language they use, especially such terms as *tactics, strategies, conflict,* and *advocacy.* Indeed, references to ethics are only rarely found in macro practice textbooks (exceptions include Netting, Kettner, & McMurtry, 1998, and Tropman, Erlich, & Rothman, 1995).

Nevertheless, macro social workers also encounter many difficult ethical dilemmas in their daily practice. The NASW *Code of Ethics* applies to all NASW members, including those in macro practice; the *Code of Ethics* states that "Social workers' primary responsibility is to promote the well-being of clients" (NASW, 1996, 1.01) and "Social workers should promote the general welfare of society" (NASW, 1996, 6.01). Further, "the social worker should engage in social and political action that seeks to ensure that all people have access to the resources, employment, services, and opportunities they require to meet their basic human needs and to develop fully"(NASW, 1996, 6.04a).

When the social worker is attempting to comply with all of these standards, many dilemmas are encountered. These dilemmas include determining who is the client to whom primary responsibility is owed as well as selecting the persons who have access to resources when not every needy person can be supplied because these resources are in short supply. Another type of dilemma occurs when there are several similarly disadvantaged groups. How does the worker choose the one who will receive her priority attention?

In the following social planning situation, the social worker has to choose between many different groups. The choices to be made clearly deal with promoting the "general welfare of society." But in this instance, who is society? Which group deserves priority consideration?

➤ **12.9 Establishing a Cancer Treatment Unit**

You are the director of social work in a large urban community hospital located in a low-income area serving people from various economic levels. You have been assigned to staff the planning committee charged with creating a plan for the future of the hospital. You grew up in the community and have family and long-standing friends who reside there. You also have relationships with many community human service administrators and staff members.

As the planning process proceeds, it becomes clear that most committee members favor the creation of a specialized cancer treatment unit, which will gain status and recognition for the hospital and also attract patients from throughout the state. But such a recommendation will make it impossible to recommend improvements for emergency and ambulatory care that are desperately needed by the neighborhood. A recommendation for a cancer treatment unit will change the nature of the available health care, who will get the jobs, use of community space, kinds of housing which will be available, and so forth.

It becomes clear to you that the local community will gain very little and lose much if a cancer treatment unit is installed. You are torn between loyalty to the hospital, to the community in general, to the social and human service agencies in the community, and to the community's population, including your friends and relatives who need a different type of service.

As a member of the planning group, you are faced with the dilemma of choosing between groups to determine who will benefit from the distribution of resources. What criteria will help you choose between the cancer patients (who do not necessarily come from the immediate community) and the health needs of your family, friends, and neighbors? Choosing between two groups, both of which have real health needs, is a typical ethical dilemma faced by social workers who are social planners. Whose good is primary? As a social worker, you owe first priority to the potential recipients of health services, but which of the groups has a higher priority? In addition, is the hospital's long-term viability a consideration that should affect the ethical decision-making process?

A review of the ethical principles screen (EPS) in Chapter 3 can be helpful as one thinks about the dilemma confronting this social planner. We would suggest that a consideration of Ethical Principles 1 and 2 is most compelling in the present case.

Principle 1—Protection of life. All medical services ultimately deal with the protection of life. Cancer patients are at a great risk, and inevitably face life-threatening situations that require early treatment—the earlier the better. On the other hand, the emergencies typically treated in a hospital ER range from routine treatments to life-threatening situations that require immediate treatment, for the latter, any delay may be a death sentence. Principle 1 does not provide unambiguous guidance, but can be used to buttress either choice.

Principle 2—Equality and inequality. Cancer is today a very high-profile disease. A cancer treatment unit will be established in at least one hospital in the state, no matter what the board of Neighborhood Hospital decides. For the neighborhood residents, however, the Neighborhood Hospital is the only chance for receiving timely emergency services; transportation to the next nearest hospital would add ten to fifteen minutes' travel time—too much time when every minute counts. Under this principle, neighborhood persons have the ethical right to expect preferred consideration. The social worker can therefore with a clear conscience support a recommendation in favor of improving emergency services.

Social workers are expected to be open and honest. Among the standards in the *Code of Ethics* is the expectation that "social workers should not participate in, condone, or be associated with dishonesty, fraud, or deception"(NASW *Code*, 1996, 4.04). At every step in their education and later in agency practice, social workers are encouraged not to engage in secretive, hidden, or disguised actions or to be manipulative. Much attention has been paid in the literature to efforts to change social agencies, always with the justification that one's efforts are designed to improve services for clients or to attain some general good. In some cases, concealed and unavowed action may be thought necessary to gain a greater good for a community or for clients. In these cases, social workers have to weigh the ethical balance between a greater good and hidden actions.

What is the best way for the worker to respond in the following situation?

➤ **12.10 How to Fight the Half-Truths of the Real Estate Lobby**

Ed Corey is a community organizer, employed by a social agency to develop new housing in a neighborhood. Ed staffs a community coalition that is vigorously working on the new housing. The early activities of the coalition were very successful. But powerful real estate interests who wanted to block the development of the new housing began to spread rumors about Ed's personal history and life. They also used deceptive and distorted facts in advertisements to destroy the coalition's efforts and to undercut Ed's potential influence.

Ed, for his part, knows about the "shady" dealings of some members of the real estate group. He senses there will be no new housing unless aggressive action is taken, but he is unsure what he should do to combat the half-truths and lies of the opponents of the new housing. How should Ed use the information he has? Should he be open and rebut the charges of the opponents? Or should he retaliate and fight "fire with fire" behind the scenes? Should he use the facts he possesses with strategically located opinion molders to undermine the influence of the real estate group?

EXERCISES

1. If you are confronted by the ethical dilemma that faces the director of social work in Exemplar 12.9, "Establishing a Cancer Treatment Unit," what do you think your decision would be? What arguments support your decision? What arguments exist contrary to your point of view?

2. What are the ways in which aging persons attempt to make health decisions in advance of medical operations? What dilemmas

occur that impact on social workers when such arrangements either have not been made or are unclear in some important way?

3. Can you identify ways in which ageism appears in American society and in social work practice? How do these relate to the social work *Code of Ethics?* What can a social worker do to minimize these?

4. The legislature of your state has been alarmed by a sudden sharp increase in the incidence of HIV-positive findings among several population groups. A bill has been introduced calling for mandatory HIV screening of all persons applying for a marriage license. The problem is a real one; the solution suggested may or may not be effective. But it does raise a number of ethical issues. Your local NASW chapter has asked you to discuss these questions at the next membership meeting.

5. You are a social worker for a hospital support group of young adults recovering from serious illnesses. The group has been told they can make decisions "within agency policy" in a democratic fashion. When the group is informed that a new member will be joining, one member recognizes the person, says she is disruptive, and the group joins in and says the new member cannot join. What should you do? Support the group or the new member?

SUGGESTIONS FOR ADDITIONAL READINGS

Hughes (1993a, b) reviews the life and death decisions facing child welfare workers when dealing with severely disabled children. Ward & Drotman (1998) systematically examine the demographics of HIV and AIDS. Yu & O'Neal (1992) analyze the issue of confidentiality that faces social workers who work with clients with AIDS. Dolgoff and Skolnik (1996) report on the findings of an empirical study of decision making by social workers with groups. Dickson (1997) reviews the complex relationships between law, ethics, social work, and self-determination among the aging. Egan (1999) reports on social workers' ethical concerns in an expanding field, home health care. Torczyner (1991) examines ethical issues in social action.

13. Whose Responsibility Are Professional Ethics?

Ethical decision making is often presented in a way suggesting that the social worker who must make a decision is completely alone and cut off from every support system that might give her guidance. Many have questioned this view. Philosopher W. D. Walsh wrote, "morality is first and foremost a social institution, performing a social role, and only secondarily, if at all, a field for individual self-expression" (Frankena, 1980, p. 33).

While every social worker is, of course, responsible for her ethical decisions, it must be recognized that she is a participant in a number of networks and social systems that support—or should support—her ethical decision making. One of the purposes of the *Code* is to help social workers "identify relevant considerations when professional obligations conflict or ethical uncertainties arise" (NASW Code, 1996, Purpose of the NASW *Code of Ethics*). Yet decision making always occurs within a social setting that influences, rewards, or guides certain behaviors and which limits, sanctions, or disapproves others. The social agency employing the social worker is one such setting, the service delivery team or office is another, and the professional association a third. Any discussion of steps designed to facilitate and strengthen ethical decision making is incomplete if it fails to take these systems into consideration.

Granted there will never be a time when clear and unambiguous guidelines will be available for every ethical decision that a social worker must make, yet over the years various societal and institutional mechanisms have been developed to provide guidance and support. Here we want to discuss a number of mechanisms that have been found particularly helpful by some social workers.

Peer review and committees on the ethics of social work practice.   Peer review permits a social worker to test her ethical decision making against that of her colleagues, either informally in groups that practitioners create for mutual aid or formally in agencies. In the past, social workers have utilized informal groupings to review their professional practice decisions. Such groupings can also be useful for reviewing ethical decisions. Peer review groups are particularly important for social workers in private practice because they are more isolated than workers in agency-based practice and because they have less opportunity for interaction with peers. Controls and accountability of private practice social workers depend almost entirely upon the sensitivity and knowledge of the individual practitioner. Peer pressures, which are so immediate in agency practice, are much less evident in private practice. Because of these considerations, social workers in private practice may want to organize peer review systems that are specifically geared to review their ethical decision making. In this way they can be certain that their decisions will be of the highest quality.

Each agency should establish a Committee on the Ethics of Social Work Practice, analogous to Committees on the Rights of Human Subjects that exist in every academic research organization. Practitioners who have an ethical question may consult with the committee about a problem. Such a committee can serve as a forum where social workers can think through thorny ethical questions occurring in everyday practice. Most important, this committee can be the locus for the routine monitoring of ethical practice within the agency.

Accountability systems.   Professional social workers, whether they work in agencies or in private practice for the foreseeable future, will practice in an environment in which they will be held accountable for their professional activities. Courts, third-party payers, governmental regulators, and empowered clients and patients as citizens play roles in regard to accountability in our increasingly litigious society. Social agencies are accountable for what they do. Social agencies that want to implement this responsibility in a positive way must develop and operate accountability systems. These systems are characterized by the following features: information systems and monitoring; methods for sampling activities and decisions; clear indicators of the desired quality of performance; clear indicators or criteria of the desired quantity; and feedback systems that permit an early alert to problem situations.

Accountability systems relate primarily to practice performance, but there is no reason why such systems could not incorporate additional indicators that focus on the ethical aspects of practice. Just as agencies evaluate the effectiveness and efficiency of the services they deliver and the social work practices of their social work employees, agencies can also track and evaluate systematically the ethical decision making of social work practitioners.

In-service training and consultation.   Most agencies make a heavy investment in providing in-service training, continuing education opportunities, and consultation for their staff. Though the focus is often on more effective practice and more efficient administration, these sessions should also include a focus on the ethical implications of practice in order to strengthen the ethical level of practice.

Agency appeals procedures and ombudsmen.   Many agencies have appeals procedures, but clients are often not aware of them. "Forgetting" to inform clients about them may simplify the life of the practitioners and administrators, but this does not make for a high level of ethical practice. The utilization of appeals procedures does more than correct mistakes made by social workers. One of their most valuable functions is to sensitize social workers to the ethical aspects of practice. An ombudsman or another type of appeals procedure should be readily available to clients, who should be able to use these procedures without any risk of stigma. Ethical social workers will welcome such strategies. Administrative review procedures also have a place in the support system, but they do not take the place of appeals procedures freely available to clients.

Clients' Bill of Rights.   Many hospitals and other service organizations distribute a Bill of Rights to new clients and patients. These brief statements inform people of the type of information they are entitled to know about their situation. They are also told that they can expect to be treated with dignity and respect, that they will participate in decision making about their situation, that they will be informed about available options, and that they have a right to speak to an ombudsman or other person if they are dissatisfied with their treatment.

Social workers should consider the use of a clear and informative statement to inform new clients about what they can expect from the professional personnel they will encounter, the mechanisms for raising questions or seeking clarification where needed, and the procedures for registering grievances. While social workers can and should inform their clients about these things, transmitting such information verbally is *not* a Bill of Rights. This must be in writing and can be issued only by the *Agency*, not by the individual social worker. The situation is different for those in private practice who can and should issue such a written document to every new client. The document should include statements about what the client can and cannot expect to happen in the professional service.

Professional associations. Professional associations, such as NASW, can play a key role in strengthening ethical practice. The promulgation and periodic revision of the *Code* needs to be strengthened through the inclusion of case references and interpretive guidelines because the standards of practice and the limits of ethical behavior are difficult to define. Jayaratne, Croxton, and Mattison (1997) found in a study of Michigan NASW members that there is much confusion and dissension as to what constitutes appropriate ethical practice. This disturbing finding suggests that NASW and other professional associations of social workers must develop additional strategies if they want to encourage the strengthening of ethical decision making within the profession. The following are some of the ways to do so:

1. Continue to revise and refine the *Code of Ethics*. It may be helpful to add case precedents.
2. Encourage the formation of formal and informal groups to study and review critical ethical decisions arising out of actual practice experiences.
3. Develop a data bank of precedents with ethical implications. Knowledge about ethical decisions is valuable, but identifying and learning about those actions found to be unethical can also have positive consequences, including being instructive and pre-warning members of the profession.
4. Schedule activities that focus on the ethical aspects of practice, both at professional conferences and as part of continuing education programs.
5. Publish an "Ethics Reporter" or a regular ethics column in *Social Work* or in the *NASW News* in order to make social workers more familar with their *Code of Ethics*.
6. Develop an ethics hotline so that practitioners, supervisors, and administrators can obtain advice on ethical issues that arise in their practice. Modern communication technologies, such as fax and electronic mail, can provide instant communication over long distances. At the same time, these technologies give the consultant sufficient time to reflect on the question or to consult with others.

7. NASW should publish an annual report, as does the American Psychological Association, regarding the number and types of ethical complaints investigated and the disposition of those cases.
8. State licensing boards can also play a part in reporting on their activities and in other ways educating practitioners, supervisors, and administrators in their respective states.

It is desirable that the professional organization and its local chapters, as well as individual social agencies, begin to collect data on ethical decision making. Such a data bank should not be limited to "success stories" but should also include errors, unanswerable questions, and embarrassing situations. Collection of this type of data will be helpful to practitioners as well as to students. This information will explicate the ethical quandaries experienced by social workers, the preferred solutions, and the results achieved. Such a data base will also be helpful in the creation of case materials, which are so necessary for the systematic development of new social work knowledge. Just as lawyers can draw on case law for guidance in making the difficult decisions, so social workers should be able to receive guidance from the suggested data bank.

Professional complaint procedures.   Nationally, from July 1986 to December 1997, 1068 charges of unethical conduct were filed with NASW chapters for adjudication. Eighty-four percent (901) of these were ethics complaints (Strom-Gottfried, 1999). NASW's complaint procedures have been criticized as cumbersome and taking too much time. The procedures provide for three levels of adjudication: A complaint is first presented to the Chapter Committee on Inquiry (COI). Once the COI has ascertained that the complaint has met the stipulated criteria (including that the social worker against whom the complaint has been filed was an NASW member at the time of the alleged violation), the complaint is accepted and a formal hearing is scheduled. Prior to the hearing, there can be a prehearing. After the COI has arrived at a decision about the complaint, it reports its findings to the parties involved and to the chapter executive committee, which may accept the report or send it back to the COI for reconsideration. Either party may appeal the decision, first to the National Committee on Inquiry and finally to the executive committee of the NASW board of directors. Revised adjudication procedures were approved in July 1991. These are designed to assure greater fairness to both parties. They also provide more comprehensive guidelines for the COI and other groups involved in the adjudication. Each of the steps in the process takes time, and the total elapsed time can be significant. It remains important to find ways to simplify the procedure and slash the time necessary to adjudicate complaints.

One effort to streamline procedures concerns resolution at the chapter level of disputes involving professional ethics and agency personnel standards. A new first step, implemented in 1998, allows chapters to determine whether a dispute meets the criteria for acceptance into the adjudication process before designating it as a complaint. This step helps to protect social workers against harm from unfounded complaints. Another effort to make the process more efficient is the proposed development of an alternative dispute resolution process (ADR) involving mediation. This will allow either party in a dispute to request the use of the ADR after a request for professional review has been filed. ADR pilot projects are being conducted by several chapters (*NASW*, 1998).

In addition to a complex process, problems also arise because there are relatively few knowledgeable colleagues from whom those charged with a violation can seek advice. Access to these knowledgeable individuals may also be difficult because they can be found only in relatively few places.

In this final chapter we have presented ideas that may help social workers in their search for more effective ethical practice. The values of the social work profession form the background for ethical decision making. In turn, ethical decision making is the cornerstone for ethical practice.

Ethical decision making begins with the clarification of one's own values. Knowledge of what one really believes is an inescapable basic step for social workers seeking to strengthen their ethical practice. Beyond this, it becomes important for social workers to clarify the values of society and of the various groups with which they work. Clarification of these values permits social workers to become more sensitive to and more aware of the values of others and of possible conflicts between different value systems.

Individual practitioners sometimes feel that they are alone when facing ethical dilemmas, but there are others who can share these ethical problems. Formal peer review, agency consultations, and the professional association must share the burden of thinking through these dilemmas. Some persons have suggested that ethics do not exist outside of community. To base ethical decisions strictly on one's individual conscience can lead a person into very difficult situations and into playing God. All ethics are integral to community. There are many reasons for a professional social worker to "connect" with the professional community. Fellow professionals can provide opportunities to think through ethical questions and dilemmas, to discuss one's ethical concerns with other social work professionals, and to gain colleague support.

EXERCISES

1. Identify your strengths and limitations in regard to ethical decision making when you are engaged in social work practice. How can you better prepare yourself for being an ethical social worker?

2. Identify in your field instruction placement, your agency of employment, or other social agency what you consider to be the limitations of the ethical decision-making patterns utilized. If you could improve one thing about ethical decision making in this organization, what would you choose to alter and how could you go about trying to improve the situation?

SUGGESTIONS FOR ADDITIONAL READINGS

Csikai and Sales (1998) report on the explosive growth of hospital ethics committees and the roles and expectations of social workers as related to them. Jayaratne, Croxton, and Mattison (1997), in "Social Work Professional Standards: An Exploratory Study," found that practitioners and those who judge practitioner behavior are making decisions with relatively little guidance from the profession. Review the *NASW Procedures for the Adjudication of Grievances* (1994b) to become familiar with the filing of a complaint with the professional association.

Appendix A:
Additional Exemplars

The exemplars in this appendix have been chosen to illustrate ethical practice problems occurring in the real world of social workers.

➤ A.1 Discriminatory Practices and an Agency Employee

Several social agencies in your city, including the one for which you work, engage in discriminatory practices against minority group children. There is now a court case about this matter. Lawyers for the plaintiff have asked you to testify about specific instances of such discriminatory practices. You oppose these practices and repeatedly have spoken against them at staff meetings, but you hesitate to testify in court because (1) you are afraid that you may be fired if you testify against your agency, (2) you are not sure whether the confidential relationship you have with your clients permits you to reveal this information, and (3) you are not certain whether it is ethical for you to use agency records for this purpose.

➤ A.2 A Multiproblem Family

Pearl Konesky, social worker at the Downriver Consultation Center, wonders what her new clients, the Spinos, are like. According to the short application form filled out by Mildred Spino at the reception desk, she is 33 years old, married, a mother of three, and employed as a clerk. She wants help in arranging an abortion. Pearl is hoping that there will not be too many other serious problems because agency policy permits only time-limited services—no more than eight counseling sessions over four weeks.

Before the first session is over, Pearl realizes that the Spinos are a multiproblem family, if there ever was one. The household consists of Walter Spino, age thirty-one, an alcoholic with no steady employment; Irma Spino, age fifteen, a school dropout and six months pregnant (according to her mother, Irma neither wanted an abortion nor was she ready to release her child for adoption); Irma's boyfriend, Mark Rehm, age eighteen, unemployed; Charlene Spino, age fourteen, severely retarded; and Sally Spino, age thirteen, expelled from elementary school because of repeated drug abuse.

By ignoring all problems other than Mildred Spino's request for an abortion, Pearl can adhere to her agency's time-limited service policy. But can a social worker overlook the many other problems that this family presents? Is this ethical?

➤ A.3 Birth Control for Teenagers

Pam Welsh, a 14-year-old teen, is not getting along with her parents. After Pam ran away from home twice, her parents took her for therapy to a social worker. During therapy, Pam told her social worker that she is sexually active. She asked the worker for help in avoiding pregnancy. She is afraid of becoming pregnant, but she is even more afraid that her puritanical parents may learn of her sexual activities.

Should the social worker help Pam obtain birth control pills, even though she knows that Pam's parents have taken a strong public stand against supplying them to teens? Is it ethical for the social worker to ignore the parents' values? Can she ignore her clients request? To whom is she accountable?

➤ A.4 Taking on a Private Client

Christine Ross is the only MSW social worker in a remote mountain community where she staffs the county welfare office. Her friend, Kay Jordan, the principal of the county high school, has told her about a very disturbed student in her school. This student has lately engaged in some very bizarre behavior and Kay has no doubt that he needs professional help. Since the nearest mental health clinic is 130 miles away, Kay asked Christine to provide therapy for this student.

The student is not eligible for service from the county welfare department (which in any case does not provide therapy). Therefore, Kay asked Christine to take him on as a private client. Christine has never before provided therapy for this kind of very disturbed person, but she is willing to try. Is it ethical for her to do so when there is no possibility of obtaining supervision?

➤ A.5 The Ethics of Team Practice

Timothy Land is a social worker in a day treatment program for deinstitutionalized persons. Professionally Mr. Land is respected by other members of the team and is viewed as a social worker of great promise who will move ahead quickly in his career.

Clients in the program are assigned to treatment groups on the basis of the decision of the psychiatrist and the social worker. There is no written contract as to what is expected of either patients or of staff. Clients are never involved in decisions about group assignment or tasks. If a client does not fulfill the assigned tasks, he or she is typically labeled "disruptive" or "decompensating." These comments are written on the clients' charts.

Land questions the ethical aspects of these procedures. He feels strongly that social work ethics require client participation in all phases of the decision-making process. But Land is not certain to whom he owes primary loyalty and responsibility. Is it to the team? To the clients? Or to his career?

➤ A.6 An Autistic Young Adult

Since Gary's family has placed him in a hostel for autistic young adults, they have just about cut all contact with him. Recently they sent him a postcard, telling him that they would no longer be able to visit him regularly since they had moved to another state.

The hostel social worker is aware that Gary misses his family greatly. He also knows that the family has not moved out of the city, but merely to another neighborhood within the city. Should he tell Gary the truth? What is the ethical thing to do?

➤ A.7 Threats from Your Client

You have been treating Jason Conger, a severely disturbed person, for several months. In recent weeks he has become increasingly aggressive toward you, claiming (wrongly) that you are planning to harm him. Today he told you that if you do not stop persecuting him, he will get even with you by harming your child.

You are very concerned since you know that Jason has been involved in the past in physically abusing children. Should you report this threat to the police? Should you arrange for a commitment to a mental hospital? Should you withdraw from this case? Or what should you do? What are the ethical dilemmas you must resolve before you can make a decision?

➤ A.8 An Interracial Marriage

Chris, age 28, has many problems. Until now he has coped with them, but now he has a problem that is too big for him to handle alone. Chris has fallen in love with Amy and wants to marry her. The problem is that both of their families are vehemently opposed to this interracial marriage—Chris is a white Anglo, while Amy is a Vietnamese-American.

The social worker to whom he has turned for help sees nothing wrong with an interracial marriage. She herself is white and has a Native American daughter-in-law. Should the worker share this information with Chris and help him deal with the prejudices of his and Amy's family? Is it ethical for the worker to talk about her own values?

What if this worker felt that interracial marriages made for many difficulties in our society and in this community in particular? Should she share with Chris the problems that her son and daughter-in-law have encountered? Is this ethical?

➤ A.9 Getting Help for Clyde Lukke

Clyde Lukke voluntarily entered Sunnyside Psychiatric Hospital on Wednesday afternoon. He complained of severe depression and was afraid that he might commit suicide. The admitting psychiatrist diagnosed his case as *depression, recurrent*. The usual treatment at Sunnyside for this diagnostic category is two to three weeks hospitalization, followed by long-term intensive individual therapy and medication.

Five days after admission, Angela Mennikke, the floor social worker, was notified by the business office to prepare the patient for discharge. Ms. Mennikke was surprised since discharge orders are usually discussed by the floor staff before they are entered. Rarely is discharge an administrative decision. Upon inquiry she learned that Mr. Lukke's HMO benefits are limited to one week of psychiatric hospitalization. She also learned that this HMO, like many similar organizations, reimburses only for time-limited group therapy, not for individual therapy.

Should the social worker prepare a routine discharge and let the HMO staff worry about how to help Lukke? Or should she take an advocate stance to ensure that Lukke will get the treatment he needs? What is expected in this situation from a professional social worker who wants to engage in ethical practice?

➤ A.10 Who's to Know?

A local psychologist has just completed a battery of intelligence tests for a teenager with mental retardation served by your agency. You have learned that this boy's test results are just above the score required to continue services for him and his family. Your supervisor, concerned about what will happen if services are cut off, asked you to suggest to the psychologist that she report a slightly lower score, thus ensuring that the agency could continue to provide services to this client.

➤ **A.11 A New Friend and Peer Consultation**

Last night social worker Mark Sussna met Valery Aylon at a party at a friend's apartment. In the course of the evening they discovered that they shared many interests. It was almost a case of "love at first sight." Mark made a date to meet Valery the following evening.

Today one of Mark's colleagues discussed a complicated case with him. Mark soon realized that the client being discussed was his new friend, Valery Aylon. What should he do? Should he tell his colleague to consult with someone else? Or should he keep silent so that he can find out more about Valery, information which will help him determine whether they are really suitable? Or should he terminate his friendship with Valery? (Note: Peer consultation is the accepted practice in this agency so that *confidentiality* is not an issue.)

➤ **A.12 One Job or Two?**

Joseph Leggio is a 25-year-old man with mental retardation. He has no living relatives and is able to live in protected environments in the community. Alice Patella, a social worker, recently placed him at a board and care home run by Mrs. Collins, a person with whom Alice has had a long relationship. Mrs. Collins has been supportive of the clients placed in her home, something that is found infrequently. Alice just discovered that Mrs. Collins—who needs the money—has not been supervising the clients placed in her home. Instead, she has hired a discharged psychiatric patient to monitor the residents while she works part-time in a local store. Alice knows that Mrs. Collins needs the income and her assistant, the discharged patient, needs both the extra money and the sense of accomplishment from performing the job. What would you suggest Alice do?

➤ **A.13 Health and Safety, or Housing for the Poor**

Amelia Pena is a social worker employed by an agency whose mission is to develop housing that is desperately needed for poor persons. Ms. Pena is a member of a special committee of staff and board members set up to review the situation that results from the discovery that some of the homes being renovated have lead paint problems. If the agency undertakes to remove the lead paint in order to ensure the safety of future residents, the agency will not be able to offer this new housing to the poor since the purchase price will be prohibitive. But if the lead is not removed, the agency will be morally and legally liable for any resulting damage. The agency does not have sufficient resources to do both—remove the lead and build the housing.

➤ **A.14 Who Makes Social Work Decisions?**

In the Whitehurst Children's Agency, the social work staff is supervised by Gloria Tabaka, a licensed social worker who is an excellent teacher and supervisor. When Ms. Tabaka has to be away from the agency, whether for a few hours or a day, the only person she trusts sufficiently to act for her is the office manager, Monica Monteleone, who is not a professional social worker nor is she trained in any human service. When Ms. Tabaka is not present and cannot be reached, the staff must go to Ms. Monteleone for decisions about the clients. Admittedly, Ms. Monteleone does know a great deal about many things, but the social work staff is not sure whether social work decisions should be made by a person who has not been certified. Today while Ms. Tabaka is away, you have to make a decision about an emergency child welfare situation that needs your supervisor's approval. Ms. Monteleone disagrees with your recommendation and instead suggests an option which you feel is not professionally defensible. What should you do?

➤ A.15 Obey the Law or Help?

Daphne Ranesco, a social work student, will graduate next week. Today one of her clients, Harry Plimkin, called distraught saying he has become violent with his wife and that he wants help. He tells her he has much respect for her since she has been very helpful to him, especially in controlling his temper. He wants to see her privately for a few sessions because he does not trust anyone else at the agency to help him in this emergency. State regulations do not allow social workers to practice privately until they have had two years of postgraduation profession experience under supervision. Does an emergency such as this one justify breaking the law? Is the prevention of violence more important than abiding by the law? What are Daphne's options? What ethical considerations must be considered for each option?

➤ A.16 No Other Way to Gather Resources

You are employed by a rural County Department of Education, which has no funds available to help Tom Bishop, your homebound young client or his family to purchase a cheap computer and modem which would enable him to communicate with many learning facilities and with other teenagers. Tom is desperate for activity but cannot travel out of his house because of his physical disabilities, which resulted from a diving accident. You have already asked your colleagues if they know how you might gather these resources, but no one had any helpful suggestions. Tom and his parents have now given you permission to advertise his needs on the electronic network. In your e-mail message you identified your client by gender, age, and a general description of his physical problems, but you did not use his name nor indicate the specific nature of his disabilities. Is this a responsible and ethical use of information? Can your client be recognized in a relatively small and sparsely populated area? What are the ethical issues involved when you use an electronic network to gain needed resources for your client?

➤ A.17 A Reporter After Death

A year ago when you were employed by St. Paul's Family Center, you served as social worker of Nicholas Karros, who had been experiencing problems on his job that affected him and his family. About eight months ago Nicholas was killed in an altercation at a local bar. You heard later that he had been the innocent victim. Roberta Frei, a reporter for the local newspaper, approached you yesterday to ask for information about Nicholas because she heard he had been abusive to his wife and children. Ms. Frei wanted this information as part of her preparation for an article on local domestic violence. What should you do? Does the *Code of Ethics* protect dead persons? What ethical issues are involved here?

➤ A.18 A Peaceful House in a New Land

Your client is a recent immigrant and has many traditional cultural values. Referred by her physician, she has been having headaches and difficulty with her husband, who is very critical of her housework and of her care for their children. She believes that the woman is responsible for a peaceful house and should put up with her husband's criticisms. In fact, she is proud that he only criticizes her and does not slap or hit her when she does things incorrectly. Your goals as the social worker differ. You think she should protect herself, gain some independence, and be more self-assertive. Should you continue to work with this person? If not, why not? If yes, why?

➤ A.19 How to Be Fair?

Your community is in the midst of an annual enrollment period for qualified aging persons to obtain tax-supported inexpensive transportation. Not every applicant will be accepted because only limited funds are available. As you help older persons fill out applications, you know some persons are needy but not providing all the income information in order to qualify. Should you confront them? Should you inform the authorities?

➤ A.20 Insider Trading

Recently Mr. Wellington, a friend and neighbor, approached you in the supermarket. You were pleased to see him. Some years ago he helped your parents several times when they were late on mortgage payments by loaning them money free of charge. He tells you that his nine-year-old child has been "acting up" and driving his wife crazy. They went for an initial interview at the local mental health clinic where you serve as the executive director and learned that it would be approximately one month before their son could be seen on a regular basis. Could you do anything to move up the appointment? What should you do?

➤ A.21 A House in a New Development

You are employed in a social agency and have developed a very positive relationship with a client, Chip, a very successful real estate agent who is appreciative of the help you have been able to provide for him. You and your wife are interested in buying a house in a new development where construction has been unable to keep up with the demand for new homes. However, you have less of a down payment than is needed, and you also are not high on the waiting list to get into this desirable area.

When you asked Chip about these two problems, he responded by telling you that he would be glad to move you up on the waiting list and would arrange for a loan for the difference in the down payment. Is there a difference between being moved up on the list and accepting the loan which you will repay? What are your choices?

➤ A.22 Christopher, Stella, or Clients?

Garnet Hinckley, a social worker in private practice, is exceptionally conscientious and an excellent practitioner, but she works too many hours and too many days because her family needs money for expensive medical care for her son, Christopher. At the same time, she is driven to provide service to her clients who have difficulty paying fees. She feels she is not paying enough attention to other family members. Her daughter, Stella, has often complained that she misses her and would like her to be home when she arrives from school in the afternoon. However, if she is home when Stella wants her to be, she will lose part of her clientele and further reduce her income. To whom does Ms. Hinckley owe priority loyalty?

➤ A.23 But I Don't Like Him

Joe Sirocco appeared for an initial interview with Marti Holmgren, social worker in the Mt. Everest Counseling Center. He explains what is bothering him. As he talks, Ms. Holmgren feels more and more negative toward him. Eventually, she tells him she can't accept him as a client, although she will help him find another therapist. Mr. Sirocco asks why he is not being accepted. Ms. Holmgren responds that her case load is too full at this time. Was she justified in giving this answer? Should she have told Joe Sirocco the real reason for her decision?

➤ A.24 Must There Be No Relationship?

Arthur Baker has been a client of Anton Forsyte for about six months. Mr. Baker feels that Mr. Forsyte has been very helpful to him and, in fact, the relationship has been very friendly. Mr. Forsyte admires Mr. Baker and enjoys his sense of humor, courage, and problem-solving ability. They also share many common interests, including music and art. But the time has come for terminating the relationship because all Mr. Baker's problems at home and work seem to have worked out well. Mr. Forsyte would like to continue the friendship but wonders at what point he can do so in terms of the *Code*'s prohibitions against dual role relationships. When does the client role end? When can they be friends? Is there a time limit?

➤ **A.25 It All Depends on the Code and How Social Work Is Defined**

Dr. Curtis Worley is a licensed social worker in private practice with extensive credentials, professional training, and a thriving private practice. At one point, he became interested in Eastern philosophies and mysticism, meditation, uses of herbs, and other alternative treatment methods. As he became more educated in these methods, he gradually began to introduce them into his practice. Some patients felt his work was appropriate and helpful. Some even were "worshipful" of his personality and skill. Others believed these new approaches were not helpful and discontinued treatment. One of these latter persons complained to the State Licensing Board that Dr. Worley is unethical and no longer practicing social work. To date, there are no reports of personal harm being done to patients. You are a member of the board and are being asked whether you believe his behavior is ethical.

➤ **A.26 To Report or Not Report a Crime**

Lindsey Robertson has been seeing Tom Bland at the Big Bend Psychiatric Outpatient Center. She was told early during his treatment that Mr. Bland had been tried and found not guilty of embezzlement. Later, he told her that he actually had committed the crime ten years ago. Ms. Robertson decided not to report these facts to anyone because she thought no one can be retried for felony crimes when he is found innocent at trial but later found to have actually committed the crime. Is her assumption correct? Does it make a difference that the worker-client relationship is occurring in a mental health setting?

➤ **A.27 The Whole Truth. . . ?**

A social worker is trying to find an adoptive family for a child. A potential adoptive family has been found. The birth mother was a heroin addict, was malnourished, and the child was born in distress but has now recovered. If you tell the entire story, you believe the family will not adopt the child. You believe that if you don't tell the whole story, they will adopt the child. How much should you tell? Is not telling "all the truth" ethical?

➤ **A.28 You're Needed in Bayville**

A social worker was attacked and killed last week at a community outreach program serving mentally ill persons in Bayville. You found this especially unnerving. Even before the death you worried because you heard that from time to time guns were fired in the neighborhood, although no one had been injured. The agency is a subunit of an overall citywide system of services for this group of people. Your supervisor talks with you and explains that your skills and experience are needed at the outreach site because the death left mainly relatively inexperienced social workers employed there. You don't want to go. What should you do?

➤ **A.29 The Foundation Has Its Own Priorities**

Southside Advocacy Center has a long history of service to the people of the southern part of the city. In fact, the agency is beloved by many persons. The center receives large grants from the Anon Foundation that enable the agency to exist. The foundation, because of its own agenda, asks the agency to move its operation to the southeast, another poor community. It is impossible for the center to serve both neighborhoods, and there has been a clear indication the foundation has developed a special concern—for whatever reason—about the southeast section. They regret having to make the demand but insist they must do so. Both neighborhoods need and deserve help. The southeast section, perhaps, may need help more because the support extended there over the years has been limited. To whom does the agency owe loyalty? Its continued existence? To the south community? Southeast?

➤ **A.30 Regina Has Cancer and Her Parents Can't Agree**

Regina Benson is a three-year-old with terminal cancer who needs palliative care until her expected death. The hospital wants the child to go home to die among her family members. When Susan Blank, social worker, discusses the situation with Patty and Carl Benson, Regina's parents, Mrs. Benson wants Regina to come home for her last months but Mr. Benson is adamantly opposed. He feels the situation will be destructive to their other children. They simply cannot agree. When Susan Blank checks with the hospital administrator, he says the insurance company will pay and the hospital would keep the child until her death. What are Ms. Blank's ethical options in view of the father's adamant position? What is best for the child? For the family? For the insurance company?

Appendix B:
Codes of Ethics

National Association of Social Workers

PREAMBLE

The primary mission of the social work profession is to enhance human well-being and help meet the basic human needs of all people, with particular attention to the needs and empowerment of people who are vulnerable, oppressed, and living in poverty. A historic and defining feature of social work is the profession's focus on individual well-being in a social context and the well-being of society. Fundamental to social work is attention to the environmental forces that create, contribute to, and address problems in living.

Social workers promote social justice and social change with and on behalf of clients. "Clients" is used inclusively to refer to individuals, families, groups, organizations, and communities. Social workers are sensitive to cultural and ethnic diversity and strive to end discrimination, oppression, poverty, and other forms of social injustice. These activities may be in the form of direct practice, community organizing, supervision, consultation, administration, advocacy, social and political action, policy development and implementation, education, and research

Reprinted with permission from NASW *Code of Ethics*. Copyright 1996. National Association of Social Workers, Inc.

and evaluation. Social workers seek to enhance the capacity of people to address their own needs. Social workers also seek to promote the responsiveness of organizations, communities, and other social institutions to individuals' needs and social problems.

The mission of the social work profession is rooted in a set of core values. These core values, embraced by social workers throughout the profession's history, are the foundation of social work's unique purpose and perspective:

- service
- social justice
- dignity and worth of the person
- importance of human relationships
- integrity
- competence.

This constellation of core values reflects what is unique to the social work profession. Core values, and the principles that flow from them, must be balanced within the context and complexity of the human experience.

PURPOSE OF THE NASW CODE OF ETHICS

Professional ethics are at the core of social work. The profession has an obligation to articulate its basic values, ethical principles, and ethical standards. The *NASW Code of Ethics* sets forth these values, principles, and standards to guide social workers' conduct. The *Code* is relevant to all social workers and social work students, regardless of their professional functions, the settings in which they work, or the populations they serve.

The *NASW Code of Ethics* serves six purposes:

1. The *Code* identifies core values on which social work's mission is based.
2. The *Code* summarizes broad ethical principles that reflect the profession's core values and establishes a set of specific ethical standards that should be used to guide social work practice.
3. The *Code* is designed to help social workers identify relevant considerations when professional obligations conflict or ethical uncertainties arise.
4. The *Code* provides ethical standards to which the general public can hold the social work profession accountable.
5. The *Code* socializes practitioners new to the field to social work's mission, values, ethical principles, and ethical standards.

6. The *Code* articulates standards that the social work profession itself can use to assess whether social workers have engaged in unethical conduct. NASW has formal procedures to adjudicate ethics complaints filed against its members.[1] In subscribing to this *Code*, social workers are required to cooperate in its implementation, participate in NASW adjudication proceedings, and abide by any NASW disciplinary rulings or sanctions based on it.

The *Code* offers a set of values, principles, and standards to guide decision making and conduct when ethical issues arise. It does not provide a set of rules that prescribe how social workers should act in all situations. Specific applications of the *Code* must take into account the context in which it is being considered and the possibility of conflicts among the *Code's* values, principles, and standards. Ethical responsibilities flow from all human relationships, from the personal and familial to the social and professional.

Further, the *NASW Code of Ethics* does not specify which values, principles, and standards are most important and ought to outweigh others in instances when they conflict. Reasonable differences of opinion can and do exist among social workers with respect to the ways in which values, ethical principles, and ethical standards should be rank ordered when they conflict. Ethical decision making in a given situation must apply the informed judgment of the individual social worker and should also consider how the issues would be judged in a peer review process where the ethical standards of the profession would be applied.

Ethical decision making is a process. There are many instances in social work where simple answers are not available to resolve complex ethical issues. Social workers should take into consideration all the values, principles, and standards in this *Code* that are relevant to any situation in which ethical judgment is warranted. Social workers' decisions and actions should be consistent with the spirit as well as the letter of this *Code*.

In addition to this *Code*, there are many other sources of information about ethical thinking that may be useful. Social workers should consider ethical theory and principles generally, social work theory and research, laws, regulations, agency policies, and other relevant codes of ethics, recognizing that among codes of ethics social workers should consider the *NASW Code of Ethics* as their primary source. Social workers also should be aware of the impact on ethical decision making of their clients' and their own personal values and cultural and religious beliefs and practices. They should be aware of any conflicts between personal and professional

[1]For information on NASW adjudication procedures, see *NASW Procedures for the Adjudication of Grievances.*

values and deal with them responsibly. For additional guidance social workers should consult the relevant literature on professional ethics and ethical decision making and seek appropriate consultation when faced with ethical dilemmas. This may involve consultation with an agency-based or social work organization's ethics committee, a regulatory body, knowledgeable colleagues, supervisors, or legal counsel.

Instances may arise when social workers' ethical obligations conflict with agency policies or relevant laws or regulations. When such conflicts occur, social workers must make a responsible effort to resolve the conflict in a manner that is consistent with the values, principles, and standards expressed in this *Code*. If a reasonable resolution of the conflict does not appear possible, social workers should seek proper consultation before making a decision.

The *NASW Code of Ethics* is to be used by NASW and by individuals, agencies, organizations, and bodies (such as licensing and regulatory boards, professional liability insurance providers, courts of law, agency boards of directors, government agencies, and other professional groups) that choose to adopt it or use it as a frame of reference. Violation of standards in this *Code* does not automatically imply legal liability or violation of the law. Such determination can only be made in the context of legal and judicial proceedings. Alleged violations of the *Code* would be subject to a peer review process. Such processes are generally separate from legal or administrative procedures and insulated from legal review or proceedings to allow the profession to counsel and discipline its own members.

A code of ethics cannot guarantee ethical behavior. Moreover, a code of ethics cannot resolve all ethical issues or disputes or capture the richness and complexity involved in striving to make responsible choices within a moral community. Rather, a code of ethics sets forth values, ethical principles, and ethical standards to which professionals aspire and by which their actions can be judged. Social workers' ethical behavior should result from their personal commitment to engage in ethical practice. The *NASW Code of Ethics* reflects the commitment of all social workers to uphold the profession's values and to act ethically. Principles and standards must be applied by individuals of good character who discern moral questions and, in good faith, seek to make reliable ethical judgments.

ETHICAL PRINCIPLES

The following broad ethical principles are based on social work's core values of service, social justice, dignity and worth of the person, importance of human relationships, integrity, and competence. These principles set forth ideals to which all social workers should aspire.

Value: *Service*

Ethical Principle: *Social workers' primary goal is to help people in need and to address social problems.*

Social workers elevate service to others above self-interest. Social workers draw on their knowledge, values, and skills to help people in need and to address social problems. Social workers are encouraged to volunteer some portion of their professional skills with no expectation of significant financial return (pro bono service).

Value: *Social Justice*

Ethical Principle: *Social workers challenge social injustice.*

Social workers pursue social change, particularly with and on behalf of vulnerable and oppressed individuals and groups of people. Social workers' social change efforts are focused primarily on issues of poverty, unemployment, discrimination, and other forms of social injustice. These activities seek to promote sensitivity to and knowledge about oppression and cultural and ethnic diversity. Social workers strive to ensure access to needed information, services, and resources; equality of opportunity; and meaningful participation in decision making for all people.

Value: *Dignity and Worth of the Person*

Ethical Principle: *Social workers respect the inherent dignity and worth of the person.*

Social workers treat each person in a caring and respectful fashion, mindful of individual differences and cultural and ethnic diversity. Social workers promote clients' socially responsible self-determination. Social workers seek to enhance clients' capacity and opportunity to change and to address their own needs. Social workers are cognizant of their dual responsibility to clients and to the broader society. They seek to resolve conflicts between clients' interests and the broader society's interests in a socially responsible manner consistent with the values, ethical principles, and ethical standards of the profession.

Value: *Importance of Human Relationships*

Ethical Principle: *Social workers recognize the central importance of human relationships.*

Social workers understand that relationships between and among people are an important vehicle for change. Social workers engage people as partners in the helping process. Social workers seek to strengthen relationships among people in a purposeful effort to promote, restore, maintain, and enhance the well-being of individuals, families, social groups, organizations, and communities.

Value: *Integrity*

Ethical Principle: *Social workers behave in a trustworthy manner.*

Social workers are continually aware of the profession's mission, values, ethical principles, and ethical standards and practice in a manner consistent with them. Social workers act honestly and responsibly and promote ethical practices on the part of the organizations with which they are affiliated.

Value: *Competence*

Ethical Principle: *Social workers practice within their areas of competence and develop and enhance their professional expertise.*

Social workers continually strive to increase their professional knowledge and skills and to apply them in practice. Social workers should aspire to contribute to the knowledge base of the profession.

ETHICAL STANDARDS

The following ethical standards are relevant to the professional activities of all social workers. These standards concern (1) social workers' ethical responsibilities to clients, (2) social workers' ethical responsibilities to colleagues, (3) social workers' ethical responsibilities in practice settings, (4) social workers' ethical responsibilities as professionals, (5) social workers' ethical responsibilities to the social work profession, and (6) social workers' ethical responsibilities to the broader society.

Some of the standards that follow are enforceable guidelines for professional conduct, and some are aspirational. The extent to which each standard is enforceable is a matter of professional judgment to be exercised by those responsible for reviewing alleged violations of ethical standards.

1.   Social Workers' Ethical Responsibilities to Clients

1.01   Commitment to Clients

Social workers' primary responsibility is to promote the well-being of clients. In general, clients' interests are primary. However, social workers' responsibility to the larger society or specific legal obligations may on limited occasions supersede the loyalty owed clients, and clients should be so advised. (Examples include when a social worker is required by law to report that a client has abused a child or has threatened to harm self or others.)

1.02   Self-Determination

Social workers respect and promote the right of clients to self-determination and assist clients in their efforts to identify and clarify their goals. Social workers may limit clients' right to self-determination when, in the social workers' professional judgment, clients' actions or potential actions pose a serious, foreseeable, and imminent risk to themselves or others.

1.03   Informed Consent

(a) Social workers should provide services to clients only in the context of a professional relationship based, when appropriate, on valid informed consent. Social workers should use clear and understandable language to inform clients of the purpose of the services, risks related to the services, limits to services because of the requirements of a third-party payer, relevant costs, reasonable alternatives, clients' right to refuse or withdraw consent, and the time frame covered by the consent. Social workers should provide clients with an opportunity to ask questions.

(b) In instances when clients are not literate or have difficulty understanding the primary language used in the practice setting, social workers should take steps to ensure clients' comprehension. This may include providing clients with a detailed verbal explanation or arranging for a qualified interpreter or translator whenever possible.

(c) In instances when clients lack the capacity to provide informed consent, social workers should protect clients' interests by seeking permission from an appropriate third party, informing clients consistent with the clients' level of understanding. In such instances social workers should seek to ensure that the third party acts in a manner consistent with clients' wishes and interests. Social workers should take reasonable steps to enhance such clients' ability to give informed consent.

(d) In instances when clients are receiving services involuntarily, social workers should provide information about the nature and extent of services and about the extent of clients' right to refuse service.

(e) Social workers who provide services via electronic media (such as computer, telephone, radio, and television) should inform recipients of the limitations and risks associated with such services.

(f) Social workers should obtain clients' informed consent before audiotaping or videotaping clients or permitting observation of services to clients by a third party.

1.04   Competence

(a) Social workers should provide services and represent themselves as competent only within the boundaries of their education, training, license, certification, consultation received, supervised experience, or other relevant professional experience.

(b) Social workers should provide services in substantive areas or use intervention techniques or approaches that are new to them only after engaging in appropriate study, training, consultation, and supervision from people who are competent in those interventions or techniques.

(c) When generally recognized standards do not exist with respect to an emerging area of practice, social workers should exercise careful judgment and take responsible steps (including appropriate education, research, training, consultation, and supervision) to ensure the competence of their work and to protect clients from harm.

1.05   Cultural Competence and Social Diversity

(a) Social workers should understand culture and its function in human behavior and society, recognizing the strengths that exist in all cultures.

(b) Social workers should have a knowledge base of their clients' cultures and be able to demonstrate competence in the provision of services that are sensitive to clients' cultures and to differences among people and cultural groups.

(c) Social workers should obtain education about and seek to understand the nature of social diversity and oppression with respect to race, ethnicity, national origin, color, sex, sexual orientation, age, marital status, political belief, religion, and mental or physical disability

1.06   Conflicts of Interest

(a) Social workers should be alert to and avoid conflicts of interest that interfere with the exercise of professional discretion and impartial judgment. Social workers should inform clients when a real or potential conflict of interest arises and take reasonable steps to resolve the issue in a manner that makes the clients' interests primary and protects clients' interests to the greatest extent possible. In some cases, protecting clients' interests may require termination of the professional relationship with proper referral of the client.

(b) Social workers should not take unfair advantage of any professional relationship or exploit others to further their personal, religious, political, or business interests.

(c) Social workers should not engage in dual or multiple relationships with clients or former clients in which there is a risk of exploitation or potential harm to the client. In instances when dual or multiple relationships are unavoidable, social workers should take steps to protect clients and are responsible for setting clear, appropriate, and culturally sensitive boundaries. (Dual or multiple relationships occur when social workers relate to clients in more than one relationship, whether professional, social, or business. Dual or multiple relationships can occur simultaneously or consecutively.)

(d) When social workers provide services to two or more people who have a relationship with each other (for example, couples, family members), social workers should clarify with all parties which individuals will be considered clients and the nature of social workers' professional obligations to the various individuals who are receiving services. Social workers who anticipate a conflict of interest among the individuals receiving services or who anticipate having to perform in potentially conflicting roles (for example, when a social worker is asked to testify in a child custody dispute or divorce proceedings involving clients) should clarify their role with the parties involved and take appropriate action to minimize any conflict of interest.

1.07 Privacy and Confidentiality

(a) Social workers should respect clients' right to privacy. Social workers should not solicit private information from clients unless it is essential to providing services or conducting social work evaluation or research. Once private information is shared, standards of confidentiality apply.

(b) Social workers may disclose confidential information when appropriate with valid consent from a client or a person legally authorized to consent on behalf of a client.

(c) Social workers should protect the confidentiality of all information obtained in the course of professional service, except for compelling professional reasons. The general expectation that social workers keep information confidential does not apply when disclosure is necessary to prevent serious, foreseeable, and imminent harm to a client or other identifiable person. In all instances, social workers should disclose the least amount of confidential information necessary to achieve the desired purpose; only information that is directly relevant to the purpose for which the disclosure is made should be revealed (revised by NASW Delegate Assembly, August 1999).

(d) Social workers should inform clients, to the extent possible, about the disclosure of confidential information and the potential consequences, when feasible before the disclosure is made. This applies whether social workers disclose confidential information on the basis of a legal requirement or client consent.

(e) Social workers should discuss with clients and other interested parties the nature of confidentiality and limitations of clients' right to confidentiality. Social workers should review with clients circumstances where confidential information may be requested and where disclosure of confidential information may be legally required. This discussion should occur as soon as possible in the social worker-client relationship and as needed throughout the course of the relationship.

(f) When social workers provide counseling services to families, couples, or groups, social workers should seek agreement among the parties involved concerning each individual's right to confidentiality and obligation to preserve the confidentiality of information shared by others. Social workers should inform participants in family, couples, or group counseling that social workers cannot guarantee that all participants will honor such agreements.

(g) Social workers should inform clients involved in family, couples, marital, or group counseling of the social worker's, employer's, and agency's policy concerning the social worker's disclosure of confidential information among the parties involved in the counseling.

(h) Social workers should not disclose confidential information to third-party payers unless clients have authorized such disclosure.

(i) Social workers should not discuss confidential information in any setting unless privacy can be ensured. Social workers should not discuss confidential information in public or semipublic areas such as hallways, waiting rooms, elevators, and restaurants.

(j) Social workers should protect the confidentiality of clients during legal proceedings to the extent permitted by law. When a court of law or other legally authorized body orders social workers to disclose confidential or privileged information without a client's consent and such disclosure could cause harm to the client, social workers should request that the court withdraw the order or limit the order as narrowly as possible or maintain the records under seal, unavailable for public inspection.

(k) Social workers should protect the confidentiality of clients when responding to requests from members of the media.

(l) Social workers should protect the confidentiality of clients' written and electronic records and other sensitive information. Social workers should take reasonable steps to ensure that clients' records are stored in a secure location and that clients' records are not available to others who are not authorized to have access.

(m) Social workers should take precautions to ensure and maintain the confidentiality of information transmitted to other parties through the use of computers, electronic mail, facsimile machines, telephones and telephone answering machines, and other electronic or computer technology. Disclosure of identifying information should be avoided whenever possible.

(n) Social workers should transfer or dispose of clients' records in a manner that protects clients' confidentiality and is consistent with state statutes governing records and social work licensure.

(o) Social workers should take reasonable precautions to protect client confidentiality in the event of the social worker's termination of practice, incapacitation, or death.

(p) Social workers should not disclose identifying information when discussing clients for teaching or training purposes unless the client has consented to disclosure of confidential information.

(q) Social workers should not disclose identifying information when discussing clients with consultants unless the client has consented to disclosure of confidential information or there is a compelling need for such disclosure.

(r) Social workers should protect the confidentiality of deceased clients consistent with the preceding standards.

1.08   Access to Records

(a) Social workers should provide clients with reasonable access to records concerning the clients. Social workers who are concerned that clients' access to their records could cause serious misunderstanding or harm to the client should provide assistance in interpreting the records and consultation with the client regarding the records. Social workers should limit clients' access to their records, or portions of their records, only in exceptional circumstances when there is compelling evidence that such access would cause serious harm to the client. Both clients' requests and the rationale for withholding some or all of the record should be documented in clients' files.

(b) When providing clients with access to their records, social workers should take steps to protect the confidentiality of other individuals identified or discussed in such records.

1.09   Sexual Relationships

(a) Social workers should under no circumstances engage in sexual activities or sexual contact with current clients, whether such contact is consensual or forced.

(b) Social workers should not engage in sexual activities or sexual contact with clients' relatives or other individuals with whom clients maintain a close personal relationship when there is a risk of exploitation or potential harm to the client. Sexual activity or sexual contact with clients' relatives or other individuals with whom clients maintain a personal relationship has the potential to be harmful to the client and may make it difficult for the social worker and client to maintain appropriate professional boundaries. Social workers—not their clients, their clients' relatives, or other individuals with whom the client maintains a personal relationship—assume the full burden for setting clear, appropriate, and culturally sensitive boundaries.

(c) Social workers should not engage in sexual activities or sexual contact with former clients because of the potential for harm to the client. If social workers engage in conduct contrary to this prohibition or claim that an exception to this prohibition is warranted because of extraordinary circumstances, it is social workers—not their clients—who assume the full burden of demonstrating that the former client has not been exploited, coerced, or manipulated, intentionally or unintentionally.

(d) Social workers should not provide clinical services to individuals with whom they have had a prior sexual relationship.

Providing clinical services to a former sexual partner has the potential to be harmful to the individual and is likely to make it difficult for the social worker and individual to maintain appropriate professional boundaries.

1.10   Physical Contact

Social workers should not engage in physical contact with clients when there is a possibility of psychological harm to the client as a result of the contact (such as cradling or caressing clients). Social workers who engage in appropriate physical contact with clients are responsible for setting clear, appropriate, and culturally sensitive boundaries that govern such physical contact.

1.11   Sexual Harassment

Social workers should not sexually harass clients. Sexual harassment includes sexual advances, sexual solicitation, requests for sexual favors, and other verbal or physical conduct of a sexual nature.

1.12   Derogatory Language

Social workers should not use derogatory language in their written or verbal communications to or about clients. Social workers should use accurate and respectful language in all communications to and about clients.

1.13   Payment for Services

(a) When setting fees, social workers should ensure that the fees are fair, reasonable, and commensurate with the services performed. Consideration should be given to clients' ability to pay.

(b) Social workers should avoid accepting goods or services from clients as payment for professional services. Bartering arrangements, particularly involving services, create the potential for conflicts of interest, exploitation, and inappropriate boundaries in social workers' relationships with clients. Social workers should explore and may participate in bartering only in very limited circumstances when it can be demonstrated that such arrangements are an accepted practice among professionals in the local community, considered to be essential for the provision of services, negotiated without coercion, and entered into at the client's initiative and with the client's informed consent. Social workers who accept goods or services from clients as payment for professional services assume the full burden of demonstrating that this arrangement will not be detrimental to the client or the professional relationship.

(c) Social workers should not solicit a private fee or other remuneration for providing services to clients who are entitled to such available services through the social workers' employer or agency.

1.14 Clients Who Lack Decision-Making Capacity

When social workers act on behalf of clients who lack the capacity to make informed decisions, social workers should take reasonable steps to safeguard the interests and rights of those clients.

1.15 Interruption of Services

Social workers should make reasonable efforts to ensure continuity of services in the event that services are interrupted by factors such as unavailability, relocation, illness, disability, or death.

1.16 Termination of Services

(a) Social workers should terminate services to clients and professional relationships with them when such services and relationships are no longer required or no longer serve the clients' needs or interests.

(b) Social workers should take reasonable steps to avoid abandoning clients who are still in need of services. Social workers should withdraw services precipitously only under unusual circumstances, giving careful consideration to all factors in the situation and taking care to minimize possible adverse effects. Social workers should assist in making appropriate arrangements for continuation of services when necessary.

(c) Social workers in fee-for-service settings may terminate services to clients who are not paying an overdue balance if the financial contractual arrangements have been made clear to the client, if the client does not pose an imminent danger to self or others, and if the clinical and other consequences of the current nonpayment have been addressed and discussed with the client.

(d) Social workers should not terminate services to pursue a social, financial, or sexual relationship with a client.

(e) Social workers who anticipate the termination or interruption of services to clients should notify clients promptly and seek the transfer, referral, or continuation of services in relation to the clients' needs and preferences.

(f) Social workers who are leaving an employment setting should inform clients of appropriate options for the continuation of services and of the benefits and risks of the options.

2.   Social Workers' Ethical Responsibilities to Colleagues

2.01   Respect

(a) Social workers should treat colleagues with respect and should represent accurately and fairly the qualifications, views, and obligations of colleagues.

(b) Social workers should avoid unwarranted negative criticism of colleagues in communications with clients or with other professionals. Unwarranted negative criticism may include demeaning comments that refer to colleagues' level of competence or to individuals' attributes such as race, ethnicity, national origin, color, sex, sexual orientation, age, marital status, political belief, religion, and mental or physical disability.

(c) Social workers should cooperate with social work colleagues and with colleagues of other professions when such cooperation serves the well-being of clients.

2.02   Confidentiality

Social workers should respect confidential information shared by colleagues in the course of their professional relationships and transactions. Social workers should ensure that such colleagues understand social workers' obligation to respect confidentiality and any exceptions related to it.

2.03   Interdisciplinary Collaboration

(a) Social workers who are members of an interdisciplinary team should participate in and contribute to decisions that affect the well-being of clients by drawing on the perspectives, values, and experiences of the social work profession. Professional and ethical obligations of the interdisciplinary team as a whole and of its individual members should be clearly established.

(b) Social workers for whom a team decision raises ethical concerns should attempt to resolve the disagreement through appropriate channels. If the disagreement cannot be resolved, social workers should pursue other avenues to address their concerns consistent with client well-being.

2.04   **Disputes Involving Colleagues**

(a) Social workers should not take advantage of a dispute between a colleague and an employer to obtain a position or otherwise advance the social workers' own interests.

(b) Social workers should not exploit clients in disputes with colleagues or engage clients in any inappropriate discussion of conflicts between social workers and their colleagues.

2.05   **Consultation**

(a) Social workers should seek the advice and counsel of colleagues whenever such consultation is in the best interests of clients.

(b) Social workers should keep themselves informed about colleagues' areas of expertise and competencies. Social workers should seek consultation only from colleagues who have demonstrated knowledge, expertise, and competence related to the subject of the consultation.

(c) When consulting with colleagues about clients, social workers should disclose the least amount of information necessary to achieve the purposes of the consultation.

2.06   **Referral for Services**

(a) Social workers should refer clients to other professionals when the other professionals' specialized knowledge or expertise is needed to serve clients fully or when social workers believe that they are not being effective or making reasonable progress with clients and that additional service is required.

(b) Social workers who refer clients to other professionals should take appropriate steps to facilitate an orderly transfer of responsibility. Social workers who refer clients to other professionals should disclose, with clients' consent, all pertinent information to the new service providers.

(c) Social workers are prohibited from giving or receiving payment for a referral when no professional service is provided by the referring social worker.

2.07   **Sexual Relationships**

(a) Social workers who function as supervisors or educators should not engage in sexual activities or contact with supervisees, students, trainees, or other colleagues over whom they exercise professional authority.

(b) Social workers should avoid engaging in sexual relationships with colleagues when there is potential for a conflict of interest. Social workers who become involved in, or anticipate becoming involved in, a sexual relationship with a colleague have a duty to transfer professional responsibilities, when necessary, to avoid a conflict of interest.

2.08 Sexual Harassment

Social workers should not sexually harass supervisees, students, trainees, or colleagues. Sexual harassment includes sexual advances, sexual solicitation, requests for sexual favors, and other verbal or physical conduct of a sexual nature.

2.09 Impairment of Colleagues

(a) Social workers who have direct knowledge of a social work colleague's impairment that is due to personal problems, psychosocial distress, substance abuse, or mental health difficulties and that interferes with practice effectiveness should consult with that colleague when feasible and assist the colleague in taking remedial action.

(b) Social workers who believe that a social work colleague's impairment interferes with practice effectiveness and that the colleague has not taken adequate steps to address the impairment should take action through appropriate channels established by employers, agencies, NASW, licensing and regulatory bodies, and other professional organizations.

2.10 Incompetence of Colleagues

(a) Social workers who have direct knowledge of a social work colleague's incompetence should consult with that colleague when feasible and assist the colleague in taking remedial action.

(b) Social workers who believe that a social work colleague is incompetent and has not taken adequate steps to address the incompetence should take action through appropriate channels established by employers, agencies, NASW, licensing and regulatory bodies, and other professional organizations.

2.11 Unethical Conduct of Colleagues

(a) Social workers should take adequate measures to discourage, prevent, expose, and correct the unethical conduct of colleagues.

(b) Social workers should be knowledgeable about established policies and procedures for handling concerns about colleagues' unethical behavior. Social workers should be familiar with national, state, and local procedures for handling ethics complaints. These include policies and procedures created by NASW, licensing and regulatory bodies, employers, agencies, and other professional organizations.

(c) Social workers who believe that a colleague has acted unethically should seek resolution by discussing their concerns with the colleague when feasible and when such discussion is likely to be productive.

(d) When necessary, social workers who believe that a colleague has acted unethically should take action through appropriate formal channels (such as contacting a state licensing board or regulatory body, an NASW committee on inquiry, or other professional ethics committees).

(e) Social workers should defend and assist colleagues who are unjustly charged with unethical conduct.

3.   Social Workers' Ethical Responsibilities in Practice Settings

3.01   Supervision and Consultation

(a) Social workers who provide supervision or consultation should have the necessary knowledge and skill to supervise or consult appropriately and should do so only within their areas of knowledge and competence.

(b) Social workers who provide supervision or consultation are responsible for setting clear, appropriate, and culturally sensitive boundaries.

(c) Social workers should not engage in any dual or multiple relationships with supervisees in which there is a risk of exploitation of or potential harm to the supervisee.

(d) Social workers who provide supervision should evaluate supervisees' performance in a manner that is fair and respectful.

3.02   Education and Training

(a) Social workers who function as educators, field instructors for students, or trainers should provide instruction only within their areas of knowledge and competence and should provide instruction based on the most current information and knowledge available in the profession.

(b) Social workers who function as educators or field instructors for students should evaluate students' performance in a manner that is fair and respectful.

(c) Social workers who function as educators or field instructors for students should take reasonable steps to ensure that clients are routinely informed when services are being provided by students.

(d) Social workers who function as educators or field instructors for students should not engage in any dual or multiple relationships with students in which there is a risk of exploitation or potential harm to the student. Social work educators and field instructors are responsible for setting clear, appropriate, and culturally sensitive boundaries.

3.03   Performance Evaluation

Social workers who have responsibility for evaluating the performance of others should fulfill such responsibility in a fair and considerate manner and on the basis of clearly stated criteria.

3.04   Client Records

(a) Social workers should take reasonable steps to ensure that documentation in records is accurate and reflects the services provided.

(b) Social workers should include sufficient and timely documentation in records to facilitate the delivery of services and to ensure continuity of services provided to clients in the future.

(c) Social workers' documentation should protect clients' privacy to the extent that is possible and appropriate and should include only information that is directly relevant to the delivery of services.

(d) Social workers should store records following the termination of services to ensure reasonable future access. Records should be maintained for the number of years required by state statutes or relevant contracts.

3.05   Billing

Social workers should establish and maintain billing practices that accurately reflect the nature and extent of services provided and that identify who provided the service in the practice setting.

3.06   Client Transfer

(a) When an individual who is receiving services from another agency or colleague contacts a social worker for services, the social worker should carefully consider the client's needs before agreeing to provide services. To minimize possible confusion and conflict, social workers should discuss with potential clients the nature of the clients' current relationship with other service providers and the implications, including possible benefits or risks, of entering into a relationship with a new service provider. (b) If a new client has been served by another agency or colleague, social workers should discuss with the client whether consultation with the previous service provider is in the client's best interest.

3.07   Administration

(a) Social work administrators should advocate within and outside their agencies for adequate resources to meet clients' needs.

(b) Social workers should advocate for resource allocation procedures that are open and fair. When not all clients' needs can be met, an allocation procedure should be developed that is nondiscriminatory and based on appropriate and consistently applied principles.

(c) Social workers who are administrators should take reasonable steps to ensure that adequate agency or organizational resources are available to provide appropriate staff supervision.

(d) Social work administrators should take reasonable steps to ensure that the working environment for which they are responsible is consistent with and encourages compliance with the *NASW Code of Ethics*. Social work administrators should take reasonable steps to eliminate any conditions in their organizations that violate, interfere with, or discourage compliance with the *Code.*

3.08   Continuing Education and Staff Development

Social work administrators and supervisors should take reasonable steps to provide or arrange for continuing education and staff development for all staff for whom they are responsible. Continuing education and staff development should address current knowledge and emerging developments related to social work practice and ethics.

3.09   Commitments to Employers

(a) Social workers generally should adhere to commitments made to employers and employing organizations.

(b) Social workers should work to improve employing agencies' policies and procedures and the efficiency and effectiveness of their services.

(c) Social workers should take reasonable steps to ensure that employers are aware of social workers' ethical obligations as set forth in the *NASW Code of Ethics* and of the implications of those obligations for social work practice.

(d) Social workers should not allow an employing organization's policies, procedures, regulations, or administrative orders to interfere with their ethical practice of social work. Social workers should take reasonable steps to ensure that their employing organizations' practices are consistent with the *NASW Code of Ethics*.

(e) Social workers should act to prevent and eliminate discrimination in the employing organization's work assignments and in its employment policies and practices.

(f) Social workers should accept employment or arrange student field placements only in organizations that exercise fair personnel practices.

(g) Social workers should be diligent stewards of the resources of their employing organizations, wisely conserving funds where appropriate and never misappropriating funds or using them for unintended purposes.

3.10   Labor–Management Disputes

(a) Social workers may engage in organized action, including the formation of and participation in labor unions, to improve services to clients and working conditions.

(b) The actions of social workers who are involved in labor-management disputes, job actions, or labor strikes should be guided by the profession's values, ethical principles, and ethical standards. Reasonable differences of opinion exist among social workers concerning their primary obligation as professionals during an actual or threatened labor strike or job action. Social workers should carefully examine relevant issues and their possible impact on clients before deciding on a course of action.

4.   Social Workers' Ethical Responsibilities as Professionals

4.01   Competence

(a) Social workers should accept responsibility or employment only on the basis of existing competence or the intention to acquire the necessary competence.

(b) Social workers should strive to become and remain proficient in professional practice and the performance of professional functions. Social workers should critically examine and keep current with emerging knowledge relevant to social work.

Social workers should routinely review the professional literature and participate in continuing education relevant to social
work practice and social work ethics.

(c) Social workers should base practice on recognized knowledge, including empirically based knowledge, relevant to social
work and social work ethics.

4.02   Discrimination

Social workers should not practice, condone, facilitate, or collaborate with any form of discrimination on the basis of race, ethnicity, national origin, color, sex, sexual orientation, age, marital
status, political belief, religion, or mental or physical disability.

4.03   Private Conduct

Social workers should not permit their private conduct to interfere with their ability to fulfill their professional responsibilities.

4.04   Dishonesty, Fraud, and Deception

Social workers should not participate in, condone, or be associated with dishonesty, fraud, or deception.

4.05   Impairment

(a) Social workers should not allow their own personal problems, psychosocial distress, legal problems, substance abuse, or
mental health difficulties to interfere with their professional
judgment and performance or to jeopardize the best interests of
people for whom they have a professional responsibility.

(b) Social workers whose personal problems, psychosocial distress, legal problems, substance abuse, or mental health difficulties interfere with their professional judgment and
performance should immediately seek consultation and take
appropriate remedial action by seeking professional help, making adjustments in workload, terminating practice, or taking any
other steps necessary to protect clients and others.

4.06   Misrepresentation

(a) Social workers should make clear distinctions between statements made and actions engaged in as a private individual and as
a representative of the social work profession, a professional
social work organization, or the social worker's employing agency.

(b) Social workers who speak on behalf of professional social
work organizations should accurately represent the official and
authorized positions of the organizations.

(c) Social workers should ensure that their representations to clients, agencies, and the public of professional qualifications, credentials, education, competence, affiliations, services provided, or results to be achieved are accurate. Social workers should claim only those relevant professional credentials they actually possess and take steps to correct any inaccuracies or misrepresentations of their credentials by others.

4.07   Solicitations

(a) Social workers should not engage in uninvited solicitation of potential clients who, because of their circumstances, are vulnerable to undue influence, manipulation, or coercion.

(b) Social workers should not engage in solicitation of testimonial endorsements (including solicitation of consent to use a client's prior statement as a testimonial endorsement) from current clients or from other people who, because of their particular circumstances, are vulnerable to undue influence.

4.08   Acknowledging Credit

(a) Social workers should take responsibility and credit, including authorship credit, only for work they have actually performed and to which they have contributed.

(b) Social workers should honestly acknowledge the work of and the contributions made by others.

5.   Social Workers' Ethical Responsibilities to the Social Work Profession

5.01   Integrity of the Profession

(a) Social workers should work toward the maintenance and promotion of high standards of practice.

(b) Social workers should uphold and advance the values, ethics, knowledge, and mission of the profession. Social workers should protect, enhance, and improve the integrity of the profession through appropriate study and research, active discussion, and responsible criticism of the profession.

(c) Social workers should contribute time and professional expertise to activities that promote respect for the value, integrity, and competence of the social work profession. These activities may include teaching, research, consultation, service, legislative testimony, presentations in the community, and participation in their professional organizations.

(d) Social workers should contribute to the knowledge base of social work and share with colleagues their knowledge related to practice, research, and ethics. Social workers should seek to contribute to the profession's literature and to share their knowledge at professional meetings and conferences.

(e) Social workers should act to prevent the unauthorized and unqualified practice of social work.

5.02   Evaluation and Research

(a) Social workers should monitor and evaluate policies, the implementation of programs, and practice interventions.

(b) Social workers should promote and facilitate evaluation and research to contribute to the development of knowledge.

(c) Social workers should critically examine and keep current with emerging knowledge relevant to social work and fully use evaluation and research evidence in their professional practice.

(d) Social workers engaged in evaluation or research should carefully consider possible consequences and should follow guidelines developed for the protection of evaluation and research participants. Appropriate institutional review boards should be consulted.

(e) Social workers engaged in evaluation or research should obtain voluntary and written informed consent from participants, when appropriate, without any implied or actual deprivation or penalty for refusal to participate; without undue inducement to participate; and with due regard for participants' well-being, privacy, and dignity. Informed consent should include information about the nature, extent, and duration of the participation requested and disclosure of the risks and benefits of participation in the research.

(f) When evaluation or research participants are incapable of giving informed consent, social workers should provide an appropriate explanation to the participants, obtain the participants' assent to the extent they are able, and obtain written consent from an appropriate proxy.

(g) Social workers should never design or conduct evaluation or research that does not use consent procedures, such as certain forms of naturalistic observation and archival research, unless rigorous and responsible review of the research has found it to be justified because of its prospective scientific, educational, or applied value and unless equally effective alternative procedures that do not involve waiver of consent are not feasible.

(h) Social workers should inform participants of their right to withdraw from evaluation and research at any time without penalty.

(i) Social workers should take appropriate steps to ensure that participants in evaluation and research have access to appropriate supportive services.

(j) Social workers engaged in evaluation or research should protect participants from unwarranted physical or mental distress, harm, danger, or deprivation.

(k) Social workers engaged in the evaluation of services should discuss collected information only for professional purposes and only with people professionally concerned with this information.

(l) Social workers engaged in evaluation or research should ensure the anonymity or confidentiality of participants and of the data obtained from them. Social workers should inform participants of any limits of confidentiality, the measures that will be taken to ensure confidentiality, and when any records containing research data will be destroyed.

(m) Social workers who report evaluation and research results should protect participants' confidentiality by omitting identifying information unless proper consent has been obtained authorizing disclosure.

(n) Social workers should report evaluation and research findings accurately. They should not fabricate or falsify results and should take steps to correct any errors later found in published data using standard publication methods.

(o) Social workers engaged in evaluation or research should be alert to and avoid conflicts of interest and dual relationships with participants, should inform participants when a real or potential conflict of interest arises, and should take steps to resolve the issue in a manner that makes participants' interests primary.

(p) Social workers should educate themselves, their students, and their colleagues about responsible research practices.

6.   Social Workers' Ethical Responsibilities to the Broader Society

6.01   Social Welfare

Social workers should promote the general welfare of society, from local to global levels, and the development of people, their communities, and their environments. Social workers should advocate for living conditions conducive to the fulfillment of basic human needs and should promote social, economic, political, and cultural values and institutions that are compatible with the realization of social justice.

6.02   Public Participation

Social workers should facilitate informed participation by the public in shaping social policies and institutions.

6.03   Public Emergencies

Social workers should provide appropriate professional services in public emergencies to the greatest extent possible.

6.04   Social and Political Action

(a) Social workers should engage in social and political action that seeks to ensure that all people have equal access to the resources, employment, services, and opportunities they require to meet their basic human needs and to develop fully. Social workers should be aware of the impact of the political arena on practice and should advocate for changes in policy and legislation to improve social conditions in order to meet basic human needs and promote social justice.

(b) Social workers should act to expand choice and opportunity for all people, with special regard for vulnerable, disadvantaged, oppressed, and exploited people and groups.

(c) Social workers should promote conditions that encourage respect for cultural and social diversity within the United States and globally. Social workers should promote policies and practices that demonstrate respect for difference, support the expansion of cultural knowledge and resources, advocate for programs and institutions that demonstrate cultural competence, and promote policies that safeguard the rights of and confirm equity and social justice for all people.

(d) Social workers should act to prevent and eliminate domination of, exploitation of, and discrimination against any person, group, or class on the basis of race, ethnicity, national origin, color, sex, sexual orientation, age, marital status, political belief, religion, or mental or physical disability.

National Association
of Black Social Workers

In America today, no Black person, except the selfish or irrational, can claim neutrality in the quest for Black liberation nor fail to consider the implications of events taking place in our society. Given the necessity for committing ourselves to the struggle for freedom, we as Black Americans practicing in the field of social welfare set forth this statement of ideals and guiding principles.

If a sense of community awareness is a precondition to humanitarian acts, then we as Black social workers must use our knowledge of the Black community, our commitments to its self-determination and our helping skills for the benefit of Black people as we marshal our expertise to improve the quality of life of Black people. Our activities will be guided by our Black consciousness, our determination to protect the security of the Black community and to serve as advocates to relieve suffering of Black people by any means necessary.

Therefore, as Black social workers we commit ourselves, collectively, to the interests of our Black brethren and as individuals subscribe to the following statements:

> I regard as my primary obligation the welfare of the Black individual, Black family and Black community and will engage in action for improving social conditions.
>
> I give preference to this mission over my personal interests.
>
> I adopt the concept of a Black extended family and embrace all Black people as my brothers and sisters, making no distinction between their destiny and my own.
>
> I hold myself responsible for the quality and extent of service performed by the agency or organization in which I am employed, as it relates to the Black community.
>
> I accept the responsibility to protect the Black community against unethical and hypocritical practice by any individuals or organizations engaged in social welfare activities.
>
> I stand ready to supplement my paid or professional advocacy with voluntary service in the Black public interest.
>
> I will consciously use my skills, and my whole being, as an instrument for social change, with particular attention directed to the establishment of Black social institutions.

Clinical Social Work Federation

PREAMBLE

The principal objective of the profession of clinical social work is the enhancement of the mental health and the well-being of the individuals and families who seek services from its practitioners. The professional practice of clinical social workers is shaped by ethical principles which are rooted in the basic values of the social work profession. These core values include a commitment to the dignity, well-being, and self-determination of the individual; a commitment to professional practice characterized by competence and integrity, and a commitment to a society which offers opportunities to all its members in a just and non-discriminatory manner. Clinical social workers examine practice situations in terms of the ethical dilemmas that they present, with a critical analysis of how the formulation of a solution fulfills the core requirements of ethical practice; non-malfeasance, (doing no harm to clients); beneficence, (helping clients), and autonomy (enhancing the self-determination of clients).

The following represents a specific codification of those ethical principles. It is intended to serve as a standard for clinical social workers in all of their professional functions, and to inspire their will to act in a manner consistent with those tenets. The clinical social worker is expected to take into consideration all principles in this code that have a bearing upon any situation in which ethical judgment is to be exercised, and to select a course of action consistent with the spirit, as well as the letter of the code.

Individual members of the Clinical Social Work Federation and of the various State Societies for Clinical Social Work agree to adhere to the precepts expressed in this Code, and to practice in a manner which is consistent with them. When the practice of a member is alleged to deviate from the Code of Ethics, the Code is to be used as a standard for the evaluation of the nature and seriousness of the deviation.

I. GENERAL RESPONSIBILITIES OF CLINICAL SOCIAL WORKERS

Clinical social workers maintain high standards in all of their professional roles, and value professional competence, objectivity, and integrity.

This *Code of Ethics* was revised in 1997 and is included here with the permission of the Clinical Social Work Federation.

They accept responsibility for the consequences of their work, and ensure that their services are used in an appropriate manner.

a) Clinical social workers bear a heavy professional responsibility because their actions and recommendations may significantly affect the lives of others. They practice only within their sphere of competence, and maintain and enhance that competence through participation in continuing professional development throughout their careers. They refrain from undertaking or continuing any professional activity in which their personal difficulties, or any other limitations, might lead to the inadequate provision of service.

b) Clinical social workers do not exploit professional relationships sexually, financially, or for any other professional and/or personal advantage. They maintain this standard of conduct toward all those who may be professionally associated with them.

c) Clinical social workers often function as employees in clinics, hospitals, and agencies, or, as providers on managed care panels. In these positions, they are responsible for identifying and actively working to modify policies or procedures which may come into conflict with the standards of their profession. If such a conflict arises, the primary responsibility of the clinical social worker is to uphold the ethical standards of the profession. These standards require that commitment to the welfare of the client(s) is the primary obligation.

d) Clinical social workers have an additional responsibility, both to the profession which provides the basis of their practice, and to those who are entering that profession. As teachers, supervisors, and mentors, they are responsible for maintaining high standards of objectivity and scholarship. In all of their professional activities they consistently examine, and attempt to expand, the knowledge base on which practice in the profession is centered.

II. RESPONSIBILITY TO CLIENTS

The primary responsibility of the clinical social worker is to the individual client, the family or the group with whom he or she has a professional relationship. Clinical social workers respect the dignity, protect the welfare, and maximize the self-determination of the clients with whom they work.

1. INFORMED CONSENT TO TREATMENT

a) Clinical social work treatment takes place within a context of informed consent. This requires that the client(s) be informed of the extent and nature of the services being offered as well as the mutual

limits, rights, opportunities, and obligations associated with the provision of and payment for those services. In order for the consent
to be valid, the client(s) must be informed in a manner which is clear
to them, must choose freely and without undue influence, and must
have the capacity to make an informed choice. In instances where
clients are not of legal age or competent to give a meaningful consent, they will be informed in a manner which is consistent with their
level of understanding. In such situations, authorization for treatment will be obtained from an appropriate third party, such as a parent or other legal guardian.

b) Clinical social workers have a duty to understand the potential
impact on all aspects of treatment resulting from participation in
various third party payment mechanisms, and to disclose fully their
knowledge of these features to the client. Such features might
include, but are not limited to; limitations of confidentiality; payment limitations related to provider choice; a summary of the treatment review process required by the plan; the comparative treatment
orientations of the plan and of the clinical social worker; the possibility that benefits may be limited under the plan; the clinical social
worker's relationship to the plan and any incentives to limit or deny
care; and, the availability of alternative treatment options.

2. PRACTICE MANAGEMENT AND TERMINATION

a) Clinical social workers enter into and/or continue professional relationships based on their ability to meet the needs of clients appropriately. The clinical social worker terminates services and
relationships with clients when such services and relationships are
no longer in the client's best interest. Clinical social workers do not
abandon clients by withdrawing services precipitously, except under
extraordinary circumstances.

Clinical social workers give careful consideration to all factors
involved in termination and take care to minimize the possible
adverse effects it might have on the client(s). When interruption or
termination of service is anticipated, the clinical social worker gives
resonable notification and provides for transfer, referral, or continuation of service in a manner as consistent as possible with the
client's needs and preferences.

b) Clinical social workers providing services which are reimbursed by
third party payers continue to have primary responsibility for the
welfare of the client(s). The failure of the third party to authorize
continued benefits does not remove the obligation of the clinical
social worker to assure necessary treatment, if this is in the client's

best interests. When benefits are ended, the clinical social worker has a number of options including; acceptance of private payment for continued services, at either regular or reduced rates; provision of services on an unpaid basis; and, referral to appropriate alternative treatment sources.

c) A clinical social worker who disagrees with the denial of continued benefits by a third party payer is responsible for discussing this action with the client(s), and for devising a clinically appropriate plan, which may or may not include appeal of the decision. Further pursuit of the appeals process will be based on such facotrs as; the degree to which the clinical social worker believes that further treatment is necessary for the client's well-being; the degree to which the client(s) wishes to pursue the appeals process, and; the degree to which there are alternative means available for the client(s) to continue treatment.

d) Clinical social workers keep records for each individual and family they treat which reflect relevant administrative rules, contractual obligations, and local and federal statutes. They are required to be knowledgeable about statutes relating to client access to records, and to fulfill their responsibility as required by law. When access to records is permitted, the clinical social worker will take appropriate, legally permitted steps to protect the privacy of all third parties who may be named in the records.

e) All requirements regarding the establishment, maintenance, and disposal of records relate equally to written and to electronic records.

Clinical social workers establish a policy on record retention and disposal, or are aware of agency policies regarding these issues, and communicate it to the client. In the event of the death or incapacity of a client, they safeguard the record, within existing statues, and the information contained therein. Clinical social workers have a plan or procedure for the proper handling of client records in the event of their own death or disability which both protects privacy, and ensures that legitimate access functions can be properly carried out.

3. RELATIONSHIPS WITH CLIENTS

a) Clinical social workers are responsible for setting clear and appropriate professional boundaries, especially in those instances in which dual or multiple relationships are unavoidable. They do not engage in dual or multiple relationships in which there is any risk of their professional judgment being compromised, or of the client being harmed or exploited. When clinical social workers provide services to two or more persons who have a relationship with each other, they clarify with all parties the nature of the professional responsibilities to each of them, and the ways in which appropriate boundaries will be maintained.

b) Clinical social workers do not, under any circumstances, engage in romantic or sexual contact with either current or former clients. Clinical social workers are also mindful of how their relationship with the family and/or friends of their clients might affect their work with the client. Consequently, they also avoid romantic or sexual involvements with members of the client's family, or with others with whom the client has a close, personal relationship.

c) Clinical social workers are aware of the authority which is inherent in their professional role. They do not engage in any activity that will abuse their professional relationships or exploit others for personal, political, or business interests. As practitioners, supervisors, teachers, administrators, and researchers their primary professional responsibility is always the welfare of the client(s) with whom they work.

d) When the clinical social worker must act on behalf of a client, that action should always safeguard the interests and concerns of that client. When another person has been authorized to act on behalf of a client, the clinical social worker should deal with that person in a manner which will safeguard the interests and concerns of the client.

e) Clinical social workers recognize and support the right to self-determination of clients who may choose not to relinquish their privacy by pursuing third party reimbursement for treatment, even when they are eligible for such reimbursement. In such instances, the clinical social worker makes every effort to assist the client in making alternative financial arrangements so that treatment can proceed.

f) When a clinical social worker determines that a conflict potentially detrimental to the treatment process has arisen, he or she should inform the individual(s) to whom he or she has a professional responsibility of the nature of the conflict and the way in which it might affect the provision of service.

4. COMPETENCE

a) Clinical social workers are aware of the scope in which they are entitled to practice. This scope is defined by their areas of personal competence; by their license or other legal recognition; and by their training and/or experience. They are responsible for confining their practice to those areas in which they are legally authorized and in which they are qualified to practice. When necessary, they utilize the knowledge and experience of members of other professions. In using such consultants or supervisors, the clinical social worker is responsible for ensuring that they are recognized members of their own profession, and are qualified and competent to carry out the service required.

b) Clinical social workers recognize that the privacy and intimacy of the therapeutic relationship may unrealistically intensify the client's feelings for them. The maintenance of professional boundaries and objectivity is crucial to effective and responsible treatment. Clinical social workers maintain self awareness and take care to prevent the possible harmful intrusion of their own unresolved personal issues into the therapeutic relationship. They take appropriate steps to resolve the situation when there is a danger of this occurring. Such steps could include, but are not limited to; seeking additional supervision or consultation; seeking additional personal treatment; and, if necessary, making alternative arrangements for the treatment of the client(s).

c) Clinical social workers recognize the responsibility to remain abreast of knowledge and developments in the field which may benefit their client(s). Ongoing involvement in supervision, consultation, and continuing education are some of the ways in which this responsibility can be fulfilled. It is particularly important for the clinical social worker to secure appropriate training, supervision, or consultation when attempting to use a treatment technique with which he or she is unfamiliar.

III. CONFIDENTIALITY

Clinical social workers have a primary obligation to maintain the privacy of both current and former clients, whether living or deceased, and to maintain the confidentiality of material that has been transmitted to them in any of their professional roles. Exceptions to this responsibility will occur only when there are overriding legal or professional reasons and, whenever possible, with the written informed consent of the client(s).

a) Clinical social workers discuss fully with clients both the nature of confidentiality, and potential limits to confidentiality which may arise during the course of their work. Confidential information should only be released, whenever possible, with the written permission of the client(s). As part of the process of obtaining such a release, the clinical social worker should inform the client(s) about the nature of the information being sought, the purpose(s) for which it is being sought, to whom the information will be released, how the client(s) may withdraw permission for its release, and, the length of time that the release will be in effect.

b) Clinical social workers know and observe both legal and professional standards for maintaining the privacy of records, and mandatory reporting obligations. Mandatory reporting obligations may include, but are not limited to; the reporting of the abuse or neglect of children or of vulnerable adults; the duty to take steps to protect or warn a third party who may be endangered by the client(s); and, any duty to report the misconduct or impairment of another professional. Additional limits to confidentiality may occur because of parental access to the records of a minor, the access of legal guardians to the records of some adults, access by the courts to mandated reports, and access by third party payers to information for the purpose of treatment authorization or audit. When confidential information is released to a third party, the clinical social worker will ensure that the information divulged is limited to the minimum amount required to accomplish the purpose for which the release is being made.

c) Clinical social workers treating couples, families, and groups seek agreement among the parties involved regarding each individual's right to confidentiality, and the mutual obligation to protect the confidentiality of information shared by other parties to the treatment. Clients involved in this type of treatment should, however, be informed that the clinical social worker cannot guarantee that all participants will honor their agreement to maintain confidentiality.

d) When confidential information is used for purposes of professional education, research, or publication, the primary responsibility of the clinical social worker is the protection of the client(s) from possible harm, embarrassment, or exploitation. When extensive material is used for any of these purposes the clinical social worker makes every effort to obtain the informed consent of the client(s) for such use, and will not proceed if the client(s) denies this consent. Whether or not a consent is obtained, every effort will be made to protect the true identity of the client. Any such presentation will be limited to the amount necessary for the professional purpose, and will be shared only with other responsible individuals.

e) The development of new technologies for the storage and transmission of data poses a great danger to the privacy of individuals. Clinical social workers take special precautions to protect the confidentiality of material stored or transmitted through computers, electronic mail, facsimile machines, telephones, telephone answering machines, and all other electronic or computer technology. When using these technologies, disclosure of identifying information regarding the client(s) should be avoided whenever possible.

IV. RELATIONSHIPS WITH COLLEAGUES

Clinical social workers act with integrity in their relationships with colleagues and members of other professions. They know and take into account the traditions, practices, and areas of competence of other professionals and cooperate with them fully for the welfare of clients.

a) Clinical social workers represent accurately the views, qualifications, and findings of colleagues. When expressing judgment on these matters they do so in a manner that is sensitive to the best interests of both colleagues and clients.

b) If a clinical social worker's services are sought by an individual who is already receiving similar services from another professional, consideration for the client's welfare is the primary concern. This concern requires that the clinical social worker proceed with great caution, carefully considering the existing professional relationship, the therapeutic issues involved, and whether it is therapeutically and ethically appropriate to be involved in the situation.

c) As supervisors, consultants, or employers, clinical social workers are responsible for providing competent professional guidance and a role model to colleagues, employees, and students. They foster working conditions that assure consistency, respect, privacy, and protection from physical or mental harm. Clinical social workers do not abuse the authority of their position by harassing or pressuring colleagues, employees, or students for sexual reasons, financial gain, or any other purpose. They refrain from actions that are unwanted by the recipient, and can resonably be interpreted as pressuring or intimidating the recipient.

d) Clinical social workers carry out their responsibility to both clients and the profession by maintaining high standards of practice within the professional community. They take appropriate measures to discourage, prevent, expose, and correct unethical or incompetent behavior by colleagues, and also assist and defend colleagues believed to be unjustly charged with such conduct. They discourage the practice of clinical social work by those who fail to meet accepted standards of training and experience, or who are practicing outside of their area of competence.

e) Clinical social workers who have knowledge of a colleague's impairment, misconduct, or incompetence attempt to bring about remediation through whatever means is appropriate. Such actions may include, but are not limited to; direct discussion with the colleague, with permission from the client(s) if this is needed; a report, if mandatory, to a regulatory body, professional organization, or employer, a report to a supervisor, or other agency administrator.

V. FEE ARRANGEMENTS

When setting fees, clinical social workers should give consideration to the client's ability to pay and make every effort to establish fees that are fair, reasonable, and commensurate with the value of the service performed.

a) In the initial contact with the client(s) fees for services and policies regarding fee collection should be clarified. This clarification should also take into account any financial constraint which may affect the treatment process.

b) It is unethical for a clinical social worker to offer, give, solicit, or receive any fee or other consideration to or from a third party for the referral of a client. They accept reimbursement from clients and from third party payers only for services directly rendered to the client(s). Clinical social workers may, however, participate in contractual arrangements in which they agree to discount their fees.

c) A clinical social worker who contracts with a third party payer agrees to abide by the conditions of the contract. If, however, the clinical social worker believes the contract contains elements which violate the ethics of the profession, the clinical social worker seeks to redress this situation through appropriate courses of action which may include; obtaining the other party's agreement to delete the clause; or, refusing to sign the contract.

d) Barter arrangements, in which goods or services are accepted from clients as payment for professional services, should be avoided as much as possible. Such plans, especially when they involve provision of services by the client(s), have the potential to constitute dual relationships which will damage the treatment. Barter arrangements may be entered into only in rare situations, and may only involve provision of goods, as opposed to services, in exchange for treatment. Such arrangements can only be entered into upon the specific request of the client, and when the following additional criteria are met; traditional payment methods are not possible; the client(s) is not coerced or exploited in any way, and; the arrangement is not detrimental to the client(s) or to the professional relationship.

e) Clinical social workers employed by an agency or clinic, and also engaged in private practice, conform to contractual agreements with the employing facility. They do not solicit or accept a private fee or consideration of any kind for providing a service to which the client is entitled through the employing facility.

VI. CLINICAL SOCIAL WORKERS' RESPONSIBILITIES TO THE COMMUNITY

Clinical social workers are aware of the social codes and ethical expectations in their communities, and recognize that violation of accepted societal, ethical, legal, and moral standards on their part may compromise the fulfillment of their professional responsibilities and/or reduce public trust in the profession.

a) Clinical social workers do not, in any of their capacities, practice, condone, facilitate, or collaborate with any form of discrimination on the basis of race, religion, color, national origin, gender, sexual orientation, age, socioeconomic status, or physical or emotional disability.

b) Clinical social workers practice their profession in compliance with legal standards, and do not participate in arrangements or activities which undermine or violate the law. When they believe, however, that laws or community standards are in conflict with the principles and ethics of the profession, they make known the conflict and work responsibility toward change that is in the public interest.

c) Clinical social workers recognize a responsibility to participate in activities leading toward improved social conditions. They should advocate and work for conditions and resources that give all persons equal access to the services and opportunities required to meet basic needs and to develop to the fullest potential.

VII. RESEARCH AND SCHOLARLY ACTIVITIES

In planning, conducting, and reporting a study, the investigator has the responsibility to make a careful evaluation of its ethical acceptability, taking into account the following additional principles for research with human subjects. To the extent that this appraisal, weighing scientific and humane values, suggests a compromise of any principle, the investigator incurs an increasingly serious obligation to observe stringent safeguards to protect the rights and well-being of research participants.

a) In conducting research in institutions or organizations, clinical social workers obtain appropriate authority to carry out their work. Host organizations are given proper credit for their contributions to the project.

b) Ethically acceptable research begins with the establishment of a clear and fair agreement between the investigator and the research participant that clarifies the responsibilities of each. The investigator has the obligation to honor all commitments included in that agreement.

c) Responsibility for the establishment and maintenance of acceptable ethical practice in research always remains with the investigator. The investigator is also responsible for the ethical treatment of research participants by collaborators, assistants, students, and employees, all of whom incur parallel obligations.

d) Ethical practice requires the investigator to inform the participant of all features of the research that might reasonably be expected to influence willingness to participate, and to explain all other aspects of the research about which the participant inquires. After the data are collected, the investigator provides the participant with information about the nature of the study in order to remove any misconceptions that may have arisen.

e) The ethical investigator protects participants from physical and mental discomfort, harm, and danger. If a risk of such consequences exists, the investigator is required to inform the participant of that fact, secure consent before proceeding, and take all possible measures to minimize distress. A research procedure must not be used if it is likely to cause serious or lasting harm to a participant.

f) The methodological requirements of the study may necessitate concealment, deception, or minimal risk to participants. In such cases, the investigator must be able to justify the use of these techniques and to ensure, as soon as possible, the participant's understanding of the reasons and sufficient justification fo the procedure in question.

g) Ethical practice requires the investigator to respect the individual's freedom to decline to participate in, or withdraw from, research and to so inform prospective participants. The obligation to protect this freedom requires special vigilance when the investigator is, in any manner, in a position of authority over the participant. It is unethical to penalize a participant in any way for withdrawing from or refusing to participate in a research project.

h) Information obtained about the individual research participants during the course of an investigation is confidential unless otherwise agreed to in advance.

i) Investigation of human subjects in studies which use drugs, are conducted only in conjunction with licensed physicians.

j) Clinical social workers take credit only for work actually done in scholarly and research projects, and give appropriate credit to the contributions of others in a manner which is proportional to the degree to which those contributions are represented in the final product.

k) Research findings must be presented accurately and completely, with full discussion of both their usefulness and their limitations. Clinical social workers are responsible for attempting to prevent any distortion or misuse of their findings.

VIII. PUBLIC STATEMENTS

Public statements, announcements of services, and promotional activities of clinical social workers serve the purpose of providing sufficient information to aid consumers in making informed judgments and choices. Clinical social workers state accurately, objectively, and without misrepresentation their professional qualifications, affiliations, and functions as well as those of the institutions or organizations with which they or their statements may be associated. In addition, they should correct the misrepresentations of others with respect to these matters.

a) In announcing availability for professional services, protection of the public is the primary concern. A clinical social worker may use any information so long as it describes his or her credentials and the services provided accurately and without misrepresentation. Information usually found helpful by the public includes the name of the professional; highest relevant academic degree from an accredited institution; specialized post-graduate training; type and level of state certification or license; any advanced certifications held; address and telephone number; office hours; type of service provided; languages spoken; and, policy with regard to third party payments.

b) In annnouncements of available professional services, information regarding fees and fee policies may also be found helpful by prospective clients. Appropriate announcements of this type could include such general terms as "moderate fees." It is unethical to make statements regarding fees or fee policies which are deceptive, or misrepresent the actual fee arrangements.

c) The clinical social worker is responsible for assuring that all advertising is in conformity with the ethical standards of the profession. Publications announcing any type of clinic social work service describe those services accurately. They do not falsely or deceptively claim or imply superior personal or professional competence.

d) Clinical social workers are free to make public appearances and engage in public discussion regarding issues such as, for example, the relative value of alternative treatment approaches. Diagnostic and therapeutic services for clients, however, are rendered only in the context of a professional relationship. Such services are not given by means of public lectures, newspaper or magazine articles, radio or television programs, or anything of a similar nature. Professional use of the media or of other public forums is appropriate when the purpose is to educate the public about professional matters regarding which the clinical social worker has special knowledge or expertise.

e) Clinical social workers respect the rights and reputation of any professional organization with which they are affiliated, and do not falsely imply sponsorship or certification by any organization. When making public statements, the clinical social worker will make clear which are personal opinions, and which are authorized statements on behalf of the organization.

Canadian Association of Social Workers

PREAMBLE

Philosophy

The profession of social work is founded on humanitarian and egalitarian ideals. Social workers believe in the intrinsic worth and dignity of every human being and are committed to the values of acceptance, self-determination and respect of individuality. They believe in the obligation of all people, individually and collectively, to provide resources, services and opportunities for the overall benefit of humanity. The culture of individuals, families, groups, communities and nations has to be respected without prejudice.

Social workers are dedicated to the welfare and self-realization of human beings; to the development and disciplined use of scientific knowledge regarding human and societal behaviours; to the development of resources to meet individual, group, national and international needs and aspirations; and to the achievement of social justice for all.

Professional Practice Conflicts

If a conflict arises in professional practice, the standards declared in this code take precedence. Conflicts of interest may occur because of demands from the general public, workplace, organizations or clients. In all cases, if the ethical duties and obligations or ethical responsibilities of this Code would be compromised, the social worker must act in a manner consistent with this Code.

Nature of this Code

The first seven statements in this code establish ethical duties and obligations. These statements provide the basis of a social worker's relationship with a client and are based on the values of social work. A breach of any of these statements forms the basis of a disciplinary action. The remaining three statements are characterized as ethical responsibilities and are to be seen as being different from the ehtical duties and obliga-

This *Social Work Code of Ethics*, adopted by the board of directors of the Canadian Association of Social Workers (CASW), is effective January 1, 1994, and replaces the CASW Code of Ethics (1983). The *Code* is reprinted here with the permission of CASW. The copyright in the document has been registered with Consumer and Corporate Affairs Canada, registration No. 427837.

tions. These ethical responsibilities are not likely to form the basis of any disciplinary action if breached. However these sections may form the basis of inquiry. These ethical responsibilities may be used in conjunction with breaches of other sections of this code and may form the basis of necessary background information in any action for discipline. Of equal importance, these ethical responsibilities are desirable goals to be achieved by the social work profession which by its nature is driven by an adherence to the values that form the basis of these desirable ethical behaviours.

Ethical Duties and Obligations

1. A social worker shall maintain the best interest of the client as the primary professional obligation.
2. A social worker shall carry out her or his professional duties and obligations with integrity and objectivity.
3. A social worker shall have and maintain competence in the provision of a social work service to a client.
4. A social worker shall not exploit the relationship with a client for personal benefit, gain or gratification.
5. A social worker shall protect the confidentiality of all information acquired from the client or others regarding the client and the client's family during the professional relationship unless
   (a) the client authorizes in writing the release of specified information,
   (b) the information is released under the authority of a statute or an order of a court of competent jurisdiction, or
   (c) otherwise authorized by this Code.
6. A social worker who engages in another profession, occupation, affiliation or calling shall not allow these outside interests to affect the social work relationship with the client.
7. A social worker in private practice shall not conduct the business of provision of social work services for a fee in a manner that discredits the profession or diminishes the public's trust in the profession.

Ethical Responsibilities

8. A social worker shall advocate for workplace conditions and policies that are consistent with the Code.
9. A social worker shall promote excellence in the social work profession.

10. A social worker shall advocate change
    (a) in the best interest of the client, and
    (b) for the overall benefit of society, the environment and the global community.

1.   PRIMARY PROFESSIONAL OBLIGATION

1.   A social worker shall maintain the best interest of the client as the primary professional obligation.

1.1   The social worker is to be guided primarily by this obligation. Any action which is substantially inconsistent with this obligation is an unethical action.

1.2   A social worker in the practice of social work shall not discriminate against any person on the basis of race, ethnic background, language, religion, marital status, sex, sexual orientation, age, abilities, socio-economic status, political affiliation or national ancestry.

1.3   A social worker shall inform a client of the client's right to consult another professional at any time during the provision of social work services.

1.4   A social worker shall immediately inform the client of any factor, condition or pressure that affects the social worker's ability to perform an acceptable level of service.

1.5   A social worker shall not become involved in a client's personal affairs that are not relevant to the service being provided.

1.6   A social worker shall not state an opinion, judgment or use a clinical diagnosis unless there is a documented assessment, observation or diagnosis to support the opinion, judgment or diagnosis.

1.7   Where possible, a social worker shall provide or secure social work services in the language chosen by the client.

2.   INTEGRITY AND OBJECTIVITY

2.   A social worker shall carry out his or her professional duties and obligations with integrity and objectivity.

2.1   The social worker shall identify and describe education, training, experience, professional affiliations, competence, and nature of service in an honest and accurate manner.

2.2   The social worker shall explain to the client her or his education, experience, training, competence, nature of service and action at the request of the client.

2.3   A social worker shall cite an educational degree only after it has been received from the institution.

2.4   A social worker shall not claim formal social work education in an area of expertise or training solely by attending a lecture, demonstration, conference, panel discussion, workshop, seminar or other similar teaching presentation.

2.5   The social worker shall not make a false, misleading or exaggerated claim of efficacy regarding past or anticipated achievement with respect to clients.

2.6   The social worker shall distinguish between actions and statements made as a private citizen and actions and statements made as a social worker.

3.   COMPETENCE IN THE PROVISION OF SOCIAL WORK SERVICES

3.   A social worker shall have and maintain competence in the provision of a social work service to a client.

3.1   The social worker shall not undertake a social work service unless the social worker has the competence to provide the service or the social worker can reasonably acquire the necessary competence without undue delay, risk or expense to the client.

3.2   Where a social worker cannot reasonably acquire the necessary competence in the provision of a service to a client, the social worker shall decline to provide the service to the client, advising the client of the reason and ensuring that the client is referred to another professional person if the client agrees to the referral.

3.3.   The social worker, with the agreement of the client, may obtain advice from other professionals in the provision of service to a client.

3.4   A social worker shall maintain an acceptable level of health and well-being in order to provide a competent level of service to a client.

3.5   Where a social worker has a physical or mental health problem, disability or illness that affects the ability of the social worker to provide competent service or that would threaten the health or well-being of the client, the social worker shall discontinue the provision of social work service to a client

    (a) advising the client of the reason and,

    (b) ensuring that the client is referred to another professional person if the client agrees to the referral.

3.6   The social worker shall have, maintain and endeavor periodically to update an acceptable level of knowledge and skills to meet the standards of practice of the profession.

4.   LIMIT ON PROFESSIONAL RELATIONSHIP

4.   A social worker shall not exploit the relationship with a client for personal benefit, gain or gratification.

4.1   The social worker shall respect the client and act so that the dignity, individuality and rights of the person are protected.

4.2   The social worker shall assess and consider a client's motivation and physical and mental capacity in arranging for the provision of an appropriate service.

4.3   The social worker shall not have a sexual relationship with a client.

4.4   The social worker shall not have a business relationship with a client, borrow money from a client, or loan money to a client.

4.5   The social worker shall not have a sexual relationship with a social work student assigned to the social worker.

4.6   The social worker shall not sexually harass any person.

5.   CONFIDENTIAL INFORMATION

5.   A social worker shall protect the confidentiality of all information acquired from the client or others regarding the client and the client's family during the professional relationship unless
   (a) the client authorizes in writing the release of specified information,
   (b) the information is released under the authority of a statute or an order of a court of relevant jurisdiction, or
   (c) otherwise authorized under this Code.

5.1   The requirement of confidentiality also applies to social workers who work as
   (a) supervisors,
   (b) managers,
   (c) educators, or
   (d) administrators.

5.2   A social worker who works as a supervisor, manager or administrator shall establish policies and practices that protect the confidentiality of client information.

5.3   The social worker may disclose confidential information to other persons in the workplace who, by virtue of their responsibilities, have an identified need to know as determined by the social worker.

5.4   Clients shall be the initial or primary source of information about themselves and their problems unless the client is incapable or unwilling to give information or when corroborative reporting is required.

5.5   The social worker has the obligation to ensure that the client understands what is being asked, why and to what purpose the information will be used, and to understand the confidentiality policies and practices of the workplace setting.

5.6   Where information is required by law, the social worker shall explain to the client the consequences of refusing to provide the requested information.

5.7   Where information is required from other sources, the social worker
  (a) shall explain the requirement to the client, and
  (b) shall attempt to involve the client in selecting the sources to be used.

5.8   The social worker shall take reasonable care to safeguard the client's personal papers or property if the social worker agrees to keep the property at the request of the client.

Recording Information

5.9   The social worker shall maintain only one master file on each client.

5.10   The social worker shall record all relevant information, and keep all relevant documents in the file.

5.11   The social worker shall not record in a client's file any characterization that is not based on clinical assessment or fact.

Accessibility of Records

5.12   The social worker who contracts for the delivery of social work services with a client is responsible to the client for maintaining the client record.

5.13   The social worker who is employed by a social agency that delivers social work services to clients is responsible
  (a) to the client for the maintaining of a client record, and
  (b) to the agency to maintain the records to facilitate the objectives of the agency.

5.14   A social worker is obligated to follow the provision of a statute that allows access to records by clients.

5.15   The social worker shall respect the client's right of access to a client record subject to the social worker's right to refuse access for just and reasonable cause.

5.16   Where a social worker refuses a client the right to access a file or part of a file, the social worker shall advise the client of the right to request a review of the decision in accordance with the relevant statute, workplace policy or other relevant procedure.

Disclosure

5.17   The social worker shall not disclose the identity of persons who have sought a social work service or disclose sources of information about clients unless compelled legally to do so.

5.18   The obligation to maintain confidentiality continues indefinitely after the social worker has ceased contact with the client.

5.19   The social worker shall avoid unnecessary conversation regarding clients.

5.20   The social worker may divulge confidential information with consent of the client, preferably expressed in writing, where this is essential to a plan of care or treatment.

5.21   The social worker shall transfer information to another agency or individual, only with the informed consent of the client or guardian of the client and then only with the reasonable assurance that the receiving agency provides the same guarantee of confidentiality and respect for the right of privileged communication as provided by the sending agency.

5.22   The social worker shall explain to the client the disclosure of information requirements of the law or of the agency before the commencement of the provision of social work services.

5.23   The social worker in practice with groups and communities shall notify the participants of the likelihood that aspects of their private lives may be revealed in the course of their work together, and therefore require a commitment from each member to respect the privileged and confidential nature of the communication between and among members of the client group.

5.24   Subject to section 5.26, the social worker shall not disclose information acquired from one client to a member of the client's family without the informed consent of the client who provided the information.

5.25   A social worker shall disclose information acquired from one client to a member of the client's family where

(a) the information involves a threat of harm to self or others,

(b) the information was acquired from a child of tender years and the social worker determines that its disclosure is in the best interests of the child.

5.26   A social worker shall disclose information acquired from a client to a person or a police officer where the information involves a threat of harm to that person.

5.27   A social worker may release confidential information as part of a discipline hearing of a social worker as directed by the tribunal or disciplinary body.

5.28   When disclosure is required by order of a court, the social worker shall not divulge more information than is reasonably required and shall where possible notify the client of this requirement.

5.29   The social worker shall not use confidential information for the purpose of teaching, public education or research except with the informed consent of the client.

5.30   The social worker may use non-identifying information for the purpose of teaching, public education or research.

Retention and Disposition of Information

5.31   Where the social worker's documentation is stored in a place or computer maintained and operated by an employer, the social worker shall advocate for the responsible retention and disposition of information contained in the file.

6.   OUTSIDE INTEREST

6.   A social worker who engages in another profession, occupation, affiliation or calling shall not allow these outside interests to affect the social work relationship with the client.

6.1   A social worker shall declare to the client any outside interests that would affect the social work relationship with the client.

6.2   A social worker shall not allow an outside interest:

(a) to affect the social worker's ability to practise social work;

(b) to present to the client or to the community that the social worker's ability to practise social work is affected; or

(c) to bring the profession of social work into disrepute.

7.   LIMIT ON PRIVATE PRACTICE

7.   A social worker in private practice shall not conduct the business of provision of social work services for a fee in a manner that discredits the profession or diminishes the public's trust in the profession.

7.1   A social worker shall not use the social work relationship within an agency to obtain clients for his or her private practice.

7.2   Subject to section 7.3 a social worker who enters into a contract for service with a client

(a) shall disclose at the outset of the relationship, the fee schedule for the social work services,

(b) shall not charge a fee that is greater than that agreed to and disclosed to the client, and

(c) shall not charge for hours of service other than the reasonable hours of client services, research, consultation and administrative work directly connected to the case.

7.3   A social worker in private practice may charge differential fees for services except where an increased fee is charged based on race, ethnic background, language, religion, marital status, sex, sexual orientation, age, abilities, socio-economic status, political affiliation or national ancestry.

7.4   A social worker in private practice shall maintain adequate malpractice, defamation and liability insurance.

7.5   A social worker in private practice may charge a rate of interest on delinquent accounts as is allowed by law.

7.6   Notwithstanding section 5.17 a social worker in private practice may pursue civil remedies to ensure payment for services to a client where the social worker has advised the client of this possibility at the outset of the social work service.

8.   ETHICAL RESPONSIBILITIES TO THE WORKPLACE

8.   A social worker shall advocate for workplace conditions and policies that are consistent with the Code.

8.1   Where the responsibilities to an employer are in conflict with the social worker's obligations to the client, the social worker shall document the issue in writing and shall bring the situation to the attention of the employer.

8.2   Where a serious ethical conflict continues to exist after the issue has been brought to the attention of the employer, the social worker shall bring the issue to the attention of the Association or regulatory body.

8.3   A social worker shall follow the principles in the Code when dealing with

(a) a social worker under the supervision of the social worker,

(b) an employee under the supervision of the social worker, and

(c) a social work student under the supervision of the social worker.

9.   ETHICAL RESPONSIBILITIES TO THE PROFESSION

9.   A social worker shall promote excellence in the social work profession.

9.1   A social worker shall report to the appropriate association or regulatory body any breach of this Code by another social worker which adversely affects or harms a client or prevents the effective delivery of a social service.

9.2   A social worker shall report to the association or regulatory body any unqualified or unlicensed person who is practising social work.

9.3   A social worker shall not intervene in the professional relationship of a social worker and client unless requested to do so by the client and unless convinced that the best interests and well-being of the client require such intervention.

9.4   Where a conflict arises between a social worker and other professionals, the social worker shall attempt to resolve the professional differences in ways that uphold the principles of this Code and the honour of the social work profession.

9.5   A social worker engaged in research shall ensure that the involvement of clients in the research is a result of informed consent.

10. ETHICAL RESPONSIBILITIES FOR SOCIAL CHANGE

10.   A social worker shall advocate change

(a) in the best interest of the client, and

(b) for the overall benefit of society, the environment and the global community.

10.1   A social worker shall identify, document and advocate for the elimination of discrimination.

10.2   A social worker shall advocate for the equal distribution of resources to all persons.

10.3   A social worker shall advocate for the equal access of all persons to resources, services and opportunities.

10.4   A social worker shall advocate for a clean and healthy environment and shall advocate the development of environmental strategies consistent with social work principles.

10.5   A social worker shall provide reasonable professional services in a state of emergency.

10.6   A social worker shall promote social justice.

Feminist Therapy Code of Ethics: Ethical Guidelines for Feminist Therapists

I. CULTURAL DIVERSITIES AND OPPRESSIONS

A. A feminist therapist increases her accessibility to and for a wide range of clients from her own and other identified groups through flexible delivery of services. When appropriate, the feminist therapist assists clients in accessing other services.

B. A feminist therapist is aware of the meaning and impact of her own ethnic and cultural background, gender, class, and sexual orientation, and actively attempts to become knowledgeable about alternatives from sources other than her clients. The therapist's goal is to uncover and respect cultural and experiential differences.

C. A feminist therapist evaluates her ongoing interactions with her clientele for any evidence of the therapist's biases or discriminatory attitudes and practice. The feminist therapist accepts responsibility for taking action to confront and change any interfering or oppressing biases she has.

II. POWER DIFFERENTIALS

A. A feminist therapist acknowledges the inherent power differentials between client and therapist, and models effective use of personal power. In using the power differential to the benefit of the client, she does not take control or power which rightfully belongs to her client.

B. A feminist therapist discloses information to the client which facilitates the therapeutic process. The therapist is responsible for using self-disclosure with purpose and discretion in the interests of the client.

C. A feminist therapist negotiates and renegotiates formal and/or informal contacts with clients in an on-going mutual process.

D. A feminist therapist educates her clients regarding their rights as consumers of therapy, including procedures for resolving differences and filing grievances.

This *Code of Ethics* is printed with the permission of the Feminist Therapy Institute, Inc. c/o Administrator Polly Taylor, 904 Irving St. #258, San Francisco, CA 94122.

III. OVERLAPPING RELATIONSHIPS

A. A feminist therapist recognizes the complexity and conflicting priorities inherent in multiple or overlapping relationships. The therapist accepts responsibility for monitoring such relationships to prevent potential abuse of or harm to the client.

B. A feminist therapist is actively involved in her community. As a result, she is especially sensitive about confidentiality. Recognizing that her clients' concerns and general well-being are primary, she self-monitors both public and private statements and comments.

C. A feminist therapist does not engage in sexual intimacies nor any overtly or covertly sexualized behaviors with a client or former client.

IV. THERAPIST ACCOUNTABILITY

A. A feminist therapist works only with those issues and clients within the realm of her competencies.

B. A feminist therapist recognizes her personal and professional needs, and utilizes ongoing self-evaluation, peer support, consultation, supervision, continuing education, and/or personal therapy to evaluate, maintain, and improve her work with clients, her competencies, and her emotional well-being.

C. A feminist therapist continually re-evaluates her training, theoretical background, and research to include developments in feminist knowledge. She integrates feminism into psychological theory, receives ongoing therapy training, and acknowledges the limits of her competencies.

D. A feminist therapist engages in self-care activities in an ongoing manner. She acknowledges her own vulnerabilities and seeks to care for herself outside of the therapy setting. She models for the ability and willingness to self-nurture in appropriate and self-empowering ways.

V. SOCIAL CHANGE

A. A feminist therapist actively questions other therapeutic practices in her community that appear abusive to clients or therapists, and when possible, intervenes as early as appropriate or feasible, or assists clients in intervening when it is facilitative to their growth.

B. A feminist therapist seeks multiple avenues for impacting change, including public education and advocacy within professional organizations, lobbying for legislative actions, and other appropriate activities.

Appendix C: Glossary

Autonomy self-determination, self-rule, being able to make free choices.

Autonomous ethics ethical systems in which humans determine the moral rules.

Client Bill of Rights a statement distributed to all clients/patients informing them of the information they are entitled to know about their situation, treatment expectations, and participation in decision making, and that they will be informed about available options and have a right to speak to an ombudsman or other person if dissatisfied with treatment.

Code of ethics a collection of aspirations, regulations, and guidelines that represent the values of a group or profession to which it applies; a compilation of ethical standards.

Competence the ability to give informed consent to some or all decisions, clients/patients are located along a range of capabilities, extending from completely competent to those who are somewhat competent to those who are not at all competent.

Competing loyalties two or more loyalties that cannot be honored at the same time.

Competing values two or more values that cannot be honored at the same time.

Confidentiality a rule or duty requiring one entrusted with private or secret matters to refrain from divulging them; a contract not to reveal information about an individual except with his or her consent.

Conflicting obligations   two or more obligations that cannot be fulfilled at the same time.

Deontology   a philosophy of ethics holding that ethical rules for the right course of action are self-evident, can be formulated, and should hold under all circumstances.

Dual role/relationship   situation in which professionals fill more than one role at a time and should avoid conflicts of interest that interfere with the exercise of professional discretion and impartial judgment, especially to protect clients' interests and not to take unfair advantage of them.

Duty to warn   an obligation to use reasonable care to protect intended victims; also referred to as the *Tarasoff* principle.

Effectiveness criterion   the degree to which a desired outcome is achieved.

Efficiency criterion   relative cost of achieving a stated objective.

Ethical absolutism   any ethical theory that claims there are ethical rules that hold regardless of society, culture, or religion; correct standards applicable to everyone everywhere.

Ethical decision making   the process of analyzing and assessing the ethical dimensions of practice in order to develop ethically appropriate professional behavior.

Ethical dilemmas   choice by the social worker between two or more relevant but contradictory ethical directives; when every alternative results in an undesirable outcome for one or more persons.

Ethical problem   identifying the right thing to do in a given practice situation.

Ethical priorities screen (EPS)   a guide for rank-ordering ethical principles and priorities.

Ethical relativism   the belief there is no absolute or universal moral standard and what is morally right or wrong is relative to an individual, group, or culture.

Ethical rules screen (ERS)   used as a step in ethical decision making by consulting the *Code of Ethics* for guidance.

Ethics   branch of philosophy that deals with the rightness or wrongness of human actions.

General ethics   the obligations that are owed by one person to another.

Group values   values held by subgroups within a society.

Heteronomous ethics   ethical systems that derive moral rules from nonhuman sources.

Informed consent   the knowledgeable and voluntary agreement by a client/patient to undergo an intervention that is in accord with the patient's values and preferences.

Least harm principle   when harm will come to someone in the situation, choice of the option that results in the least harm, the least permanent harm, or the most easily reversible harm.

Malpractice   professional negligence or misconduct; failure to exercise a degree of care that a similar professional of ordinary prudence would demonstrate under the same circumstances.

Morality   a concern with personally held ethical beliefs, theories of obligation, and the social elements that reinforce ethical decisions.

Paternalism   the act of overriding the autonomous decisions of a person or making decisions for the person with the intention of benefiting that person.

Personal (individual) values   the values held by one person but not necessarily by others.

Prima facie correct   apparently correct upon first viewing.

Privacy   a zone of individual autonomy in which people ought to be free to behave as they wish; the constitutional right protecting individuals from unwarranted governmental interference in intimate personal relations or activities.

Privileged communication   a legal concept protecting against forced disclosure in legal proceedings that would break a promise of privacy—based on ethical principles of confidentiality and privacy.

Professional code of ethics   a compilation of values, ethical principles, and ethical standards of a particular profession (see Appendix B for examples).

Professional ethics   codification of the special obligations that arise out of a person's voluntary choice to become a professional, such as a social worker.

Professional social work ethics   those ethical standards promulgated by the social work profession through its *Code of Ethics* and other publications.

Professional values   those values proclaimed by a professional group.

Religious ethics   ethics based upon a religion and its beliefs.

Self-determination   a person's right to make his or her own decisions.

Situational ethics   the position that all ethical decisions must be made in the light of individual circumstances and not according to moral rules or universal laws.

Societal values   values recognized by major portions of the entire social system, or, at least, by the leading members or spokespersons of that system.

Teleology   philosophy of ethics that justifies ethical decisions on the basis of the context in which they are made or on the basis of the consequences that they create.

Unethical behavior   violations of the profession's principles established by the profession's *Code of Ethics*.

Utilitarianism   a philosophy of ethics that defines right action as that which results in the greatest happiness for the greatest number.

Value dilemmas   two or more values that cannot be reconciled and simultaneously enacted.

Values   preferences that serve as guides or criteria for selecting good or desirable behaviors.

Voluntariness   acting on the basis of meaningful and free consent obtained without coercion.

Appendix D:
Selected Internet Sources of
Information About Values and Ethics

www.naswdc.org/code.htm *NASW Code of Ethics*—Overview *Code of Ethics.* Effective 1/1/97.

www.naswnyc.org/ethics.html Ethics and professional liability. Material on a variety of topics related to the *Code.*

http://www.globalethics.org Institute for Global Ethics.

http://condor.depaul.edu/ethics/harvard.htm Harvard University Program for Ethics and the Professions.

http://www.ethics.ubc.ca/overview/ Centre for Applied Ethics, University of British Columbia.

http://www.nyu.edu/socialwork/wwwrsw/ World Wide Web Resources for Social Workers codes of ethics, ethics on the Web, ethics updates, journals and newsletters, professional associations, social work values and ethics.

http://www.cswf.org/ethframe.htm *Code of Ethics* (1997), Clinical Social Work Federation.

www.php.indiana.edu~appe/home.html Association for Practical and Professional Ethics.

http://www.ifsw.org/2.4dir.html International Federation of Social Workers *Code of Ethics*, Ethical Committee.

http://www.nbcc.org/ethics/wcstandards.htm National Board for Certified Counselors Standards for the Ethical Practice of Web Counseling.

Bibliography

This bibliography lists the books and articles cited in this book, as well as additional literature on ethical problems in professional practice that may be of interest to the reader.

Abramson, M. (1984). Collective responsibility in interdisciplinary collaboration: An ethical perspective for social workers. *Social Work in Health Care, 10* (1), 35–43.

Abramson, M. (1985). The autonomy-paternalism dilemma in social work practice. *Social Casework, 66,* 387–93.

Abramson, M. (1989). Autonomy vs. paternalistic beneficence: Practice strategies. *Social Casework, 70,* 101–5.

Abramson, M. (1990). Keeping secrets: Social workers and AIDS. *Social Work, 35,* 169–73.

Abramson, M. (1996). Toward a more holistic understanding of ethics in social work. *Social Work in Health Care, 23* (2), 1–14.

Adler, S. S. (1989). Truth telling to the terminal ill. *Social Work, 34,* 158–60.

Agbayani-Siewert, P. (1994). Filipino American culture and family: Guidelines for practitioners. *Families in Society, 75,* 429–38.

Albert, R. (1986). *Law and social work practice.* New York: Springer Publishing.

Aldarondo, E., & Straus, M.A. (1994). Screening for physical violence in couple therapy: Methodological, practical, and ethical considerations. *Family Process, 33,* 425–39.

Alexander, Jr., R. (1997) Social workers and privileged communication in the federal legal system. *Social Work, 42,* 387–91.

Algana, F. J., et al. (1979). Evaluating reaction to interpersonal touch in a counseling interview. *Journal of Counseling Psychology, 26,* 465–72.

Almason, A. L. (1997). Personal liability implications of the duty to warn are hard pills to swallow: From *Tarasoff* to *Hutchinson v. Patel* and beyond. *Journal of Contemporary Health Law and Policy, 13,* 471–96.

Altman, L. K. (1999). Focusing on prevention in fight against AIDS. *New York Times,* August 31, 1999, F5.

American Medical Association (1997). *Code of Ethics.* http://www.aaem.net/ama_ethics.html. March 17, 1999.

American Psychiatric Association. (1994). *Diagnostic and statistical manual of mental disorders* (4th ed.). Washington, DC: Author.

Anderson, S., & Mandell, D. (1989). The use of self-disclosure by professional social workers. *Social Casework, 70,* 259–67.

Andrews, A. B., & Patterson, E. G. (1995). Searching for solutions to alcohol and other drug abuse during pregnancy: Ethics, values, and constitutional principles. *Social Work, 40,* 55–64.

Austin, J. B., & Dankwort, J. (1999). Standards for batterer programs. *Journal of Interpersonal Violence, 14,* 152–168.

Baier, K. (1958). *The moral point of view: A rational basis of ethics.* New York: Random House.

Barker, R. L. (1988a). "Client dumping": Some ethical considerations. *Journal of Independent Social Work, 2,* 1–5.

Barker, R. L. (1988b). Just whose code of ethics should the independent practitioner follow? *Journal of Independent Social Work, 2* (4), 1–5.

Barker, R. L. (1992). Social Work in Private Practice (2nd ed.). Washington, DC: NASW Press.

Barksdale, C. (1989). Child abuse reporting: A clinical dilemma. *Smith College Studies in Social Work, 59,* 170–82.

Basham, K. K., Donner, S., Killough, R. M., & Rozas, L. W. (1997). Becoming an anti-racist institution. *Smith College Studies in Social Work, 67,* 564–85.

Bauman, Z. (1996). Morality in the age of contingency (pp. 49–58). In P. Heclas, S. Lash, & P. Morris (Eds.), *Detraditionalization: Critical reflections on authority and identity.* Cambridge, MA: Blackwell Publishers.

Bayer, R. (1998). AIDS and the ethics of prevention, research, and care (pp. 799–807). In G. Wormser (Ed.), *AIDS and other manifestations of HIV infection* (3rd ed.). Philadelphia: Lippincott-Raven Publishers.

Bayles, M. D. (1981). *Professional ethics.* Belmont, CA: Wadsworth Publishing.

Beck, J. C. (1998). Legal and ethical duties of the clinician treating a patient who is liable to be impulsively violent. *Behavioral Sciences and the Law, 16,* 375–389.

Beder, J. (1998). The home visit, revisited. *Families in Society, 79,* 514–522.

Beit-Hallahmi, B. (1975). Encountering orthodox religions in psychotherapy. *Psychotherapy, 12,* 357–59.

Bem, D. J. (1970). *Beliefs, attitudes and human affairs.* Pacific Grove, CA: Brooks/Cole Publishing.

Berliner, A. K. (1989). Misconduct in social work practice. *Social Work, 34,* 69–72.

Berman-Rossi, T., & Rossi, P. (1990). Confidentiality and informed consent in school social work. *Social Work in Education, 12,* 195–207.

Bernstein, S. (1960). Self-determination: "King or citizen in the realm of values." *Social Work, 5,* 3–8.

Bernstein, S. B. (1993). What happened to self-determination? *Social Work with Groups, 16* (1/2), 3–14.

Bernstein, S. R. (1990). Contracted services: Issues for the nonprofit agency manager. In *Towards the 21st century: Challenges for the voluntary sector.* Proceedings of the 1990 Conference of the Association of Voluntary Action Scholars. London, England.

Besharov, D. J., & Besharov, S. H. (1987). Teaching about liability. *Social Work, 32,* 517–22.

Besharov, D. J., & Laumann, L. A. (1996). Child abuse reporting. *Society, 33* (4), 40–46.

Beyerstein, D. (1993). The functions and limitations of professional codes of ethics (pp. 416–25). In E. R. Winkler & J. R. Coombs (Eds.), *Applied Ethics*. Cambridge, MA: Blackwell Publishers.

Black, D. (1972). The boundaries of legal sociology. *Yale Law Journal, 81*, 1086–1101.

Bloom, M. (1975). *The paradox of helping: Introduction to the philoso phy of scientific helping*. New York: John Wiley & Sons.

Bogodanoff, M., & Elbaum, P. L. (1978). Touching: A legacy from the encounter movement to social work practice. *Social Work in Health Care, 4*, 209–19.

Bonosky, N. (1995). Boundary violations in social work supervision: Clinical, educational, and legal implications. *The Clinical Supervisor, 13* (2), 79–95.

Borenzweig, H. (1983). Touching in clinical social work. *Social Casework, 64*, 238–242.

Borys, D. S., & Pope, K. S. (1989). Dual relationships between therapist and client: A national study of psychologists, psychiatrists, and social workers. *Professional Psychology: Research and Practice, 20*, 283–93.

Bowers v. Hardwick, 106 S. Ct. 2841 (1986).

Brager, G. A. (1968). Advocacy and political behavior. *Social Work, 13* (2), 5–15.

Brandeis, L. D., & Warren, S. D. (1890). The right to privacy. *Harvard Law Review. IV* (5), December 15.

Broadie, S. (1991). *Ethics with Aristotle*. New York: Oxford University Press.

Brown, B. S. (1968). Social change: A professional challenge. Unpublished paper.

Brown, H. J. (1970). Social work values in a developing country. *Social Work, 15* (1), 107–12.

Bullis, R. K., & Harrigan, M. P. (1992). Religious denominational policies on sexuality. *Families in Society: The Journal of Contemporary Human Services, 73*, 304–12.

Butz, R. A. (1985). Reporting child abuse and confidentiality in counseling. *Social Casework, 66*, 83–90.

Cain, L. P. (1979). Social worker's role in teen-age abortion. *Social Work, 24,* 52–56.

Callahan, D. (1987, October/November). Terminating treatment: Age as a standard. *Hastings Center Reporter,* 21–25.

Callahan, J. (1988). *Ethical issues in professional life.* New York: Oxford University Press.

Callahan, J. (1994). The ethics of assisted suicide. *Health and Social Work, 19,* 237–44.

Canadian Association of Social Workers. (1994). *Code of Ethics.* Ottawa, Ontario: Author.

Canda, E. R. (1988). Spirituality, religious diversity, and social work practice. *Social Casework, 69,* 238–47.

Caputo, Richard K. (1991). Managing information systems: An ethical framework and information needs matrix. *Administration in Social Work, 15* (4), 53–64.

Carlton, W. (1978). *In our professional opinion: The primacy of clinical judgment over moral choice.* Notre Dame, IN: University of Notre Dame Press.

Carpenter, M. C., & Platt, S. (1997). Professional identity for clinical social workers: Impact of changes in health care delivery systems. *Clinical Social Work Journal, 25,* 337–51.

Cervera, N. J. (1993). Decision making for pregnant adolescents: Applying reasoned action theory to research and treatment. *Families in Society: The Journal of Contemporary Human Services, 74,* 355–65.

Chow, J. (1999). Multiservice centers in Chinese American immigrant communities: Practice principles and challenges. *Social Work, 44,* 70–80.

Christensen, K. E. (1986). Ethics of information technology. In G. R. Geiss & N. Viswanathan (Eds.), *The human edge* (pp. 72–91). Binghamton, NY: Haworth Press.

Clemens, E. L. (1995). Multiple perceptions of discharge planning in one urban hospital. *Health and Social Work, 20,* 254–61.

Clinical Social Work Federation (1997). *Code of ethics.* Arlington, VA: Author.

Cohen, R. (1980). The (revised) NASW Code of Ethics. *NASW News, 25* (April), 19.

Coleman, E., & Schaefer, S. (1986). Boundaries of sex and intimacy between client and counselor. *Journal of Counseling and Development, 64,* 341–44.

Congress, E. P. (1992). Ethical decision making of social work supervisors. *Clinical Supervisor, 10,* 157–69.

Congress, E. P., & Lynn, M. (1997). Group work practice in the community: Navigating the slippery slope of ethical dilemmas. *Social Work with Groups, 20* (3), 61–74.

Conrad, A. P. (1988). Ethical considerations in the psychosocial process. *Social Casework, 69,* 603–10.

Conte, H. R., Plutchik, R., Picard, S., & Karasu, T. B. (1989). Ethics in the practice of psychotherapy. *American Journal of Psychotherapy, 43,* 32–42.

Conte, C. K., Fisher, D. S., Callahan, L. E., & Roffman, R. A. (1996). Training and supporting the telephone intake worker for an AIDS prevention counseling study. *Social Work, 41,* 314–19.

Corey, G., Corey, M. S., & Callanan, P. (1998). *Issues and Ethics in the Helping Profesions* (5th ed.). Boston: Brooks/Cole Publishing Co.

Coughlin, B. J. (1966). Interrelationship of governmental and voluntary welfare services. *The Social Welfare Forum 1966.* New York: Columbia University Press.

Council on Social Work Education (1982, 1992, 1997, 1998 Revised). *Curriculum Policy Statement.* Alexandria, VA: Author.

Courtney, M. E., Barth, R. P., Berrick, J. D., Brooks, E., Needell, B., & Park, L. (1996). Race and child welfare services: Past research and future directions. *Child Welfare, LXXV,* 99–137.

Csikai, E. L., & Sales, E. (1998). The emerging social work role on hospital ethics committees: A comparison of social worker and chair perspectives. *Social Work, 43* (3), 233–42.

Curtis, P. A., & Lutkus, A. M. (1985). Client confidentiality in police social work settings. *Social Work, 30,* 355–60.

Cwikel, J. G., & Cnaan, R. A. (1991). Ethical dilemmas in applying secondwave information technology to social work practice. *Social Work, 36* (2), 114–20.

Cyrns, A. G. (1977). Social work education and student ideology: A mul-tivaiiate study of professional socialization. *Journal of Education for Social Work, 13* (1), 44–51.

Daro, D. (1988). *Confronting child abuse: Research for effective program design.* New York: Free Press.

Davidson, J. R., & Davidson, T. (1996). Confidentiality and managed care: Ethical and legal concerns. *Health and Social Work, 21,* 208–15.

Davis, K. (1997). Managed care, mental illness and African Americans: A prospective analysis of managed care policy in the United States. *Smith College Studies in Social Work, 67,* 623–41.

Dean, H. (1998). The primacy of the ethical aim in clinical social work: Its relationship to social justice and mental health. *Smith College Studies in Social Work, 69,* 9–24.

Dean, R. G., & Rhodes, M. L. (1992). Ethical-clinical tensions in clinical practice. *Social Work, 37,* 128–32.

DeSmidt, G., & Gorey, K. M. (1997). Unpublished social work research: Systematic replication of a recent meta-analysis of published intervention effectiveness research. *Social Work Research, 21,* 58–62.

Deutscher, I., Pestello, F. P., & Pestello, H. F. G. (1993). *Sentiments and Acts.* New York: Aldine de Gruyter.

DeYoung, M. (1988). The good touch/bad touch dilemma. *Child Welfare, 67,* 60–68.

Dickson, D. T. (1997). Law, ethics and social work with the elderly: Self-determination. *Journal of Law and Social Work, 7* (2), 105–25.

Diggs, B. J. (1970). Rules and utilitarianism. In K. Pahel & M. Schiller (Eds.), *Readings in contemporary ethical theory* (pp. 260–82). Englewood Cliffs, NJ: Prentice-Hall.

Dobrin, A. (1989). Ethical judgments of male and female social workers. *Social Work, 34,* 451–55.

Dolgoff, R., & Skolnik, L. (1992). Ethical decision making: The NASW Code of ethics and group work practice: Beginning explorations. *Social Work with Groups, 15* (4), 99–112.

Dolgoff, R., & Skolnik, L. (1996). Ethical decision making in social work with groups: An empirical study. *Social Work with Groups, 19* (2), 49–65.

Dumont, M. P. (1996). Privatization and mental health in Massachusetts. *Smith College Studies in Social Work, 66,* 293–303.

Dunkel, J., & Hatfield, S. (1986). Countertransference issues in working with persons with AIDS. *Social Work, 31,* 114–17.

Dworkin, G. (1985). Behavioral control and design. *Social Research, 52,* 543–54.

Edward, J. (1999). Is managed mental health treatment psychotherapy? *Clinical Social Work Journal, 27,* 87–102.

Egan, M. (1999). The social worker in the emerging field of home care: Professional activities and ethical concerns. *Health & Social Work, 24* (1), 43–55.

Egley, L. C. (1992). Defining the *Tarasoff* Duty. *Journal of Psychiatry and Law, 19,* 93–133.

Ellis, A. (1973). *Humanistic psychotherapy: The rational-emotive approach.* New York: McGraw-Hill.

Ewalt, P. L., & Mokuau, N. (1995). Self-determination from a Pacific perspective. *Social Work, 40,* 168–75.

Feldman, K. A., & Newcomb, T. M. (1994). *The impact of college on students.* New Brunswick, NJ: Transaction Publishers.

Feminist Therapy Institute (1987). *Feminist code of ethics.* San Francisco: Author.

Festinger, L. (1957). *A Theory of cognitive dissonance.* New York: Harper & Row.

Finkelhor, D. (1990). Is child abuse over-reported? *Public Welfare, 48,* 22–29.

Finkelhor, D. (1998). Improving research, policy, and practice to understand child sexual abuse. *Journal of the American Medical Association, 280,* 1864–1865.

Finn, J. (1990). Security, privacy, and confidentiality in agency microcomputer use. *Families in Society: The Journal of Contemporary Human Services* (May), 283–90.

Fisher, D. (1987). Problems for social work in a strike situation: Professional, ethical, and value considerations. *Social Work, 32,* 252–54.

Fishkin, J. S. (1982). *The limits of obligation.* New Haven, CT: Yale University Press.

Fleck-Henderson, A. (1991). Moral reasoning in social work practice. *Social Service Review* (June), 185–202.

Fletcher, J. F. (1966). *Situation ethics, the new morality.* Philadelphia: Westminster Press.

Flexner, A. (1915). Is social work a profession? *Proceedings of National Conference of Charities and Corrections* (pp. 576–90). Chicago: Hindman.

Fodor, J. L. (1999, February). Computer ethics in higher education. *Syllabus,* 12–15.

Frank, J. (1991). *Persuasion and healing* (Rev. ed.). New York: Schocken Books.

Frankena, W. K. (1973). *Ethics* (2nd ed.). Englewood Cliffs, NJ: Prentice-Hall.

Frankena, W. K. (1980). *Thinking about morality.* Ann Arbor: University of Michigan Press.

Frankl, V. (1968). *The doctor and the soul.* New York: Alfred A. Knopf.

Frans, D. J., & Moran, J. R. (1993). Social work education's impact on students' humanistic values and personal empowerment. *Arete, 18* (1), 1–11.

Freedberg, S. (1989). Self-determination: Historical perspectives and effects on current practice. *Social Work, 34,* 33–38.

Freedman, T. G. (1998). Genetic susceptibility testing: ethical and social quanderies. *Health & Social Work, 23,* 214–22.

Galambos, C. M. (1997). Resolving ethical conflicts in providing case management services to the elderly. *Journal of Gerontological Social Work, 27* (4), 57–67.

Glainsky, M. J., Schopler, J. H., & Abell, M. D. (1997). Connecting group members through telephone and computer groups. *Health & Social Work, 22,* 181–88.

Gambrill, E., & Pruger, R. (Eds.). (1997). *Controversial issues in social work ethics, values, and obligations.* Boston: Allyn and Bacon.

Garb, H. N. (1994). Cognitive heuristics and biases in personality assessment (pp. 73–90). In L. Heath (Ed.), *Applications of heuristics and biases to social issues.* New York: Plenum Press.

Gerhart, U. C., & Brooks, A. D. (1985). Social workers and malpractice: Law, attitudes, and knowledge. *Social Casework, 66,* 411–16.

Gewirth, A. (1978). *Reason and morality.* Chicago: University of Chicago Press.

Gibelman, M., & Schervish, P. H. (1997). *Who we are: A second look.* Washington, DC: NASW.

Gillis, J. S. (1974). Social influence therapy: The therapist as manipulator. *Psychology Today, 8* (7), 90–95.

Girardi, J. A., Keese, R. M., Traver, L. B., & Cooksey, D. R. (1988). Psychotherapist responsibility for notifying individuals at risk for exposure to HIV (AIDS). *Journal of Sex Research, 25,* 1–27.

Givelber, D., Bowers, W., & Blitch, C. (1984). *Tarasoff:* Myth and reliability. *Wisconsin Law Review, 2,* 443–97.

Glasser, P. H. (1984). Being honest with ourselves: What happens when our values conflict with our clients? *Practice Digest, 6* (4), 6–10.

Glassman, Carol. (1992). Feminist dilemmas in practice. *Affilia, 7,* 160–66.

Gochros, H. L. (1988). Risks of abstinence: Sexual decision making in the AIDS era. *Social Work, 33,* 254–56.

Goffman, E. (1959). *The presentation of self in everyday life.* Garden City, NY: Doubleday Anchor Books.

Goldberg v. Kelly. (1970).

Goldstein, E. G. (1997). To tell or not to tell: The disclosure of events in the therapist's life to the patient. *Clinical Social Work Journal, 25,* 41–58.

Goldstein, H. (1973). *Social work: A unitary approach.* Columbia: University of South Carolina Press.

Goldstein, H. (1987). The neglected moral link in social work practice. *Social Work, 32,* 181–86.

Goldstein, H. (1998). Education for ethical dilemmas in social work practice. *Families in Society: The Journal of Contemporary Human Services, 79,* 241–53.

Golton, M. (1971). Private pratice in social work. In R. Morris (Ed.), *The encyclopedia of social work.* New York: National Association of Social Workers.

Goodban, N. (1985). The psychological impact of being on welfare. *Social Service Review, 59,* 403–22.

Gorey, K. M., Thyer, B. A., & Pawluck, D. E. (1998). Differential effectiveness of prevalent social work practice models: A meta-analysis. *Social Work, 43,* 269–78.

Green, S. L., & Hansen, J. C. (1989). Ethical dilemmas faced by family therapists. *Journal of Marriage and Family Therapists, 15,* 149–58.

Greenhouse, L. (1998). High court curbs claim on privacy in a house. *New York Times,* December 2, A11.

Greenhouse, L. (1999a). Check out your driver. *New York Times,* April 11, 4, 2.

Greenhouse, L. (1999b). Supreme court roundup; police searching car may include passenger's things. *New York Times,* April 6, A19.

Greenwood, E. (1957). Attributes of a profession. *Social Work, 2* (3), 45–55.

Grisso, T., & Appelbaum, P. S. (1998). *Assessing competence to consent to treatment: A guide for physicians and other health professionals.* New York: Oxford University Press.

Group for the Advancement of Psychiatry. (1994). *Forced into treatment: The role of coercion in clinical practice.* Report No. 137. Washington, DC: American Psychiatric Press.

Haley, J. (1976). *Problem-solving therapy.* New York: Harper & Row.

Halmos, P. (1965). *Faith of the counselor.* London: Constable.

Handler, J. E., & Hollingsworth, E. J. (1971). *The deserving poor.* Chicago: Markham.

Haney, C., Banks, C., & Zimbardo, P. G. (1973). Interpersonal dynamics in a simulated prison. *International Journal of Criminology and Penology, 1,* 69–97.

Harris, G. C. (1999). The dangerous patient exception to the psychotherapist-patient privilege: The *Tarasoff* duty and the *Jaffee* footnote. *Washington Law Review, 74,* 33–68.

Hayes, D. D., & Varley, B. K. (1965). The impact of social work education on students' values. *Social Work, 10* (4), 40–46.

Healy, T. C. (1998). The complexity of everyday *ethics* in home health care: An analysis of social workers' decisions regarding frail elders' autonomy. *Social Work in Health Care, 27* (4), 19–37.

Hiratsuka, J. (1994). When it's a helper who needs help. *NASW News* (June), 3.

Hokenstad, M. C. (1987). Preparation for practice: The ethical dimension. *Social Work Education Reporter, 25*, 1–4.

Holmes, S. A. (1998). Right to abortion quietly advances in state courts. *New York Times*, December 6, 1, 1.

Holroyd, J., & Brodsky, A. (1977). Psychologists' attitudes and practices regarding erotic and nonerotic physical contact with patients. *American Psychologist, 32*, 843–49.

Houston-Vega, M. K., Nuehring, E. M., & Daguio, E. R. (1997). *Prudent Practice*. Washington, DC: NASW Press.

Howard, M. O., & Jenson, J. M. (1999). Clinical practice guidelines: Should social work develop them? *Research on Social Work Practice, 9*, 283–301.

Howe, E. (1980). Public professions and the private model of professionalism. *Social Work, 25*, 179–91.

Hughes, E. C. (1965). Professions. In K. S. Lynn (Ed.), *The professions in America*. Boston: Beacon Press.

Hughes, R. C. (1993a). Child welfare services for the catastrophically ill newborn: Part I—A confusion of responsibility. *Child Welfare, 72*, 323–40.

Hughes, R. C. (1993b). Child welfare services for the catastrophically ill newborn: Part II—A guiding ehtical paradigm. *Child Welfare, 72*, 423–37.

Imre, R. E. (1989). Moral theory for social work. *Social Thought, 15* (1), 18–27.

Iserson, K. V. (1986). An approach to ethical problems in emergency medicine. In K. V. Iserson et al. (Eds.), *Ethics in emergency medicine* (pp. 35–41). Baltimore: Williams & Wilkins.

Ivanoff, A., Blythe, B. J., & Tripodi, T. (1994). *Involuntary clients in social work practice: A research-based approach*. New York: Aldine de Gruyter.

Jayaratne, S., Croxton, T., & Mattison, D. (1997). Social work professional standards: An exploratory study. *Social Work, 42*, 187–99.

Jones, W. T., Sontag, F., Beckner, M. O., & Fogelin, R. J. (1977). *Approaches to ethics*. New York: McGraw-Hill.

Jory, B., Anderson, D., & Greer, C. (1997). Intimate justice: Confronting issues of accountability, respect, and freedom in treatment for abuse and violence. *Journal of Marital and Family Therapy*, 399–419.

Joseph, M. V. (1983). The ethics of organization. *Administration in Social Work*, 7, 47–57.

Joseph, M. V. (1985). A model for ethical decision-making in clinical practice. In C. B. Germain (Ed.), *Advances in clinical social work practice* (pp. 207–17). Silver Spring, MD: NASW.

Judah, E. H. (1979). Values: The uncertain component of social work. *Journal of Education for Social Work*, 15(2), 79–86.

Kadushin, A. (1992). What's wrong, what's right with social work supervision. *The Clinical Supervisor*, 10 (1), 3–19.

Kagle, J. D., & Gielbelhausen, P. N. (1994). Dual relationships and professional boundaries. *Social Work*, 39, 213–20.

Karis, J. M., & Wandrei, K. E. (1992). PIE: A new language for social work. *Social Work*, 37 (1), 80–85.

Kaslow, F. (1998). Ethical problems in mental health practice. *Journal of Family Psychotherapy*, 9 (2), 41–54.

Keith-Lucas, A. (1977). Ethics in social work. *Encyclopedia of social work* (pp. 350–55). Washington, DC: National Association of Social Workers.

Kirk, S. A., & Kutchins, H. (1988). Deliberate misdiagnosis in mental health practice. *Social Service Review*, 62, 225–37.

Kitchner, K. S. (1984). Intuition, critical evaluation and ethical principles: The foundation of ethical decisions in counseling psychology. *Counseling Psychology*, 12, 43–55.

Kluckhohn, C. (1951). Values and value-orientations in the theory of action: An exploration in definition and clarification. In T. Parsons & E. A. Shils (Eds.), *Toward a general theory of action* (pp. 388–433). Cambridge, MA: Harvard University Press.

Kohlberg, L. (1984). *The psychology of moral development*. New York: Harper & Row.

Kopels, S., & Kagle, J. D. (1993). Do social workers have a duty to warn? *Social Service Review*, 67, 101–26.

Kugelman, Wendy (1992). Social work ethics in the practice arena: A qualitative study. *Social Work in Health Care*, 17 (4), 59–80.

Kuhse, H., & Singer, P. (1985). Ethics and the handicapped newborn infant. *Social Research*, 52, 505–42.

Kupperman, J. J. (1999). *Value...and what follows*. New York: Oxford University Press.

Kurzman, P. A. (1995). Professional liability and malpractice (pp. 1921–27). *Encyclopedia of social work* (19th ed.). Washington, DC: NASW Press.

Kurzweil, Z. (1980). Why heteronomous ethics? In M. Kranzberg (Ed.), *Ethics in an age of pervasive technology* (pp. 68–71). Boulder, CO: Westview Press.

Kutchins, H. (1991). The fiduciary relationship: The legal basis for social workers' responsibilities to clients. *Social Work, 36*, 106–13.

Kutchins, H., & Kirk, S. A. (1987). DSM-III and social work malpractice. *Social Work, 32*, 205–11.

Kutchins, H., & Kirk, S. A. (1988). The business of diagnosis: DSM-III and clinical social work. *Social Work, 33*, 215–20.

Kutchins, H., & Kirk, S. A. (1995). Review of *Diagnostic and statistical manual of mental disorders* (4th ed.). *Social Work, 40*, 286–87.

Kutchins, H., & Kirk, S. A. (1997). *Making us crazy*. New York: The Free Press.

Laing, R. D. (1967). *Politics of experience*. New York: Pantheon Books.

Levy, C. (1976a). Personal versus professional values: The practitioner's dilemma. *Clinical Social Work Journal, 4*, 110–20.

Levy, C. (1976b). The value base of social work. *Journal of Education in Social Work, 9*, 34–42.

Levy, C. (1982). *Guide to ethical decisions and actions for social service administrators*. Binghamton, NY: Haworth Press.

Lewis, H. (1984). Ethical assessment. *Social Casework, 65*, 203–11.

Lewis, H. (1989). Ethics and the private non-profit human service organization. *Administration in Social Work, 13* (2), 1–14.

Lewis, K. N., & Walsh, W. B. (1980). Effects of value-communication style and similarity of values on counselor evaluation. *Journal of Counseling Psychology, 27*, 305–14.

Loewenberg, F. M. (1987). Another look at unethical professional conduct. *Journal of Applied Social Sciences, 11*, 220–29.

Loewenberg, F. M. (1988). *Religion and social work practice in contemporary American society*. New York: Columbia University Press.

Loewenberg, F. (1992). Notes on ethical dilemmas in wartime: Experiences of Israeli social workers during Operation Desert Shield. *International social work, 35* (4) 429–39.

Lyden, J. (1998). Christian ethics, Protestant. In R. Chadwick (Ed.), *Encyclopedia of Applied Ethics* (pp. 457–69). Boston: Academic Press.

Lystad, M., Rice, M., & Kaplan, S. J. (1996). Family violence. In S. J. Kaplan (Ed.), *Domestic violence* (pp. 139–80). Washington, DC: American Psychiatric Press.

MacIver, R. (1922). The social significance of professional ethics. *Annals, 101*, 5–11.

MacMurray, J. (1961). *Persons in relation.* Atlantic Highlands, NJ: Humanities Press.

Maesen, W. A. (1991). Fraud in mental health practice: A risk management perspective. *Administration and Policy in Mental Health, 18*, 431–32.

Manning, R. C. (1992). *Speaking from the heart: a feminist perspective on ethics.* Lanham, MD: Rowman & Littlefield Publishers.

Manning, S. S. (1997). The social worker as moral citizen: Ethics in action. *Social Work, 42*, 223–30.

Manning, S. S., & Gaul, C. E. (1997). The ethics of informed consent: A critical variable in the self-determination of health and mental health clients. *Social Work in Health Care, 25* (3), 103–17.

Manstead, A. S. R. (1996). Attitudes and behavior. In G. R. Semin & K. Fiedler (Eds.), *Applied Social Psychology.* Thousand Oaks, CA: Sage Publications.

Marcuse, P. (1976). Professional ethics and beyond: Values in planning. *Journal of the American Institute of Planners, 42*, 264–74.

Maritain, J. (1934). *Introduction to philosophy.* London: Sheed & Ward.

Marson, S. (1993). Social work discussion list (SOCWORK@UMAB.BITNET). October 18, 1993.

Maslow, A. H. (1962). *The farther reaches of human nature.* New York: Penguin Books.

Maslow, A. H. (1969). Toward a humanistic biology. *American Psychologist, 24*, 724–35.

Mason, R. O. (1994). Morality and models. In W. A. Wallace (Ed.), *Ethics in modeling* (pp. 183–94). Tarrytown, NY: Pergamon.

May, L. (1992). *Sharing responsibility*. Chicago: University of Chicago Press.

McCann, C. W. (1977). The codes of ethics of the NASW: An inquiry into its problems and perspectives. In B. E. Olvett (Ed.), *Values in Social Work Education* (pp. 10–19). Salt Lake City: University of Utah Graduate School of Social Work.

McGowan, B. G. (1995). Values and ethics. In C. H. Meyer & M. A. Mattaini (Eds.), *The foundations of social work practice* (pp. 28–41). Washington, DC: NASW Press.

McMahon, A., & Allen-Meares, P. (1992). Is social work racist? A content analysis of recent literature. *Social Work, 37*, 533–539.

Melton, G. B. (1988). Ethical and legal issues in AIDS-related practice. *American Psychologist, 43*, 941–47.

Meyer, C. H. (1985). Different voices: Comparable worth. *Social Work, 30*, 99.

Meyers, C. J. (1997). Expanding *Tarasoff*: Protecting patients and the public by keeping subsequent caregivers informed. *The Journal of Psychiatry & Law, Fall*, 365–75.

Mickelson, J. S. (1995). Advocacy. In R. L. Edwards (Ed.), *Encyclopedia of social work, Volume 1* (19th ed.) (pp. 95–100). Washington, DC: National Association of Social Workers.

Miller, D. J., & Thelen, M. H. (1986). Knowledge and beliefs about confidentiality in psychotherapy. *Professional Psychology: Research and Practice, 17*, 15–19.

Miller, H. (1968). Value dilemmas in social casework. *Social Casework, 13*, 27–33.

Miller, L. (1990). Voluntary organizations in turbulent times. In *Towards the 21st century: Challenges for the voluntary sector*. Proceedings of the 1990 Conference of the Association of Voluntary Action Scholars. London, England.

Mitchell, C. G. (1998). Perceptions of empathy and client satisfaction with managed behavioral health care. *Social Work, 43*, 404–11.

Mitchell, C. G. (1999). Treating anxiety in a managed care setting: A controlled comparison of medication alone versus medication plus cognitive-behavioral group therapy. *Research on Social Work Practice, 9*, 188–200.

Moran, J. R. (1989). Social work education and students' humanistic attitudes. *Journal of Education for Social Work, 25* (1), 13–19.

Moser, C. (1980). Letter. *NASW News,* 25 (9), 6.

Muehleman, T., Pickens, B. K., & Robinson, F. (1985). Informing clients about the limits to confidentiality, risk and their rights: Is self disclosure inhibited? *Professional Psychology: Research and Practice, 16,* 385–97.

Murdach, A. D. (1996). Beneficence re-examined: Protective intervention in mental health. *Social Work, 41,* 26–32.

Murphy, M. J., DeBernardo, C., & Shoemaker, E. (1998). Impact of managed care on independent practice and professional ethics: A survey of independent practitioners. *Professional psychology: Research and Practice, 29,* 43–51.

Myers, L. L., & Thyer, B. A. (1997). Should social work clients have the right to effective treatment? *Social Work, 42,* 288–98.

National Association of Black Social Workers. (n.d.). *Code of ethics.* 1994 Annual Report, NABSW, Detroit, MI.

National Association of Social Workers. (1985). *Compilation of public social policy statements.* Silver Spring, MD: National Association of Social Workers.

National Association of Social Workers. (1987). *AIDS: A social work response.* Washington, DC: National Association of Social Workers.

National Association of Social Workers. (1990a). People in the news. *NASW News, 35* (5), 17.

National Association of Social Workers. (1990b). *Standards for Social Work Personnel Practices.* Washington, DC: National Association of Social Workers.

National Association of Social Workers. (1993). A study of trends in adjudication of complaints concerning violations of NASW's code of ethics—overview of results.

National Association of Social Workers. (1994a). Client self-determination in end-of-life decisions. In *Social work speaks* (pp. 58–61). Washington, DC: Author.

National Association of Social Workers. (1994b). *NASW Procedures for the Adjudication of Grievances* (3rd ed.). Washington, DC: Author.

National Association of Social Workers. (1995a). Lawsuits: No more immunity. *NASW News, 40* (1), 7.

National Association of Social Workers. (1995b). A study cites most reported ethics breaches. *NASW News, 40* (4), 4.

National Association of Social Workers. (1996). *Code of ethics.* Washington, DC: Author.

National Association of Social Workers. (1998). Adjudication's first step is altered. *NASW News,* November, 8.

National Association of Social Workers. (1999). Assembly lowers BSW's dues, alters ethics code, eyes itself. *NASW News, 44* (9) (October), 1, 10.

NASW Ad Hoc Committee on Advocacy. (1969). The social worker advocate: Champion of social victims. *Social Work, 14* (2), 16–23.

National Research Council. (1993). *Child abuse and neglect.* Washington, DC: National Academy Press, Author.

Netting, F. E. (1987). Ethical issues in volunteer management and accountability. *Social Work, 32,* 250–252.

Netting, F. E., Kettner, P. M., & McMurtry, S. L. (1998). *Social work macro practice* (2nd ed.). White Plains, NY: Longman Publishing Group.

Newhill, C. E. (1992). Assessing danger to others in clinical social work practice. *Social Service Review, 66* (1), 64–84.

North, R. L., & Rothenberg, K. (1993). Partner notification and the threat of domestic violence against women with HIV infection. *New England Journal of Medicine, 329,* 1194–96.

Nyberg, D. (1996). Deception and moral decency. In R. A. French, T. E. Vehling, Jr., & H. K. Wettstein (Eds.), *Midwest studies in philosophy, vol. XX, moral concepts.* Notre Dame, IN: University of Notre Dame Press.

Padilla, Y. C. (1997). Immigrant policy: issues for social work practice. *Social Work, 42,* 595–606.

Parrott, C. (1999). Towards an integration of science, art and morality: The role of values in psychology. *Counselling Psychology Quarterly, 12* (1), 5–24.

Pellegrino, E. D. (1991). Trust and distrust in professional ethics. In E. D. Pellegrino, R. M. Veatch, & J. P. Langan (Eds.), *Ethics, trust, and the professions* (pp. 69–85). Washington, DC: Georgetown University Press.

Pemberton, J. D. (1965). Is there a moral right to violate the law? *Social Welfare Forum, 1965* (pp. 183–96). New York: Columbia University Press.

Perlman, H. H. (1965). Self-determination: Reality or illusion? *Social Service Review, 39,* 410–22.

Perlman, H. H. (1976). Believing and doing: Values in social work education. *Social Casework, 57,* 381–390.

Perry, C., & Kuruk, J. W. (1993). Psychotherapists' sexual relationships with their patients. *Annals of Health Law, 2,* 35–54.

Pike, C. K. (1996). Development and initial validation of the social work values inventory. *Research in Social Work Practice, 6,* 337–52.

Planned Parenthood of Southeastern Pa. v. Casey, 505 U.S. 833 (1992).

Pope, K. S., & Bouthoutsos, J. C. (1986). *Sexual intimacy between therapist and patient.* New York: Praeger Publishers.

Pope, K. S., Levenson, H., & Schover, L. R. (1979). *American Psychologist, 34* (8) (August), 682–89.

Pope, K. S., Tabachnick, B. G., & Keith-Spiegel, P. (1987). Ethics of practice: The beliefs and behaviors of psychologists and therapists. *American Psychologist, 42,* 993–1006.

Powell, W. E. (1994). The relationship between feelings of alienation and burnout in social work. *Families in Society, 75,* 229–35.

Proctor, E. K., Morrow-Howell, N., & Lott, C. L. (1993). Classification and correlates of ethical dilemmas in hospital social work. *Social Work, 38,* 166–77.

Pumphrey, M. W. (1959). *The teaching of values and ethics in social work education.* New York: CSWE.

Rabkin, J. G., & Struening, E. L. (1976). *Ethnicity, social class and mental illness.* New York: Institute on Pluralism & Group Identity.

Raines, J. C. (1996). Self-disclosure in clinical social work. *Clinical Social Work Journal, 24,* 357–75.

Rawls, J. (1971). *A theory of justice.* Cambridge, MA: Harvard University Press.

Reamer, F. G. (1983). Ethical dilemmas in social work practice. *Social Work, 28,* 31–35.

Reamer, F. G. (1988). AIDS and ethics: The agenda for social workers. *Social Work, 33*, 460–64.

Reamer, F. G. (1993). *The philosophical foundations of social work.* New York: Columbia University Press.

Reamer, F. G. (1995). Malpractice claims against social workers: First facts. *Social Work, 40*, 595–601.

Reamer, F. G. (1998). The evolution of social work ethics. *Social Work, 43*, 488–500.

Regehr, C., & Antle, B. (1997). Coercive influences: Informed consent in court-mandated social work. *Social Work, 42*, 300–306.

Reid, W. J. (1997). Research on task-centered practice. *Social Work Research, 21*, 132–37.

Reiser, S. J., Burstajn, H. J., Applebaum, P. S., & Gutheil, T. G. (1987). *Divided staffs, divided selves: A case approach to mental health ethics.* Cambridge, England: Cambridge University Press.

Rhodes, M. L. (1986). *Ethical dilemmas in social work practice.* London, England: Routledge & Kegan Paul.

Rice, D. S. (1994). Professional values and moral development: The social work student. Unpublished Dissertation. University of South Carolina.

Roberts, C. S. (1989). Conflicting professional values in social work and medicine. *Health and Social Work, 14*, 211–18.

Roberts, L. W., Battaglia, J., & Epstein, R. S. (1999). Frontier ethics: Mental health care needs and ethical dilemmas in rural communities. *Psychiatric Services, 50*, 497–503.

Robertson, J. A. (1985). The geography of competency. *Social Research, 52*, 555–79.

Rogers, C. R. (1951). *Client-centered therapy.* Boston: Houghton Mifflin.

Rogers, C. R. (1977). *Carl Rogers on personal power.* New York: Delacorte.

Rooney, R. H. (1992). *Strategies for work with involuntary clients.* New York: Columbia University Press.

Rosa, L., Rosa, E., Sarner, L., & Barrett, S. (1998). A close look at therapeutic touch. *Journal of the American Medical Association, 279*, 1005–10.

Ross, J. W. (1992). Editorial: Are social work ethics compromised? *Health and Social Work, 17*, 163–64.

Rothman, J. (1989). Client self-determination: Untangling the knot. *Social Service Review, 63*, 598–612.

Rothman, J., Smith, W., Nakashima, J., Paterson, M. A., & Mustin, J. (1996). Client self-determination and professional intervention: Striking a balance. *Social Work, 41*, 396–405.

Roy v. Hartogs. 366 N. YS. 2d297 (1975).

Royce, D., Dhooper, S. S., & Rompf, E. L. (1999). *Field instruction: A guide for social work students* (3rd ed.). New York: Longman.

Rubin, A., Cardenas, J., Warren, K., Pike, C. K., & Wambach, K. (1998) Outdated practitioner views about family culpability and severe mental disorders. *Social Work, 43* (5), 412–22.

Rust v. Sullivan. (1992).

Sammons, C. C. (1978). Ethical issues in genetic intervention. *Social Work, 23*, 237–42.

Schamess, G. (1996). Who profits and who benefits from managed mental health care? *Smith College Studies in Social Work, 60*, 209–20.

Schild, S., & Black, R. B. (1984). *Social work and genetic counseling: A guide to practice.* Binghamton, NY: Haworth Press.

Schlossberger, E., & Hecker, L. (1996). HIV and family therapists' duty to warn: A legal and ethical analysis. *Journal of Marital and Family Therapy, 22*, 27–40.

Schopler, J. H., Abell, M. D., & Galinsky, M. J. (1998). Technology-based groups: A review and conceptual framework for practice. *Social Work, 43*, 254–67.

Schultz, L. G. (1975). Ethical issues in treating sexual dysfunction. *Social Work, 20*, 126–28.

Schutz, W. C. (1967). *Joy.* New York: Grove Press.

Sedlak, A. J., & Broadhurst, D. D. (1996). *Third national incidence study of child abuse and neglect: Final report.* Washington, DC: U.S. Department of Health and Human Services.

Selznick, P. (1961). Sociology and natural law. *Natural Law Forum, 6*, 84–108.

Sharwell, G. R. (1974). Can values be taught? *Journal of Education for Social Work, 10*, 99–105.

Shaw, G. B. (1932). *The doctor's dilemma.* London, England: Constable.

Shillington, A. M., Dotson, W. L., Faulkner, A. O. (1994). Should only African-American community organizers work in African-American neighborhoods? In M. J. Austin & J. I. Lowe (Eds.), *Controversial Issues in Communities and Organizations*. Boston: Allyn & Bacon, 128–41.

Shirk, E. (1965). *The ethical dimension*. New York: Appleton-Century-Crofts.

Siegel, M. (1979). Privacy, ethics, and confidentiality. *Professional Psychology, 10*, 249–58.

Simon, R. I., & Gutheil, T. G. (1997). Ethical and clinical risk management principles in recovered memory cases: Maintaining therapist neutrality. In P. S. Appelbaum, L. A. Uyehara, & M. R. Elin (Eds.), *Trauma and memory* (pp. 477–95). New York: Oxford University Press.

Siporin, M. (1982). Moral philosophy in social work today. *Social Service Review, 56*, 516–38.

Siporin, M. (1983). Morality and immorality in working with clients. *Social Thought, 9* (Fall), 10–28.

Siporin, M. (1985a). Current social work perspectives for clinical practice. *Clinical Social Work Journal, 13*, 198–217.

Siporin, M. (1985b). Deviance, morality and social work therapy. *Social Thought, 11* (4), 11–24.

Siporin, M., & Glasser, P. (1986). Family functioning, morality and therapy. In P. Glasser & D. Watkins (Eds.), *Religion and social work*. Newbury Park, CA: Sage Publications.

Sloan, L., Edmond, T., Rubin, A., & Doughty, M. (1998). Social workers' knowledge of and experience with sexual exploitation by psychotherapists. *Social Work, 43*, 43–53.

Smyer, M. A. (1993). Aging and decision-making capacity. In M. A. Smyer (Ed.), *Mental health and aging: Progress and prospects*. New York: Springer Publishing.

Social Work, (1991). Volume 36, issue 2, 106–144. This issue contains a series of articles on the theme "Ethics and Professional Relationships."

Soderfeldt, M., Soderfeldt, B., & Warg, L. E. (1995). Burnout in social work. *Social Work, 40*, 638–46.

Sokolowski, R. (1991). The fiduciary relationship and the nature of professions. In E. D. Pellegrino, R. M. Veatch, & J. P. Langan (Eds.), *Ethics, trust, and the professions* (pp. 23–39). Washington, DC: Georgetown University Press.

Soyer, D. (1963). The right to fail. *Social Work, 8* (3) (July), 72–78.

Specht, H., & Courtney, M. E. (1994). *Unfaithful angels: How social work has abandoned its mission.* New York: Free Press.

Spero, M. H. (1990). Identification between the religious patient and therapist in social work and psychoanalytic psychotherapy. *Journal of Social Work and Policy in Israel, 3,* 83–98.

Steinberg, K. L., Levine, M., & Doueck, H. (1997). Effects of legally mandated child-abuse reports on the therapeutic relationship: A survey of psychotherapists. *American Journal of Orthopsychiatry, 67,* 112–22.

Stevens, J. W. (1998). A question of values in social work practice: Working with the strengths of black adolescent females. *Families in Society, 79,* 288–96.

Strean, H. S. (1997). Comment on James C. Raines, "Self-Disclosure in Clinical Social Work." *Clinical Social Work Journal, 25,* 365–66.

Strom, K. (1992). Reimbursement demands and treatment decisions: A growing dilemma for social workers. *Social Work, 37,* 398–403.

Strom, K. (1994). Social workers in private practice: An update. *Clinical Social Work Journal, 22,* 73–89.

Strom-Gottfried, K. (1998a). Informed consent meets managed care. *Health and Social Work, 23,* 25–33.

Strom-Gottfried, K. (1998b). Is "ethical managed care" an oxymoron? *Families in Society: The Journal of Contemporary Human Services, 79,* 297–307.

Strom-Gottfried, K. (1999). When colleague accuses colleague: Adjudicating personnel matters through the filing of ethics complaints. *Administration in Social Work, 23* (2), 1–16.

Sunley, R. (1997). Advocacy in the new world of managed care. *Families in Society, 78,* 84–94.

Tarasoff v. Regents of the University of California. (1976).

Taylor, L., & Adelman, H. S. (1989). Reframing the confidentiality dilemma to work in children's best interest. *Professional Psychology: Research and Practice, 20,* 79–83.

Taylor-Brown, S., & Garcia, A. (1995). Social workers and HIV-affected families: Is the profession prepared? *Social Work, 40,* 14–15.

Timms, N. (1983). *Social work values: An enquiry.* London, England: Routledge & Kegan Paul.

Tong, R. (1998). Feminist ethics. In *Encyclopedia of applied ethics*, Vol. 2 (pp. 261–68). New York: Academic Press.

Torczyner, J. (1991). Discretion, judgment, and informed consent: Ethical and practice issues in social action. *Social Work, 36*, 122–28.

Toren, N. (1972). *Social Work: The Case of a Semi-Profession*. Beverly Hills, CA: Sage Publications.

Tower, Kristine D. (1994). Consumer-centered social work practice: Restoring client self-determination. *Social Work, 39* (2), 191–96.

Towle, C. (1965). *Common human needs*. New York: National Association of Social Workers.

Trolander, J. A. (1997). Fighting racism and sexism: The CSWE. *Social Service Review, 71*, 110–34.

Tropman, J. E. (1984). *Policy management in the human services* (pp. 226–27). New York: Columbia University Press.

Tropman, J. E., Erlich, J. L., & Rothman, J. (1995). *Tactics and techniques of community intervention* (3rd ed.). Itasca, IL: F. E. Peacock Publishers.

Tully, C. T., Craig, T., & Nugent, G. (1994). Should only gay and lesbian community organizers operate in gay and lesbian communities? In M.J. Austin & J. I. Lowe (Eds.), *Controversial Issues in Communities and Organizations* (pp. 86–96). Boston: Allyn & Bacon.

Ulrich, B., & Beck-Gernsheim, E. (1996). Individualization and "precarious freedoms." In P. Heclas, S. Lash, & P. Morris (Eds.), *Detraditionalization: Critical Reflections on Authority and Identity* (pp. 23–48). Cambridge, MA: Blackwell Publishers.

U.S. Census. (1999a). The elderly population. August 24, 1999. http://www.census.gov/population/www/pop-profile/elderpop.html

U.S. Census. (1999b). Sixty-five plus in the United States. http://www.census.gov/socdemo/www/agebrief.html, August 24, 1999.

VandeCreek, L., Knapp, S., & Herzog, C. (1988). Privileged communications for social workers. *Social Casework, 69*, 28–34.

Van Hoose, W. H., & Kottler, J. A. (1985). *Ethical and legal issues in counseling and psychotherapy* (2nd ed.). San Francisco: Jossey-Bass.

Varley, B. K. (1963). Socialization in social work education. *Social Work, 8* (4), 102–9.

Varley, B. K. (1968, Fall). Social work values: Changes in value commitment of students from admission to MSW graduation. *Journal of Education for Social Work, 4,* 67–76.

Verschelden, C. (1993). Social work values and pacifism: Opposition to war as a professional responsibility. *Social Work, 38,* 765–69.

Videka-Sherman, L. (1988). Metaanalysis of research on social work practice in mental health. *Social Work, 33,* 325–38.

Vigilante, J. L. (1974). Between values and science: "Education for the profession during a moral crisis or is proof truth?" *Journal of Education for Social Work, 10,* 107–15.

Vigilante, J. L. (1983). Professional values. In A. Rosenblatt & D. Waldfogel (Eds.), *Handbook of clinical social work* (pp. 58–69). San Francisco: Jossey-Bass.

Wagner, L., Davis, S., & Handelsman, M. M. (1998). In search of the abominable consent form: The impact of readability and personalization. *Journal of Clinical Psychology, 54,* 115–20.

Wakefield, J. (1988). Psychotherapy, distributive justice and social work (Parts 1 and 2). *Social Service Review, 62,* 187–209, 353–81.

Walden, T., Wolock, I., & Demone, H. W., Jr. (1990). Ethical decision making in human services: A comparative study. *Families in Society, 71,* 67–75.

Walrond-Skinner, S., & Watson, D. (1987). *Ethical issues in family therapy.* London, England: Routledge & Kegan Paul.

Ward, J. W., & Drotman, D. P. (1998). Epidemiology of HIV and AIDS. In G. P. Wormser (Ed.), *AIDS and other manifestations of HIV infection* (3rd ed.) (pp. 1–17). Philadelphia: Lippincott-Raven.

Watt, J. W., & Kallmann, G. L. (1998). Managing professional obligations under managed care: A social work perspective. *Family and Community Health, 21* (2), 40–49.

Weick, A., & Pope, L. (1988). Knowing what's best: A new look at self-determination. *Social Casework, 69,* 10–16.

Wheeler, D. L. (1993). Physician-anthropologist examines what ails America's medical system: Instead of treating patients, Melvin Konner probes health care in general. *Chronicle of Higher Education,* June 2, A6–A7.

Wicclair, M. R. (1993). *Ethics & the elderly.* New York: Oxford University Press.

Wigmore, J. (1961). *Evidence in trials at common law* (Rev. ed.). Boston: Little, Brown.

Williams, R. M., Jr. (1967). Individual and group values. *Annals, 371,* 20–37.

Willis, C. (1987). Legal and ethical issues of touch in dance/movement therapy. *American Journal of Dance Therapy, 10,* 41–53.

Wilson, C. A., Alexander, J. F., & Turner, C. W. (1996). Family therapy process and outcome research: Relationship to treatment ethics. *Ethics & Behavior, 6,* 345–52.

Wineburgh, M. (1998). Ethics, managed care, and outpatient psychotherapy. *Clinical Social Work Journal, 26,* 433–43.

Witkins, S. L. (1998). The right to effective treatment and the effective treatment of rights: Rhetorical empiricism and the politics of research. *Social Work, 43,* 75–80.

Wodarski, J. S., Pippin, J. A., & Daniels, M. (1988). The effects of graduate social work education on personality, values and interpersonal skills. *Journal of Social Work Education, 24,* 266–77.

Woody, J. D. (1990). Clinical strategies to promote compliance. *American Journal of Family Therapy, 18,* 285–94.

Yu, M., & O'Neal, B. (1992). Issues of confidentiality when working with persons with AIDS. *Clinical Social Work Journal, 20,* 421–30.

Yurkow, J. (1991). Abuse and neglect of the frail elderly. *Pride Institute Journal of Long Term Home Health Care, 10* (1), 36–39.

Zygmond, M. J., & Boorhem, H. (1989). Ethical decision-making in family therapy. *Family Process, 28,* 269–80.

Index

ETHICAL DECISIONS FOR SOCIAL WORK PRACTICE
Sixth Edition
Edited by John Beasley
Production supervision by Kim Vander Steen
Cover design by Lucy Lesiak Design, Park Ridge, Illinois
Composition by Point West, Inc., Carol Stream, Illinois
Paper, Finch Opaque
Printed and bound by McNaughton & Gunn, Saline, Michigan